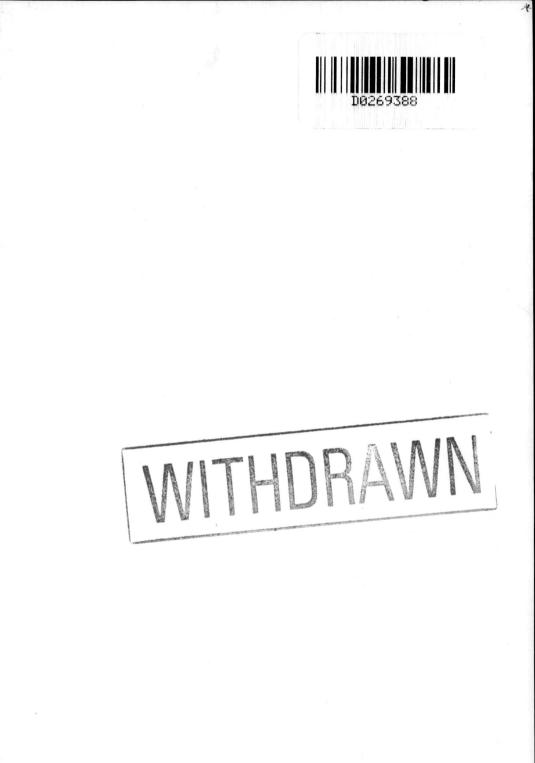

ACTION LEARNING IN PRACTICE

Third Edition

Edited by

Mike Pedler

Published by
Gower Publishing Limited
Gower House
Croft Road
Aldershot
Hampshire GU11 3HR
England

Gower
Old Post Road
Brookfield
Vermont 05036
USA

British Library Cataloguing in Publication Data

Action learning in practice. – 3rd ed.
1. Active learning   2. Organizational learning   3. Executives –
Training of
I. Pedler, Mike, 1944 –
658.4′07′1245

ISBN 0 566 07795 7

Library of Congress Cataloging-in-Publication Data

Action learning in practice / edited by Mike Pedler. – 3rd ed.
    p. cm.
  Includes bibliographical references and index.
  ISBN 0–566–07795–7 (hardcover)
  1. Executives–Training of.   2. Organizational change–Study and
teaching.   I. Pedler, Mike.
HD30.4.A3   1997
658.4′07124–dc21   97–20724
                                                                       CIP

Phototypeset in Century Old Style by Intype London Ltd and printed in Great Britain by Biddles Ltd, Guildford

Contents

Part III   Questions of Practice

Part IV   Evaluating Action Learning

Appendices

List of Figures and Tables

Figures

Tables

A Conversation with Reg Revans

Salford, 17 December 1996

This conversation with Reg Revans, Mike Pedler, David Bothams, John Morris and Diane Asher and Hazel Barker, two members of an MPhil/PhD group, took place at the Revans Centre for Action Learning & Research in the University of Salford. We met to discuss the idea of action learning – its vision, central values, progress to date and likely future. This version of the conversation is derived from a much longer transcript[1] and is loosely structured around questions put to Reg by those present. His contributions are indented.

The conversation begins with Reg picking up a card showing two monks – the one labouring on an illustrated manuscript, the other at a word processor – both producing the message 'Peace & Goodwill To All Men'...

> This Christmas card, this is exactly saying it. One chap is merely tapping the keys on a whatever it is... that's where we are. Have you heard of Leopold Aurhenbrugger? He was the first man to discover and use percussion of the chest. Two hundred and fifty years ago he wrote a paper saying... 'unless your ideas are ridiculed by experts, they can have no merit whatsoever'. But he went a lot further than that... because he had been using percussion of the chest in the Allgemeineskriegenshause – the big general hospital in Vienna... and he'd showed that if you tapped people's chests and listened, and interpreted what you were hearing you could cure them. And this idea was so ridiculed by the other people who were making their livings by making sure the patients died....

> ... merely circulating strings of words around and imagining that these strings of words also reflect or manipulate or ensure their practice in reality... well... this is where we are.

MP: Can you say more of what you see in the card, what do you mean by 'people imagining that words circulating reflected actual practice'?

[1] Available from the Revans Centre for Action Learning & Research, Continuing Education, Maxwell Building, The University of Salford, Salford M5 4WT.

Are you familiar with the Thirty Years War? It reduced Germany to cannibalism. Because a century before a chap had invented the printing press and was printing the Bible – previously the Bible had been handwritten by all kinds of people, and in writing it, the chap who was writing it said, well, I don't quite believe this, so he altered it . . . so all the Bibles had previously reflected their opinions or religions or morality. . . .

The Thirty Years War ran from 1618 to 1648. It's true it wasn't until the beginning of January 1649 that we cut Charles' head off . . . but when the Bible was printed, exactly the same signs, words, letters appeared page after page and every copy was absolutely identical and when the words in the Bible were read by Catholics, they said 'they mean this' and when they were read by Protestants they reckoned they meant something else, so they found themselves – it's true not in England where we were so busy working out how we should deal with the Royal family – but for most other countries in Europe their fundamental problem was what are the meaning of these words? And you may find this hard to believe but it then reduced Germany to cannibalism because all the farms were destroyed, and fighting was so appalling, that the only meat they could get was from the corpses.

And this is where we are at the moment – all kinds of people, who are now claiming – it's true they're saying 'Good God do you mean that riff raff there only charge £5000 for a lecture? Ours is £50,000, we are much better than they are!' – all kinds of organizations are now calling themselves not Action Learning but 'active learning'. But we must expect this because as Leopold Aurhenbrugger pointed out unless your ideas are exploited and ridiculed by experts, they can have no intrinsic merit. This is something which Action Learning is going through at the moment. It's being picked up, imitated, sold!

. . . and I think that only those who are not experts, who have never been professors or management consultants, but have been themselves, not only acquainted with it but responsible for treating patients or looking after children or managing a factory . . . unless that's their very first motivation or understanding of reality, then we're not going to get very far.

But I'm not saying anything new, you'll find all these ideas are being expressed a few thousand years ago by other people.

MP: In the history of an idea like Action Learning . . . and history has always been important to you . . . you've always said that it is not a new idea, what are your thoughts on where we are now with the idea – perhaps in terms of its recent incarnation since you came back from Belgium 20 years [ago] or so?

Well I think the present conditions don't have much or anything to do with what I've been saying or urging or writing about. I think the whole world is now in so precarious a position that even the professional politicians are beginning to notice it. When that happens then there may be hope for humanity. When all these mountebanks who go rushing into this place called Westminster and out again, when they begin to see that the world may be in a mess then there's hope for humanity. That's all.

MP: Do you see the idea as having developed since you came back to England?

All I can say is that I've noticed all over the country, even as far away as Cornwall and right up into the north of Scotland, people are now interested in Action Learning . . . when I say they're interested in Action Learning . . . they're expressing the view that perhaps so-and-so – the boss – isn't correct, he should be thinking afresh. I think that this is now visible everywhere . . . people are now beginning to say 'it's high time we asked ourselves fresh questions about how this organization is being run'.

Let me give a simple example. It must be getting on for 17 or 18 years ago after I'd left Belgium and come back here to Manchester, I found all kinds of people were disagreeing with each other and fighting and so forth. Not very far from the University of Manchester, in Moss Side, there were all kinds of people quarrelling and I said, 'yes, well it's all very well to have a police force that can arrest them for fighting each other and even have a law court which sends them to jail, but shouldn't we be asking ourselves why are they quarrelling with each other so much?

. . . I recommended that what we should be doing is getting all these black chaps and these Chinese and these Arabs together and saying 'you're all living here together in Moss Side, don't you think there are a lot of things you might be doing to each other except fighting?' And it so happened that the Deputy Chief Constable of Manchester, who was a Welshman, he agreed with me and said yes, let's have a meeting and we got a whole lot of people together, a big public meeting at the old Manchester Poly-technic, and I said 'what I think we should be doing is talking to each other about can't we do a few constructive things? After all if you walk round Moss Side you see that a few things are needed – houses in pretty poor shape, let's put a few tiles on the roof, or we might even get a factory to open and provide a few jobs.

This went very well but of course you know what happened. When the report came out all the professors of economics and sociology said listen to this bloody nonsense, here's this feller, what's his name Revans? saying only if you get this riff raff to work together do we get anywhere! What do you think happened? nothing happened . . . until the Moss Side riots broke out. The Moss Side riots had an enquiry run by a chap called Bennett Hytner QC and he said had the people listened to what Revans was saying this wouldn't have happened.

It wasn't anything I was saying which had created this, it was the fact that the world itself is now in the hands of experts who just send messages to each other without any explanations of what the messages might really mean.

ACTION LEARNING AND MANAGERS

MP: One of the areas where Action Learning has had a big impact is in management education, but when you're talking about Moss Side you're not just talking about managers, and you've never talked just about managers . . . (but) managers or the people who organize management education have been one of the more receptive audiences – do you think that's true?

Don't forget that the most successful businessman – successful as judged by economics

– in this country, Arnold Weinstock saw me on a television programme and he immediately asked me if I would go and meet with his . . . he said he had 136 companies which he'd taken over in the last 15 years . . . would I go and meet with them and tell them what I'd been talking about. The advance of Action Learning in industry isn't due to me, it's Arnold Weinstock who saw the point straight away.

MP: When you opened the Revans Centre here at Salford, only a year ago, the way you described Action Learning then was 'helping each other to help the helpless' and I hadn't actually heard you use those exact words before?

I think they're in my report to the Bennett Hytner enquiry in Moss Side *[actually in a paper on social workers helping each other to improve what can be done for the mentally handicapped – 'Helping each other to help the helpless' Chapter 37 in The Origins & Growth of Action Learning, Bromley: Chartwell Bratt 1982 pp. 467–492]*.

MP: I suppose managers are experts in a way – they organize the work of others – are the people you want to reach beyond managers?

I was telling Diane about my recent visit to South Africa. I was asked out by Nelson Mandela and had a long conference with his deputy, Walter Sisulu, and as part of the visit was asked to go to Natal and meet the little children who were supposed to be doing arithmetic. I discovered that at school they had become very interested in Action Learning because a big nearby manufacturing firm, a Japanese motor car company, had introduced Action Learning for training their own workforce and the fathers had said, if this is such a good idea that we in the workforce get together and talk to each other, it's true the managers asked us to get together, but we get together and talk about our difficulties with people who share those difficulties or our relationship with them, why not with the children in the school? So the school had started Action Learning.

The fact was that the South Africans said that the factory where they make motor cars might be more efficient if people learn with and from each other by action learning, and the people themselves said, why don't our little children understand better what life is about by learning with and from each other? Let's introduce this idea into schools.

So you say managers, yes managers certainly have done a great deal to get Action Learning started, but I think also that the Moss Side Report and the little children in the school and all kinds of nurses in hospitals, not merely industrial managers. So, to me what you're all raising is even more important; why is it that ordinary people, like ourselves, who realize that life, society, is becoming more and more complicated and, if we're not careful, more and more unstable – why aren't they themselves getting together and saying, shouldn't we be developing action learning?

This is what I regard as the most important current question. How is this simple idea . . . that it is high time we asked ourselves fresh questions of each other about what it is we're doing here and now – not what other people are telling us – though that may be important to understand what others are saying to us, but not as important as asking ourselves and each other what we think we're doing. I think that you lot here in Salford have a moral responsibility to see that something is done about this.

HB: Are there cultural differences which influence the acceptability of Action Learning?

> Once conditions get so complex, so uncertain, so unstable that those who say 'we're in charge here, we're the boss, you do exactly what we tell you' – once they begin to say, 'hey hold on a minute, this is what I want to tell them but I'm not absolutely certain that they'll either understand what I'm trying to say, or if they do understand and then start acting on it, whether it will work'.

> It's only when the people in charge begin to get this degree of self-awareness, self-criticism if you like, self-understanding ... and I think that most cultures that I'm aware of have now got this in interaction between all the cultures – look what's happening in Turkey compared with what's happening in Romania and what's happening in California compared with what's happening in Ceylon – the interaction between these cultures is now so great, so essential that I think that this notion that those who think they're in charge should be asking themselves fresh questions about whether what they're saying is all that correct as they think it is.

> I think, to give a practical illustration of your point, if somehow, a group here in Salford could say we think things are changing so much in and around ... we've had bombs in Manchester, all kinds of things.... you can't be sure what's going to happen tomorrow, next week or next year, we feel that this uncertainty demands or requires or suggests that we should be doing so-and-so. If they could do that, if they could write their vision of what they think is happening around them and what their uncertainty is of what's happening around them, and let people in Southampton or Los Angeles read it, then the people in Southampton or Los Angeles could say well it's extremely interesting how the people in Salford are asking themselves fresh questions, we've been on about it for some time, we don't quite agree with them, with this, this and this – this is what I think the world needs at this moment.

MP: Talking about uncertainty and going back to my theme about managers, some managers respond to this uncertainty by trying to create stability and security. For example in some hospitals they have implemented the 'Brunel System' based on Eliott Jaques' levels of work and they tell them whether they're level 2s, or 3s or 5s. Now all this in my view militates against people asking themselves fresh questions about what they're doing. If managers are charged with creating order, is this often at the cost of the conditions that lead people to ask fresh questions of each other and indeed to treat each other as colleagues, as comrades, as equals as opposed to relating hierarchically?

> Well, I used to argue exactly this same concept – what do you mean by being the manager? This was the thing which we somehow managed to develop in Belgium – the Belgian managers, it's true they came largely from industry but not just from industry, from insurance companies, banks, even department stores selling expensive clothing for fashionable ladies, but they all got together and did Action Learning in a very, very profound way. The senior managers from one company gave up their job in that company for six months and went and worked as a senior manager in another company about which they knew absolutely nothing.

So we had fellows who were senior managers in Sabena Airlines going off and working in an insurance company, and people who were in charge of a department store leaving that and going to work in a hospital. They [looked at] the troubles of some totally different enterprise altogether, and before you can understand what the problems of that different enterprise are, you've obviously got to learn a great deal yourself. You haven't come in here merely to tell your industrial or commercial colleagues what they should be doing, your first responsibility is to come here and try to understand what it is they're saying about what they're doing.

So [I said to them] all I want to ask you is what is the most important question you've learned to ask yourselves as a result of this? It's been going on for 10 years and at least 100 big enterprises had been involved, and I asked them to write down what they thought was the most important question . . . and you know the answer . . . at the end of it the one they voted for – and we said that you mustn't vote for your own question – was what is an honest man and what need I do to become one?

What they had learned from studying other people's problems . . . was were these other people who said these were their problems really being honest about it or were they not pretending and their problems were something else altogether? And this is it. I think if we go around the world pretending that we're something that we're not, we just have to ask the question – what is our real problem?

HB: In unstable conditions, don't some managers exploit instability for people whose jobs are under threat – that stifles this honesty that you're looking for, because to admit that you don't know something or that you've got a problem could be against you in a controlled environment?

This is what Roger Bacon said when he spent a few years in Oxford, he said what these professors at Oxford are doing is concealing their own ignorance from themselves beneath a veneer . . . I think the word he used was . . . cleverness. This is it – so many people are trying to pretend that they understand.

ACTION LEARNING AND UNIVERSITIES

MP: Turning to the university, Action Learning has now become involved with degrees and with academic qualifications. In the Blond and Briggs book *Action Learning: New Techniques for Managers* you talk about leaving Manchester and of action learning as an antidote to university or business school management education. One of the ways that action learning has developed over the last few years is that it's almost become orthodox for some degree programmes to have 'learning sets' and for people to be using the experience of working with a small group of people and learning in a cooperative way as part of their qualification work. What do you think about this marriage of academia and practice?

All I can say is, if you point out to someone that they write their name and put MBA after it, that might be Master of Business Administration but it also might be 'Moral

Bankruptcy Assured!' All you're pretending all the time is that certain letters mean this, that or the other. This is something inherent in our methods of communicating with each other. We send a signal across but that signal may have more than one interpretation ... what we do about it I don't know. I think it's only when people get to know themselves that we get anywhere.

MP: Is there a contradiction in your mind between Action Learning and getting a degree?

If the Action Learning is genuine, involving other people who aren't professors of Action Learning, and if it demands that those people who are claiming now to understand Action Learning that they must have done something about it, done it and exhibited it or made it visible in such a way that other people can judge whether it's genuine or not ...

I think the point you're raising Mike is very, very fundamental indeed. Not merely to do with are we being honest about Action Learning, but goes right to the heart of what we mean by understanding or comprehension. It's all very well emitting words about something, a lot of people are very good at that, actors ... some actors who have never heard of Shakespeare can stand up and announce it, but whether they themselves behave towards other people in the same spirit is another question altogether.

When I started Action Learning in a practical sense was during the war when I was working in the pits. One reason why in the end I finished up in Cannock Chase was that the pits were sufficiently close together, and sufficiently compact to get the staff of one pit to agree to stop working in their particular pit and get working in another one. So they were all working in each other's pits, and they were all miners of course and all working the same seams of coal, but in different places and they were different in that their histories were different, they belonged to 14 separate companies, owners and so forth. So, although they had in common that they were all coal miners working coal, they had different histories, they inherited different concepts ...

... and then when I went to Belgium we went even further, there people left responsible jobs running department stores to go into responsible jobs in a factory making glass windows or something like that, totally different. What they had in common of course was that they spoke the same languages, German, French, Dutch.

... it wasn't just a question of the person who was responsible understanding why a system wasn't working, but understanding also that the systems were themselves differently organized and the people who were working in those systems were different people. What I was on about, and all my early writings I hope should be reflecting this, was that although all these activities had one thing in common, namely how does humanity mix with its fellow members in order to achieve something ... yet I think it was the differences between the different industries which was to me the fundamental.

MP: The economy of this Centre rests on people coming here and getting diplomas and degrees; whatever the academic test, which is usually a piece of writing, words produced on the word processor, there is another test that must be applied – a test of practical application or action to change the way something is actually done. What is distinctive about a qualification which has Action Learning associated with it? Does it worry you that the future of the Revans Centre rests on people getting degrees?

> Well I think the question is, what are the conditions which the university has demanded of people to whom it awards degrees. Does the university recognize and also make clear to the whole world that it recognizes what Roger Bacon said about the Professors at Oxford 750 years ago – they're just concealing their own self-ignorance under a veneer of cleverness?

> When you're entering any kind of competition, including academic competition and going through a degree, your first motivation is to say how can I give the impression that I'm much higher than anybody else? The notion that it might be a good thing to stop for a moment and say what I should be doing now is trying to explain to the examiners how ignorant I am, how deeply I misunderstand this, this just isn't encouraged.

> That's why I said that I think a genuine interpretation of Action Learning goes very very deeply indeed . . . asking what really are universities claiming to do?

THE VISION OF ACTION LEARNING

HB: When you started this idea of Action Learning, what was your vision? Where did you think it might end up? And do you feel you've achieved any of that?

> Well, all I was aware of at that time was something which a chap I used to listen to, a fellow called Einstein, he said 'there's no such thing as whole truths, all truths are half truths'. So that whatever it is you think you're doing, you may make a little progress, but there's no final goal which you can attain . . . you might say well, this is what I thought I knew, now I know a little more and so forth, and you can go on. So you can be quite sure that when I wrote my first paper on this topic, which is just 60 years ago next year – 1937 – it was called 'The Entry of Girls into the Nursing Profession' . . . what I was concerned with was 'what do we mean by training nurses?' But at that time I had no idea where this curiosity to know what we should be doing to try and help girls who, for some reason or another, which only they themselves might understand, that they had decided they wanted to train as nurses. In what way should the local hospital be helping them?

> I had no idea, and certainly no conviction, that my curiosity would lead me . . . all I can remember was that a year or two later when I was asked to go and work in the coal industry, and I chose this because I can't imagine any organization more different from the hospital ward than a pit . . . it's true that a lot of people die in hospitals and they also get killed in coal mines so there might be something in common there . . . only if those people who actually live there and work there and gave their lives to it, could we get anywhere . . . nothing I was telling them, all I wanted to do was to try

and understand what they were doing that's all. But I was aware that a lot of people had been interested in this topic, if you read what Bhudda had to say about what the people who lived in India should be doing about . . . or what Mohammed had said . . . they were all equally concerned with understanding why people were doing the things they were.

But to me what is most interesting now is that . . . and before I say what I am going to say, let me explain that this is not, not in any circumstances the consequence of what I've been talking about for the last 60 years . . . people all over the world – I've even been asked to go to New Zealand to meet Maori women, just think of that! – are now beginning to see that life has a few problems and that they should be . . . it's all very well listening to what the expert is telling you about what you should be doing, but it's also a good thing just to pause for a moment and say 'do I agree with this? do I understand it? have I got any suggestions of my own?'

That's coming out now in so many different places that all I'm saying is that those to whom this idea has already occurred, as it must have done to all you sitting around here saying to yourselves from time to time 'just what do we mean by trying to run something or improve the way we're doing it?' . . . this is now of such universal interest, that I'm curious to know what's going to happen next. And what's going to happen next won't be the last thing that's going to happen . . . all that's happening next will be preparing the world to ask themselves the same question in ten years time, fifty years time – what are we going to be doing tomorrow?

MP: Is it to do with reaching the limits of expert knowledge? The mess which you say that people are now acknowledging is partly to do with acknowledging the limitations of expertise?

I think the fundamental problem is to stress Action Learning, not as something which I have thought about, but which is now apparent to people all over the world in all kinds of different cultures. I think it's arising in this way because the problems facing the world are now so great that people are beginning to ask themselves fresh questions. This is not a single idea.

I can remember Lord Rutherford saying at the end of a conference on action research, he said 'what's impressed me most about the past three and three-quarter hours is my own bloody ignorance – what does yours look like to you yourselves?' This is another statement of truth. This is why when you're really going to understand the world, you'd better understand that it isn't quite as mechanical, as mechanistic as we're being taught it is. All kinds of unexpected things happen.

But I think if you're in a group of people of whom you are not the only person present who may be wondering whether they understand what it is they are trying to say, somehow you become aware that this other person is a bit dubious, a bit doubtful about what they're saying, may be clarifying to you yourself what it is you don't know, don't understand. I think it's only by bartering our own misunderstandings that we learn better how to understand.

Notes on Contributors

Doris Adams is an Assistant Professor at Trinity College in Burlington, Vermont. The focus of her teaching and consulting has been on development in the workplace. Dr Adams's dissertation from the University of Texas researched problem-solving approaches of small groups utilizing the concepts of Argyris, a framework she has continued to explore in her consulting and teaching.

Richard Baker is the president of Baker & Company, a Dallas based management consulting firm specializing in working with clients to strengthen their competitive positions. Mr Baker's firm has worked with recognized leaders in their industries including American Airlines, General Motors Corp., Xerox Corp., American National Can Co., Rockwell International, and AT & T.

Liz Beaty is Principal Lecturer in staff and management development at the University of Brighton Business School. She is responsible for a Masters programme and for staff development for teachers in higher education. Her special interests are in learning theory and educational development.

George Percy Boulden is currently Chairman and Managing Director of ALA International Ltd which he founded in 1980 with Professor Reg Revans and Alan Lawlor to promote the use of Action Learning in solving business problems. His work involves such clients as Motorola, ICL and Lucas Industries who he helps to design and deliver people development programmes. His international work takes him to Japan, where he advises a major Japanese consultancy organization, the US and Central and Eastern Europe. He works with many of the international agencies including the International Labour Organisation, EC-PHARE, UNDP, WHO and the Know How Fund. George is a member of the International Foundation for Action Learning and the Institute of Management Consultants.

He has written a number of papers and articles on Action Learning and human resource productivity.

Tom Bourner is Principal Lecturer at the University of Brighton Business School's Centre for Management Development, where most programmes are based on Action Learning. He is currently the centre's research coordinator. There is no time since the mid-1980s when he has not been a participant member of an Action Learning set; he has been set adviser to about 20 sets.

John Burgoyne is Professor and Head of the Department of Management Learning at Lancaster University. He is well known for his work on evaluation, self-development and the Learning Company.

David Casey is changing from a consultant who does the odd bit of painting in watercolour to a watercolour artist who does the odd piece of consulting. Having been a teacher (St Benedict's Ealing), research scientist (Berger Paints), manager (Reed International) and freelance consulant (25 years), he is finding his fifth career the most difficult and interesting of all.

Ian Cunningham is Chairman of the consultancy Strategic Developments, Chairman of the Centre for Self Managed Learning, and an independent consultant. Ian has been a research chemist, a manager, a trainer, a business school academic and chief executive of a management college. He has served on the boards of companies in the travel and the insurance sectors. He has also been a visiting professor in the USA and in India.

Nancy M. Dixon is Associate Professor of Administrative Sciences at The George Washington University in Washington DC. She has written extensively on how organizations learn from their experience. Her book, *The Organizational Learning Cycle: How We Can Learn Collectively* (McGraw-Hill, 1994) summarizes many of those concepts. Her most recent publication is *Perspectives on Dialogue: Making Talk Developmental for Individuals and Organizations* (The Center For Creative Leadership, 1996). She serves on the editorial board of *Management Learning* and is an editorial reviewer for the *Human Resource Development Quarterly.* Dr Dixon has served as a consultant to numerous organizations assisting them to design processes through which collectives learn.

Otmar Donnenberg is working as an independent management consultant in the Netherlands (where he lives), in Germany and in Austria. He studied law in Austria and political science in the US. Since 1980 he has undertaken projects in the field of health care. He focuses on 'learning in the working-situation'. He is chairman of the Dutch Action Learning Association and is affiliated with the Austrian Trigon Consultancy.

Mark Easterby-Smith is Professor of Management Learning at Lancaster University. He has been conducting evaluation studies since the mid-1970s in a wide range of settings including universities, companies and public sector organizations and this work has been published in numerous papers and a book which is now in its second edition.

Meg Elliott is a Senior Lecturer in Management Development at Manchester Metropolitan University. The main focus of her work is the development and management of the Department of Management's corporate programmes. She has been involved in working with a number of corporate clients to develop and deliver programmes that can be accredited at Certificate, Diploma and Masters levels.

Paul Frost is Head of the Centre for Management Development at the University of Brighton Business School and a partner in a development consultancy. He has worked in the USA as a human resources executive and as a chief executive for an international education and development charity.

Bob Garratt is Chairman of Media Products International and of Organisation Development Ltd. in Hong Kong. He advises on director development and strategic thinking and is the author of *The Learning Organisation* (HarperCollins) and series editor of Fontana's *Successful Manager Series*. He is a visiting faculty member of the Management School at Imperial College, London and an Associate of the Judge Institute of Management at Cambridge University.

David L. Giles works as an independent consultant/trainer principally with supervisory and management groups, a contact with the shopfloor that he has retained since his early days of working in the aircraft industry. Following a spell in full time youth and community work, Dave moved into further education where he was able to develop his interest and ability in working with issues related to motivation. This continued into organizational learning when he encouraged his most recent employer Rolls Royce and Associates to join the Learning Company Consortium. He continues to be happiest when at work with a developmental group.

Larry Hales is the Manager of Advanced Learning at General Motors Corporate Education and Training in Warren, Michigan. His responsibilities include the identification, development and transfer of innovative learning processes into organizational change strategies, leadership development programmes and furthering a corporate learning culture.

Zhou Jianhua is a lecturer in China's National Centre for Management Development at Wuxi. He has ten years experience as personnel manager of Wuxi Electric Equipment Company and joined the China-EEC Management Programme for three years. His recent interest has focused upon Sino-foreign enterprises on which he has published several papers including 'The Cultural Discrepancy and Mixtures in Joint Ventures' and 'China's Joint Ventures and Their Environment'.

Alison Johns is Director of Staff Development at Plymouth University where she has initiated and run a major initiative with senior managers based on the principles of Action Learning.

Robert Kolodny is a consultant working with companies in western and eastern Europe and throughout the United States on organization and management development. He has a Master's Degree from the University of Pennsylvania and a PhD from Columbia University. A LIM Associate, he teaches in the graduate Human Resources Management Program at the New School for Social Research and is a founding member of its Leadership Center. He is on the visiting staff of the Gestalt Institute of Cleveland, and for 13 years was on the full-time faculty of the Columbia University School of Architecture, Planning and Preservation.

Alan Lawlor co-founded Action Learning Associates in 1978 to earn his living from applying the principles of Action Learning. He worked with many different management groups in large and small organizations and also with unemployed managers. He was a chartered engineer and had previously been Head of Department of Management Studies at Redditch College. He died in 1988.

Jean Lawrence is a Managing Partner in the Development Consortium, an Associate of Henley Management College, and Chair of the International Foundation for Action Learning. She was earlier a production manager at Cadburys, a staff member at the Manchester Business School for fifteen years, and a previous Chair of the Association for Management Education & Development. Since 1972, she has based all her organization and management development consultancy work on Action Learning principles, and works regularly overseas, particularly in Africa.

Ronnie Lessem is Reader in International Management at City University Business School and Academic Director of the consortial MBA. He has used Action Learning all over the world with small and large concerns to facilitate self, organization and business development. He has written a number of books, including *Managing in Four Worlds* (Blackwell, 1997).

Alec Lewis has been an independent management consultant since 1984 and concentrates his Action Learning endeavours in the insurance and banking sectors. After graduating in economics he worked in sales and market research with Cadbury-Fry before joining Bristol Polytechnic in 1968 where he was Principal Lecturer in the South West Regional Management Centre.

Victoria Marsick is an Associate Professor of Adult and Continuing Education at Teachers College, Columbia University, and chair of the Department of Higher and Adult Education. She holds a PhD in adult education from the University of California, Berkeley, and an MPA in international public administration from Syracuse University. Dr Marsick consults with both private and the public sectors on planning and design of strategies to create learning organizations. Through LIM Ltd she assists in the design and implementation of Action Reflection Learning programmes aimed at management development and organizational change. She is co-author with Karen Watkins of *Sculpting the Learning Organization* and *Informal and Incidental Learning in the Workplace*. She has authored and co-authored many articles on organizational learning and adult education.

John Morris is a Visiting Professor at Salford University, working at the recently established Revans Centre for Action Learning and Research. He left Manchester Business School in 1982 to work as a consultant in action learning and organizational change. He lives in Chester and is increasingly involved in activities that bring family and community, work and learning congenially together.

Alan Mumford has been a management development specialist for over 30 years. He has had experience as a full time adviser in a variety of organizations, a leader in an innovative business school based on action learning, and now as an independent consultant. His specialist knowledge has resulted in numerous publications; two on director development – *Developing Top Managers* (Gower, 1988) and *Making Experience Count* (Institute of Directors, 1990). Other books include *Management Development: Strategies for Action* (IPM, IPD edition 1997) and *How Managers can Develop Managers* (Gower, 1993), *Action Learning at Work* (Gower, 1997), and with Peter Honey, *The Manual of Learning Styles* (Honey, 3rd edition 1992).

Glenn Nilson is Chair of the Department of Sociology and Applied Social Relations and an associate professor of sociology at Eastern Connecticut State University. He holds an MA in sociology from the California State University-Chico and a PhD in sociology from the University of Massachusetts. Dr Nilson has written many articles and papers relating to learning organizations and learning communities. He is a specialist in collective behaviour and culture construction theory. Dr Nilson consults with both private and public organizations.

Judy O'Neil of Partners for the Learning Organization and Leadership in International Management, works with companies, in the US and internationally, interested in development and change through Action Learning and in becoming learning organizations. She has over 25 years experience in corporate training and development. She plays a leadership role in IFAL-USA, has published several articles on Action Learning, and is studying the role of set advisers for her doctoral work at Columbia University.

David Pearce is a consultant in management and organization development working in the UK and Europe. He was previously management development adviser with GEC where he worked on the introduction of Action Learning to the senior management development programme. With David Casey, he edited *More Than Management Development: Action Learning at GEC,* Gower, 1977.

Mike Pedler is a writer, researcher and consultant and a partner in the Learning Company Project and Whole Systems Development. He is an author of a number of books on learning and organizational development including *Action Learning for Managers* (Lemos & Crane 1996); *A Manager's Guide to Self-development*; *The Learning Company: A Strategy for Sustainable Development; 'Perfect plc?'; The purpose & practice of organisational learning* (all with McGraw-Hill). He is currently Revans Professorial Fellow in the Centre for Action Learning and Research at Salford University, Visiting Professor in the Department of Health Studies, University of York and Honorary Senior Research Fellow at the Department of Management Learning at the University of Lancaster.

Reg Revans wrote his first paper on Action Learning in 1937 and as an education officer in Essex was asked by the County Medical Officer why so many girls were abandoning hospital training that wards were threatened with closure. From this pre-war study he moved to the coal industry where he recommended the first non-expert-directed staff college on record and has since developed the Action Learning idea of concentrating upon the talents and motivations of the managers themselves in fifty countries. He has long forecast the uselessness of traditional 'management education' and is now concerned that, because this forecast is verified, genuine Action Learning will be replaced by 'established futilities being marketed at still higher fees as "advanced Action Learning" and under scores of different names, such as "quality assurance" and "clinical evaluation" '.

Vlasta Safarikova is currently Director of the Institute of the Confederation of the Czech Industries. Dr Safarikova founded the institute, which provides a training and management development service to confederation member companies, in 1993. From nothing she has built the institute into one of the leading training institutes in the Czech Republic. Prior to joining the institute Dr Safarikova was Director of the Economic Research Institute at the Prague School of Economics and before that, she was a lecturer then Assistant Professor in the Economics faculty.

Maggie Taylor was Senior Lecturer in Management Development at the former Manchester Polytechnic and a course team member of the MSc in Management by Action Learning. In 1990 she moved to Chester College to manage their Enterprise in Higher Education initiative. She is currently Development Project Manager at University College, Chester working on staff development and training, continuing vocational education and external relations. Previously her career has centred on personnel management as a practitioner, lecturer, consultant and course manager in the UK and USA.

Richard Thorpe is Professor in Management at Manchester Metropolitan University. Richard has been involved in Action Learning in the Department of Management almost from its inception. His main interests lie in the areas of action research and organizational change. He is committed to methods of management development that link management development with organizational change and the Action Learning approach is one way in which this is being developed at Manchester.

Krystyna Weinstein first encountering Action Learning while at Manchester Business School, has been running AL programmes since the mid-1980s as an independent consultant. She is Secretary of the International Foundation for Action Learning, and produces their quarterly newsletter. As an ex-journalist/editor she still writes – on 'frivolous' subjects, as well as management development – and applies the principles of Action Learning on writing programmes she runs.

Tony Winkless is a chartered occupational psychologist specializing in assessment, selection and development of managers and professionals within the public and private sectors. He held senior personnel and management positions for over twenty years in industry before establishing his own consulting practice. He has worked extensively within the NHS. This has involved long-term development programmes, workshops and research and evaluation projects for Chief Executives, Board Directors, Operational Managers, Senior Registrars, Consultants, Clinical and Medical Directors. A particular interest is in assessment and guidance to support the transition of the professional to the management role.

Lyle Yorks is Chair of the Department of Business Administration and Professor of Management at Eastern Connecticut State University. He also serves on the executive development faculties of the University of Tennessee, Knoxville and Louisiana State University. He holds master of arts degrees from Vanderbilt and Columbia Universities and an Ed.D. from Columbia University. He is author or co-author of several books, and his articles have been published in *The Academy of Management Review, The California Management Review, The Sloan Management Review,* and many other professional journals. Dr Yorks regularly serves as a consultant for companies worldwide.

Introduction

Mike Pedler

It has been suggested that we are reaching the end of certainty. The end of a shortish period in history when we believed we could control the world and manage our affairs. 'Scientific management' and the rationalistic nature of the management teaching which has grown out of it, are one aspect of an era in which the study and practice of science has seemed to promise that every problem is but a puzzle waiting to be solved.

Reg Revans has long distrusted this perspective, smelling danger when those in power come armed with right answers on their side. Revans imbibed the methods and values of science in the 1920s from Lord Rutherford and his colleagues, and in his early career approached the problems of management and organization from this standpoint – as an operational researcher – in coal mines, schools, hospitals and factories. The title of his 1965 book *Science and the Manager* acknowledges this heritage, although long before this he had become interested in learning, and what blocks learning, both in individuals and enterprises seen as whole organisms. Now 90 years old, he remains optimistic that ordinary people like you and me, being wary of those who seek to impose solutions, and putting our trust in each other as fellow learners, can question our way forwards from what troubles us:

> ... perhaps so-and-so – the boss – isn't correct, he should be thinking afresh ... people are beginning to say 'it's high time we asked ourselves fresh questions about how this organization is being run'. (From *A conversation with Reg Revans*.)

Since this book first appeared in 1983, Action Learning has continued to grow in popularity with management developers worldwide. Not all of this usage seems well informed; a senior management adviser said to me recently 'I use Action Learning all the time but I've never been in a set'. Practice also varies widely. For example, *Management Learning*, **27** (1) 1996 contains three articles and an editorial which either feature or cite Action Learning. One of these describes it as a way of teaching via simulation or 'experiential' methods, with no apparent awareness of the requirement for action on organizational problems and accountability to clients or sponsors.

The appeal of Action Learning is even reaching some academic management educators, who see in it the possibility for a more *Critical Management Education*.[1,2] This is welcome but ironic given Action Learning's origins in reaction to what Revans saw as the sterility and worse of Business School management education. It is also ironic that none of Revans' books is currently in print. Such texts as *Developing Effective Managers* (1971); *Action Learning: New Techniques for Managers* (1980); *The Origins and Growth of Action Learning* (1982) and *The ABC of Action Learning* (1983) can now only be found in libraries (especially IFAL and the Revans Centre at Salford University – see Appendix 3).

This absence of Revans from the bookshelves may help to explain some of the variability in interpretation and usage of Action Learning, but more likely the difficulty stems from the apparent simplicity and elusiveness of the idea itself. Revans has always resisted a single definition, and in so doing has both preserved Action Learning as a philosophy, preventing it from becoming just another management technique, and contributed to the plethora of activities claiming membership of the family. Newcomers seek in vain for a simple definition of Action Learning which, as I suggest in Chapter 6, is capable of being interpreted in various ways. Despite the difficulties, here is one short definition:

> Action Learning couples the development of people in work organizations with action on their difficult problems. It is based on the premise that there is no learning without action and no sober and deliberate action without learning. This contrasts with the principles underlying most of our formal education. Action Learning makes the task the vehicle for learning and has three main components – *people*, who accept the responsibility for action on a particular task or issue; *problems*, or the tasks which are acted on; and the *set* of six or so colleagues who meet regularly to support and challenge each other to take action and to learn. Action Learning implies both organization development and self-development – action on a problem changes both the problem and the actor.

However, this definition can be argued with – for example in the Hospital Internal Communications Project,[3] where groups of 30 or more doctors, nurses, porters and administrators met on a regular basis to share information, ask questions and plan action. These large groups have much in common with the related ideas of search conferencing (see for example Weisbord[4]). While small sets of six or so peer learners are a splendid social invention, apposite to our times, neither they, nor any other specific form which Action Learning may take, can be said to fully define the idea. In the book which most pretends definition, *The ABC of Action Learning*,[5] it is significant that Revans does not address the question 'What is Action Learning' but only the reciprocal 'What Action Learning is not'.

As he says in Chapter 1 there, 'Action Learning takes so long to describe . . . because it is so simple!'

As suggested above, this lack of definition is what vivifies Action Learning – demanding that those who practise it must create their own forms from the principles and experience available. This third edition of *Action Learning in Practice* provides some of those foundations by presenting the thoughts and findings of experienced practitioners from around the world. Action Learning continues to develop its practice – reflected in the changes in this edition since the second one appeared in 1991. Of the thirty or so chapters here, a third are entirely new, with several authors being published for the first time; of the remainder, half have been extensively revised, while the others, including some classic papers, stand the test of time.

The contents of this third edition are in four parts, with the new emphasis in Part IV reflecting both the maturing of the idea and the growing academic interest:

Part I What is Action Learning?
Part II Applications
Part III Questions of Practice
Part IV Evaluating Action Learning

In addition there are three Appendices. David Pearce's Action Manual has appeared unchanging in each edition of this book and continues to be praised and valued for its straightforward and practical advice in a field where much is ifs and buts as well as Ps and Qs.

Alan Mumford contributes his wide-ranging Review of the Action Learning Literature called from many years of reading and commenting. As a review it is rightly personal and evaluative and different in character and content from Nelson Coghill's Bibliography of Action Learning which it replaces. For Nelson's Bibliography you now have to consult the second edition, but updated versions and alternatives can be had from IFAL and the Revans Centre, which are listed in the brief Appendix 3.

It is my hope that, in this revised and updated version, *Action Learning in Practice* will continue to serve as a source of knowledge, guidance and inspiration.

REFERENCES

1 McLaughlin, H. and Thorpe, R. (1993) 'Action Learning – a paradigm in emergence: the problems facing a challenge to traditional management education and development', *British Journal of Management*, **4**(1), 19–27.

2 Willmott, H. (1995) 'Management education: provocations to a debate', *Management Learning*, **25**(1), 105–136.
3 Revans, R. W. (1972) *Hospitals: communications, choice and change*, London: Tavistock.
4 Weisbord, M. R. (1992) *Discovering common ground*, San Francisco: Berrett Koehler.
5 Revans, R. W. (1983) *The ABC of Action Learning*, Bromley, Kent: Chartwell-Bratt.

Part I
What is Action Learning?

INTRODUCTION

Part I of this book is devoted to understanding and defining the idea of Action Learning. It does this via examining the origins of the idea, its fields of application, the details of its method and the biography of its founder. It attempts some of the early questions which people bring when they approach the idea of Action Learning, particularly *What is action learning*? *What is the core of the idea*? *What survives beyond any given form or context*?

The Part begins with two contributions from Reg Revans: Chapter 1 is an early account of Action Learning's origins and nature and Chapter 4 is his brief but powerful prescription for a learning organization. Between them, they illustrate the ambition as well as the underlying values of Action Learning.

The other chapters in Part I are by experienced practitioners seeking to express the essence of Action Learning for themselves. Bob Garratt's applied and well-illustrated chapter sets out what needs to be done to unleash the power of Action Learning in the organizational context. John Morris unpicks some of the key processes of working with the Action Learning idea, especially the notion of P (Programmed Knowledge) and Q (Questioning Insight). Chapter 3 stresses the moral philosophy and purposes of Action Learning, and draws out the implications for the value-laden practice of management development in work organizations, while Chapter 6 explores three ways in which Action Learning may be differently interpreted, suggesting some benefits which may be had from a multiple perspective. Part I ends with Ronnie Lessem's fine essay on Revans' Action Learning depicting an idea forged over a long life in a man's successive encounters with the world.

1 Action Learning: Its Origins and Nature

Reg Revans

In 1971 Action Learning circumnavigated the globe; in the summer of that year I visited New York (to discuss the publication of *Developing Effective Managers*, where it had appeared), Dallas (where Southern Methodist University was initiating a programme), Sydney (to lay the foundations of future programmes), Singapore (where discussions about starting a programme continue), Delhi (now the headquarters of a programme run by the Government of India) and Cairo (to follow up the Nile Project).

In this chapter I try to explain what Action Learning may be, but this is not easy when those who read my lines have not tried Action Learning themselves. There is nothing in this chapter about what teachers of management ought to do about getting started, for that is dealt with by others. My only suggestion to those running the management schools is, over and above what they are already teaching, they should set out to contrive the conditions in which managers may learn, with and from each other, how to manage better in the course of their daily tasks.

Action Learning takes so long to describe, so much longer to find interesting, and so much longer still to get started because it is so simple. As soon as it is presented as a form of *learning by doing* the dismissiveness pours forth. 'Not unlike *learning by doing?* . . . But that's precisely what everybody here has been up to for donkeys' years! Anybody in management education can tell you that lectures and bookwork alone are not sufficient for developing people who have to take decisions in the real world. We all know that practice alone makes perfect, and ever since our first programmes were set up we've made all our students, however senior, do a lot of case studies. Some we fit into practical projects, and others do job rotation in their own firms. What's more, all our staff have been managers themselves, averaging over ten years of business experience, so they can get in on local problems to write up as our own cases. Quite often the initiative for this comes from the firms down on the industrial estate;

3

one man has a quality problem, another is trying to cut his stock levels, and they ask us if we'd like to help both them and our own students.... So, what with one thing and another going on here, we don't see what this excitement is about. Action learning? Learning by doing? What's so new? And who wants another book about it?'

We may all agree that learning by doing is, in many forms, nothing very new. It is one of the primary forces of evolution, and has accompanied mankind since long before our ancestors came down from the trees. Even the most primitive creatures must have learnt from their own experience, by carrying on with what they found good for them and by refraining from what they found to be harmful. The earliest living things, without any memory worth mentioning, also learnt by doing; if it was fatal to their life style they died, and if it was agreeable they flourished. Their behaviour was self-regulatory and its outcomes either 'Yes' or 'No'. But, as evolution went forward and the brain developed, the results of more and more experiences were remembered and the organisms grew more and more discriminating: outcomes were no longer just black or white, life or death, go or no-go. They took on more subtle differences of interpretation, like 'good' or 'bad'; 'try again' or 'that's enough for now'; 'carry on by yourself' or 'ask someone to help you'. These experiences are enshrined in our proverbs: 'The burned child dreads the fire'; 'Once bitten, twice shy'; and (Proverbs ch. xiv, v. 6) expresses clearly the regenerative nature of learning, knowledge building upon knowledge in a true desire to learn: 'A scorner seeketh wisdom and findeth it not: but knowledge is easy unto him that understandeth'. Once the first point has been grasped the others readily follow: 'Nothing succeeds like success' is, perhaps, a more modern way of saying the same thing. Even the failure to learn has its aphorism: 'There's no fool like an old fool' tells of those to whom experience means little, and who go on making the same mistakes at 70 that might have been excused at 17. With so much common testimony to learning by doing, therefore, what can be said for Action Learning that we find it necessary to keep on about it?

One reason is that it is a social process, whereby those who try it learn with and from each other. The burned child does not need to be told by its mother that it has been hurt, nor that the fire was the agent of pain. Action Learning has a multiplying effect throughout the group or community of learners. But this effect has also long been known: 'Iron sharpeneth iron; so a man sharpeneth the countenance of his friend' (Proverbs ch. xxvii, v. 17) expresses well one aspect of Action Learning today. The best way to start on one's really difficult problems is to go off and help somebody else with theirs. To be sure, the social strength of Action Learning (as I believe it to be) has a subtlety of its own: it is more than mutual growth or instruction, whereby each partner supplies the manifest deficiencies of the others with the knowledge or skill necessary to

4

complete some collective mission. Lending a hand to the common cause may well be part of any Action Learning project – but it remains incidental, rather than central, to it. Nor is Action Learning the essence of the mutual improvement societies so morally essential to the Victorians and still, to some degree, the contract tacitly uniting all communities of scholars. We must applaud the free exchange of what is known between the experts who know it; the sophisticated approach of operational research, in which teams of scientists, engineers and mathematicians work together on the complexities of vast undertakings, such as international airports, new towns, atomic energy plants and so forth, demands that one professional shall learn with and from the other. Nevertheless, what they are doing, for all its intricate teamwork, may be far from Action Learning – and may even be flatly opposed to it. For in true Action Learning, it is not what a man already knows and tells that sharpens the countenance of his friend, but what he does not know and what his friend does not know either. It is recognized ignorance, not programmed knowledge, that is the key to Action Learning: men start to learn with and from each other only when they discover that no one knows the answer but all are obliged to find it.

In practice, we find small groups are more effective at learning than simple pairs, provided that every member can describe his need to learn to the others in his set. The explanation of our paradox – that the learning dynamic is the recognition of a common ignorance rather than of some collective superfluity of tradeable knowledge – is both simple and elusive. Action Learning, as such, requires questions to be posed in conditions of ignorance, risk and confusion, when nobody knows what to do next; it is only marginally interested in finding the answers once those questions have been posed. For identifying the questions to ask is the task of the leader, or of the wise man; finding the answers to them is the business of the expert. It is a grave mistake to confuse these two roles, even if the same individual may, from time to time, occupy them both. But the true leader must always be more interested in what he cannot see in front of him, and this is the mark of the wise man; the expert's job is to make the most of all that is to hand. To search out the meaning of the unseen is the role of Action Learning; to manipulate to advantage all that is discovered is the expression of programmed teaching. Action Learning ensures that, before skills and other resources are brought to bear in conditions of ignorance, risk and confusion, some of the more fertile questions necessary to exploring those conditions have been identified: there is nothing so terrible in all human experience as a bad plan efficiently carried out, when immense technical resources are concentrated in solving the wrong problems. Hell has no senate more formidable than a conspiracy of shortsighted leaders and quickwitted experts. Action Learning suggests that, only if a man, particularly the expert, can be persuaded to draw a map of his own ignorance, is he likely to develop his full potential. In an epoch

5

of change, such as that in which the world now flounders, there is no handicap to exceed the misconception of past experience – particularly that on which present reputations are founded. The idolization of successes established in circumstances unlikely to recur may well guarantee one's place in The Dictionary of National Biography, but it is of little help in the fugitive present; there are times when we do well to put our fame aside:

> At the same time came the disciples unto Jesus, saying, Who is the greatest in the kingdom of heaven? And Jesus called a little child unto him, and set him in the midst of them and said, Verily I say unto you, Except ye be converted and become as little children, ye shall not enter into the kingdom of heaven. Whosoever therefore shall humble himself as this little child, the same is greatest in the kingdom of heaven. (Matthew ch. xviii, v. 1)

In times such as now, it is as imperative to question the inheritance of the past as it is to speculate upon the uncertainties of the future. As indicated in the quotation above Jesus warns of the need to be converted, to become once more as little children, since there is little hope for those who cannot unclutter their memories of flattery and deceit. It is advice most worthy of attention among all peoples with such tremendous histories as the British, although its classical illustration is in the parable of David and Goliath (I Samuel ch. xvii); here the experts, the warriors of Israel, faced with an adversary unknown in their experience (an armoured giant), could do nothing. They could only imagine what they had been taught: a bigger and stronger Israelite was needed to crush Goliath. Since no such man existed they were facing disaster. But the little child, David, proved himself the greatest among them; he was a child who had no experience of armour and could see that the search for the bigger and stronger Israelite was misconceived, so that Goliath had to be dealt with in some other fashion. The way was therefore open for him to pose the key question: 'Given that there is no man to throw at Goliath, how else do we kill him?' It is a fair statement of Action Learning to paraphrase this question as: 'Now all of us can see – even the experts, too – that our ideas simply do not work, what we need is to look for something that is quite new'. No question was ever more important to the denizens of this Sceptred Isle; somebody should launch a campaign to change its patron saint to David from Saint George.

We must not give the impression that it is only traditionalists such as the soldiers who have trouble in changing their conceptions; on the contrary, many of the greatest inventions are the products of conflict, for then we are obliged to think to save our skins. Nor must we imagine that our (supposed) intellectual leaders will necessarily come up with the new ideas; for example, an extrapolation of the current unemployment figures recently made by some professor suggests that 90 per cent of the population will be out of work by the year 2000 – although he does not say how many of these will be professors. What can be done to deflect the course of history, so as to avert this terrible calamity with but one person out of ten in work? The academic seer, exactly like the Israelites, finds the answer in his own past experience: more education. At the very moment in which the country needs as many Davids as possible, to help the rest of us become again as little children and to enter the kingdoms of heaven of our choice, we are to be exposed still more mercilessly to the dialectic of scholars and the sophistry of books.

So far Action Learning has been presented merely as another interpretation of well-known historical events and biblical quotations. It is as old as humanity, illustrated in the Old Testament, justified in the New and implicit in classical philosophy. What, then, is original about it? Only, perhaps, its method. But, before we dismiss this as incidental, let us recall that every branch of achievement advances only as fast as its methods: without telescopes there could be no astronomy, without computers no space missions, without quarries and mines no walls, no houses, no tools and therefore not much else.

This relation of what can be done to the richness of the means of doing it is, of course, another statement of Action Learning itself; its specifically useful method for the 1990s is not only in making clear the need for more Davids, but in setting out to develop them. It may, in essence, be no more than learning by doing, but it is learning by posing fresh questions rather than copying what others have already shown to be useful – perhaps in conditions that are unlikely to recur. Most education, and practically all training, is concerned in passing on the secrets and the theories of yesterday; before anything can be taught, or before anybody can be instructed, a syllabus must be prepared out of what is already known and codifed. But if today is significantly different from yesterday, and tomorrow is likely to be very different from today, how shall we know what to teach? Does not the parable of David and Goliath justify this question? Action Learning is not opposed to teaching the syllabus of yesterday, nor of last year, nor even of antiquity; Action Learning merely asks that, in addition to programmed instruction, the development of our new Davids will include the exploration of their own ignorance and the search for fresh questions leading out of it. Action Learning is a method of building on the academic tradition, not (as some seem to fear) a simplistic challenge to that tradition. As another authority has it:

> Think not that I am come to destroy the law, or the prophets: I am not come to destroy, but to fulfil (Matthew Ch v, v. 17)

The search for innovation began at the nationalization of the British coal industry, when it emerged that much less was known about how to run a pit than the experts would admit to – particularly when they were overwhelmed by the political hurricane that had struck their ancient culture. The colliery managers themselves were soon able to recognize that their new problems were beyond their individual capabilities, and in those early days they had little confidence in the administrative hierarchies established as their new masters. Thus, the suggestion made to the colliery managers' professional organization by its former president, Sir Andrew Bryan, that the managers themselves should work together, despite their self-confessed shortcomings, upon the here-and-now troubles of their own mines, was discussed with a cautious curiosity and accepted with a confident determination.

For three years a representative sample of twenty-two managers, drawn from pits all over England and Wales, worked together to identify and to treat their own problems; they were helped by a small team under the technical leadership of a seconded manager (who returned to run his own pit again) and by a dozen graduate mining trainees. Together with the staffs of the twenty-two pits themselves, the team worked through the symptoms of trouble indicated by the managers themselves, who met regularly at each other's mines to review not only the evidence that had been collected, but also the use made of it to improve the underground performances of the systems to which that evidence referred. Learning by doing took on both a structure and a discipline: identifying the problem by following up the symptoms, obliging those who owned the emergent problem to explain to their colleagues how they imagined it to have arisen, inviting proposals about early action to deal with it, reporting back to those same colleagues the outcome of such proposals for evaluation, and reviewing progress and prospects. The managers met regularly in stable sets of four or five; they were constrained by the nature of their operations and by the discipline of observation not only to examine with their own underground officials what might be going on around them, but also to disclose to their learner-colleagues why they might have held the many misconceptions uncovered by these practical exercises.

One manager agreed to study in depth the system by which he maintained his underground machinery; he encouraged interested parties from other pits to share his results, not merely to instruct him on how to do a better job but because they had to understand more clearly some troubles of their own. In this way he is launching a community of self-development whose credentials are the ultimate values of the managers themselves. There are many forms, no doubt, of education and training that enable the well-informed to make a point or two for the benefit of others, but invariably it is not clear that the points so made are also for the benefit of the here-and-now conditions in which those others may work. Facts that are incontrovertible in discussion may be ambiguous in application, and those unskilled in application may, simply by instructing others, nevertheless deceive themselves. There can be no place for this in Action Learning: all statements, whether of fact or of belief, whether of observation or of policy, whether about one's problems or about oneself, are all subject to the impartial responses of nature and to the sceptical judgements of relentless colleagues. Only those who have suffered the comradeship in adversity of an Action Learning set, each manager anxious to do something effective about something imperative, can appreciate the clarifying influences of compulsory self-revelation. This alone can help the individual to employ better his existing talents and internal resources, revealing why he says the things he says, does the things he does, and values the things he values. As one of the fellows in an early Belgian programme remarked at its final review: 'An honest man, did you suggest? What is an honest man? And what ought I to do to become one?' It is the participants themselves, each wrestling with his own conditions of ignorance, risk and confusion, who drag such questions from the newly-explored doubts of their macerated souls: they have no need for case leaders nor for programmed instruction (save on such technical details as they themselves can spot), since their growth is symbiotic, with and from each other, out of their own adversities, by their own resources and for their own rewards.

The reference to how Action Learning (as a specific social process) began in the collieries offers the chance of its further description. First, we notice that it was intended, not as an educational instrument, but as an approach to the resolution of management difficulties; the principal motivation to Action Learning was not a desire to teach anybody, nor even the hope that somebody else might learn: it was to do something about the tasks that the colliery managers were under contract to master. The argument was simple: the primary duty of the National Coal Board is to ensure that coal is drawn up the shafts of its pits at a reasonable price and in adequate amount; the training of colliery managers to help the Board fulfil this duty is quite incidental. Action Learning maintains the proper priorities by suggesting that the managers continue with their contractual obligations of drawing coal, which they now do in such fashion that they succeed in doing it better tomorrow by reporting to their colleagues how well they are doing it today. The managerial task itself is both the syllabus and the lesson.

Secondly, the learning of the managers, manifested by the improvement in productivity, consists mainly in their new perceptions of what they are doing and in their changed interpretations of their past experiences; it is not any fresh programme of factual data, of which they were previously ignorant but which they now have at their command, that enables them to surge with supplementary vigour through the managerial jungles. Perhaps for the first time in their professional lives they are able to relate their managerial styles (how to select objectives, evaluate resources and appraise difficulties) to their own values, their own talents and their own infirmities. If, as will at times occur, any particular member of an Action Learning set recognizes that he has need of technical instruction or programmed knowledge, he may make such arrangements as he can to acquire it. But his quest need no longer be seen as cardinal to Action Learning, even if his further success in treating his problems must depend upon the accuracy of his newly-to-be-acquired techniques; Action Learning will soon make clear the value of his latest lessons, and may even encourage him to be more discriminating in any future choice of technical adviser.

Thirdly, we see from this distinction between the reinterpretation of what is already known on the one hand, and on the other, the acquisition of knowledge formerly unfamiliar, another characteristic of Action Learning: it is to attack *problems* (or opportunities) and not *puzzles*, between which there is a deep distinction, yet one frequently overlooked. The puzzle is an embarrassment to which a solution already exists, although it may be hard to find even for the most accomplished of experts. Common examples are the crossword puzzle, the end game at chess, and the A-level examination question demanding a geometrical proof. Many technical troubles of industrial management are largely puzzles, such as how to speed work flow, measure costs, reduce stock levels, simplify delivery systems, optimize maintenance procedures and so forth; industrial engineering and operational research are systematic attacks upon manufacturing puzzles more often than not. The problem, on the other hand, has no existing solution, and even after it has been long and deliberately treated by different persons, all skilled and reasonable, it may still suggest to each of them some different course of subsequent action. This will vary from one to another, in accordance with the differences between their past experiences, their current values and their future hopes.

In the treatment of problems, therefore, as distinct from puzzles, the subjectivities of those who carry out that treatment are cardinal. All who treat the same puzzle should arrive at much the same conclusion, consonant with some observable outcome. But, in the treatment of a problem, none can be declared right or wrong; whether any particular upshot is acceptable or not, and to whom, depends (and must depend) upon the characteristics of the individual to whom that upshot is made known. While it may be a substantial *puzzle* to measure how many unemployed persons there will be in Britain next New Year's Eve, those who set out to do the measurement should be in significant agreement. But the managerial (political, governmental) *problem* as to what, if anything, to do about it will scarcely be an object of agreement. Such proposals for action will be strongly coloured by all manner of personal beliefs and interests, ranging from bank balances to international sentiments, and from the estimate of oneself being out of work to the (possibly subconscious) appreciation of what a power of good this experience would do to those who write so eloquently about its reinvigorating effects.

However, Action Learning makes no claim to develop the skills for solving puzzles: this is the role of programmed instruction in the appropriate profession,

10

trade or technology; the mission of our method is to clarify the problems that face managers, by helping them to identify, through the enticing distortions and deceitful recollections of their own past triumphs and rebuffs, what possible courses of action are open to them. It is when these are then surveyed in detail that the puzzle solving expertise is called for. Our experience of many Action Learning programmes then suggests that this expertise is generally at hand in the very organization tormented by the problem to be resolved; if it is not, then there is almost invariably another organization represented in the Action Learning programme that will be most happy to supply it.

All may learn with and from each other, not just the participants alone but on a larger scale; the concept of a *learning community*, that emerged from the Inter-University Programme of Belgium, is perhaps the highest expression of the social implications of Action Learning that we can find. The ease with which such a community may be formed out of the organizations that choose to work together in an Action Learning programme is evidently a measure of the readiness with which they communicate both within and between themselves. It has long been known that high morale and good performance are marked by speedy and effective systems of communication, and it is these which enable their managements to learn. When tasks are carried out in settings that soon make clear the consequences of those tasks, then life becomes not only intelligible, but is in itself a learning process and an avenue to self-respect and confidence.

So far this chapter has concentrated on the advantages of working in the set of manager-colleagues, each of whom is endeavouring to understand and treat some problem allocated to him. It may be (as it was with the participants in the pioneering programme among the mining engineers) a series of troubles arising in his own command, so that, if the manager is to carry on with his own job, he is able to work only part-time on his assignment; on the other hand, the manager (as in the first top level exchange programme in Belgium) may be working full-time in some other enterprise and upon a problem in some functional field remote from his own. There are many different options available to the designer of Action Learning programmes, but all must be characterized by two criteria: the set, in which real managers tackling real problems in real time are able freely to criticize, advise and support their fellows, helped as the participants feel appropriate by external specialists; and the field of action, wherein the real problem exists to be treated by other real persons in the same real time. In other words, Action Learning demands not only self-disclosure of personal perception and objective, but the translation of belief and opinion into practice; all that goes on in the set must have its counterpart in the field of action, and the progress of this counterpart activity is constantly reviewed within the set.

Thus, action learning not only makes explicit to the participant managers their own inner processes of decision, but makes them equally attentive to the

11

means by which those processes effect changes in the world around them. After twenty years observing what the set members have to say to each other about success and failure in the field of action, it is possible to suggest that what might reasonably be called the 'micropolitical' skills needed by managers to judge what is relevant to building into a decision, on the one hand, and to secure what is essential to implementing that decision, on the other, can be significantly developed by Action Learning. In other words, those who participate in successful sets can also learn to penetrate the mists of field diagnosis more clearly and to bring a surer touch to their field achievements.

This is not the place to enter into a detailed discussion of what these micropolitical skills may be, but an understanding of them seems cardinal to any general theory of human action. For the present, it is sufficient to summarize the successful diagnosis in the three questions: 'What are we trying to do? What is stopping us from doing it? What might we be able to do about it?' (and it is interesting to write down what David might have answered to them all); and to perceive effective therapy as a campaign of allies who answer to the specification: 'Who knows about this problem? Who cares about it? Who can do anything about it?' It is the quality of the successful fellow to identify these allies and to recruit them throughout his project into an action team (known in Belgium as the *structure d'accueil*) to serve whoever may own the problem on which the fellow is to exercise and develop his managerial skills.

The literature of project design and negotiation must be consulted by those who wish to take Action Learning beyond the report writing stages that many see as its conclusion, for the complexities of taking action (which demand commitment and anxiety) go far beyond those of suggesting what action might be taken by others (which call only for intelligence and loquacity); all that must be observed now is that exercises that call only for (supposed) analysis of field problems, and are completed without the (supposed) analysis being put into action, are simply not Action Learning as it is defined in this chapter. This, of course, is no reason whatsoever for regarding them unfavourably; as with the case study, in which the participants neither collect the evidence from the field before discussing it nor, after their discussion, do anything to implement their conclusions, much may still be gained – in particular, dialectical skill in knocking the arguments of others to bits. For many of life's occasions such skill may be a most useful asset. It is, all the same, a mistake to imagine that the facts of nature in all her raw relentlessness are quite as readily disposed of as are the arguments of one's more vulnerable opponents in the classroom. It is not enough for managers to know what is good, nor even to convince other managers that they know what is good: they must also be able to do it in the real world. In this life it is generally a mistake to confuse *talking about* action with action itself.

The other contributions to this book will give some indication of the present condition of our subject; the central thesis – that responsible action is our greatest disciplinarian as well as our most sympathetic helper – will appear in every light, in every setting and in every culture. It will do so, not because Action Learning has any claim to greatness nor to originality, but because it is in the very nature of organic evolution. Nevertheless, so numerous are the possible variations upon the themes that run through this book that Action Learning may seem to be all things to all men. Certainly, I for one am often confused by reading of some development that is what I would have called pure Action Learning, but that is described by some other name, such as 'activity learning', or 'action teaching', or 'participative management', or 'management action teamwork', or any of a score of other titles; it is only when I refer to the date of publication of such accounts (usually in the past couple of years) that I can be assured that my writings of the 1940s are not unconscious plagiarism. I am also mystified, from time to time, to read confident reports of successful achievements in the field of management education that are listed as Action Learning, but later perusals still confirm my inability to detect in them what I have set forth in this chapter as characteristic (for me) of Action Learning. But of what importance is my failure? If we give our attention to the main process by which mankind has dragged itself up from the abyss to which some of its representatives seem so anxious to return, we must not be surprised if there is disagreement as to the nature of that process. For all that, however, I cannot put out of my mind two references, whenever the nature of Action Learning is compared with what, during my spell as President of the European Association of Management Training Centres, was for a generation regarded as management education. The first is from Plutarch's *Lives* (Agesilaus p. 726):

> Agesilaus being invited once to hear a man who admirably imitated the nightingale, he declined, saying he had heard the nightingale itself

The origin of the second I can no longer recall, except as a threat by my mother when I was inclined to stray beyond the garden wall; it was that I might be stolen by the gipsies and then so disfigured that even she would be unable to recognize me were I offered back to her on sale. It is astonishing to discover, so late in life, how vividly I remember her words on reading yet one more article on what is new in Action Learning.

2 The Power of Action Learning

Bob Garratt

Action Learning is a process for the reform of organizations and the liberation of human vision within organizations. The process is based on taking one or more crucial organizational problems and, in real time, analysing their dynamics; implementing proposed solutions derived from the constructive criticisms of colleagues; monitoring results; and through being held responsible for these actions, learning from the results so that future problem solving and opportunity taking is improved. In theory this is little different from the logical procedure of any rational person attempting to solve organizational problems. But organizations rarely behave rationally. In practice irrationality is generated by misunderstanding the complexities and uncertainties of modern organizations. Such irrationality interferes with achieving the blend of logic and emotionality necessary to transcend organizational difficulties. The Action Learning process attempts to achieve this blend through giving rigour and pace to the cycle of learning and, through using the positive powers of small groups, to sustain this discipline and rhythm. Structural elements of Action Learning are that the authority and responsibility for analysis and implementation are given to those people who have psychological ownership of the problem and must live with their proposed solution. The whole is underpinned by the proven assumption that people learn most effectively with and from colleagues in the same position.

As such it is a very powerful organizational tool for the reform of working systems and the subsequent restating of organizational objectives. Its power derives from releasing and reinterpreting the accumulated experiences of the people who comprise the organization. The combination of this released energy and the act of moving the authority for problem solving to those people who must live with the consequences is a deliberate devolution of organizational power. Such devolution has two major benefits. First, giving responsibility to those who own the problem gains commitment to any proposed solution, offers participants the chance to consciously develop their own learning, and demonstrates to all concerned the benefits of more autonomous group working. Second, the learned autonomy and reintegration of work groups allows the top managers

15

to concentrate on the increasingly necessary roles of monitoring the uncertain environment, and designing the future to ensure the organization's continuity, with the time released from not having to watch constantly day-to-day activities.

Action Learning can be seen as so powerful by perceptive but faint-hearted souls that they will not allow its use in their organizations because of the perceived risks to the organization and their careers. The fear is usually that uncovering the inadequacies of the organization, and the blocks to reform, will unsettle the stability of all concerned. This is part of the process. Action Learning is concerned with risk and uncertainty, but its focus is not on the destructive aspects of negative criticism and buck passing often associated with them. It concentrates on managing risks and uncertainties and on learning from them for the benefit of the stakeholders of the organization. As the recession in the West continues and the uncertainties and risks in just surviving become painfully clear, many people are realizing that there are no risk free remedies for their organizational ills. They are, therefore, looking for processes of organizational learning and adaptation which though incurring risks are creative, motivating, and cost-effective. Action Learning meets these criteria, but it needs some organizational clout to get it started effectively enough to sustain itself as the style of managing and thinking suitable for the turbulent 1990s. One of the few constructive things to come out of the present economic and social recession is that it is creating crises in organizations. As this is the only condition under which truly radical rethinking of the means and ends of an organization can be undertaken, and the results implemented systematically and rapidly, it bodes well for Action Learning, for Action Learning thrives in crises.

Given that Action Learning is a powerful process of organizational reform; that it involves the devolution of powers and the recasting of managerial roles; and that it is often instigated in conditions of crisis; it is essential that the present holders of organizational power understand both logically and emotionally what is likely to happen in their own backyard if they use this process. It has long been an axiom of management that for any significant changes to occur in an organization the top management must be committed to, and informed of, the proposed changes. Action Learning goes a step further and says the top management must be willing to learn from the resulting analyses and implementation in their turn, i.e. that they need become part of the total organizational learning system and must play a continuing part in the development of it.

This is essential for Action Learning as it is based on the synergy of simultaneous development at the personal, organizational, and business levels to achieve its powerful impact. Such synergy is beneficial both to top management who see it as a suitable and socially acceptable return made on their investment in people – the learning resource of their organization – and to the employees of the organization as it allows them to reform their ways of working by removing the sources of frustration whilst also developing themselves as more rounded people. So for any simultaneous development to occur through Action Learning, no matter what the level of entry to the organization, it is essential that top management is prepared for the opportunities and risks they face.

Top management commitment and the consequent change in their behaviour is necessary because it symbolizes that changes in all the stakeholders' attitudes are to be encouraged as the meaning of what is meant by 'work' in their organization is reconsidered. This process will often seem uncomfortable, even alien, to the people concerned. Hence any evidence, however flimsy, that top management is not serious in their commitment will be used to abort the process. It is the role of top management to provide sufficient personal and organizational 'cover' for those people participating in an Action Learning programme to ensure they are not punished under the existing organizational rules whilst they strive to develop new ones. Time is needed for any significant behavioural and attitudinal changes to occur so carefully monitored 'pilot projects' are a useful way of signalling that change is being encouraged from the top and the authority for day-to-day problem solving devolved.

Many people feel that they would like to use Action Learning in their organization but have not sufficient power or rhetoric to make the case. In the next few paragraphs I have outlined the arguments I have found effective in convincing top managements of the benefits of using Action Learning to reform their organizations. It is not 'pure' Action Learning theory because it draws pragmatically on the work of many people where this has been found to make a point effectively, but the structure and logic of the argument is very much Action Learning's own.

CONVINCING TOP MANAGEMENT

I assume that top managers are interested in the survival and growth of their organizations. In the present age of uncertainty and discontinuity both aspirations are increasingly difficult to attain using current organizational thinking and structures. One is looking, therefore, for a way of thinking and acting which helps cope with these uncertainties and discontinuities. We know from the study of ecology that the essential formula for the continuing survival of an organism is that its rate of learning must be equal to, or greater than, the rate of change in its environment. (See Fig 2.1.) If its rate of learning is less than the rate of change, then it dies. This formula is usually symbolized in the Action Learning writings as $L \geqslant C$. It seems to hold good from the simple amoeba to the largest trans-national corporation. Its usefulness is in its focus on learning as the crux of surviving environmental change. In organizations this argues for the development and maintenance of a system of organizational learning to monitor environmental change and take appropriate avoiding action.

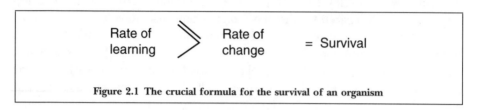

Figure 2.1 The crucial formula for the survival of an organism

The only resource capable of learning within an organization is the people who comprise it. The very diversity of the experience of the people in the organization is a valuable asset, if one can learn to use it. No technology can learn to cope with the managerial problems of organizations because it is designed to cope with the solution of technical 'puzzles' rather than managerial 'problems'. Problems are rooted in the quality and quantity of the organizational learning resource and, therefore, reflect the quality of top management's investment in that area.

Action Learning is most effective when used to confront organizational problems rather than technical puzzles. As learning is at the core of its process it is particularly valuable in developing the structures and dynamics of organizational change. It is, therefore, immediately attractive to top managers as an obvious way out of the present organizational difficulties. But their acceptance is often without sufficient consideration to the unique strengths and weaknesses of their organization. For a system of organizational learning to be developed for effective organizational problem solving, it is essential that top management accept there are no cut-and-dried answers to what are seen as common organizational problems. The different social history, personalities, and organizational culture, will determine the boundaries of resources and values within which any possible solutions will lay. Encouraging the employees to find effective solutions within these boundaries is a task of top management. They have available to them a highly cost-effective set of tools – the talents and experiences of the people they employ. It is vital that they release and tap the springs of self-sufficient learning within their organization, establishing the atmosphere in which reinterpretation and constructive criticism of people's experiences is encouraged on a regular basis which is central to this style of managing, so that failure to meet targets can be discussed openly and more realistic targets be mutually agreed. This will enable employees to rise above the usual interpersonal bickering and subscribe to important common tasks which transcend the petty politics and concentrate on the survival of their organization.

It takes time to change organizational culture, management styles, and organizational structures. Action Learning is significantly faster and more effective in achieving these ends than other forms of organizational change. However, the interim period is always difficult so 'cover' within the business for the first projects is essential. Whether these are called 'pilot programmes', 'management action groups' or other such names is unimportant. What is essential is that the top managers are sufficiently committed intellectually and emotionally to want to become part of the organizational learning system. However, it is often alarming how quickly top managers 'buy' the Action Learning idea intellectually without having bought it emotionally. Then, as information is uncovered that does not fit their stereotypes, they withdraw co-operation or react negatively to the initiative. Questioning their assumptions and work processes is an essential part of the organizational learning process. Once they can be seen to change when faced with authentic information which questions their operating assumptions, then the change in organizational attitudes will disseminate rapidly through the organization.

The organizational learning of which I am talking is not just the acquisition of impersonal and codified knowledge. It is not just a matter of collecting as much data as possible on any problem area. Data, the ocean of facts available in the world, is useless on its own. What are needed for effective managerial decisions are the attitude and skill to select from that sea of data the specific pieces which form the information needed to resolve the problem. So I am looking for a meaning for 'learning' in an organization which integrates attitudes, knowledge, and skills through action on live problems into a process of reflection and reinterpretation that develops higher quality question posing and answering. This I see as the core of the learning organization.

Built into organizational learning in a rapidly changing world is an ever present element of risk taking. This is why developing higher quality questioning is central to managing such risks. We have seen that the application of technical knowledge alone is insufficient to resolve complex organizational problems. Even if it were, the intervention of a single variable, time, is sufficient to ensure that managers are usually unable to have sufficient learning to take risk free decisions. It seems to be an axiom of management that decisions have to be taken always before one has had time to gain the full facts. The consequence is that the difference between the level of learning held by a manager, or an organization, and the level needed theoretically for a totally risk free decision is a measure of the amount of risk being taken. (See Figure 2.2.)

My argument is that it is impossible to avoid risks in the present economic climate so a prime role of top management is to create the organizational climate in which thoughtful risk taking and subsequent learning are encouraged. Top managers face the same risk taking dilemmas as the employees they lead. We all fantasize about the amount and consequences of the risks we face. Recent work has shown that there are three main categories of risks about which people concern themselves – physical; financial; and emotional. In an unsupportive or destructively critical organizational environment fantasies about all three types breed with each other and stifle action. 'Dynamic conservatism', or creative inactivity, are common causes of learning loss in organizations. Action Learning counters learning loss by encouraging supportive and constructively critical behaviour within individuals first, and then disseminated it throughout the organization.

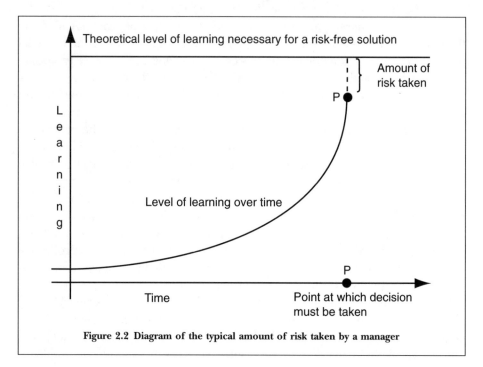

Figure 2.2 Diagram of the typical amount of risk taken by a manager

An essential foundation of the Action Learning argument is that of ensuring that the authority and responsibility for action and learning is passed to the lowest appropriate part of the organization for the work in hand. This is usually in direct contrast with most behaviour in organizations. The argument for doing this is that a system that encourages people at all levels of their organization to be as self-sufficient as possible is inherently healthy in itself as it will keep up the necessary rate of learning. But more than that it also releases the time and energy of top managers to look upwards and outwards to undertake the strategic aspects of their jobs which are often neglected in times of crisis. It assumes that the daily operational problems are dealt with by the people who must live with them and any proposed solutions; whilst senior managers get on with monitoring the environment and integrating the boundaries between the internal operational world and the external environment. (See Figure 2.3.)

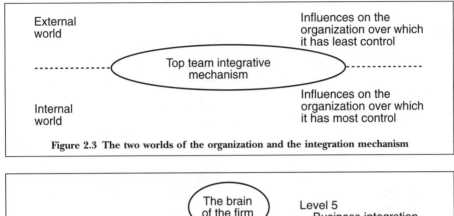

External world

Influences on the organization over which it has least control

Top team integrative mechanism

Internal world

Influences on the organization over which it has most control

Figure 2.3 The two worlds of the organization and the integration mechanism

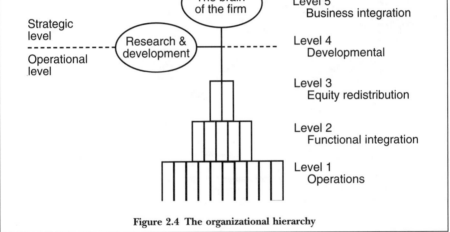

Strategic level

Operational level

The brain of the firm

Research & development

Level 5
Business integration

Level 4
Developmental

Level 3
Equity redistribution

Level 2
Functional integration

Level 1
Operations

Figure 2.4 The organizational hierarchy

Two models seem to help top managers clarify their thinking in relation to what will be an appropriate launching and development Action Learning strategy for them. The first concerns the organizational structure and roles of their business. It is a highly simplified version of Stafford Beer's excellent 'Brain of the Firm' (see Figure 2.4), where the notions of what should happen at the equity distribution and business integration levels can be usefully debated. Most Action Learning interventions in the UK have happened at level 3 as this is typically the area where externally or internally-generated crises are felt. Action here can usually be disseminated downwards, to where the work is happening, very fast. With the time then released top management can give better thought, and develop better questioning, about the strategic levels, reasonably secure in the knowledge that the operational side is self-regulating within its agreed plans.

This can be represented by a simplified adaptation of Argyris' model of 'double loop learning' (see Figure 2.5) i.e. the idea that the internal operational sphere and the external strategic sphere need integration through a learning mechanism. In terms of an intervention strategy for the use of Action Learning by top management this could be seen as:

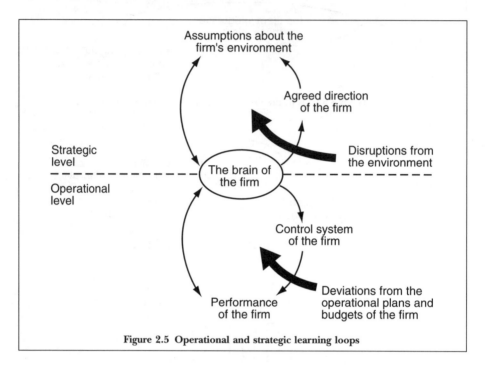

Figure 2.5 Operational and strategic learning loops

1. Activation of senior functional managers to tackle key organizational survival projects.
2. Dissemination of the approaches learned by senior managers to the wider employee base, to encourage their reconsideration of present work practices and structures, in preparation for the devolution of authority to become self-learning and self-regulating within the plans agreed with top managers.
3. Activation of the top management to reconsider their thinking and roles following the devolution of most daily operational problems; and their need to concentrate on environmental monitoring and the integration of strategy with operations.

These simple models and arguments proved sufficient to convince a range of top managers to launch pilot activities for the reform of their organizations in many parts of the United Kingdom, France, and The Netherlands in the early 1980s.

MAKING IT OPERATIONAL

If such arguments are powerful enough to cause debate amongst the top team and demands for subsequent action, then the focus turns to 'What do we do from here?'

The four key elements of the Action Learning process:

1. a crucial organizational problem
2. people willing to take risks to develop themselves and their organizations
3. authority to take action on the problem
4. a system for learning reflectively

are all that are needed to guarantee success with the pilot programme. The reader should now be able to design his/her own programme subject only to the personalities and history of their organization. The rest of what I have to say is, therefore, more anecdotal and may overshadow the simplicity of the above elements. What follows is a distillation of my experiences over the last ten years. It is not a series of formulae the application of which will guarantee that what you are doing is Action Learning. Only you can decide that through your learning.

One thing I have learned is that there is a need for a 'programme manager'. This is not necessarily a personnel or training department person. Line managers are just as competent to do it. The role is arduous and political – a good training for general managership. It is the link between the logic of top management's Action Learning strategy and the emotional responses, positive or negative, of the employees. It is therefore not an easy job, but any risk taking manager can do it. Perhaps one of the most regular surprises for people taking the programme manager role for the first time is just how fast top managers grasp the idea of getting cost-effective development launched in their business. Within this enthusiasm for the logic of the idea there are a series of traps for the unwary programme manager. There is no direct connection between the acceptance of the logic of an idea and its emotional acceptance. This latter aspect requires an attitude and behavioural change which the former does not. So, rather than just accepting top management's verbal acceptances of the logic, the programme manager must be courageous and keep a firm link with the top team to gain their emotional commitment to the practice of Action Learning within their organization.

Whilst this can appear initially as a daunting prospect to a new programme manager it is a necessary test of the resolve of each side in the process. An honest and humble approach to working alongside the top team to research their views as to what are the crucial problems of the organization can build the credibility of the programme manager rapidly with them. The selection of key problem areas by individual top team members usually generates a varied list which needs debate and comparison by the whole team before they can focus on the structural elements of policy and strategy for their organization. From this debate it is usually easy to identify one or more managerial problems that need resolution within, say, twelve months and would, therefore, make suitable Action Learning projects. Once the top team has selected these projects the programme manager is locked into a line manager role. He or she needs to operate within the time and money budgets agreed with the top team to achieve the stated performances. Any deviations from the required targets will need careful monitoring and reflection by the top team to determine whether their target setting is unrealistic, or whether the failure to achieve lies with their employees. In either case there is a need to develop a system of organizational learning which allows the business to do significantly better next time.

ELEMENTS OF PROGRAMME DESIGN

Having gained the commitment and operational targets of the top team, the next stage is essentially one of design. Dogmatism can raise its ugly head at this point as to what is the nature of 'real' Action Learning. Rather than become embroiled in a fruitless game of restrictive definition I prefer to take a contingent stance and stress that, if there exist the four key elements mentioned above (p. 23), the appropriate design will depend on the history and resources of the organization, the personalities involved, and the wit and creativity of those charged with the programme design.

Central to an appropriate design is an awareness of the processes by which adults learn. Reg Revans in *The ABC of Action Learning* describes four typical managerial blockages to the problem of deciding honest sources of information in conditions of uncertainty and risk – the four corrigible handicaps:

1. the idolization of perceived past experiences
2. the charismatic influences of (other) successful managers
3. the impulsion to instant activity
4. the belittlement of subordinates

Within the employee's energy and enthusiasm for actions based on ill-considered learned responses – their action fixation – lays both the blockage and opportunity for true learning. We know that adults learn best from live projects; from the support and constructive criticism of colleagues; from rigorous self-reflection leading to serious reinterpretation of their previous experiences; and from a willingness to test their hypotheses in action.

We need to design, therefore, an organizational learning process that links analysis, prognosis, implementation, and testing, with a group of colleagues facing similar problems who will respect the personal experimentation and reconsideration that lies at the heart of the Action Learning process. This grouping of colleagues is called the 'project set'. It is a group of comrades in adversity who will give, and expect as a reciprocal, personal support and honest, constructive criticism as the rights and duties of each project set member. The set gives the rigour and pace through the regularity of its meetings for each individual to develop the ability to reflect upon both proposed plans of action and the consequences of them. Then it encourages reinterpretation of the realities of that plan and its implementation as they unfold.

The Action-fixated cycle of learning can be characterized as shown in Figure 2.6 and can be contrasted with the Action Learning cycle shown in Figure 2.7. At this point in the design the programme manager can link the projects, as agreed with the top team, with the participants in the project set. We can then characterize the basic logistics as shown in Figure 2.8. The elements I have now added are those of the 'client' and the 'set adviser'. The client is the person who ultimately owns the problem under investigation – the person who will finally be held responsible for the resolution of the project on which the participants work. In pilot programmes the client is typically the top team member with responsibility for the key problem area. The set adviser is usually a person external to the organization who helps with the developmental processes of the individuals and the set. Whilst theoretically unnecessary because the experiences already reside within the employees and simply need reinterpretation, they are usually helpful for a first programme both to 'legitimize' the Action Learning process within the organization and to help participants experiment with the changes in learning and management style demanded.

There are characteristics of successful programmes which depend on a combination of project type and situation. The simple matrix which describes these can be shown as in Figure 2.9. Observation of the effectiveness of each part of this quadrant seems to show that:

1. Own job projects tend to be effective for personal (role) development and the reinterpretation of specific jobs within an organization.
2. Internal exchanges tend to be effective for personal development and establishing better links between specialist functions within an organization.
3. External exchanges tend to be highly effective for personal development and in helping the client organization learn to value different experiences and views.

25

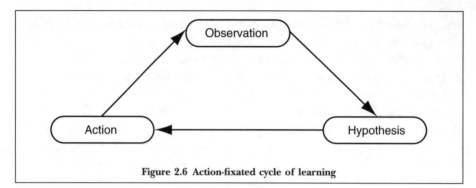

Figure 2.6 Action-fixated cycle of learning

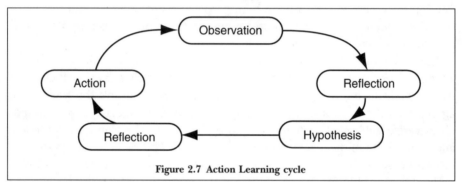

Figure 2.7 Action Learning cycle

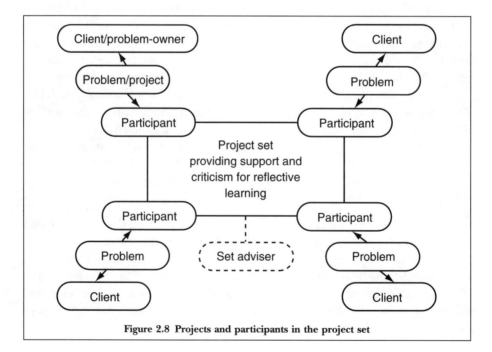

Figure 2.8 Projects and participants in the project set

4. Technical exchanges tend not to be effective for the development of managerial problem solving because of their over-concentration on technical puzzles but are useful for the dissemination of best practice.

The programme designer has a number of permutations of personal and/or organizational development to negotiate with the top team using this quadrant. Many highly successful programmes have been completed over the past twenty years using the individually-orientated approach mentioned above. However, in the present economic conditions, it has been noticeable that top managers have been keen to get fast and cost-effective results throughout their organizations. In these conditions the personally-orientated approaches tend to be seen as too slow and other approaches are needed. Within the last two years there has been a rise in the number of team based programmes. In these small teams – typically four or five participants usually but not exclusively from one organization – work on a crucial problem of the business as a single project. As a team they form a much stronger political force for change in the organization than an individual. This increased strength usually guarantees that changes will disseminate fast once the Action Learning process is under way. Team projects are, therefore, a powerful tool for organizational renewal.

This demand for increasing the scale and speed of dissemination of Action Learning within organizations, and its focus away from individual development

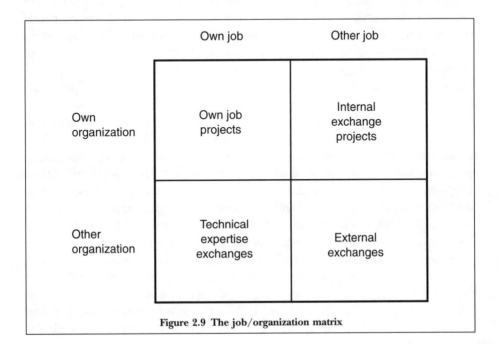

Figure 2.9 The job/organization matrix

towards the reform of the total organization, brings into sharp relief the earliest and rather neglected work of Reg Revans in the National Coal Board, the Hospital Service, and West Africa. These emphasized the need to develop a 'learning community' attitude at all levels of the organization. This change of scale does not negate the fundamental idea of using intelligent people, naive to the functional specialism that forms the basis of the project they are confronting, asking basic questions about fundamental organizational problems. The power of 'intelligent naivety' in questioning the working assumptions of an organization is the leading edge of the Action Learning process. The rigour and pace of the project set forms the plane; and the motive force for organizational take-off is the energy released through the devolution of authority to solve problems. With this combination it is possible to truly undertake organizational reform.

THE CHANGING ROLES OF TRAINERS AND DEVELOPERS

Other chapters in this book will deal with life in project sets, the processes of personal development and organizational change, and the advantages and disadvantages of using advisers for the project sets. What interests me is the significant change in roles 'traditional' trainers or developers need to embrace if they are to become effective practitioners of Action Learning. Systems of organizational learning are much too important to be left to trainers. They are central to the survival and growth of any organization and therefore reside ultimately with the top team. The practice of developing such a learning system is a line management job in its own right and needs, therefore, line management skills. Perhaps the biggest trauma for a trainer or developer to face is that the programme manager need not be a trainer; but any trainer undertaking the running of an Action Learning programme must be a line manager. An entrepreneurial, risk taking, stance is essential if the programme manager is to be successful. I use the word 'entrepreneurial' here both in the sense of selling to top managers the cost-effectiveness of the proposition and, more importantly, in its original French sense of a 'stager of dramas'. The use of the Action Learning process with its resultant release of hitherto untapped energies is most certainly a drama to be staged and managed. This is easily understood by line managers but often proves more difficult for trainers and developers to assimilate, particularly if they have been running courses or programmes which have been hermetically sealed from the real time pressures of their organizations.

In addition to the entrepreneurial role, there is that of programme designer. Here it is not sufficient to be just a technical expert on Action Learning or the processes of the project set because both lock the trainer back into the easy stereotype expected by participants. This will inevitably lead to the rejection of the trainer and the possibility of rejection of the total process. A more appropriate stance for a programme designer seems to be that of the contingent consultant working from the problems as they exist and, through using a wide and flexible range of behavioural, attitudinal, and cognitive inputs, working towards the assimilation of the Action Learning process within the brain of the firm through the demonstration of its effectiveness.

Parallel with the entrepreneurial and design stages, and continuing throughout the programme, is the adviser and counsellor role which helps everyone involved in the process interpret it through their own experiences. This calls for the ability to explain what is proposed and expected in a language appropriate to each part of the organization. An essential part of this role is the ability to demystify the fantasies of the participants as to why 'they' (top management) wish to launch the Action Learning process, and then following through the process by highlighting the individual and group learning as it develops. As the total strategy unfolds, then the programme manager needs to ensure the development of the top team's strategic role and ensure that it links into the operational learning systems as they grow.

In all these new roles it is impossible for the trainers to maintain a safe, off-line, role. Commitment to launching Action Learning processes in an organization is undoubtedly more risky than traditional stances. But the reward is in bringing the trainer directly into the line functions as part of their career development. It seems that the management of an Action Learning programme is a useful test of general management competence. Perhaps in the future we shall see this as a natural move in any manager's career path as the acid test before general managership.

3 Managing as Moral Art

Mike Pedler

In this chapter managing and management development is put forward as a moral art. Following Snell 'moral' is taken to refer to any position adopted with regard to 'right' or 'wrong' purposes, actions, ways of living and so on.[1] Significant learning, which changes both the person and the world, must always be concerned with moral values. Managerial action influences both the world in which it takes place and the responsible actor, and is an 'art of the possible' going beyond individual action to creative collaboration in organizing.

The chapter begins by addressing the relationship of management and morality. Growing concerns over the environment, questions of ethical business behaviour and the unequal trading relationship between rich and poor countries contribute to a rising interest in this issue. 'Right' managerial action seems to involve a wider accountability than that of any single 'bottom line', but how may this happen? Assuming that we wish to, how can we learn to exercise better moral judgement, set higher standards for ourselves and a better example for others?

It is argued that Action Learning, with its emphasis upon manager development taking place within the context of managerial action (and vice versa), provides the appropriate conditions for developing the capacity for making moral judgements. Finally the argument is extended beyond the individual to the organization. Does the extent to which individual managers can make moral choices depend upon the 'ethical climate' of the organization? Does 'ethical' management development lead to ethically sound organizations?

MANAGING AND MORALITY

From the polluting and alienating businesses of the northern hemisphere to the poverty and famine of the south the costs of bad managing become ever more serious in our increasingly interconnected world.[2] The burgeoning business of management development has plenty of advice, elixirs and 'new' ideas on offer.

Recent suggestions include searching for 'excellence', seeking 'total quality management', 're-engineering your business' and becoming a 'lean' or a 'learning organization'. In a world described by pundits as hyper-competitive and turbulent, characterized by uncertainty, chaos and complexity, beset by megatrends and so on, there is much temptation to purchase.

In so many ways the Action Learning idea stands against consumerist values. Where we are exhorted to buy the latest package, Action Learning sharply questions its validity, suggesting instead, in David Casey's words, that each manager needs to re-invent the wheel of their own managerial practice. In Action Learning the emphasis is on the courageous struggle to act and understand; not on short cuts and quick fixes. Yet 'Action Learning sets', 'management action groups' or 'learning sets' are increasingly popular. The small, self-managed group meeting members' needs for peer support and advice, with a 'bias to action', has now become a familiar aspect of management development programmes.

Good managing can often seem to be equated with achieving action in the short term:

> Most managers, tormented by the ticking of the office clock and the fall of the days from the factory calendar, will respond sooner to the urgencies of the moment, however inconsequential, than to the suggestion that they ought to clear the decks and heed the long-term warnings; this is Gresham's law of management: 'Short-term issues drive out the long'. Thus one observes the managerial chefs singing as they peel the managerial spuds or roll up their sleeves to scour out the administrative pans.[3]

Weighing long-term consequences against short-term advantage can create moral dilemmas. MacLagan provides evidence of increasing interest in moral and ethical issues in business management.[4] First, there is a move towards the 'professionalization' of management including the need for better management education called for by various UK reports. Ethical conduct is a concern for all professions with guidelines usually enshrined in codes, policed by committees and so on. These alone, of course, do not guarantee high standards of behaviour, and indeed, codes of ethical practice, by apparently tackling the issue, may even take genuine ethical questions off the agenda.

There are doubts as to whether management can be a profession, given the diversity of roles and tasks undertaken. There are also questions as to whether it should strive for this status. Commenting on British management education, Reed and Anthony S. criticize its 'unreflective pragmatism', the lip service it pays to issues of morality and power and call for a new type of 'organisational professionalism'.[5]

Secondly, the idea of management competence itself poses ethical questions. Although Boyatsis[6] is vague on the link between competence and ethical conduct but allows that competences 'could be associated with higher stages of moral and cognitive reasoning', Burgoyne[7] suggests that the competences movement overemphasizes the technical and understates the ethical. MacLagan holds that 'maturational processes hold the key to moral development' and that competence, individual maturity and moral development go together.[8]

Finally, as Solomon points out, whether managers behave ethically or not depends crucially upon their business environment:

> As the Greeks used to say, 'to live the good life one must live in a great city' . . . In business ethics the corporation becomes one's immediate community and, for better or for worse, the institution that defines the values within which one lives much of one's life. A corporation that encourages mutual cooperation and encourages individual excellence as an essential part of teamwork is a very different place to work and live than a corporation that incites 'either/or' competition, antagonism and continuous jostling for status and recognition. . . .[9]

LEARNING TO BE BETTER MANAGERS

How may the ethical and moral development of individuals and organizations take place? Kohlberg[10] has suggested three stages of moral development from the *pre-conventional* where 'right' action is determined by rewards/punishments by authorities, through the *conventional* (conforming to social norms/being 'well behaved') to the *post-conventional* or *autonomous* stage where the individual attempts independent, reasoned judgement. Boydell has developed these ideas into seven modes of being and learning.[11] Moving towards autonomy with its associated higher levels of moral development is necessary not just for doing good business in the commercial sense but also in the wider arenas of citizenship. For example, Bettelheim[12] links the achievement of autonomy in individuals with avoiding the re-emergence of Fascism and authoritarianism.

Movement between stages is not, however, automatic and many researchers suggest that some 'crisis' or 'perturbation' is necessary to cause us to question our current mode of operation and trigger a learning process. This is also central to Argyris and Schon's thinking about organizational learning; for organizations to engage in 'double loop learning' the current operating norms and assumptions must be challenged and transformed.[13]

Revans' statement that ' . . . there can be no learning without action, and no (sober and deliberate) action without learning'[14] makes it clear that we are not to escape from the responsibility for our acts, and that it is from these acts that we learn. While the simple imperative to act may well lead to leisurely repentance, defining what constitutes 'action' in managerial settings is problematic. For managers, action can often take the form of words. If words constitute action then why not thoughts? As Braddick and Casey note, what managers often need to do is to 're-frame', to re-order their thoughts.[15] Right thinking is an inseparable part of right action.

Learning, as something that changes us and our relationships with others and the world, is part of what shapes our actions – past, present and future. If what we learn over the years is part of what forms us and goes to make us what we are, then it follows that management development is concerned both with right managerial action and with the continuing development of the manager as a person. Both these aspects, the outer action in the world and the inner becoming of the person, are matters which are finally judged against moral and ethical criteria. In Revans' writings, issues of value – of right and wrong – are always at the heart, as in his reporting of the Belgian managers' most profound question: 'What is an honest man, and what need I do to become one?'[16]

The acid test is that you can tell whether this is Action Learning or not by whether people are exercising moral imagination. How often do they question their own and each other's actions? How much are they striving towards integrity for themselves and their colleagues? The method of Action Learning – of 'outer' (actions) and 'inner' (learnings) – is one in which questions of value and the practical matters of managing interact continuously. This is a tough and demanding script.

MANAGING THE VISIBLE AND THE INVISIBLE

The positivist traditions have encouraged a view of 'knowledge' as that which can be perceived via the 'five senses'. Powered by advances in the natural and then the social 'sciences' we have learned to direct our attention to observing and discriminating outwardly in the physical world. We have come to know the world, as it were, from the outside; as if we ourselves were not part of it. Inheriting this tradition, managing is something done to others – in popular terms a manager is defined as someone responsible for the work of others and who achieves results through others.

Management development has commonly concerned itself with outer knowledge, of marketing and production, of planning and organizing, of motivating and so on. The inner processes of the manager – thinking, feeling and willing – are not visible, and can only be inferred. Yet moral choices about right actions are made within. In seeking to make good decisions these invisible aspects of us are most important:

> We can all see another person's body directly. We see the lips moving, the eyes opening and shutting, the lines of the mouth and the face changing, and the body as a whole expressing itself in action. The person himself is invisible. . . . All our thoughts, emotions, feelings, imaginations, reveries, dreams, fantasies are invisible. All that

belongs to our scheming, planning, secrets, ambitions, all our hopes, fears, doubts, perplexities, all our affections, speculations, ponderings, vacuities, uncertainties, all our desires, longings, appetites, sensations, our likes, dislikes, aversions, attractions, loves and hates – are themselves invisible. They constitute 'oneself'. (Maurice Nicoll quoted by Schumacher.[17])

To illustrate the interaction of the invisible inner processes and the visible outer actions, consider the case of Gordon, a 34-year-old quarry manager, member of an Action Learning set, whose problem was to increase profitability and reduce waste:

JOHN: If these piles of waste have been here longer than you, why hasn't anything been done about them before?

GORDON: Well, it's obvious that when you quarry you get waste . . . depending on the product, you can get up to 90 per cent. . . . I started in this quarry 12 years ago as a graduate trainee and in that time I should think I've worked every job here – boy and man you might say! (*laughs*)

FIONA: How big are those piles?

GORDON: Very big! (*laughs again*)

FIONA: I mean, how many tons? How much is added each day . . . each week?

GORDON: Blimey. I've no idea. How should I know . . . they were here before my time remember.

FIONA: But they're getting bigger every day . . .

GORDON: Of course they are!

DAVE: Don't you think that the manager of a quarry ought to know how much waste is being created each week!?

Here is a good example of that everyday occurrence which Revans has called 'the idolization of past experience':

> . . . but there are those who *soberly and deliberately refuse to learn*, because the new knowledge, whilst consonant with the scientific method, is inconvenient for other reasons. . . . New ideas suggesting new behaviours may be soberly and deliberately suppressed because they contradict established values and accepted traditions.[18]

Here what we already know blocks us from new knowledge; an inner transformation is needed before a changed outer performance is possible. Managerial work is inseparable from the person who does it and matters of personality, style, experience and preferences come to the fore.

To learn something new, Gordon has to accept that the mountains of waste are worth his attention. To do this he has to overcome much within him. Those piles of waste have been there for ever. They are outside his office window, outside of him, yet they are mirrored by something inside him that accommodates them. He has an inner block analagous to the tipping zone of the quarry.

DEFENCES AND THE NEED TO KNOW

Is he really blind or is he turning a blind eye? For Gordon to be able to act he has first to come clean with himself. This involves a willingness to explore oneself, one's motives, the unforeseen consequences of one's actions and inactions. It also involves being able to bear the truths of others. The revelation of blind spots comes as a shock; the concealments, deliberate evasions and the old lies about ourselves are the hardest to open up. As Harrison has pointed out, to a large extent we *are* our defences – they stabilize us and keep us going.[19]

Action Learning stresses the interaction of inner and outer as a primary motif. In Action Learning, development of problem and person proceeds via a continuous passing from outer actions to inner processes to outer actions and back. This accords with Snell's 'holistic ethical education'[20] in which people 'examine managerial decision making as they engage in it daily in the conduct of their lives' and which he recommends as the best way forward for management education; a view echoed by Willmott in his call for a 'critical action learning' for the moral regeneration of management education.[21]

THE SOUL GOES OUT AND RETURNS

This is a modern managerial application of old wisdom. Writing in 1916 on the necessary unity of Eastern and Western approaches to knowledge, Edward Carpenter put it well:

> The Indian methods and attitude cause an ingathering and quiescence of the mind, accompanied often by great illumination; but if carried to excess, they result in over-quiescence, and even torpor. The Western habits tend towards an over-activity and external distraction of mind, which may result in disintegration. The true line is not in mediocrity, but in a bold and sane acceptance of both sides, so as to make them offset and balance each other, and indeed so that each shall make the extension of the other more and more possible. Growth is the method and the solution. The soul goes out and returns, goes out and returns; and this is its daily, almost hourly, action. . . .[22]

The epistemology of Action Learning holds that person and problem are defined and redefined in continuous interaction. Neither inner self nor outer world is sovereign; they are, in a sense, co-creations. One of Revans's key teachings is that no problem can exist independently of some human being who knows, cares or can do something about it. The designation 'problem', part of which is out there, part in here, signifies my ability to do one or more of these three things. Equally it is our ability to engage with problems which shapes us and ultimately confers on us our personhood.

From the Action Learning perspective the end is not the solution of this or that problem (only puzzles get solved in any case) nor the specific learning of the actor. These are usually hoped for and desirable consequences of Action Learning, but they are not what is ultimately signified. Our reward for transforming a problem and ourselves is that we are thus enabled to go on to our next step and the next problem.

If Gordon agrees to pit himself against the piles of limestone, in order to help him we have to work with both the limestone and with Gordon. Outside – How much is being wasted? Why is it wasted? What happens to the non-waste? and so on; and inside – How is it that you've done nothing before? What do you want to do now? Who else can help to move these piles?

As the search passes to and fro, the thread thus spun creates, out of the former duality of Gordon and the limestone, a new entity which contains the part of Gordon which is to do with the limestone and the part of the limestone which is to do with Gordon. Thus, when we manage to connect, we extend our mind.

AT LAST – SOME PROPER ACTION

Passing backwards and forwards, Gordon begins to see things differently. He sees that what goes on inside him – his thoughts, fears, likes, dislikes, prejudices and so on – are intimately connected with the piles of limestone outside the window. Having made this connection the observable action looks simple: in this case he agrees to come back with some figures. Before the meeting breaks he is asked for his estimates. Two weeks later, to his shame and surprise, the weekly additions to waste turn out to be three times his own rough estimates. This new knowledge increases his connection with the 'problem'; he can no longer proceed on the old assumption.

Subsequently Gordon begins to work on ways of reducing the waste. This is mainly done by seeking new products and new markets. He forms a 'think tank' with other managers to see what can be done. Over a few months various ideas are put into practice, which indeed result in decreased waste and increased profits. Gordon learns that 'we can improve anything we choose to look at'.

This happy tale has everyone winning. Many moral dilemmas faced by managers are not so conveniently resolved. Where managers may increase safety at increased cost, or decrease environmental damage with a lower quality product, there is no such happy coincidence. Yet we can try to be as good as we can afford to be. Whether we will or not depends a lot on whether we are encouraged or expected to by the wider 'ethical climate' of the company, the industry, the country – 'to live the good life one must live in a great city'.

GOOD COMPANY

Yet right action starts with the individual. Revans has called his Principle of Insufficient Mandate – Those unable to change themselves cannot change what goes on around them – the prime principle of action learning.[23] In the quarrying company, Gordon and his people have agreed that things are like such and such, and have then acted for years in a way which sustains that belief rather than challenges it. Over those years we have built up a joint picture, supported and elaborated it in our conversations, gossiping and stories, and now we are stuck with it. Believing that environment to be unfriendly – cut-throat, unpredictable, unsympathetic – it is a long time since anyone has been out to test the theory. 'We just know it.'

> Human beings . . . show remarkable ingenuity for self-protection. They can create individual and organisational defences that are powerful and in which that power is largely in the service of the poor to mediocre performance as well as of antilearning. . . . The result of these countless everyday actions is to deaden individuals' awareness to the ethical pollution they are generating. . . . It makes little sense to enact laws and rules against organizational defensive routines. . . . The equivalents of such laws are already in place and they do not work. The answer, as in the case of prohibition, lies in each one of us becoming self-managing and helping to create organizations that reward such self-responsible action.[24]

The revival of interest in organizational learning may bring about some much needed developments here. Important as it is to improve the actions and learning of individuals, we also need to develop our understanding and practice of learning at this level if these individuals are to flourish. Amongst others,[25,26] Revans has pointed to the need for organizational learning with his 'The enterprise as a learning system' (1969) [see chapter 4].

Applying the adjective 'learning' to the collective creates some problems. We must define terms carefully if we are to claim learning (often seen as an individual activity) on the part of any collectivity. Also, what are we to make of organizations that 'learn' to engage in corporate misdemeanours? If we are going to get better at learning, then we must also increase our capacity for making moral judgements. Does it make sense to talk about a 'bad' learning organization?

A QUESTION OF BALANCE

Ethical trading means moving towards Morris' view of the 'good company' by seeking to balance the interests of all stakeholders.[27] The 'stakeholder model' of organizations is one way to tackle the issue of corporate morality. For Morris, the company which operates to the 'mutual advantage' of all stakeholders – capital, employees, customers, community and so on – is the 'good company'. This approach offers a way forward for managers who aim at increased professionalism and for companies who aim at developing rather than exploiting their environments. Here the company and the manager seeks to provide different sorts of quality to their stakeholders, e.g.

- *quality of business performance* for owners
- *quality of service* for consumers
- *quality of working life* for employees
- *quality of social responsibility* for the public

Perhaps such notions find it hard to stand up to commercial pressures, to the drive for 'competitive advantage' and so on? However such considerations may help with what MacLagan[28] sees as the need for 'Ethical thinking in organisations'; namely to appreciate the detail of actual situations, and to undertake the arguments and negotiation with all concerned before policies and actions are implemented.

If the bottom line remains as an essential condition of doing business, it is an insufficient one for doing good business. There is a countervailing moral imperative to be as good as we are able to be. This is not just to leave questions of moral action to 'individual conscience', so often a convenient form of corporate 'blind eye-ism'. Ways forward may include both a new form of managerial professionalism with ethical codes of practice and government and international action to create the climate in which individuals and individual organizations can exercise judgement.

The 'ethical climate' of an organization or a nation constrains or encourages particular actions on the part of individuals. Just as we learn better where there is an enabling learning climate, so we are likely to behave better in a climate which supports a high standard of ethics. However, it is only through the actions of individuals learning to exercise judgement, choosing this over that, that progress towards better managing can be maintained. No-one is ever 'ethically competent' or becomes a master of morality – managing as moral art requires

39

that we are continually examining our practice and frequently having our assumptions and decisions challenged in the good company of those who want us to do well.

REFERENCES

1 Snell R. S. (1993) *Developing Skills for Ethical Management*, London: Chapman & Hall.
2 Hawken P. (1993) *The Ecology of Commerce*, New York: HarperCollins.
3 Revans, R. W. (1983) *The ABC of Action Learning*, Bromley, Kent: Chartwell-Bratt, p. 38.
4 MacLagan, P. (1989) 'Management development & moral development', pp. 3–5. Paper presented at the *British Academy of Management Conference*, Manchester Business School, UK, 11 September.
5 Reed M. and Anthony P. (1992) 'Professionalising management and management professionalisation: British management in the 1980's', *Journal of Management Studies*, **29**(5), 291–316.
6 Boyatsis R. (1982) *The Competent Manager*, New York: Wiley.
7 Burgoyne, J. G. (1989) 'Creating the managerial portfolio: building on competency approaches to management development', *Management Education and Development*, **20**(1), 55–61.
8 MacLagan, P. op. cit. p. 4.
9 Solomon R. (1993) *Ethics and Excellence: Cooperation and Integrity in Business*, New York: Oxford University Press, p. 148.
10 Kohlberg L. (1969) 'Stage and sequence: the cognitive developmental approach to socialisation', in Goslin, D. A. (ed.) *Handbook of Socialization Theory and Research*, Chicago: Rand McNally.
11 Boydell T. H. (1996) 'Modes of being and learning', Chapter 21 of Pedler, M. J., Boydell, T. H. and Burgoyne, J. G. (eds), *The Learning Company: A Strategy for Sustainable Development*, 2nd edn, Maidenhead: McGraw-Hill.
12 Bettelheim, B. (1986) *The Informed Heart*, Harmondsworth: Penguin.
13 Argyris, C. and Schon, D. (1978) *Organizational Learning: A Theory in Action Perspective*, Boston: Addison-Wesley, Chapter 1.
14 Revans, R. W. op. cit. p. 54.
15 Braddick W. and Casey D. (1981) 'Developing the forgotten army – learning and the top manager', *Management Education and Development*, **12**(3), 169–80.
16 Revans, R. W. op. cit. p. 13.
17 Nicoll, M. *Living Time* quoted by Schumacher, E. F. (1978), *A Guide for the Perplexed*, London: Abacus, p. 43.
18 Revans, R. W. op. cit. p. 55.
19 Harrison, R. (1996) 'Defenses and the need to know', in *The Collected Papers of Roger Harrison*, London: McGraw-Hill, pp. 286–291.
20 Snell R. S. (1990), 'The development of ethical awareness & personal morality by managers through work experiences: an agenda for research', *Personnel Review*, **19**(1), 13–20.
21 Willmott H. (1994) 'Management education: provocations to a debate', *Management Learning*, **25**(1), 105–36.
22 Carpenter, E. (1916) *My Days and Dreams*, London: Allen & Unwin, pp. 144–5.
23 Revans, R. W. op. cit. p. 55.
24 Argyris C. (1990) *Overcoming Organizational Defences: Facilitating Organizational Learning*, Boston: Allyn & Bacon, pp. 157–61.
25 Senge P. (1990) *The Fifth Discipline: The Art & Practice of the Learning Organisation*, New York: Doubleday Currency.
26 Pedler, M. J., Boydell, T. H. and Burgoyne, J. G. (eds), (1996), *The Learning Company: A Strategy for Sustainable Development*, 2nd edn, Maidenhead: McGraw-Hill.
27 Morris, J. (1987), 'Good company', *Management Education & Development*, **18**(2), 103–115.
28 MacLagan, P. (1995) 'Ethical thinking in organisations', *Management Learning*, **26**(2), 159–77.

4 The Enterprise as a Learning System*

Reg Revans

This paper was written in the last months of the Inter-University Programme of the Fondation Industrie-Université of Belgium. It had been discovered during the course of that momentous experiment how the presence of a visiting manager within an enterprise whose management had become convinced of the need for a lot of those employed there to learn, particularly when supported by a band of allies, could in fact engender an enlightenment previously unsuspected. Our key assumption was that the presence within each enterprise of an outsider undisguised, simply behaving as the intelligent learner about some problem he had never before encountered, soon set off a secondary, but nonetheless powerful, campaign of learning among the subordinates on the spot and with whom he regularly discussed his lines of enquiry.

Since the visitor was not only trying to understand his own approach to conditions of ignorance, risk and confusion, but was also the agent of the home management equally concerned to make sense of what appeared to them an intractable difficulty, a very simple question arose: Was the secondary (autonomous) learning process engendered merely because the majority of subordinates had become aware that the problem existed, and that it was seen by their top management to be serious? Or was the visitor more than an agent, in the sense that without him there could not possibly have started any autonomous curiosity among the home subordinates at all?.... If there is in most organizations staffed with normally intelligent persons a latent desire to behave sensibly in front of colleagues (as the visiting fellows of the programme seemed to have discovered) could this desire not be identified and turned to constructive use without needing to go through the elaborate ceremonies of exchanging senior managers? If the enterprise was, in fact, already a potential learning system

* This chapter originally appeared in Revans, R. W. *The Origins and Growth of Action Learning*, Chartwell-Bratt, 1982.

could its capacity for self-development be exploited autonomously by the top management taking the lead? Why, except when the learning of the senior managers was the cardinal objective, do more than get the local staffs and their existing subordinates running their own enquiries?

Alas, the suggestion was grossly premature; it was rejected even by those who had had the courage to open their secrets to the exchanges of the Inter-University Programme. Not until the Japanese menace of the late 1970s introduced the Q-circle to Europe could the issue once more be raised.

THE ENTERPRISE AS A SYSTEM OF SYSTEMS

Many persons concerned with the business enterprise, whether as director, employee or adviser, will have their own professional reasons for perceiving it as some manner of system: for example, the controller, who needs to ensure that its total revenue exceeds, one year with another, its total expenditure, without the specific costs of such-and-such a department necessarily being met by its own specific income; the manufacturing superintendent, who will expect some overall balance between its flow of goods and materials, not being embarrassed at one moment by a chronic shortage of stock to meet his orders, nor at another by a sharp reminder that too much capital is tied up in a super-abundance of raw materials; the personnel director, who hopes that, five years hence, the enterprise will still be able to rely upon eighty per cent of the staff now serving it, each and every one richer by five intervening years of precious experience . . .

All these senior men, to ensure continuity and balanced effectiveness, need to think in terms of inputs, flows and outputs; none must envision the enterprise as a series of isolated and independent jerks of activity, springing at random into local effect and unrelated to any larger and continuous totality. Such systemic approaches would be readily claimed by most departmental heads: to ensure such organic thinking there exists a vast range of professional teaching and qualification, embracing such arts as budgetary control and standard costing; production scheduling and inventory control; manpower planning and staff development, and an inexhaustible army of managerial techniques marching in acronymic procession across the prospectuses of the business schools – PERT, CPA, DCF, TWI, MBO, OD, OR, X or Y, and a score of others.

THE INDIVIDUAL AND THE TASK

Such unifying ideas arouse little contention. They have, indeed, entered deeply into the planning both of the working organizations themselves, and of many education programmes enticing managers to think of their firms or departments as 'systems' with many interacting parts. It would hardly be rash to suggest that one-third of all published management literature is concerned with such issues of functional organization, nor that an even larger proportion of time is devoted to them on management courses.

But there is now evidence that, however useful, however valid, may be this functional approach, the concept of the enterprise as a system has quite other but no less significant interpretations. The tasks that every person carries out in the course of his daily employment, whether at first sight concerned with purchasing, design, manufacture, marketing, transport, accountancy, personnel development or wages payment, contain another systemic element, the potential power of which is only of late becoming recognized. As the chief executive of one of Britain's largest firms recently remarked:

> Our main concern is no longer to ensure that we find, train and keep the biggest share of Britain's leading chemists; nor is it solely to concentrate on the maximum return on our investment. These are necessary ends, but of themselves are insufficient. Our need in the 1970s is to see ourselves as a developing system of two hundred thousand individuals.

A DIGRESSION ON MANAGEMENT TECHNIQUES

We see there is little new in this expression of need; almost the same sentiment was declared by Robert Owen a century and a half ago; similar things are said in Eastern Europe and by Chairman Mao. But we do not here interpret the enterprise as a human system in the light of this nor that political doctrine. Nor are we suggesting the need for some super-system, stored in a gigantic computer, to which the controls of orders, purchases, production, quality, cost and so forth alike report. For, in whatsoever political system, whether in the countries of OECD, in Eastern Europe or in the Third World, we now observe some impatience with – indeed, a revolt against – the systematizing experts who, during the past century, have over-regulated the tasks of men at all levels.

Industrial engineering, work study, incentive payment schemes, task specialization, timetabling and scheduling and, above all, the machine pacing of human work are now held up as a caricature of Charlie Chaplin's *Modern Times*, and all carry within themselves the seeds of their own destruction in proportion to the authority of the experts who exploit them. The latest casuality among these managerial bailiffs is, it seems, productivity bargaining; this rigmarole of wage assessment, exalted three years ago into the very diadem of behavioural science, was recently appraised by some jaundiced personnel expert as a dead duck.

THE ENTERPRISE AS A LEARNING SYSTEM

We observe that all the expert systems here referred to must now be imposed upon the enterprise from above or from outside. But Action Learning must seek the means of improvement from within, indeed, from the common task. An essential quality of human behaviour is that, although in some degree innate or inherited, it is in great part learned: present conduct is largely our visible response to past experience newly interpreted. It follows, first, that the daily round offers constant learning opportunities and, second, that these opportunities should be of great interest to managers. When, moreover, we discover that the quality of such learning is largely determined by the morale of the organization that offers it, that interest becomes profound. Indeed, we may now assert that the observable differences between organizations otherwise comparable in technical, financial or environmental character, are determined by whether or not their members are likely to develop in and from the course of their daily employment. One enterprise can, in short, behave as a learning system, constantly and fruitfully working out autonomous solutions to its own problems: its neighbour, built to the same technical specifications, engaged in the same tasks and reporting to the same higher authority, may be an organizational sore, running with irresoluble conflict and unendurable frustration. (Many years after the note was first drafted in 1951, we may now see that the great differences in accident and strike rates between geologically identical adjacent collieries, noted in *Group Factors in Mining Accidents*, are the differences between managed systems that either learn or do not learn from their daily crises.) It is thus to the enterprise as a learning system that we need to attend; we must understand how it is that one management continuously act to encourage such an elevation of the spirit, while their colleagues across the way live under the constant threat of rebellion from their own subordinates.

THE QUALITIES OF AUTONOMOUS LEARNING SYSTEMS

Our research evidence to suggest whether or not its management policies are likely to develop an enterprise as an autonomous learning system may still be incomplete. But the conditions for success seem to include the following:

1. that its chief executive places high among his own responsibilities that for developing the enterprise as a learning system; this he will achieve through his personal relations with his immediate subordinates, since the conduct of one level of a system towards any level below it is powerfully influenced by the perception that the higher level has of its own treatment

44

from above; in the consortium of hospitals described in this series (*Action Learning takes a Health Cure*) the correlation between systematic development (attitudinal change, learning) and interest of top management as +0.91; in the secondary modern schools of Lancashire the correlation between the estimates made by the children of their teachers' skills, on the one hand, and their assessment of them as approachable human beings, on the other, was +0.87; both of these add a veneer of quantitative cunning to the immemorial verse: 'As the judge of the people is, so are his officers; and what manner of man the ruler of the city is himself, so are all they that inhabit therein,' (Ecclesiasticus ch 10 v 2);

2. the coalition of power that runs the enterprise has clear ideas about delegation, with the maximum authority for subordinates to act within the field of its own known policies *that become known by interrogation from below*; systems of delegation, in other words, are constantly worked out as part of the contract between the person, his task and his superior; the success of delegation depends significantly upon the quality of the data/ information made available; in one experimental enterprise the correlation among fifty graduate senior managers between the perceived quality of their information system, on the one hand, and their own personal satisfactions as departmental managers, on the other, was +0.78;

3. in consequence, codes of practice, standard rules and procedures, works orders and other such regulations are to be seen as norms around which variations are deliberately encouraged as learning opportunities; they will therefore contribute to the improvement of the data/information flow and may even bring into a common learning experience different members of an organization who, under codes rigorously observed, might rarely, if ever, meet;

4. any reference of what appears an intractable problem to a superior level should be accompanied by *both* an explanation as to why it cannot be treated where it seems to have arisen *and* a proposal to change the system so that similar problems arising in future could be suitably contained and treated;

5. persons at all levels should be encouraged, with their immediate colleagues, to make regular proposals for the study and reorganization of their own systems of work; such proposals should generate discussion between vertical levels and horizontal departments of how the work is currently managed, and of how its outcome is determined, such as by the content, order and distribution of individual tasks, the use and maintenance of equipment and supplies, and the flow of information essential to performing the tasks; above all, in any suggestions about the reorganization of the work, first attention should be given to its group or

45

autonomous aspects (see particularly *Worker Participation as Action Learning* and *Project 'Management Efficiency'*).

AUTONOMOUS LEARNING NOT MANAGERIAL ABDICTION

A management that interprets the employment of its staff as a continuous opportunity for their self-development does not, by setting aside the mythologies of 'scientific management' about commanding, coordinating and controlling, thereby resign to the understrappars all responsibility for running the enterprise. It merely acknowledges that the enterprise is the setting in which the staff spend most of their active lives, and that the total contract between it and its employees is wider than an agreement about who is to be paid for doing what.

This wider bargain, even if not explicit, has deep implications for personal development and personal autonomy: outstanding persons should be encouraged to develop themselves to the limits of their capacities and ought not to be restricted entirely by ingenious mechanistic programmes devised by quickwitted experts trained not to ask questions outside their own fields. Indeed, the present relation between those who perform and those who plan calls often to be stood upon its head; it is for the individual worker, as a member of a wealth-creating group, to suggest his optimum conditions of work and to set his personal standards of achievement, and for the expert to solve (with the help of the group) whatever problems the worker may introduce.

Such new approaches to work organization will offer managements their own opportunities to learn; they are certainly no invitation to their subordinates to take over and run the whole show. (Some senior managers may, of course, offer to take over, or even to buy out from the main shareholders, their section of the total enterprise; this will be a measure of the present need for the enterprise to learn.) The most precious asset of any organization is the one most readily overlooked: its capacity to build upon its lived experience, to learn from its challenges and to turn in a better performance by inviting all and sundry to work out for themselves what that performance ought to be.

LIMITED FIRST APPLICATIONS

Although the general arguments of this paper, and the experimental evidence on which they are based, apply not only to senior management, but also to supervision and the shop floor, it would be prudent to confine any discussion aimed at developing an enterprise as an autonomous system, *in the first instance*, to managers not below works level or its equivalent. Any attempt, however reasonable its factual illustration and however secure its logic, to influence managerial opinion in this totally new sense is bound to be met with all manner of unforeseeable objections. These will differ greatly from one senior management to the next; their collisions will be highly instructive to all parties, but should be kept, to begin with, from the subordinates. It should, however, be possible to employ the ideas of *Para.* 5 above to heighten the learning processes of the seniors called upon to discuss this paper for the first time.

5 Minding our Ps and Qs

John Morris

Whatsoever we pursue, some ways of saying or doing fresh things can be got from others – whether we like it or not. . . . Throughout life one is told by endless authorities what to do next, and one learns to obey. Much so picked up has already long existed, so it is here called programmed, and is denoted by 'P'. Yet much other learning also comes, neither from command nor example, but from one's own experience. Finding out for oneself may also be very mixed . . . Knowledge, ideas, attitudes, skills, new perceptions of what goes on are always turning up; what is so discovered, moreover, generally tells one something new about the self. 'Well, I must say! You do live and learn!' is so often said after the shock of finding out from one's own experience that some hallowed belief was long untrue . . . Learning of this nature comes from questioning insight, and is denoted by 'Q' . . . Simplistically, we may say that fresh learning is the sum of programmed instruction and questioning insight. . . .[1]

You may have recognized the distinctive tones of Reg Revans, the formulator of Action Learning, making one of his many useful distinctions. For Revans, education and training have placed far too much dependence on P, taught by accredited experts, rather than Q, initiated by people questioning their own direct experience, and honestly revealing the depth of their ignorance.

Fresh experience comes from trying something new, rather than repeating ourselves and a major contribution to human understanding has come from Revans's work on Action Learning, with its emphasis on voluntary commitment to learning from personal experience and to forming Action Learning groups, with fellow learners who are similarly committed.

Action Learning offers many advantages to the busy practitioner, notably its immediate relevance to the challenges and demands of real life in a period of unprecedented change. It is also immensely flexible, and attractive to adult learners because it respects their independence and experience. In particular, the questioning approach[2] adopted by Action Learning is essential in those situations where ready-made answers are clearly inadequate. A significant problem of Action Learning is one that is shared with all approaches that take learning seriously (as distinct from indoctrination or other forms of conditioning). It is no respecter of potentates or hierarchies, since it seeks to

49

empower everyone to learn from personal experience, and to find the confidence (and possibly the courage) to act in the light of that experience, as the living spirit encounters the dead letter. Fearless questioning is at the heart of Action Learning and those who rule through fear know a threat to their power when they see one.

Having stressed the vital importance of Q, as discriminating questioning, to Action Learning, it is necessary to refer to the indispensability of P as the context of Q. No one faced with a challenging situation, and hard pressed to find a way of coping with it, is likely to ignore P in the form of wise guidelines, useful know-how, and good practice. P may have much that is out of date or downright misleading, but it also contains the wisdom of the past, which we ignore at our peril. P – as the total stock of established knowledge – is also being added to constantly, especially in the fields of science and technology (much less, alas, in morals, politics and even common sense).

So the question arises: how can we gain a deeper understanding of the contributions of P and Q, as two basic approaches to the kind of learning that practitioners need and value? P attracts the busy practitioner, keen to save time and energy, by providing the ready-made answers to many questions, and Q puts into a useful and pertinent form the questions that, as yet, have no such answers. There is no doubt that for Action Learning, with its concern for coping with fresh challenges, Q is the senior partner. The situations that appear to demand action often confront us mysteriously, even in disguise. They are not readily identifiable, except perhaps as a 'mess' or, more positively, 'could this be an opportunity?' And they are most certainly not labelled with the right amounts of P and Q to be used in each situation, let alone the sequence or combination in which they are to be deployed.

Therefore, we have to remain fully alert, giving our whole attention to whatever it is we are trying to understand. We have to keep minding our Ps and Qs, taking care to get the best value from each of these approaches to learning. Action often seems urgently needed in the ever-rolling present. P, on the other hand, always seems to be pulling us towards the past, with its established answers, while Q keeps its options open and looks to the future which its decisions will shape. How can P and Q be used to help us bring past and future to the service of the present?

THREE LESSONS FROM PRACTITIONERS

In the difficult and delicate process of learning from 'real-time' challenges, Action Learning can play a distinctive and valuable part. The conventional forms of education and training have been inclined to establish their own institutions, separated from the daily flux and urgent demands of work. In striking contrast, Action Learning makes a virtue of its constant association with making things happen. This is particularly useful in the development of 'learning organizations', which seek to foster learning throughout the whole organization.[3,4,5]

In these notes, I have drawn on experience of working as a consultant and adviser to many different kinds of organization. My work has been concerned with the development of experienced practitioners, in professional fields such as managing, medicine, higher education, architecture and technology. Over many years of such activity I have learned three lessons that seem particularly relevant to the issue of Ps and Qs. The lessons have come from seeing, within and beyond the flexible framework of Action Learning, how effective practitioners develop 'good practice', both in doing their work and in learning from it.

First, the most effective practitioners are strongly biased towards using any form of P that seems to work in the challenging situations confronting them. P may take a strikingly condensed form ('Keep it simple, stupid!', 'Keep skills on tap, not on top'), or it may take the form of an elaborate display of 'state of the art' professional competence (such as the latest approach to Intellectual Property Rights, or the right configuration for one's business). In contrast to P as it appears in the often fixed forms of educational programmes, the P applied by effective practitioners is limited only by their resourcefulness and ingenuity. Metaphors, slogans, myths and legends all play their part, together with solid stuff from science and technology. P is strongly preferred in the form of knowing how rather than knowing about, and is especially valued when it helps to specify a particular line of action, rather than merely staying on the level of an airy generality.

These practitioners are constantly stirring up P, keeping it lively, as a useful stock of knowledge and skill. For them, P is seldom if ever rigorously organized into the intellectual disciplines so dear to academics. Rather, it is part of an organic network that relates to personal experience, and to the key events, incidents and episodes that have become, as it were, nodes in that network. Of course there is often room within the network for innumerable lists – check lists for action, price lists, stock lists, lists of do's and don'ts for various situations – which form part of an active store, merely grist to the mill of a constantly working conversion process of turning each and every occasion to advantage.

Action Learning is happy to take part in this unceasing process of seeking relevant information and using it to serve practice as fully as possible. My experience has been that its distinctive contributions to P quickly become evident, even to reflective practitioners. Questioning from colleagues tests the relevance and adequacy of established ideas and opinions. Differences of perception are valued, rather than ignored or attacked, and may turn out to add new facets to one's understanding of a situation. Time is made available for considering connections between different parts of one's experience, so that 'theorizing' gains new substance as useful patterns emerge. Not least, the practice of making notes on matters of interest, including feelings as well as ideas and activities, may be found to give a new dimension to the everyday flow of events. These can all be grouped under the broad heading of 'raising awareness' but that can sound rather diffuse. The essence is in the clarity of this kind of awareness: a clarity that is both critical and constructive.

The second lesson is that effective practitioners are completely committed to a questioning approach, but it has often moulded itself around their particular practice. Within this habitual mould, they question as naturally as breathing. This approach tends to be much more limited than the wide-ranging, discriminating questioning that forms Q. Nevertheless, it reveals a fruitful mental set which can provide a strong support for the later development of Q. Action Learning encourages this development by observing that discriminating questions act to re-organize knowledge, rather than merely add to it. Such questions are most effective when they focus on basic assumptions and beliefs that are taken for granted.

This is one reason why Action Learning, unlike the many 'quick fixes' available to the busy practitioner, can create moments of truth that stick in the memory and may prove to be turning points in one's life. Re-organization of one's experience can be painful, and an essential part of Action Learning is that it provides the opportunity of learning, in a fellowship of co-learners, how to provide one another with the most fruitful combination of challenge and support.

The third lesson is that effective practitioners display remarkable skill in balancing the Ps and Qs that are constantly arising. It is not only different requirements and options that must be balanced, within and between the various Ps and Qs, but those that are apparently incompatible and contradictory.

The keyword here is 'apparently'. The great value of bringing P and Q together is that Q can constantly search for information that will reconcile apparent contradictions. Q quickly detects false dilemmas, which ignore the middle ground between absurd extremes. Q recognizes that the conventional 'either/ or' can often be replaced by an innovative 'both/and'. P can be fruitfully enlarged by recognizing that feelings and values are enduring features of difficult situations. Re-framing contentious concepts can open up unexpected options. For example, Charles Hampden-Turner[6], in a recent overview of his work along these lines, has taken the dominant corporate criterion of 'profit' and shown that it can be better understood if it is considered in different contexts. He concludes, 'There are two kinds of profitability. There is profit as private gain and profit as a somewhat rough guide to mutual satisfaction between the corporation and its stakeholders. It is the latter which has kept the west far ahead of statist economies. An imperfect feedback loop is better by leagues than no feedback loop at all. Yet multiple feedbacks are more effective still.'

The task is to achieve a continuing balance between different interests, looking for common ground wherever it can be found, and innovating and adapting wherever agreement is possible. And since these interests are now on a world scale, this is a task for everyone, and not only the inflated individuals whose colossal failures are rapidly making 'Super' into a term of derision.

To return to our earlier quotation from Reg Revans. The penetrating and valuable kind of Q called 'questioning insight' is linked with 'finding out for oneself', while much of P comes from 'endless authorities'. Revans has argued, therefore, that P is the domain of experts, and Q is the practice of leaders. However, if effective practitioners are constantly using both P and Q, separately and in fruitful combination, we must recognize the need for a fruitful balance between leaders and experts; or putting the matter slightly differently, a balance between leadership and expertise. In this domain, we must watch our Ps and Qs with special care.

THE CONFUSION OF LEADERSHIP AND EXPERTISE

In our rapidly changing and confused era, which often places far more emphasis on hasty and unconsidered action than reflective learning, we are in grave danger of confusing leadership and expertise. This is perhaps not surprising, because we are obsessed with various versions of both. Experts, with their dependence on the authority of P, draw their strength from the past, from their demonstrated effectiveness in knowing what to do in situations that either repeat themselves or can be brought under the control of an established technique. Leaders commit themselves to creating a possible future, rather than waiting for one to arrive. Experts are inclined to follow a well-trodden path, while leaders, when necessary, make tracks in uncharted territory. But the best of them will always use whatever maps are around. Some experts – particularly dangerous – promise to make the present a comfortable extension of the best aspects of the past, a kind of heritage for perpetual tourists. And there are leaders – even more dangerous – whose apocalyptic vision of the future promises perpetual domination for their loyal followers.

In our hunger for security in these difficult times, we demand 'expert leaders', often in an idealized form that is humanly impossible to provide. We want guaranteed (and preferably simple) answers to newly arising and complex questions, and 'charismatic' leadership that is democratically acceptable. This provides a splendid opportunity for poseurs and charlatans who neither provide useful answers nor an inspiring and empowering vision. True leaders evoke responsibility rather than credulity, a sense of adventure rather than the arrogance of certitude. Such a leader engages others in a fellowship, bringing people together through strong personal ties based on shared values, a strong sense of direction and a recognition of the contribution that each can make in achieving the common cause. The key characteristic of this kind of leader is the provision of a visible example, a living and inspiring demonstration to others, who come to recognize that they are not mere followers, but are being encouraged to give a lead themselves.

Of all the manifold needs that the different forms of learning must meet, surely the greatest is the need for widely diffused, effective leadership, at all levels and in all forms of organization. It is just this need that Action Learning meets, with its combination of discriminating questioning related to the key opportunities and problems facing us, guided by relevant information and know-how. Just as the members of sets find their learning is enhanced when they bring both challenge and support together, the resources of leadership and expertise need to work and learn in partnership.

THE GROWING CHALLENGE TO CONVENTIONAL ORGANIZATIONS

We live in a time when, world wide, there is great impatience with established, but clearly incompetent, authority. Many of the questions asked are ill-considered and confused. But now the nuggets of gold are gleaming among the gravel (to borrow an inspired phrase from a managing director in a recent Action Learning set), and truly discriminating questions are being asked and given wide attention. I have encountered them most frequently in the domain of business enterprise:

- In whose interests are those 'at the top' acting?
- If it is the shareholders, how interested are they in the other stakeholders of the organization that provides their income? (For example, the managers and workers, the suppliers, and the public at large.)
- What place is there in the organization for 'quality'? (Not only quality of service and product, but quality of working life, for example.)
- What value is placed in the conventional form of organization on those who actually do the work of the business?
- What place is there for fairness in the conduct of the business and the allocation of rewards?
- What place is there for loyalty being given by those at the top to those at the bottom?

GOOD COMPANIES AND 'GOOD COMPANY'

We note that the organizations which find sensible and even inspiring responses to these questions are those which are widely seen as effective, not only by single interest-groups such as shareholders, but by all those 'stakeholders' associated with the business. I call these 'good companies', because *they demonstrably provide good company for this whole range of fellow human beings*.

Good companies achieve an acceptable and continuing balance between these interests, and are particularly concerned with the interests of those who use the products of the company and those who provide those products and services. Unfortunately, these companies, together with other forms of organization that provide 'good company' for those associated with them, are still a relatively tiny minority. Others are too embattled or too unreflective to see the relevance of the knowledge about good all-round performance that is piling up and to be aware of the questions that are being asked of them.[7]

The nature of the modern media of communication, with their incessant hunger for dramatic contrast, makes both the example of the good companies and the dismal performance of the bad increasingly visible. So we can expect the widespread unease to grow and be expressed more vigorously, until the strong concerns of those who are directly interested in the activities of the companies are responded to.

It is no use trying to answer these challenging questions in the conventional fashion; that is, by chopping them up into recognizable categories and handing them over to groups of experts. In modern Britain, beset with confusions about its role, we have experienced not only the ill-feeling, poor quality and confusion that arise from an over-dependence on narrowly technical expertise, but also the invasion of human qualities and values by such expertise when it goes beyond its proper bounds. Now is the time for a change of focus. By taking responsibility for our own actions, we become 'self-managing' rather than conventional role-players. We are then more likely to take difficult initiatives, rather than constantly depending on answers from above.

In taking initiatives we may find that we are seen by others as leaders; but we will not be solitary 'leaders', beset by constantly unsatisfactory followers. We will be taking our share of leading within a learning community, which is based on fellowship, working and learning close to the truth of our own fresh experience, and helping others to do the same. By continually minding our own Ps and Qs, in a working partnership with others similarly engaged, we learn to bring these two great approaches to learning into a mutually supporting balance.

Through constant questioning, we see more clearly just who we really are and what remarkable resources we have access to. We will also be more aware of what is really facing us, and we will become more capable of accepting and responding to change. By looking attentively at the relevance of best practice for our own conduct, we may learn to emulate the spirit of others who have gone beyond us, using our intelligence and ingenuity to the full rather than just copying the shells of their achievements.

ACTION LEARNING AND 'GOOD COMPANY'

As I contemplate this vision of good company, I see that this is exactly what has been pioneered on a small scale in the initiatives of Action Learning. The basic unit of Action Learning, the 'set' of about five or six co-learners, becomes a living demonstration of mutual support, drawing on the values of both co-operation and individual achievement. Because the members of the set are primarily engaged in learning from work that goes on outside the set, they are constantly required to consider the nature of their own relationships. This provides a continual spur to learning, and favours a constant, challenging relationship between P and Q. Not least, it encourages members to compare their experience of being in the set with the more familiar experience of their working groups. Commonly, members feel more relaxed in the sets, more able to carry out new ideas and be listened to. Above all, they enjoy asking and being asked questions that are supportive as well as challenging. The experience makes a welcome change from being overwhelmed with well-meaning answers. The students at an Australian high school caught the mood when they called their action learning work a 'Q Factory' and printed this slogan on their T-shirts.

I have tried to include these elements of action learning, together with other elements, in a Good Company model (see Figure 5.1) derived from earlier work on a 'development spiral'.[8] A weakness of the development spiral, from the point of view of organizations that provide good company, is that it did not specify the distinctive quality of the purpose animating the organization. So it could refer to the development of efficient death camps or the nefarious operations of millionaire drug barons. Putting it less dramatically, it could also apply to the multitude of conventional bureaucratic organizations – public, private and voluntary – that survive by making incremental changes to a loosely integrated collection of 'standard operating procedures' (otherwise known as control loops).

In such organizations, each variation from the procedures is properly defined as an error and the learning that is then activated is intended to bring about a prompt correction of the error. It could also result in a decision to introduce yet another 'mechanism' to ensure future compliance. In this way, Q is efficiently suppressed by P, in systematic procedures that are far from the mutuality and fellow feeling of good company.

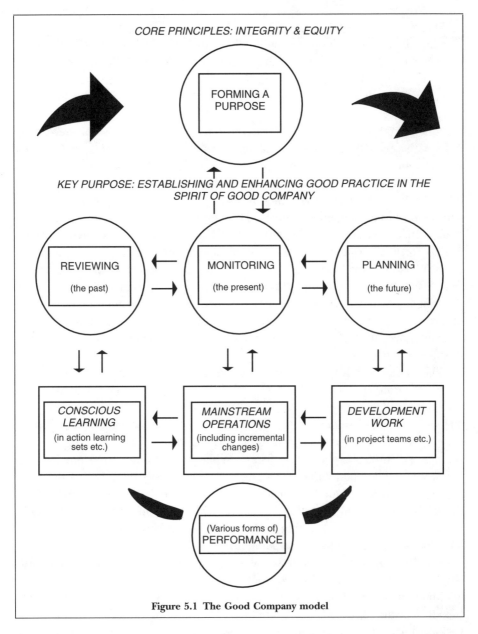

Figure 5.1 The Good Company model

Fortunately, the dialogue between Q and P does not necessarily take the form of 'efficient' P constantly quarrelling with 'developmental' Q in a kind of Punch and Judy show. Current polarized arguments might suggest this, with Crazy Organizations battling it out with Yesterday's Company. But other possibilities offer themselves. The augmented model offered here draws on the experience of different types of good company to suggest that three vital units can combine to bring about a continuing and fruitful dialogue between P and Q: (1) a network of project teams engaged in various forms of development work; (2) a network of action learning sets, or similar groups focused on learning in the context of good practice; (3) mainstream operations, including incremental changes to ensure good practice.

Rather than being controlled from 'the top', these vital units will have close links with many forms of organizational 'core', which will act as a focus for organizational integrity and equity. Each core itself constitutes a fourth vital unit. The term 'core' avoids the conventional assumption that it is 'top' in the sense of controlling the basic three units. It also avoids the assumption that it forms some kind of self-contained 'centre'. The key function of the 'core' is to relate good company to good practice, through a strong and evident sense of purpose.

This form of organization provides plenty of opportunity for leadership at every phase of development. This is not the conventional form of leadership that demands unquestioning followers, but the newer form of leadership already described, in which everyone is enabled to give a lead where appropriate. Instead of organizational purpose being restricted to a small group of owners, the constant flows of changing activity stimulate a clear sense of purpose throughout the varied networks.

Mike Pedler and Kath Aspinwall[9], in a recent study of varied forms of good company, bring out this wider sense of purpose particularly clearly: 'Purpose seems particularly important in today's organisations – what is the company for, why does it exist? Many companies are centred on one stakeholder (some, indeed, seem mere extensions of their owners' egos), while others are more mutual and multi-stakeholder in focus'. While shying away from precise definition, the implicit and contentious position taken in this book is that the latter are more likely to be 'good companies' (p. 4). Their book illuminates this contentious issue by covering a wide range of organizations, and examining the links between organizational learning and 'a growing concern with business ethics and issues of right behaviour in public life'.

With this emphasis on leadership, good company and the purpose of learning, we have come far from the conventional meaning of the traditional phrase 'minding our Ps and Qs'. This refers to a strategy of prudent compliance, under the surveillance of over-bearing authority. That kind of authority still has to be reckoned with, but as change disrupts old structures of power, and offers new and unexpected opportunities, the old phrase now shines with new meanings. If we mind our Ps and Qs skilfully and whole-heartedly enough, in good company, engaged in good practice, we will really be learning to good purpose.

REFERENCES

1 Revans, R. W. (1987) 'The learning equation: an introduction in Action Learning', *Journal of Management Development*, **6** (2).

2 Lawrence, J. K. (1994) 'Action Learning – a questioning approach', in A. Mumford (ed.), *Handbook of Management Development*, 4th edn, Aldershot: Gower.

3 Garratt, B. (1994) *The Learning Organisation*, London: HarperCollins.

4 Burgoyne, J. G. H., Pedler, M. and Boydell, T. (eds) (1994) *Towards the Learning Company*, Maidenhead: McGraw-Hill.

5 Senge, P. (1990) *The Fifth Discipline*, New York: Century Business.

6 Hampden-Turner, C. M. (1994) 'Charting the corporate mind' in W. Bennis *et al.* (eds), *Beyond Leadership*, Oxford: Blackwell.

7 Morris, J. F. (1987) 'Good Company', *Management Education & Development*, **18**, 103–115.

8 Morris, J. F. (1994) 'Development work and the learning spiral' in A. Mumford (ed.), *Handbook of Management Development*, Aldershot: Gower.

9 Pedler, M. and Aspinwall, K. (1996) *Perfect plc?*, Maidenhead: McGraw-Hill.

6 What do We Mean by Action Learning? A Story and Three Interpretations

Mike Pedler

It is ironic that as Action Learning grows in influence with both practitioners and academics, none of Revans' main texts – *Developing Effective Managers* (1971); *Action Learning: New Techniques for Managers* (1980); *The Origins and Growth of Action Learning* (1982) and *The ABC of Action Learning* (1983) – remains in print.

This may or may not explain why some current usage seems ill-informed. 'I use Action Learning all the time but I've never been in a set', a senior organizational development adviser confessed. A recent issue of *Management Learning* (Vol. 27, No 1, 1996) has three articles and an editorial which either feature or cite Action Learning. One of the papers (endorsed in the editorial) interprets Action Learning as *teaching* via simulation or 'experiential' methods, with no apparent awareness of its being rooted in learning from action in tackling intractable, organizational problems whilst being accountable to clients and sponsors, or indeed to its origins in opposition to, and as an antidote for, classroom expertise.

On the other hand Action Learning seems very much alive and evolving, a fertile idea spawning new forms and vivifying old ones. This book abounds with variations even from those who take their inspiration directly from the founder. By resisting any given form or technique, Action Learning must always re-invent itself and has emerged as a creative source of *generative* theory and practice for management and organizational learning over the last twenty years.

Different interpretations of Action Learning may have their roots in the broader idea of learning itself. This chapter begins by attempting to define learning, considering four aspects of this notion. An Action Learning story is then subjected to three interpretations; to Action Learning as problem solving and/or self-development is added the possibility of Action Learning as *collaborative enquiry*. This third possibility illuminates some problems of the earlier interpretations and also enables the exploration of how Action Learning can go beyond the limitations of individual action and learning.

WHAT DO WE MEAN BY *LEARNING?*

What do we mean by *learning*? Why is it important? George Kelly, for example, who shares Revans' commitment to action as a defining characteristic of being human, takes learning for granted and sees no reason for splitting it off; to live means to learn:

> Man lives best when he commits himself to getting on with his life. Since I see the concept of learning as nothing less than this, the term seems redundant when applied to a living creature.[1]

Yet as Senge has recently emphasized, learning difficulties – in individuals or in organizations – can have tragic consequences.[2] The case for a separate study of learning rests partly on this – that living today requires so much of it. For the person, lack of learning may deny access to an independent life, to work, to becoming fully human; for the organization, the inability to evolve and develop may lead to loss of productivity, purpose, identity, and even existence.

What we *mean* when we talk about learning varies by time and place. A 1963 undergraduate psychology lecture defined learning as 'a relatively enduring change in actual or potential behaviour as a result of experience' – reflecting the positivist, behaviourist theories holding sway then. Contrast this with Illich's (1971) iconoclastic counter – 'learning is unhampered participation in a meaningful situation'.[3] Such very different perspectives may cause us to wonder in what other ways learning might be described. Separated from living, learning turns out to be a diffuse even problematic concept. Pedler and Aspinwall suggest four different aspects: we can learn . . .[4]

1. . . . *about* things   or KNOWLEDGE
2. . . . to *do* things   or SKILLS, ABILITIES, COMPETENCES
3. . . . to *become ourselves, to*   or PERSONAL DEVELOPMENT
    achieve our full
    potential and . . .
4. . . . to *achieve things together* or COLLABORATIVE ENQUIRY

The first two of these are perhaps most familiar. *Knowledge* or learning *about* things is another wide spectrum word ranging from the memorizing of simple facts to the deep understanding of complex ideas; from knowing 'this or that' to knowing 'why'. *Skills, abilities, competences* or learning to *do* things include mental and manual skills, social abilities with others and competence in complex situations. Although knowledge and skills (or 'theory and practice' or 'thinking and doing') are often paired, they are also often split as in the diagnosis of 'academic' versus 'vocational' used as a basis for the different formal education of young people. Revans has long criticized this splitting – 'There is no learning without action, and no (sober and deliberate) action without learning'.

The splitting of learning types is even more problematic in the context of the third. *Personal development* – to become ourselves, to achieve our full potential in life – has long been valued in primary schools, adult education and now is increasingly recognized elsewhere. Theories of lifelong learning, adult development, biography and andragogy add much to the ideas of pedagogy.[5] Learning *within* the stages of development may be seen as incremental, whereas moving *between* stages – from crawling to walking; from being a professional to becoming a manager; from being a 'controller' to becoming a 'facilitator' – requires more of a step-jump or transformation. As personal development, learning focuses on questions of purpose and identity as part of intellectual growth and skilled competence.

In these first three meanings, learning is something which individuals do, largely on their own. *Collaborative enquiry* – learning to *achieve things together* – suggests that learning can also take place in relationships. Terms such as 'team learning', 'learning community' or 'learning organization', 'situated learning' in 'communities of practice' involve collective learning, cooperating in understanding and acting to do things together on behalf of the whole.[6–8] Here learning outcomes are not fully measured in terms of what individuals achieve, but by what is jointly created.

This brief sketch shows how definitions of learning may change over time. The shift from seeing learning as an individual phenomenon to seeing it as something which can result from people-in-relationship seems particularly relevant now. This new meaning is generative of a view of learning beyond the individual making isolated sense of the world to that of people jointly engaged in a collective social process of sense making and meaning creation.

THREE INTERPRETATIONS OF ACTION LEARNING

If the meanings we can ascribe to learning vary over time, is this also the case with Action Learning? Here is an Action Learning story with some alternative readings:

> David Docherty is the 29 year old director of a small but rapidly expanding engineering business. In fact, Harbourne Engineering now employs 60 men and has been tripling its turnover in every year of its five-year existence. There are three directors, including the MD, who all helped found the company. David is mainly responsible for site work

and equipment whilst his fellow directors handle the manpower and selling aspects. Harbourne Engineering does all its work on other people's premises and may be working on 30 or 40 jobs at any one time throughout the British Isles and abroad.

David Docherty has an engineering background but no formal management training. He came to an Action Learning group because his boss, Bill Harbourne, was concerned about two things:

1. The company's rapid rate of growth was putting 'pressure' on existing management and their 'systems' which were very *ad hoc* and depended very much on David and Graham Anderson chasing men and equipment around personally.
2. David was spending far too much time on the equipment side of his job. It could take 30 or 40 hours out of a week and he was not infrequently spending 12 hours on Sundays checking equipment for safety, loading trucks and generally being at the heart of the action.

David saw himself as a straight talker with an open relationship with Bill Harbourne. Bill was almost a peer rather than a boss. David had an inbuilt 'crap detector' and if he thought the group was wasting his time, he said so. At an early meeting he said he would not attend unless he got value out of it.

One of the first things he was asked by the group was how many items of equipment the company had. 'About 800' was his estimate as he had been the man directly responsible since the founding of the company. He was pushed, a bit unwillingly, into making an inventory for a future group meeting. Such a thing had not existed before – to the amazement of the 'big company' engineers in the group. His inventory got to over 2000 items before he gave up, admitting that there was other equipment on various sites that he had not been able to trace. With items varying from a few pounds for a chock or sledgehammer to several hundreds for a 30 ton chain or block and tackle, there was a large amount of money involved.

David then had to go abroad on business for a month and his problem was shelved in his absence. When he returned to the group a number of sessions were devoted to attacking his problem. Numerous suggestions were put forward from the group involving systems to solve his equipment problem. There was no shortage of ideas but it seemed that none fitted the bill. There was always a good reason from the hard-headed David which effectively meant the system would not work. Eventually the group lost patience. After going round in circles for some time and after five hours of tiring discussion, one member said 'You don't really want to solve this problem, do you, David?' This was said and meant aggressively. David was not ruffled – he was used to violent arguments. He reiterated all the reasons he had for resolving the problem – it was taking all his time; as the company expanded it would take more time unless a system was instituted; his wife was complaining about him working 60 or 70 hours each week. But the group was not satisfied and he did get ruffled and rather angry and eventually the meeting broke up.

A few weeks later the problem was resolved. A simple form, a simple filing system, a part-time old age pensioner and some meetings with the fitters were the components of it. The details are not important – all of them had been thrown up by the group weeks beforehand. Most of the other participants worked with far more complicated paperwork systems. So, why wasn't the problem resolved in week one?

The answer to this is not simple. When someone begins to tackle a problem in their own company they are often part of it themselves and if they are not personally involved then their boss usually is. Before it can be resolved they may have to look at the problem and themselves from a new angle. This is what takes the time and, in normal day-to-day managerial routine, rarely happens. David had to see for himself the paradox of his time pressures on the one hand, and his own need to hang on to what made him feel important and indispensable. He had to admit that a paperwork system – 'an alien thing which only happens in big bureaucracies' – could take over *some* aspects of what he did at present all on his own.

Finally he had to face the consequences of what would happen if he got rid of half his workload – what would he replace it with? If he was selling and meeting clients could he do it as well as Bill Harbourne? At the end of the action learning group, David was left with some of these questions still unanswered. One problem was resolved, but it had uncovered several more.

So, what happened here? Three interpretations, borrowing generously from Blantern, define action learning differently:[9]

1. ACTION LEARNING AS *CHANGING THE EXTERNAL WORLD*

As one manager puts it 'To me . . . Revans has a simple message: in action learning real managers share ideas and tackle real problems with their counterparts, which effects change in the real world by helping each other'.[10] There is plenty of support for this perspective in the story of David Docherty and Harbourne Engineering. Not included in the story is the sequel that, as a result of discovering how much equipment it had, scattered all over the country, the company set up a profitable contract hire business. You can't get much more 'real world' than that.

Here Action Learning confronts the person with a 'stern external reality . . . (which) . . . implies a very "realist" stance and an empiricist/logical positivist faith in sense data breaking through the conceptual frameworks that we use to interpret experience . . .'[11] The world is real; it is the individual's perception of it which needs to change – and for the better – for the problem to be resolved.

Much of Revans' own work supports this perspective. As first Director of Education at the Coal Board (1947–55) and as Professor of Industrial Administration at the University of Manchester Institute of Science & Technology (1955–65), Revans' work displays the concerns of the operational researcher. His studies in mines, hospitals, schools and factories measure accident levels, patient length-of-stay rates, children's classroom behaviour and the link between communication levels and supervisory satisfaction with work.[12] The early Action Learning programmes, notably the Belgian Inter-University Programme, are based on scientific models. Thus 'The system alpha paradigm is the basis of many operational research models'[13] and system beta (survey, decision, action,

65

WHAT IS ACTION LEARNING?

audit & control) is ... 'the structure, not only of the negotiation aspects of a decision, but also of the general learning process ... and of the scientific method'.[14]

Claims for Action Learning as changing the 'real world' reach their peak in Revans' quixotic view of Belgium's manufacturing productivity between 1965 and 1983. Comparing this period with the previous 15 years he concludes ' ... Belgium appears in a class by herself. And, perhaps quite coincidentally, 1965 was the year Reg. Revans left for Belgium to start action learning at the highest level'.[15]

2. ACTION LEARNING AS *SELF-DEVELOPMENT*

In contrast to action learning as *changing the external world*, the story can be read as one of individual *self-development*. In the antepenultimate paragraph, we are told that 'the problem was resolved'. Yet this is a dénouement after the dramatic climax in the previous paragraph where David is faced by his actions as seen by other set members – and ultimately by himself. The drama is in the self-development, not in the 'real world' problem-solving.

> (the aim is to) ... help people become more aware of their own processes and their own working models and suchlike ...[16]

This is the romantic, humanistic and personal face of Action Learning, in contrast to the modernism, empiricism and positivism of the previous view. Here what matters is the *inner* person where the *outer* world provides a healthy reality against which individuals, through the questioning of others and their own self-questioning, can perturb themselves and reach a healthier self. This accords with the heroic narrative where after many ups and downs our hero emerges triumphant at last, the world a backcloth to individual exploits.[17]

By the time he is reporting on his Belgian experiences, Revans is providing plenty of evidence for this interpretation. Although the scientist/operational researcher is still strongly present in the most formal and 'scientific' account he ever gives of Action Learning[18], Revans now raises the profile of what has been a lesser theme, looking for *'a general theory of human action, for a science of praxeology'*[19] [added emphasis]. Here Action Learning rests fundamentally upon the discovery and clarification of the person and of their values:

> To be obliged ... to answer the question, 'And who do you think you are?' in return for the right to put it to others, is a useful exercise in self-recognition. In a climate of mutual support, it can bring to a man's notice any latent talents that, beneath his defensive disguises, had previously been unknown to him.[20]

and ...

66

Thus it was that the single idea uncovered by the top managers in the First Inter-University Programme of Belgium to be of greatest interest to them was that of the value *system*. What were the standards of integrity against which all final judgements were made by those with whom they worked – including themselves? It was a notion bound to arise out of the set discussions in which the fellows stripped each other naked, an experience which led them to define the most valuable question they had learned as 'What is an honest man, and what need I do to become one?'[21]

This 'stripping naked', self-questioning and personal change is only achieved after great persistence by other set members. Frustration, conflict and expressions of anger are important in breaking through David's 'defensive disguises' and bringing him to see the self-deceptions which have so far made the many previous sensible suggestions for action unworkable. This self-development process is made critical to action learning in Revans' challenging *Principle of Insufficient Mandate*:

Those unable to change themselves cannot change what goes on around them.[22]

Action learning as *changing the external world* and as *self-development*

From first encountering Action Learning in the mid-1970s, I have tended to see it as being *both* about changing the world *and* the self-development of the person. The entity which is Action Learning is a flow of consciousness, of action and learning, between the inner (person) and outer (organizational problem) and vice versa, in a continuous, iterative process. Though central to my practice for many years, this view is not without its practical problems.

Drawn in 1980 by a participant in an Action Learning set, Figure 6.1 reflects Anne's personal experience of being pulled one way, then the other. It elicited the stern response from the visiting Revans: 'Doesn't this young woman know that she has to do both!'.[23] Yet in practice, it may often be difficult to hold the two in balance. Individual participants or alliances in a set may urge one view rather than the other; sponsors, managers or the context itself may push one way rather than the other. Examining some Action Learning-based Masters degree dissertations recently, I noted a common bias to emphasizing learning and self-development and much less interest in the external change projects. Perhaps, as people, we tend to work out of the values and motives we hold at a given time, choosing this over that, committing ourselves in the act. It is in this sense that the 'naive' problem-solver *or* the earnest self-developer willing to have a go sometimes seems to accomplish more than those who aim to do a bit of both.

As a footnote to this *both . . . and . . .* view of action learning we can even talk of the 'early Revans' (as scientist/ operational researcher) and the 'later Revans' (more humanistic/concerned with a general theory of action) reflecting his altered emphasis over time. This is a reversal of Karl Marx's developmental

Figure 6.1 Action Learning: task vs. self-development

biography; he moved from the romantic, humanistic poet or 'dichter' protesting the alienation of the human spirit (species-being) by capitalist production to the later more mechanistic, dialectical materialist, seeing humaness as the product of economic and social forces. Marx did not entirely lose his earlier concerns, but the individual becomes far less important in his 'science of praxeology'.[24]

3. ACTION LEARNING AS *COLLABORATIVE ENQUIRY?*

To *changing the external world* and *self-development*, a third argument can be made for action learning as *collaborative enquiry*. Here the focus is on the relationship of people in the set, and by extension with the wider context, rather than upon the individual actors and their organizational problems. The action learning set is seen as a 'community of practice' of shared work, knowledge and ways of knowing where new social meanings and realities are collectively constructed.[25]

This argument is made on the basis of three points: (i) the difficulties of taking individual and personally authentic action in work organizations; and (in any case) (ii) the problematic nature of individual action in organizations; and (iii) that Action Learning as collective meaning-making provides a bridge from individual to organizational learning.

(i) The difficulty of personally authentic action

Revans recognizes that much of what is learned in action is about the 'micropolitics of the organization' listing the blocks which top managers may put in the path of the action learner – 'lack of interest; manipulative guidance, tactical procrastination, diagnostic flexibility, evasion and vacillation, directive autocracy, defensive rationalisation'.[26] Yet he remains optimistic that these can be overcome; if not without some suffering.

This view may be too heroic for some grown wary or weary of the motives of owners and senior managers. How many modern managers will take possibly 'career limiting' risks in questioning the assumptions and practice of their bosses? Questions of voice, power, influence and participation are a key part of the enquiry, and the ubiquitousness and omnipresence of these factors in social life makes the straightforward practice of Action Learning a most demanding activity. Perhaps this makes it much rarer than is sometimes assumed?

In his ethnographic study of managers, Watson suggests that, faced with the difficult or 'intractable' problems, people typically respond by turning them over, time and time again, in their heads, seeking a way through.[27] In this view we are always working out what we might do in particular situations via internal arguments or dialogues, which are linked closely with our personal values and identity. In the action learning context, this is likely to happen, possibly for a considerable time, long before we ever get to the set. These internal 'conversations with yourself' may precede and continue alongside any learning conversations with others.[28]

Assuming that people seek to act in a way which is congruent with their personal values and beliefs, of how the world 'should be', then it may not be possible to act authentically in line with any conclusions from these internal conversations, or indeed from the deliberations of any learning conversations with others. We are not wholly free agents. For example, managers in work organizations will encounter many 'real world' reasons why they might not be able to do what they think they should. The inability to act authentically or the requirement to act inauthentically, in a way which affronts reason or personal beliefs, can cause great perturbation. Not to act in accordance with my personal values, renders my actions incongruent with 'the sort of person I am' and makes it harder to become the 'honest man' of the Belgian managers.

Watson suggests a third, intermediate category of managerial thinking falling halfway between Argyris and Schon's 'espoused theory' and 'theory in use':

> It is a kind of personal theory which can be seen as a *potential theory in use* because it contains the guidelines for action which managers would follow if they were allowed to.[29]

Rather than condemn when we see a gap between what another says and what they do, the *potential theory in use* concept suggests we can see any espoused claim as a statement of *sincere aspiration* rather than as empty rhetoric.[30]

The Action Learning group may thus become a place for sharing these internal dialogues and sincere aspirations with others, perhaps preserving a sense of self as honest person in circumstances where it is not possible to act authentically. In sets people do say things like 'I don't have anywhere else where I can say things like this' or 'there is a quality of listening here which I have not experienced before'. Braddick and Casey report that their chief executives appeared not particularly interested in taking action on their problems though they greatly valued the set as a place where they could think differently and re-frame their issues.[31]

(ii) The problematic nature of individual action

Yet even when action is desired and possible, is it a good thing? Task urgency rewards decisiveness and quick action, rather than thought and reflection. In densely interconnected organizations, actors may seek to change situations which they only partially understand. Harrison has criticized 'the bias to action' in which organizations find it easier to act than to learn; in his view, we are more than biased to action and problem solving; we are addicted.[32] Compounding this, leaders also tend to underestimate the extent of negative emotions in the organization – fear, anxiety, anger, resentment and betrayal – which inhibit and limit learning to low risk endeavours at best. In this context, encouraging individuals to take action on problems may make things worse:

> ... in complex and closely-coupled systems, local problem solving quickly creates many unintended effects in other parts of the system, some of which will become problems for the people involved in those parts. Those people, in turn, engage in more local problem solving, creating more problems elsewhere.[32]

This is 'the illusion of taking charge' where 'proactiveness' is actually *reactive*-ness – 'true proactiveness comes from seeing how we contribute to our own problems'.[33] Seeing how we contribute to our own problems can only happen at a level beyond the individual – in terms of the web of interrelationships or of the whole system. For anyone committed to frenetic action, these acts of understanding are unlikely.

(iii) Action Learning as collective meaning-making

The focus here is not upon individual action and learning (which continues to happen elsewhere) but on collective processes which may have a greater potential to transform the whole. Instead of individuals trying to change things on their own, this perspective has the person participating in a shared process of meaning-making, creating frameworks of understanding within which all may act.

A social constructionist perspective questions the assumption of the independent, self-contained self and of the primacy of the 'self' as origin. What we see and attribute to the self are 'social processes realized on the site of the personal'.[34] For Blantern, Action Learning is 'relational learning' where 'individuals participate in the communal conventions where language and constructs mutually arise and become intelligible through "movement" in relationships'.[35] As in Bohm's notion of dialogue, 'the flow of consciousness (in action learning) is not 'outer to inner', nor is it 'inner to outer' but in 'mutual arising'.[36]

The quality of 'learning relationship' in the set allows for new thoughts to be thought, new words to be spoken, new perspectives, possibilities and worlds to be glimpsed – all done jointly, cooperatively produced, communally owned.

But is this action learning?

Yet (engaging in a conversation with myself) if this is *all* the set did then how could it meet a key Revans test of Action Learning, that ... 'There can be no learning without action and no (sober and deliberate) action without learning.'? Surely 'support groups', valuable though they may be, fall short of what we mean by Action Learning? How might such a set be distinguished from an 'ain't it awful' assembly which produces little in the way of action or learning? Is it possible that sets functioning in this way can produce profound effects and results which are not picked up by normal efforts at monitoring individual project outcomes?

EXTENDING ACTION LEARNING

In the story of David Docherty's Action Learning set (which met in 1976/7), the account presented above is the original version.[37] As I saw it then, this was an heroic tale of individuals tackling persistent organizational problems and growing wiser in the process.

I notice now all manner of embarrassments in that account; the rather earnest teaching in the penultimate paragraph; the dated 'old age pensioner' label; the invisibility of the (admittedly few) women in the company, and also of the world outside work (at 29, 'David Docherty' had already been married three times and was under pressure here). This last I knew at the time but didn't include it. To tell any story much has to be left out, to 're-search' is to look again. The story could have been told in other ways, there is no single version; but now this old tale seems uncritical to me, with too much ignored or simply not seen.

Another relative silence in the story is what is said about the set. Revans has pointed out the power of the set as conspiracy – of 'comrades in adversity'. As a 'community of practice' the set may create new and influential shared realities by offering people opportunities to share, explore and co-create in good company. Arguably, this may be more subversive to current practice than any number of individuals attempting to change things on their own.

THE SET AS A COMMUNITY OF PRACTICE

Collaborative enquiry and action may lead to outcomes which are measured at least partly by what is created together. In recent empirical work on workplace learning, Brown and Duguid, arguing particularly on the basis of Orr's study of service technicians, think that workplace learning is best understood as a process in which communities are joined and personal identities are changed.[38] Knowledge and meaning are constructed by members of particular communities of practice working collaboratively to understand, to act and to learn via 'bricolage' – out of what is to hand – in the local conditions of the problem.[39] The notion of 'situated learning'[40] challenges the transfer model of individual learning (from my head to yours) which not only isolate the learner, but abstract knowledge from the context in which it is practised.

In this view learning is inseparable from working and from the process of becoming a member of a given community, be it one of doctors, TV repairers or people who sleep on the streets. The central issue is one of *becoming* a practitioner and not learning *about* practice. This is accomplished via 'legitimate peripheral participation'[40] where the learner's participation grows in from the periphery as a function of their developing understanding.

As in Action Learning, becoming a practitioner requires far more than formal 'expert knowledge'. TV repairers for example can only learn what is not in the 'programmed knowledge' of the repair manuals by accessing the local and 'non-canonical' knowledge of the community. Learning about new devices or non-standard situations involves a good deal of what is not explicit or explicable. This sort of know-how is developed and framed in a particular communal context especially through members collaborating, telling work-related stories and collectively constructing meaning: 'To acquire a store of appropriate stories and, even more importantly, to know what are appropriate occasions for telling them, is then part of what it means to become a midwife' (Jordan quoted in Brown and Duguid).[41]

CONCLUSION: ACTION LEARNING AND ORGANIZATIONAL LEARNING

This view of learning accords with Dixon's definition of organizational learning as a shift in the 'collective meaning structures' held jointly by members.[42] Where members share a common interpretation or a common way of making sense, a change in this can only come about through a dialogue which involves them all. An organization may contain many communities of practice, each with its unique collective meaning-making structures. There is little hierarchy in a community of practice, membership being essentially a single status concept, and this aids the joint construction of meaning through equal 'voice', diverse opinion, story telling and so on. The most valuable, non-canonical knowledge is not available to outsiders, and this has clear implications for their organization and management. This view offers an explanation for why so many top-down organizational change programmes fail (Argyris quoting a study by Beer, Eisenstat and Spector 1988).[43]

To reach more than the six or so commonly assumed to make up the 'set' (though not, be it noted, by Revans who resists any 'right' form or number of comrades), this may have to be larger than usually thought; linking with and extending to, for example, 'search conferencing' or 'whole systems change' methodologies, where 'public learning' can occur as senior managers face and act on questions and challenges from participating members[44, 45]. Action Learning shares many characteristics with these increasingly popular methods for bringing about 'dialogue' in the whole organization[46].

As an idea rather than a method, Action Learning is capable of taking many forms. A social constructionist perspective makes problematic the nature of the individual, of individual action in organizations and of the set as six colleagues working in isolation. Action Learning as collaborative enquiry can build on the Action Learning project and offers some ways forward in organizations seen as whole systems and as composed of communities of practice. Centred on relationship, on novel social realities and on collective understanding, this perspective on Action Learning emerges as one likely to be generative of new possibilities and practices, especially in the light of the current interest in organizational learning.

REFERENCES

1 Kelly, G. A. (1968) 'The autobiography of a theory', in *Clinical Psychology and Psychotherapy*, Maher, B. (ed.) New York: Wiley, p. 65.
2 Senge, P. M. (1990) *The Fifth Discipline: The art & practice of the learning organisation*, New York: Doubleday Currency, p. 18.
3 Illich, I. (1971) *Deschooling Society*, London: Calder and Boyars.
4 Pedler M. and Aspinwall K. (1996) *'Perfect plc?': The purpose and practice of organisational learning*, Maidenhead: McGraw-Hill, pp. 25–7.
5 Knowles M. S. (1970) *The Modern Practice of Adult Education: Andragogy versus Pedagogy*, New York: Association Press.
6 Senge, P. M. op. cit. pp. 233–69.
7 Pedler, M. J. (1981) 'Developing the learning community', in Boydell T. H. and Pedler, M. J. (eds), *Management Self-development: Concepts and Practices*, Aldershot: Gower, pp. 68–84.
8 Brown, J. S. and Duguid P. (1991) 'Organizational learning and communities-of-practice: towards a unified view of working, learning and innovation', *Organization Science*, **2**(1), February, 40–57.
9 Blantern, C. (1992) *Inter-Action Learning: Action Learning as a 'communal language' for negotiating reality*. Research Dissertation for the MA in Computer Mediated Management Learning, University of Lancaster (unpublished).
10 Newbould, D. V. (1982) Foreword to Revans, R. W. (1982) *The Origins and Growth of Action Learning*, Bromley: Chartwell-Bratt.
11 Burgoyne in Blantern, (1992) p. 14.
12 Revans, R. W. (1980) *Action Learning: New Techniques for Managers*, London: Blond & Briggs, Chapters 10–13.
13 Revans, R. W. (1971) *Developing Effective Managers*, New York: Praeger, p. 36.
14 Revans, R. W. (1971) op. cit. p. 41.
15 Revans, R. W. (1985) *Confirming Cases*, Manchester: RALI (Revans Action Learning International), p. 42.
16 Hughes J. in Blantern, (1992) p. 30.
17 Gergen, K. (1994) *Realities and Relationships: Soundings in Social Construction*, London: Harvard University Press, p. 197.
18 Revans, R. W. (1971) op. cit. pp. 28–70.
19 Revans, R. W. (1971) op. cit. p. 58.
20 Revans, R. W. (1971) op. cit. p. 132.
21 Revans, R. W. (1983) *The ABC of Action Learning*, Bromley: Chartwell-Bratt, p. 55.
22 Revans, R. W. (1983) op. cit. p. 55.

23 Roff, A. (1981) in Pedler, M. J. (ed.) *The Diffusion of Action Learning*. Occasional Paper No. 2, Department of Management Studies, Sheffield City Polytechnic, Sheffield UK.

24 Solomon R. (1993) *Ethics and Excellence: Cooperation and Integrity in Business*, New York: Oxford University Press, pp. 94–6.

25 Drath, W. H. and Palus, C. J. (1994) *Making Common Sense: Leadership as meaning-making in a community of practice*, Greensboro NC: Center for Creative Leadership, p. 11.

26 Revans, R. W. (1983) op. cit. pp. 43–48.

27 Watson, T. J. (1996) 'Motivation: that's Maslow, isn't it?' *Management Learning*, **27**(4), pp. 447–64.

28 Pedler, M., Burgoyne, J. G. and Boydell, T. (1994) *A Managers Guide to Self-Development*, 3rd edition, Maidenhead: McGraw-Hill, pp. 262–3.

29 Watson, (1996) op. cit. p. 325.

30 Watson, (1996) op. cit. pp. 338–9.

31 Braddick, W. and Casey, D. (1981) 'Developing the forgotten army – learning and the top manager', *Management Education and Development*, **12**(3).

32 Harrison, R. (1995) *The Collected Papers of Roger Harrison*, Maidenhead: McGraw-Hill, p. 403.

33 Senge, P. M. op. cit. pp. 20–21.

34 Gergen, K. op. cit. p. 210.

35 Blantern, C. op. cit. p. 88.

36 Blantern, C. op. cit, p. 82.

37 Pedler, M. J. (ed.) (1983) *Action Learning in Practice*, Aldershot: Gower, pp. 57–59.

38 Brown, J. S. and Duguid, P. op. cit. p. 30.

39 Drath, W. H. and Palus, C. J. op. cit. p. 11.

40 Lave, J. and Wenger E. (1991) *Situated Learning: Legitimate peripheral participation*, Cambridge: Cambridge University Press.

41 Jordan, quoted in Brown, J. S.and Duguid, P. op. cit. p. 48.

42 Dixon, N. M. (1994) *The Organisational Learning Cycle*, Maidenhead: McGraw-Hill, pp. 36–43.

43 Argyris, C. (1990) *Overcoming Organizational Defences: Facilitating Organizational Learning*, Boston: Allyn & Bacon, pp. 3–4.

44 Weisbord, M. R. (1992) *Discovering Common Ground*, San Francisco: Berrett Koehler.

45 Wilkinson, D. and Pedler, M. J. (1996) 'Whole systems development in public service', *Journal of Management Development*, **15**(2), pp. 38–53.

46 Dixon, N. M. (1996) *Perspectives on Dialogue: Making talk developmental for individuals and organisations*, Greensboro NC: Center for Creative Leadership.

7 A Biography of Action Learning*

Ronnie Lessem

Each person must take the risk of creating a life of his own. . . . When you think about it, you are the thread that holds the events of your life together[1]

INTRODUCTION

Dedicated athlete, follower of the Bible, scientific analyst. Action, feeling, thought. Reg Revans has taken the risk, over seventy-five years, of creating his own life. In the course of doing so, and in the face of continuous scepticism and hostility – particularly in his own country – Revans has woven together a rare fabric. The fabric is made up of the physical, emotional and intellectual strands that constitute his own self. Bringing this three-fold self to bear upon the task, Revans has woven together, in a masterful and evolving synthesis, the basic polarities that are a feature of our social fabric (see Figure 7.1). In trying to

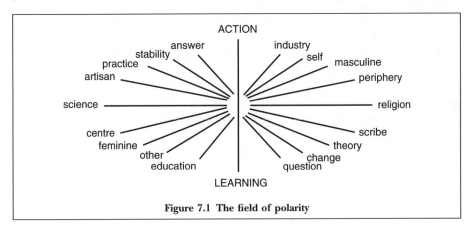

Figure 7.1 The field of polarity

* This chapter originally appeared in Revans, R. W. *The Origins and Growth of Action Learning*, Chartwell-Bratt, 1982.

resolve the conflicts, dualities and paradoxes of his own personality, Revans has attempted to heal the schisms within his society. In describing the way Action Learning has evolved, I hope to convey the intricacy, harmony and significance of Revans's synthesizing activity.

SCRIBE AND ARTISAN: MIND AND BODY

In his early years Revans gave parallel attention to the development of body and mind. He became an Olympic long-jumper and a Cambridge physicist. This particular duality was never to leave him. After this career as both athlete and physicist, he joined the Essex education authority, on the outskirts of London, soon to find himself trying to bridge the gap between body and mind, first within the health service. In 1938, while looking into 'The entry of girls into the nursing profession' he became preoccupied with the divisions between consultants and administrators on high ('scribes') and nurses on the shopfloor ('artisans'). It was this duality between matter (physical achievement) and spirit (conceptual attainment) that attracted Revans to a training and development role in the coalmining industry.

EDUCATION AND INDUSTRY: IVORY TOWER AND COLLIERY SHAFT

The mind-body split revealed itself, not only in the divisions between scribe and artisan, but also in the conflict between education and industry at large. In fact, the remoteness of the ivory tower from muck and brass has been very apparent in Great Britain, if not in the world as a whole. The recent call for the regeneration of British industry, accompanied by the urge to make education more relevant, is symptomatic of this split. Times have not changed since Revans was writing about 'A staff college for the mining industry' in 1945 – or even much earlier, 'The overture to 1945'.

Revans's starting point at the time was the need he perceived, in the wake of increased mechanization, for people to be trained to understand both the limitations of machines and how best to use and take care of them. He was quick to point out, however, that

> ... technical progress is made only by the cutting edge of the weapon of general understanding. If the temper of that body of general knowledge is poor then no amount of sharpening will make it hold an edge.[2]

Here we get a first tangible token of Revans's relentless synthesizing activity. For example, he does not advocate the teaching of English as a language to miners, as something worthwhile in itself. Rather, he claims, that only the man who commands his language can use it to describe what he sees in front of him: his powers of description grow with the knowledge of his own tongue. If by improved command of his words he can send in a more lucid telephone report of some accident or breakdown, he may save valuable time in arranging for it to be dealt with.

Revans, by implication, is bridging the gulf between the 'two cultures', rather than merely setting them up side by side. He is weaving one culture into the other to create a whole that is greater than the sum of the parts. So many attempts at so-called interdisciplinary education or multinational enterprise have failed because there has been no genuine synthesis. Separate 'apartheid' regimes have been manipulated into mutual opposition rather than developed in a mutually reinforcing way:

> It is simplifying the problem too much to say that the education authorities will deal with the theory and industry with the practice. That, in theory, might be an administrative formula, but, in fact, each side of the programme is woven into the other[3]

So, the interweaving of education and industry is accompanied by the integration of theory and practice. Revans had sown the seeds, in the 1940s, of 'The Theory of Practice in Management', which was to appear in the mid-1960s. But something else was going on in his mind and body, still concerned with the connection between the two. For the conflict between education and industry was paralleled by the man-technology duality. Revans argued that the boy who drives heavy nails near the end of a hardwood board and is angry when it splits is the boy who will later hit a conveyor bearing with a hammer after, through neglect, it has been allowed to seize up. Furthermore, ignorance breeds hostility to innovation: men may refuse to adopt new machines simply because they do not know how they work. It is for such reasons that education and industry, training and tools, people and technology, need to be united. The coming together of the ivory tower and the colliery shaft starts with a nut and a bolt. Or does it?

SELF AND OTHER: MINERS AS TEACHERS

The split between body and mind, head and limb, is one thing; the division between thoughts and feelings, head and heart, is another. In looking into the recruitment and training of young boys as miners, Revans's heart reached out to the new recruits. He emphasized that the persons with whom the boys came in contact should treat them as personal friends. But there were further implications:

... it is evident that, in an industry as human as mining, there are the men to be found who are genuinely interested in the boys, who can remember, sometimes painfully, perhaps, their own introduction to the pits, and who have a little insight into the adolescent mind . . .[4]

The miners themselves, then, should 'carry the educational can', particularly when able to combine the technical know-how with an interpersonal sensitivity. In fact, Revans marked these out as the essential qualities which the manager of any large undertaking should also possess. In so doing, he became a fore-runner of the whole 'sociotechnical' school of management which was to blossom in the 1960s. But there was more to follow. . . . For Revans went a step beyond friendship and interpersonal awareness to propose that miners and managers should also learn with and from each other. He suggested that a Staff College be formed, through which people with common problems would be brought together:

... in relating their difficulties or successes to their colleagues, those who come into contact with these questions have much both to learn and to give . . .[5]

For people engaged with similar work tend to encounter similar difficulties, and can often suggest practical solutions to each other. Learning is thus enhanced by the coming together of people in the same boat to work on live problems of common concern.

CENTRE AND PERIPHERY: INDUSTRIAL MORALE AND SIZE OF UNIT

In what context then are people able to work on (and to learn from) live problems of mutual concern? This question led Revans to consider the effect of size of unit on morale. For he had noticed, in the collieries, that management that was psychologically or physically remote inclined the miners to see their own employment as an insult to their self-respect. Throughout the 1950s he under-took extensive researches in the pits, in industry and in hospitals, to discover that there was a significant correlation between the size of the work unit, on the one hand, and, on the other, the level of absenteeism, accidents and disputes. He was led to conclude that

... it is the big organisation that suffers, for it is in the big organisation that the centre of decision and the periphery of action face the greatest risk of mutual misunder-standing[6]

Revans's major contribution has not been to make out that small is beautiful, although it is revealing to learn that he was writing about it long before Schuma-cher, his colleague at the Coal Board. What does make Revans unique is the way he has linked together industrial relations (artisan and scribe), human relations (self and others), technological change (education and industry), and the whole question of scale (centre and periphery) with information processing, problem solving and learning.

In the early 1960s, when Revans was achieving this synthesis, management education was already in full swing, both in Europe and America. While Business Schools were offering separate programmes in production, financial and personnel management, attempts were also being made to integrate these functions under one overall umbrella. A central or core programme (usually the so-called 'business policy') was supposed to help the student hang the separate business functions together. The predominant educational form was the case study, with the university courses tending to be peripheral to industry and commerce themselves. Business policy was taught in an impersonal way, remote from the actual student of management, so that no attempt could be made to bring together learner and learning. This also prevailed in the so called 'management sciences', where only what was quantifiable was also permissible.

Revans, meanwhile, placed at the centre of things the 'springs of human action'. It is one's perception of the problem, he said, one's evaluation of what is to be gained by solving it, and one's estimate of the resources at hand to solve it, that supply these action springs. Since these judgements, moreover, are largely based on one's relations to others, and since current rates of technological change the problems to be solved one day to the next, it follows that

> ... everybody in the organisation, from those who frame the policies to those who manipulate the ultimate details of technique, *must be endowed to the greatest possible extent with the means of learning* ...[7] [The stressing in this quotation, as in all the others in my paper, is my own: R. L.]

Such learning must demand not only information about the latest shift of policy; it must also demand the power to get the knowledge needed to see one's part in what is going on, and, in particular, to know the effect of one's behaviour upon those with whom one works. So problem solving, human relations, information, learning, change and proximity all come together under the springs of human action.

SCIENCE AND RELIGION: THOUGHT AND ACTION

A lot of modern management theory considers human action in terms of either tasks or relationships. Back in the 1940s Revans was talking about technical knowledge and interpersonal sensitivity as the two prime managerial attributes. However, by 1957, he maintained that any division between industrial 'processes' and 'people' was an illusion. In his 'Analysis of Industrial Behaviour' he showed that human relations in the factory were strongly influenced by the extent to which men perceived themselves to be economically and effectively organized. Or, to put it another way, whereas the overcontrolled factory impairs freedom of thought and local decision, that which is too often haphazard fritters away men's valuable time . . . the one thing that can never be recalled. So, in essence, tasks and relationships are inextricably intertwined, as are personal consciousness and management technique, religious faith and organizational science.

In the mid-1960s Revans published his first book *Science and the Manager*. He had carried his scientific past along with him and had never let it go. He particularly ensured that it was never cut off from the 'feeling life' nor from personal consciousness. The following illustrates the point:

> There are four forces bearing upon management today that encourage a new approach to its primary task of making decisions. The first is the need for *economy of managerial time and effort* . . . the age of science is one of economy, of prudent thought, precise design, exact calculation . . . The second . . . is the entry into management of the *analytical approach*, familiar for over three centuries to the scientist: while intuition, or the unremembered urges of the past, must always be the first weapon of the manager, he must also be able to grasp the underlying structures of the situations that challenge him. Thirdly, the *study of variability* through the language of statistics has brought to the manager a language to describe the unexpected, the capricious and the random elements of these tasks. Fourthly, the *social sciences* have thrown a little light on the human forces that, in the final analysis, determine whether or not any enterprise will succeed.[8]

Revans's language flows in and out of the subject and object like a stream of dual consciousness. At the same time, moreover, as he was writing about *Science and the Manager*, he was also dealing with *The Bible as Appointed to be read by Industry*.

The idea that there can be no comfort in external solutions to one's own intimate problems of security, Revans claims, comes from the earliest annals of our race. Taking this belief a step further, he maintains that the 'Kingdom of God' is to be found within a nation's own shores and within the wills of its own people. In other words, on the one hand, the salvation of Britain is not to be found by observers scanning the world in the hope of turning up some miracle; and, on the other hand, the educational task of the West, in relation to the developing nations, is not to instruct them in the records of its own achievements. It is rather to help them, the developing nations, to tackle their own problems as they perceive them, to strive after the goals they have set for themselves, and to offer such help as is appropriate to the points that they have reached and to the ends for which they seek. Thus a lesson drawn from the Bible has alike personal, national and international implications.

The Theory of Practice in Management, published in 1966, is a true synthesis of thought and action. In this book, Revans explains that the scientific method is merely a model built out of thought, just as thoughts themselves are models built from consciousness. In his next book, *Developing Effective Managers*, which came out in 1971, Revans turned this general statement into a specific method of achieving managerial objectives. The model, which he calls System Beta, involves five distinct steps:

- survey, a stage of observation
- hypothesis, a stage of theory, of conjecture
- experiment, in which practical tests are carried out
- audit, during which actual and desired results are compared
- review, relating the particular result to the whole context.

These stages in fact constitute a learning cycle popularized by David Kolb from M.I.T., and published two years after Revans's visit there with a consortium of twenty managers, described in *Developing Effective Managers*.

Contrasted against System Beta is System Gamma, based on the individual manager's subjective consciousness, or 'predisposing mental set' as this bears upon a particular problem in a particular setting. In between the subjective and the objective is System Alpha, which moves from personal values to external circumstances and internal resources:

- by what values am I guided?
- what is blocking their fulfilment?
- what can I do against such blockage?

Whereas System Alpha is concerned with the manager's use of information in designing objectives (strategies), System Beta is oriented to achieving them (negotiation), and System Gamma monitors the outcomes for adapting to experience and change (learning).[9] While all three circumscribe the processes of management, another six elements constitute what Revans calls the 'media of management analysis'. These serve to highlight once again the interactions between thought and action, intellect and faith, scientific method and personal conviction.

A real *decision*, firstly, is always that of a particular person, with his own ends not to be neglected, his own fears to amplify his problems, his own hopes a mirage to magnify his own resources, and with his own prejudices, often called experience, to colour the data with which he works. A choice of *goals*, secondly, so much bound up with decision theory, is yet distinct from it, in that the ends for which one strives, deliberately or unconsciously, as an individual or with others, are but partly determined by the calculations of economic strategy: behind them jostle the egocentric drives of the individual as the person he is. Thirdly, the relevance of *information*, that product of which the raw material is data and the creative process the personal sensitivities of the manager himself. Fourthly, the theory of *systems* describes the web in which the world-line of that particular manager is entangled. The assessment of *probability* is, fifthly, that farrago of mathematical statistics and simple guesswork, by which we attempt to assess our forgotten experiences, our present wishfulness, and our future hopes. And, sixthly, the *learning process* ... integrating everything that one has so far become, and one's sole hope for future improvement.[10]

ACTION AND LEARNING: CHANGING SYSTEM AND SELF

Back in the 1950s Revans had stated that the study of industrial behaviour was still awaiting its Faraday or its Chadwick. He confessed the metaphor might oversimplify the problem because, whereas Chadwick called up one single entity and Faraday no more than three, industrial behaviour must take into account scores of independent factors. But this, in itself, he said, should not prevent the discovery of simple laws. Whether or not Revans has discovered even one such, he has certainly evolved a method that is, in one sense, inordinately simple and, in another, extraordinarily complex. But first let me retrace steps, before elaborating further.

In the 1940s, Revans had worked on the dualities between artisan and scribe, education and industry, self and other, with particular reference to the coalmining industry. In the 1950s he was principally concerned with questions of scale and their implications for communications and learning, in both the mines and the hospital service. The 1960s saw him establish management education programmes, most particularly in Belgium, while evolving both a management science and a managerial consciousness. In the 1970s the action learning concept was hardened out and applied, for the first time with discipline and design, in British industry.

Action learning, at its simplest, is an approach to management education. At its most profound it is a form of personal therapy, a means of social and economic transformation, and even a way of life. Let me try to reconstruct Revans's argument, step by step.

We start with the symbolic amalgamation of 'artisan' and 'scribe'. Knowledge, for Revans, can be only the outcome of action. By wrestling (as artisan) with live problems, and subsequently reflecting (as scribe) upon the results of his achievements, the learner acquires knowledge. Revans continues with the symbolic intermingling of 'education' and 'industry'. For the knowledge acquired is not so much the facts or techniques imparted by an educator, but, more appropriately, the reinterpretation of the practitioner's own existing knowledge. This reinterpretation is best achieved through the meeting of 'self' and 'other', that is of 'comrades in adversity'. It is not a question of the blind leading the blind,

84

but that . . . the blindfold shall help the blindfold to strip away the veils and bandages of custom and practice.[11] Action Learning employs the social process by which a 'set' of four or five learners, by the apparent incongruity of their exchanges, frequently cause each other to examine afresh both 'project' design and its implementation.

Action Learning is also a personal activity which combines objective analysis ('science') and subjective commitment ('religion'). Its logical foundation is the structural identity of the scientific method, of rational decision making, of the exchange of sound advice and fair criticism, and of the learning of new behaviour.[12] Yet, while talking and argument call only for intelligence or quickness of wit, doing and action call for commitment or true belief. For, in taking action, Revans claims, especially after one has clearly exposed one's motives to close and critical colleagues, one is obliged to explore that inner self otherwise so often taken for granted. In seeking answers to difficult work-related questions, especially in conditions of risk and confusion, miners, nurses and managers begin to learn who they themselves may be: to answer their 'work-questions' they must, at the same time, explore their 'self-questions'. The fundamental law of industrial behaviour, that Revans was seeking in the 1950s, may well have been discovered by him in the 1970s: ' . . . knowledge is the consequence of action, and to know is the same as to do,'[13] or, to elaborate: ' . . . the underlying structures of successful achievement, of learning, of intelligent counselling, and of what we call the scientific method, are logically identical'.[14]

STABILITY AND CHANGE: TODAY AND TOMORROW

Revans has developed another law, which can be associated with that already cited. Learning, he says, for the individual or for society at large, must be greater than the rate of change. To put it another way, you cannot change the 'system' unless you also change your 'self'. In other words, external impact and internal development go hand in hand. He has called this 'the principle of insufficient mandate'.[15]

In an article on 'Management, Productivity and Risk', published in 1981, Revans has described the relationship between learning and change, at individual and societal levels. When the world does not change, the son may follow in his father's footsteps, by repeating what is already in the books. But, on the precipice of change, taking the climber into a new world at every rising of the sun, the primary need for learning is no longer programmed knowledge, but an ability to pose the questions proper to the microcosm of uncertainty now to be entered:

Our ability to adapt to change with such readiness that we are seen to change may be defined as learning.[16]

Those able to do tomorrow what there is no need to do today will have learned, just as have those who can do today what was unknown yesterday.

THE SIGNS OF OUR TIMES: MASCULINE AND FEMININE

In epochs of convulsion, Revans maintains, such as the present, there is nothing more necessary than that we should understand the conditions of our own learning:

> ... *programmed knowledge* can be acquired through the published syllabus of the teaching institution, while *questioning insight* comes only from a recognition within oneself that one's perception of what is going on in the here-and-now falls short of one's responsibility for doing something about it. Programmed knowledge is the product of technical instruction; questioning insight is to be sought through Action Learning. If we call the first 'P' and the second 'Q', we might write the general learning equation: L is f(P, Q).[17]

Learning, and the fundamental law that Revans has developed out of it, involves a programmed push and a questioning pull. Erich Jantsch, in his revealing work on *Design and Evolution*, has identified 'planning' and 'love' as the two essential complementary aspects of 'human design':

> Where planning, the MASCULINE element, aims at stabilisation which in turn makes it possible to act out power or focussed energy, love, the FEMININE element, introduces the instabilities which elevate the plane of human action to ever new dynamic regimes, thereby ensuring the continuously renewed conditions for human creativity, for the life of human systems[18]

It is, surely, no accident that Revans has done most of his work with nurses and in the National Health Service, on the one hand, and with managers in industry, on the other. Anima and animus: together constituting the whole person or society. In searching relentlessly for the *Gestalt*, Revans has brought together masculine and feminine, and this, perhaps, becomes most apparent in his work on human and industrial relations.

In the early 1970s Revans, having first run the international project for The Organization for Economic Cooperation and Development (OECD) on *The Emerging Attitudes and Motivations of Workers*,[19] then edited its proceedings. Already at that stage he chose to comment on one Japanese example of work relations. He referred particularly to its establishment of small work groups, not only with a high degree of autonomy, but organized in such a way as to endow their members with a continuous opportunity to learn and to develop. The groups were constituted, in other words, not only for effective PRODUCTION, but also for continuous LEARNING. Production and learning, which can be associated with animus and anima, can also be related to Alan Watts's description of masculine and feminine traits:

> ... all philosophical dispute can be reduced to an argument between those who are tough-minded, rigorous and precise and like to stress differences and divisions between things (PRODUCTIVITY), and those tender-minded romanticists who like wide generalisations and round syntheses, and stress the underlying unities (LEARNING).[20] [Bracketed insertions by R. L.]

In a subsequent article, *'Worker Participation as Action Learning'*, Revans refers to the great changes that top managers will need to face in the 1970s:

> The qualities to be called for ... will be temperamental and emotive rather than intellectual and cognitive; they must be involving rather than detached, questioning the self no less than quantifying the situation.[21]

He goes on to proclaim, on the one hand, that autonomy is the central theme in participation and, on the other, that the vitality of participation is its local relevance. In other words, the individual must be able to relate his autonomous part to the accessible and integral whole. Thus, participation is linked not only with the impact of scale, but also with the immediacy of task:

> The talisman that will release the enthusiasm of those who do the work is the specific difficulty of that work in the here-and-now.[22]

That work must be neither too difficult and challenging, nor too easy and unchallenging. Risk and innovation need to be balanced by support and accommodation. We need both to confront and to accommodate change; to hunt for solutions and to bring home the answers to share.

The desirability of harmonizing technological and innovative assertiveness (masculine) with a social and nurturing receptivity (feminine) was stressed by Revans already in the early 1960s. In his research paper, 'Industry and Technical Education', he lamented the shallowness of the roots of technical education in the British soil. On the one hand, he contrasted the twentieth century with those earlier times, when the master craftsman ' ... was enjoined by his guild to treat the apprentices as members of his own family ...'[23] and, on the other, he asks why technical education should have been so neglected in an industrial nation like Britain? Whereas success itself has detracted from introspection, more importantly:

> We have overlooked the price, in social disintegration, of that final triumph of Eighteenth Century rationalism, the Division of Labour.[24]

The social and economic disintegration already apparent when those lines were written has become much more apparent now.

Action Learning has, indeed, come into its time. As educational method, form of personal therapy, and vehicle for social transformation, its time is ripe. For as our society stands on the watershed between breakdown and breakthrough, so action learning has evolved to accommodate both. Revans, in synthesizing his own thoughts, feelings and actions has brought a holistic approach to bear upon our society's physical, social and economic problems. Action Learning, in addressing itself to artisan and scribe, education and industry, I and thou, centre and periphery, science and religion, stability and change, and to male and female consciousness, serves both a multitude and a singleness of purpose.

Two things, finally, stick out in my mind when recalling my own conversations with Revans. The first was his saying that Action Learning and Buddhism were one and the same thing. The second was his thanking me for sparing half an hour of my time to listen to him. The philosophy is the man. . . .

REFERENCES

1 Viscott, D. (1977), *Risking*, p. 131, Pocket Books.
2 Revans R. W. (1945) *Plans for Recruitment, Education and Training for the Coalmining Industry*, Mining Association of Great Britain, October p. 5.
3 Revans, R. W. op. cit., p. 8.
4 Revans, R. W. op. cit., p. 5.
5 Revans, R. W. op. cit., pp. 111, 112.
6 Revans, R. W. (1964), 'Bigness and Change' *New Society*, 2 January.
7 Revans, R. W. op. cit.
8 Revans, R. W. (1965), *Science and the Manager*, Macdonald pp. 55, 56.
9 Revans, R. W. (1969), 'The Managerial Alphabet' in 'Approaches to the Study of Organisational Behaviour' Tavistock Publications.
10 Revans, R. W. 'A Vocabulary of Managerial Debate', unpublished memorandum used in The Inter-University Programme of Belgium.
11 Revans, R. W. (1981), 'The Psychology of the Deliberated Random,' unpublished paper, p. 1.
12 Revans, R. W. (1971), *Action, Creativity and Learning*, Prakseologia, Polish Academy of Sciences.
13 Revans, R. W. See 11 above.
14 Revans, R. W. (1981), 'The Nature of Action Learning' Omega, International Journal of Management Science, **9** (1) p. 22.
15 Revans, R. W. op. cit., p. 16.
16 Revans, R. W. (1981), 'Management, Productivity and Risk', Omega, International Journal of Management Science, **9** (2) p. 136.
17 Revans, R. W. op. cit., p. 137.
18 Jantsch, E. (1975), *Design and Evolution*, Brazillier.
19 Revans, R. W. (1972), *The Emerging Attitudes and Motivations of Workers*, Directorate of Manpower and Social Affairs: OECD, Paris.
20 Watts, A. (1972), *Book on the Taboo Against Knowing Who You Are*, Random.
21 Revans, R. W. (1971), 'Seminars for Top Management', unpublished memorandum Fondation Industrie-Université, Brussels.
22 Revans, R. W. (1975), 'Worker Participation as Action Learning, Part III'; unpublished paper.

23 Revans, R. W. (1962), *Industry and Technical Education*, University of Leeds, Institute of Education October p. 1.
24 Revans, R. W. op. cit., p. 2.

Part II
Applications

INTRODUCTION

Part II describes some of the ways in which Action Learning is being applied to problems of managing and organizing. Some of these are most ambitious – George Boulden and Vlasta Safarikova's account of using Action Learning to bring about industrial re-structuring in the Czech Republic being one example here. A different sort of ambition is evident in Otmar Donnenberg's story of an Austrian hospital seeking to overcome the after-effects of a corrupt administration. Zhou Jianhua's account of action and learning in Chinese Joint Venture companies is another example of the use of Action Learning to tackle situations where fundamental change is required.

Several of the case studies in this part of the book illustrate how Action Learning may be applied in organization settings to pursue people development through tackling intractable problems. Alec Lewis supplies an example of a classic in-company programme from the UK, whilst Doris Adams and Nancy Dixon discuss work at the Digital Equipment Company in the USA. Tony Winkless' thoughtful account of doctors in the UK National Health Service offers some alternatives to the 'herding cats' approach to managing with professionals, and David Giles' exciting tale of Williams Grand Prix shows the need for persistence and risk-taking in getting Action Learning established over a period of several years and how it can be mixed with some more standard training approaches.

Taken together these chapters should provide any would-be organizer of Action Learning with enough examples and inspiration to start on most problem situations which they are likely to confront. However, a final chapter in this Part, by Richard Thorpe, Maggie Taylor and Meg Elliott, tackles one of the most problematic areas for Action Learning – how to apply it in the academic context. This account of the Manchester Metropolitan University's MSc in Management Programme raises many of the issues met in this burgeoning area of Action Learning activity, and of how they may be resolved.

There are some important questions about Action Learning and academia which are not adequately addressed in this part of the book. Two in particular spring to mind. The first is posed by those academics who are calling for a more 'critical management education'. Their questions can be summed up as 'Can Action Learning serve as a way of adequately critiquing management?' and 'What does Action Learning have to say about power and its distribution in organizations and society?' As noted in the main introduction, Action Learning is seen by some as a route to achieving a more critical management education albeit with some added teaching of critical theory to provide managers with an adequate basis for making this sort of analysis.

A second area of questioning is 'How does Action Learning fit with academic qualifications?' The use of Action Learning as part of higher education qualification programmes has become commonplace with people completing diplomas, masters' degrees and PhD's by (rather than in) Action Learning. To achieve this it seems they have to complete two tests – that posed by the values and principles of Action Learning and also the meeting of the appropriate academic standards. Clearly much more needs to be done here.

8 Teamworking at Williams Grand Prix Engineering

David Giles

This chapter gives an account of introducing Action Learning to foremen at Williams Grand Prix Engineering, manufacturers of motor racing cars. During its 19 years Williams has won the 'Formula 1 World Constructor Championships' eight times and grown rapidly from a small band of enthusiast engineer/ craftsmen into a leading high-tech engineering company of approximately 250 employees, half of whom are engaged in manufacture.

In the production department those who were good at their jobs and solving technical problems were promoted to foreman while continuing to make their full contribution as master craftsman. But with the company's growth the traditionally informal approach began to show some strain and things were not always 'right' by their exacting standards.

In early 1993 David Williams, the General Manager and Tony Pilcher, the Production Manager for the company invited me to provide an initial one day training course to increase the effectiveness of the foremen in the production department. The aim was to encourage greater appreciation of the foreman's role and influence, and to assist them in their ability to solve problems, handle discipline and build teams.

EARLY DAYS

The initial one-day programme was designed to be as participative as possible, encouraging the 13 foremen who came to use their own language and experience and to explore their current position, gain insights, suggest options for improvement, and then by working in support groups to attempt some individual improvement of their own choice within the next month. The day was followed up with a personal tutorial four weeks later.

At the tutorials I asked: 'What have you learnt from this about yourself, the others and the organization?' The response was gratifying. They were cautiously pleased that the training had been offered and that someone was listening to what they had to say. But for the most part they had found it difficult to put their plans into action, as they had found it difficult to think and talk about themselves. The most frequently heard remark was: 'Somehow I'm just expected to do it'.

Before we could plan an appropriate follow-up, the production department was into the build phase for next year's car. As soon as one Grand Prix season ends production work to produce next year's car begins and from that time until March the workload is crushing, a 60-hour week for everyone is not uncommon. This was my introduction to the reality of working with Williams Grand Prix!

However, the feedback in the following March was encouraging. David Williams said that there was a perceptible difference throughout the department on how the foremen were going about things and in what was being said and done. Attitudes were more positive. It was difficult to pin down but it could be sensed. Even the Technical Director had commented on it, so there was every intention to continue with the training.

The 1994 Grand Prix season opened and at San Remo in early May the Williams lead driver Ayrton Senna crashed and died as a result of his injuries. The shock and reverberations of this meant that it was to be the end of August before we met again to talk about training. At that meeting we spoke of interface issues between the Technical Engineers and the Production Foremen which were about:

- Straight talking – being assertive rather than aggressive or compliant.
- Tackling unpopular issues – gaining the confidence to do so.
- Managing conflict – squarely, as opposed to deflecting problems or short-cutting the system.
- Being accountable – facing the responsibilities associated with a given role.

From this, planning went ahead for concurrent training on the 'People' issues for both engineers and production staff. For the first time I spoke of the possibility of using Action Learning which I described as: 'Individuals working in small groups of five or six, where they each select a significant task or piece of personal development; take ownership of that task and progress it using the group as both critic and mentor. The approach is a disciplined one sticking closely to agreed rules. It promotes learning by requiring the individual to account for his progress and in learning how to support and challenge others in an acceptable manner'.

But again plans were thwarted because of the pressure of their work so that it became impossible to meet with the engineers in October and after that it was too late – they were completely committed to the design work for the following year. We did, however, run a very useful day of assertiveness training for the foremen – again with emphasis on working together in supportive teams. As before, the day was followed up four weeks later at the beginning of December with an individual tutorial for all concerned.

By now I had got the message. I was pretty sure from the difficulties we were experiencing that *we had to move* to Action Learning if we were to offer anything like a consistent level of support for staff development. Similarly I felt convinced that this could only work on the shop floor with a volunteer group. But would this be acceptable?

With the support of David Williams and Tony Pilcher I called a meeting for volunteers for an Action Learning programme and nine of the original thirteen foremen turned up to discuss the idea and at the end of the discussion to commit themselves to this approach for 1995. Specifically we agreed to work together on trying to resolve a pool of workshop and/or personal development problems. Each foreman was free to choose the problem he wished to work on. Then 'owning' that problem in the sense of project managing it. Trying to resolve the problem was to be the shared duty of the whole group, as was helping with actions between meetings and offering support to one another. We planned to meet for five days through the Summer months of 1995.

THE ACTION LEARNING SET

Six members of the production department made the inaugural day in July and stayed the course until November. They were:

Tony: Production Manager
Bob: Senior Foreman & Production Controller
Les: Foreman Machine Shop
Jim: Foreman Machine Shop
Robert: Foreman Composite Shop
Brian: Assistant Foreman Pattern Shop

Our negotiated rules for the workshop were: everyone is a volunteer, create opportunities for others to speak, and we are all equal here.

With such a long interval since our last meeting I split the first day into two. In the morning we ran a 'problem solving' mini workshop as an icebreaker, which worked well, and in the afternoon we had our first shot at describing the problems we wished to discuss within the group. However, my initial record of that meeting didn't give anything of the flavour of how things happened, or the emphasis with which things were said – which in later meetings I tried to catch and record.

For example: it didn't indicate the 'messiness' of the process: the hesitancy with which ideas were put forward, or the circular nature of the narrative or that people put forward initially 'soft cases', only to change their 'problem' as their confidence grew.

Or the surprises, as when Robert said: 'I wish I was better at knowing what to say; sometimes I keep quiet when I feel I should say something and sometimes I only work out what I want to say after the event. Do other people feel like that, or is it just me?' There were nods around the group. 'How often does it happen to you in a week?' We went around the group: about 16 times, about 12, about 18, about 10 and so on. Now that surprised everyone.

It also resulted in Robert agreeing the action of keeping a log of future occasions when this occurred and of the others supporting by contributing to it. We had learnt we weren't alone in feeling at times inadequate. Future meetings were recorded in greater detail, in an attempt to capture these moments of significance, but they were notes and not minutes.

Typically we would begin by reading through the notes of the previous meeting to agree that they were a true record. Then each person would complete an individual record sheet to form the starting point for their input into the day. This told us what had happened – and where we were now – so that the group could continue to work together on the problem. Our model for this process was based on a four-stage joint problem-solving model we had used in an earlier workshop:

- listen while they tell the story
- share perceptions for insight
- suggest and review options
- choose one as an agreed action.

In each case, before moving on, we logged the agreed action, the names of those offering support with this, and what we had learnt from the discussion (see Appendix 8B). By experience we came to believe that we worked best as a group of five or six; any more was too much to fit into one day, any less and we missed the variety in the input. Two examples will give a flavour of this work:

THE 5-AXIS MACHINE PROBLEM

Example one: Bob's problem (shared by Brian) was on the face of it a technical problem to do with the efficient loading and running of the 5-axis machine – a crucial piece of equipment in the car build programme. However, that's not how it was told:

'Its a people problem' we were told, 'and there are four key people involved':

The foreman: who apart from the status of it being his area, was not particularly interested in the problem and wanted the minimum involvement. His interests were elsewhere and his expressed views were 'Production control is a waste of time' and 'Sack the leading operator'.

The programmer: who works alone, likes to do one job at a time, works with a VDU so needs a break now and then, likes to always have another job in the pipeline, possibly feels guilty if there is nothing to do.

The operator: who frequently expressed the view that the foreman doesn't care, his colleague doesn't work hard enough, and that production control is a waste of time. He is of the opinion that two machines are needed.

The senior operator: who dislikes the foreman, they 'bad-mouth each other', gets on well with others, would like to be boss and mostly does his own thing. However, the two operators are opposites that complement each other.

The group discussed the situation at some length without actually appearing to resolve anything, it was just seen as a people/personality problem of considerable size. I attempted to focus our deliberations by asking that they help me in attempting to write down a statement describing the problem. If we took the personalities out it could be described as:

The problem: Production control are unable to confidently estimate work flow through the 5-axis machine area.

A satisfactory
solution   Production control being confident that the machine
would be: is being used to maximum efficiency.

The barriers: Lack of clear accountability
              Lack of liaison
              Lack of team work
              Self-interest
              Personality clashes (history)

It had taken us approximately $2\frac{1}{2}$ hours to reach this point so we took a break for lunch.

After lunch we started to construct a matrix of possibilities, but in so doing quickly refined the 'alternatives' until we had a statement that seemed to be entirely workable, plus the idea of running it as an 'experiment'. By calling it an experiment, suggested by the foremen's group, it was felt that there was a good chance that everyone could buy into it, and no-one would lose face in its implementation. If it was a success – Bingo – and if it wasn't well it was only an experiment and no one was 'handcuffed' by it. We felt good about that. We agreed and recorded:

Action: Brian volunteered to run the experiment (of scheduling a job through the pattern shop from beginning to end by asking all concerned for their estimate of time required). Tony volunteered, as manager, to launch the idea at a meeting of all concerned. Bob would then monitor the results and report back.

Support: Bob and Brian would work together.

Learning: We can tackle seemingly insurmountable problems together.

UNCOMFORTABLE SITUATIONS

Example two: Robert had been asked to continue to record situations where one felt it uncomfortable or difficult to say what we really thought. Everyone in the group had agreed to contribute to this.

However nobody had! Why was this? Everyone looked genuinely sheepish and recognized that we had a problem here of not putting into action what we had previously agreed.

We listed the recorded situations on the board for everyone to see. They included:

1. Overhearing conversations that should have included me.
2. Coping with an over-the-top reply from a member of staff.
3. I didn't ask, it might seem to be too pushy.
4. I went along with him, but I was unhappy.
5. 'Arse-about-face work'.
6. Work not finished and nothing said to me.

Everyone recognized these situations and the discussion was about: not avoiding confrontation, 'bollockings', and being appropriately assertive. As a group they worked towards what as foremen they wanted: 'Jobs to be tackled in a sensible way, with no nasty surprises and finished to time'. Getting in the way of this it was suggested could be: 'Personalities, attitudes, individual styles of working and our inability to explain or justify the way we would like to see things done'. It was recognized that the foremen had to give the workforce freedom where they could, because they wanted their involvement, but there were some issues that couldn't be avoided.

Clearly from the level of participation everyone was keen to join in the discussion. Reflecting on this I came to the conclusion that it was vital for everyone to practise trying to handle these situations rather than talk around them as we had been. I didn't expect this to be popular but by sharing my reasons I got everyone to 'give it a go'.

The group decided on the situations from Bob's list that they wished to practise and split into two groups of three. One person being 'difficult', one 'handling it', and the third being an observer. Just 10 minutes each. With no further prompting both groups plunged in. Some of the 'actors' were being very difficult, but individuals playing themselves were coping well.

As foremen they were: confronting the situation
consciously staying 'cool'
establishing reasonable limits
getting things out in the open
aiming to finish without the relationship becoming damaged

Everyone felt pleased with the outcome of the exercise.

Action: Robert to continue logging situations.
Support: Everyone to send in two examples to Robert.
Learning/comments: We can do it here – so why can't we do it out there?

SHARING LEARNING IN THE ORGANIZATION

Sometimes in Action Learning things just happen, opportunities occur and development blossoms. Which is what happened when the investigative work of one set member caused him to speak with the General Manager. In the beginning Jim didn't feel he had any particular problems or strong feelings other than feeling somewhat disenfranchised, so he opted to investigate possible improvements to the foremen's meetings. From his enquiries and liaison with David Williams, he picked up that both 'sides' would like to see better meetings. The foremen wanted to be asked for their opinion, to join in the resolution of problems and to feel they had some influence. While David, for his, part wanted meaningful contributions from the foremen, less pettiness in some of the debate and to avoid the feeling of 'alienation' he sometimes got.

The group saw that they had uncovered a common problem: 'How to support the kind of meetings both parties wanted to see in future' and decided to encourage more foremen to join in a further programme of Action Learning in the following year, to which management agreed.

The focus for the fifth and last meeting of the year was to invite all of their non-participating colleagues to a meeting where the group would give an account of itself. Ten invitations were sent and five guests joined us. The agreed agenda for the morning included: everyone to be honest, to hear what has been happening, everybody to join in, and to work as a team today.

So by invitation, each of the group spoke of their problem. It forms a good summary of our first years work together as an Action Learning group:

SHARING THE LEARNING

Tony started by saying why, although he was the Production Manager, he was involved as an equal; of how we had as a group moved away from the teacher/student event style to one where we shared and worked on problems together, and of how we had built on small victories to build confidence in ourselves and in the team. Tony's problem had been to change the perception of the Technical Director and the drawing office. From 'production are holding up the job' – through a more user friendly production schedule – to one where they accepted the true time to build and the need for the timely release of drawings. Relationships had improved from being disbelieved to the creation of liaison meetings.

And in the process, Brian added, we (the foremen) had come to understand the bigger picture and the pressures put upon Tony. He had been encouraged by the support of the group. Everyone was listening to each other more, and 'management' was beginning to notice that things were different.

Bob spoke of his wish to improve efficiency through the 5-axis machine shop where the 'people problems' of conflicting personalities and lack of mutual respect were effecting production. Our approach to this difficult situation had been to come up with the idea of an 'experiment' whereby we involved all concerned in that area with estimating production times. By this means sufficient agreement and commitment was achieved that estimates were accurate to within a day. It had been a technical solution to a people problem (which was still there). But it was a solution to a previously intractable problem which we had thought of and implemented as a group. 'And what is more,' said Bob, 'I wouldn't have had the confidence to talk about it like this last year'.

Brian carried on the story with his account of trying to improve relationships in the same area, between the composite and pattern shops. Relationships here were described as unhelpful. This effected production, an example would be where a worker in one shop would not stop on a little bit longer to finish his part of a job so that the other shop could pick it up first thing the next day. This problem remains as an ongoing situation, but it's one where the group is beginning to feel collectively strong enough to do something about it at a departmental level.

Les spoke about his problem of knowing how the jobs in his shop were prioritized. There wasn't any apparent order to it. The priorities themselves changed and he didn't know what was going to happen next. Breaking down jobs on the machines upset the operators, it was generally getting everyone down. We had analysed this as a group and established how the true changes came about. Liaison with the people concerned had led to a new, better and faster method of controlling work going through the shop. In addition there was now a superior 'fast track' pathway for really urgent jobs which were appropriately identified.

Jim shared with us how he had decided to try to do something about improving the foremen's meetings. He thought the communication process poor; meetings were infrequent, management talked *at* the foremen and the response was poor – as was the quality of the topics discussed. Following discussion in the group and on the shop floor, Jim had gone to David Williams with a number of suggestions. From their joint deliberations a number of changes had been implemented and the improvement process was ongoing.

Robert spoke of his willingness to try to deal better with situations which as a foreman he found 'difficult'. Everyone in the group had joined in on this one, or to be more accurate had said that they would. In the event everyone admitted to having similar problems and equal difficulty in actually doing something about it. We were still struggling with our inadequacies here. We said we would do something but we didn't. This was a real issue for us that we were beginning to tackle without recrimination and with a good deal of mutual support. Of all the problems this was agreed to be the 'toughie'.

All five guests signed up to form a new group in 1996 and the original group agreed to maintain a 'low-level' programme of self-development through the winter months.

TACKLING A COMMON PROBLEM TOGETHER

If at times things 'go well' in Action Learning, they can equally 'go wrong' as I was about to discover. I set off on my first visit in 1996 with a light heart, but on arrival I was shocked to find a state of disillusionment. Events in the company (I was never told exactly what) had seemed to mock the values which the group had sought to establish; contrary to my understanding little development had taken place; and three of the original group said they wanted to drop out. It took a lot of concentration, listening and encouragement to get the group started again but we succeeded. From the review we held came the decision to spend the remaining four meetings working together on issues associated with the setting of standards for staff on the shop floor. This required: looking at 'competence' to agree what was necessary; looking at 'behaviour' to agree what was acceptable; and looking at 'individual responsibility' to agree what was reasonable. Steadily but surely this major piece of work led to the development by the group of their own suggestions for a Company Staff Performance Review procedure.

Much of what we had learnt together went into the design and testing of the procedure they proposed to use. The review was to be honest, it was to be open, and those involved were to meet (as far as was possible) as equals. The review process was to be a joint one and culminate in a joint statement. If there proved to be any unresolved disagreement of views, then these would simply be recorded.

THE SECOND ACTION LEARNING GROUP

Meanwhile the new volunteers created a second Action Learning set, the numbers being made up to six by Tony, whose involvement as their manager was invaluable. The group worked on entirely new problems. But we did seem to be able to unfold (or develop) the problems more quickly than before.

We learnt that expressions of feeling were often an indicator that we were moving to another level with a problem. Simple examples would be: 'And another thing' – 'The cheeky sod' – 'It makes my blood boil' – 'It's better than Coronation Street' – 'Hang on a minute I don't understand what's going on here'.

'You're right' said Phil, 'It's like peeling an onion. What starts as a simple problem like trying to find a drawing when people are away – ends up by looking at the way we handle sub-contact work in a culture that says "Do It" '.

Issues which were originally put forward as their individual 'problems' led this group into the much deeper waters of 'cultural change' and the part they could play in it. A table showing the individual problems of both groups and their outcomes is shown in Appendix 8A.

THOUGHTS ON WORKING WITH AN ACTION LEARNING GROUP

My reflections on four years (two + two) of working with the foremen at Williams Grand Prix are that the key elements in the Action Learning were most probably: courage, preparation and honesty.

Courage is required because it is undoubtedly different. It is less scripted, more uncertain, which in the end means that the only way to know about it is to do it. There will never be . . . a 'right time' . . . a 'right group', or your feeling . . . 'fully prepared'. It's like a parachute jump – which means of course that you prepare as carefully as you can!

Preparation, I found, could be described in three phases:

- starting-up and establishing the ground rules
- finding an acceptable framework by which to run the meetings
- creating a record in sufficient detail that it could be used by both the facilitator and the group as a reflective tool.

Letters of invitation were sent and explanations about Action Learning were made as were reassurances about the operation of the group including creating our own ground rules. In every case the person who raised a problem had to be prepared to do something about it.

I found it helpful to have a framework for the initial start-up and then to keep us on track at each of our meetings. I found just three pieces of A4 paper could do this. The first two come from Mike Pedler's *Action Learning for Managers* and are called 'the problem brief', a start-up sheet which enables the individual to state his problem in one sentence, say why it is of importance to himself and the company and to expand it sufficiently for everyone to get to grips with it; and the 'set meeting review worksheet', which helps members to reflect about their problem, themselves, their impending action, and what they had learnt about the other people's problems in the group. The third sheet was a simple home grown document called an 'action learning record sheet' which, after reading and agreeing the notes of the previous meeting, the group members used to record what had happened to the action and support and what they had learnt as a consequence (see Appendix 8B).

Together sheets 2 and 3 created the base script for the member to continue his story, and retained the focus on the learning – the difference between Action Learning and just another progress meeting.

The 'Notes' as we called our record of the meetings were essential for continuity, for credibility, and as a final reference to our work. The key points and the breakthroughs I tried to record verbatim so that they would be recognized at the next meeting.

Honesty: great significance was placed by the members on the creation of an environment where concerns could be shared openly and honestly in the knowledge that they would gain serious and supportive response. In achieving this we succeeded in creating a microcosm of the kind of foremen's meetings all parties wished to see.

CONCLUSIONS

We had been tasked with looking at the 'people' issues and this we did through looking at work-related problems. We called it 'Action Learning', but it drew on the elements of many other disciplines. It differed from a Quality Circle in that it focused on the people, the process and the learning. It was evident from what was achieved that individual skills and teamwork had improved. At the same time our work together improved a number of shop-floor situations which made for cost-effective training. We worked out the total costs (including delegate time) based on the company's hourly rate and then compared it to the time that the group estimated that we had saved through our efforts. On this basis the training had more than paid for itself – it had added value.

REFERENCE

1 Pedler, M. J. (1996) *Action Learning for Managers*, London: Lemos Crane.

APPENDIX 8A Individual problems worked on in the two Action Learning sets at WGPE in 1995–6

Initial problem	What it became	Actions	Outcomes
Getting engineering to believe build times and that drawings were required earlier	About gaining credibility	Introducing a more easily understood production control system	Gaining credibility Initiating liaison meetings Prod dept seen as the 'good guys'
Working out what you want to say and feeling confident about it	An 'eye opener' A common problem An issue for everyone	To collect examples Role play in the group Difficult to implement	Everyone became more assertive and supportive with one another
M/c shop loading Priorities Irritated workforce	A 'people problem'	Analysis of the situation Liaison meeting	Simpler, superior system plus new 'fast-track'
Feeling he was not consulted by management	Improving the foremen's meetings	Collecting views and liaising with the General Manager	Better meetings Feeling better personally
The efficient loading and running of the 5-axis m/c	A 'people problem'	Devising an experimental solution	Initial improvement – then fell back again Fundamentally unchanged We have learnt from this
Improving relationships between pattern and composite shops	An attempt at a technical solution to a people problem	Supporting the experiment on getting more accurate estimating times on the 5-axis m/c	Personal development and enhanced reputation for the individual
'Where does my time go'?	Issues associated with delegation and changing his management style	Keeping and analysing a timelog Reviewing personal style	Greater awareness. Investigating career development and change
Timesheets	An issue of responsibility and control The need to define his role	Liaising with peers to clarify dep't issues. Confronting situations	Gaining in personal confidence and helping to define the foreman's role
'What am I responsible for'?	Defining his role in the new plant Sorting sub-contract issues Delegation	Analysing a timelog Reviewing the competence of the team. Delegation	Changing personal style Delegating more Becoming less stressed
Finding drawings	A culture change issue over sub-contract work. Clarifying internal and external customer relations	Pursuing inefficient work practices Gaining cooperation for better ways of working	Gained in self-esteem and respect of others. Improved efficiency. Assisting with the Culture change
Knowing the manufacturing priorities	Becoming more assertive and less aggressive in style. Gaining cooperation	Learning and applying a more appropriate liaison style	Better control over priorities More essential work done to time
How to report on safety aspects with a new building	Investigating H & S procedures in a new plant	Listing concerns and liaising with the general manager	Detailed safety features incorporated

APPENDIX 8B

Supervisor Training at WGPE 1996
Action Learning Record Sheet

Name: Date:

Problem:

Agreed Action:

Agreed Support:

What happened to the Action:

What happened to the support:

Learning:

9 Industrial Restructuring in the Czech Republic

George P. Boulden and Vlasta Safarikova

This chapter describes the use of action learning in a large industrial restructuring project in the Czech Republic in 1995. The project came within the terms of reference of the EC-PHARE programme to support Czech Industrial Privatization and Restructuring. The project was run jointly by ALA International Ltd who took responsibility for the design and delivery of the project and The Institut Svazu Prumyslu (ISP) – The Institute of the Confederation of the Czech Industries – who were responsible for the recruitment of the companies and local consultants, and the day to day management of the project.

The project was designed to provide:

- a selected group of Czech companies with direct help in restructuring their organizations to meet the business conditions imposed by the introduction of the market economy;
- a group of Czech consultants, selected from amongst CAMETIN (Czech Association of Management Education and Training Institutes Network) member companies, with the expertise to use an action learning approach to carry out business audits, run business development programmes, provide support in specialist consultancy projects and to facilitate action learning groups, called business clubs in the project.

The programme was designed to run for twelve months with fifteen companies participating (in the event twelve took part) and to develop twenty-five Czech consultants (twenty-two participated). The design envisaged a four-stage programme using an Action Learning approach; companies would be helped to help themselves, not told what to do through traditional consultancy interventions. In our view Action Learning was the only way to ensure the transfer of the

107

business management knowledge and skills required to the client companies; a traditional consultancy approach may have helped in the short term but would not have created a belief system which ensured the development of the management team or left the expertise behind.

The programme started with a 'whole company' needs analysis. This was designed to enable us to quantify the issues facing each company and to agree these with the management team before starting the intervention. It also provided us with benchmarking information against which to evaluate the success or otherwise of our efforts. This was to be followed by an organizational development programme supported by appropriate management training. The fourth stage of the programme was to be a plenary review to evaluate the achievements and the learning. The objectives of the programme were to

- develop participating companies management teams and equip them to manage their organizations more effectively, and
- to train Czech consultants to facilitate the OD process.

THE PROJECT

The recruitment of companies for the project was carried out by ISP in October 1994. Some 40 companies expressed an interest and were invited to attend an introductory day on 25th October 1994. From these, 12 companies applied to join the project. These ranged in size from one company with over 3000 employees, which was still state owned, to a newly restituted company with 150 people. Most were in the engineering sector although we had one large chemical producer, a paper manufacturer and the largest map-making company in the Czech Republic.

The next step was to recruit the consultants, which was done by ISP through the CAMETIN network. Twenty-two people expressed an interest in working with us. We ran an introductory day for them on the 5th of December during which they were introduced to the project and the Action Learning style of working.

We visited all participating companies during December 1994 and briefed the management teams on how the project would work and their role in it. We stressed that we were there to 'help them to help themselves', not to do things for them and outlined what they could expect in terms of outputs.

The needs analysis was carried out in January 1995 using seven western consultants, four British and three German, each a specialist in one of the following areas, general management, finance, sales, marketing, quality, information technology, human resource management and production. The western consultants were partnered by fourteen Czech counterparts who were also experienced in the functional specialisms. The western consultants provided needs analysis questionnaires which were used for all audits thus ensuring that they were carried out consistently and objectively, allowing us to use the data for reference purposes. The audit teams spent one day in each company working with the relevant functional team to assess the current situation, and produced individual reports.

We categorized the consultants findings in terms of training needs, those things which could be resolved through training, and non-training needs, those things, usually organizational issues, which could only be resolved through direct intervention in the firm.

The main training needs identified were as below:

Training needs	Companies with the need
Finance – management accounting	7
Communication skills	7
Marketing and sales – management and skills	6
Top team development	6
Management skills, managing meeting, case presentations, performance appraisal, etc.	6
Marketing awareness for all managers	5
Understanding IT	5
Customer awareness – all staff	4
Negotiation skills	4
Using financial ratios	3

The main non-training needs identified were as below:

Non-training needs	Companies with the need
Top team development – senior managers needed to learn how to manage the business	All
Develop effective sales and marketing functions	10
Financial restructuring – particularly management accounting	9
Strategic planning	8
Integrated IT strategy	8
Modernize the HR function	8

Understand and apply the principles of 'world class' manufacturing	8
Develop a quality mentality (ISO 9000)	8
Carry out job evaluation and develop a competitive remuneration policy	4
Become market/customer driven	2

From our analysis of the non-training needs it was clear that all companies needed some form of business development/top team building programme and all had needs for consultancy support to resolve specific problems. We decide to offer all companies the opportunity to participate in a Business Development Programme which was designed to build the management team through helping them to resolve the structural and managerial problems they faced. We offered selected companies projects in the areas of finance, sales and marketing, human relations and quality. In addition we offered all companies the opportunity to participate in monthly business club meetings in each of the specialist areas. Analysis of the training needs indicated the need to provide formal training in ten areas. In the event we designed and ran training programmes for all companies in the areas of finance, communication skills, marketing and sales, management skills, and information management.

The audit teams reports were incorporated into a composite report for each company accompanied by specific recommendations. The reports were presented to all of the management teams during February and March 1996. They were well received and with the exception of one company which decided to withdraw from the project, all companies accepted all of our recommendations.

USING ACTION LEARNING

We used Action Learning as the basis for satisfying all of the non-training needs. In the Business Development Programme we organized the management teams to work as Action Learning sets. They had a common project, to re-structure their company to meet the changing needs brought on by the introduction of the market economy. The programme started with a three-day Business Development Workshop for all companies. We ran two of these, one covering five companies and the other six. The workshop was used to help the teams to:

- develop their vision and values
- agree business goals, organization structure, key responsibilities, performance targets

110

- decide business management systems they needed to put in place to control their businesses effectively
- build the management team.

Each company had its own Czech facilitator who worked with the management team during the introductory workshop and for three days a month over the three-month life of the programme. We co-ordinated these groups through monthly on site reviews and the general management business club meetings.

All of the consultancy interventions were carried out by in company project teams. The foreign consultant worked in the dual role of 'expert' providing specialist advice and guidance and took responsibility for developing his/her Czech counterpart who worked with the groups as the 'local' expert, interpreter and facilitator. *Note*. We took the view that using the Czech counterpart as an interpreter would not only develop his/her language skills but would ensure their understanding of the material, and this proved to be the case.

We could not provide specialist consultancy to all companies in all areas. We therefore decided to share the learning by offering 'business clubs' open to all project companies, in the specialist areas. We offered seven business clubs:

- General managers
- Quality managers
- Finance managers
- Manufacturing managers
- IT managers
- HR managers
- Sales and marketing managers

The clubs ran monthly along 'Action Learning' lines. Each club, apart from the general management club, was attended by managers from at least one company in which we were running a specialist project plus the local and foreign consultants who were working on the project. We had made it a condition of the original offer of consultancy support that the managers receiving the support would attend the clubs and share the learning. Typically meetings opened with the manager, in some cases there were more than one, from the company with the specialist project reporting on what was happening, what they had learnt, and their plans for the next month. For example the Sales Director for JIP Cerepa reported on his experiences with his marketing project which was to test market a new product in one region of the country, something which he did very successfully, to the other managers attending the sales and marketing club. The other participants were encouraged to question both the company personnel and the project consultants. A number of managers from other companies ran parallel projects using the learning from the project company and

111

the consultancy resources available through the club. The average attendance at club meetings was twelve with many people undertaking an eight hour return journey just to be there. The most popular clubs were the quality, sales and marketing and the finance clubs.

The general management club differed from the others in that all of the general managers had a common project as all were participating in a Business Development Programme and this formed the focus for the group. Participants reported in turn on their experiences and the other managers questioned them to discover the learning. Once this process was complete the group chose a particular area of interest to debate, topics included things like annual performance appraisal, customer care, performance related pay, etc. These meetings were facilitated by the authors.

EVALUATION

By the time the project ended in December 1995 we had successfully:

- run the Business Development Programme for all companies
- provided every company with specific consultancy support in a key area of need
- run over forty business clubs
- delivered five modular training programmes in which all companies participated *Note*. These programmes are still being run by ISP as open courses under the sponsorship of the National Training Fund
- trained our counterparts in the audit process and the use of the questionnaires which they retained for use in their own practice
- developed our counterparts facilitation skills.

As a final assessment we invited the managing directors of all participating companies to Prague and asked their views of the programme and specifically what it had achieved for their companies. Many said that they were sceptical about the project when they started. Jan Rydl of TOS Varnsdorf probably expressed the group's feelings best when he said that he thought the project was:

A waste of time . . . and money . . . probably more concerned with industrial espionage than helping companies.

To his surprise the company received practical help to:

- develop its vision and values
- make organizational changes

- agree functional roles and responsibilities
- introduce modern HR practices
- manage external consultants.

This help has enabled the company to:

- introduce a completely new management structure
- change its managing style from directing to participative
- achieve West European productivity standards.

When the project started the company was significantly less productive than its West European competitors. Management committed itself to doing something about this and we helped them to identify five key indicators, benchmarks, through which they could achieve West European performance standards. The management set themselves a target to do this over twelve months starting in August 1995 and they have done it (see table below).

Ratio	August 1995	Target	Actual July 1996
Return on capital employed	3.5%	>12%	13.5%
Average debtor days	90	70	80
Sales per employee	750K	1.5M	1.53M
Order cycle time (months)	7	6	5
Rate of stock turn	2	3	3.5

Most people, even some in the TOS management team, believed that this was impossible at the outset. The knowledge that others had achieved it and better (the Japanese machine tool manufactures are nearly twice as efficient as the European average) motivated Jan and his team to achieve these remarkable results.

Kelment Horak, Managing Director of Bratri Horak focused on the 'holistic' nature of the project. He had recently taken over the family firm after forty years in state hands and was trying to decide what to do for the best. In his view *'The project took a "whole organisation approach"; it enabled us to see the issues we were facing in context for the first time'*. During the life-time of the project Klement and his management team have restructured their company from the traditional 'centralized' structure it had under state control into three lines of business and have been helped to develop new management accounting systems to support this.

Lubenece tovorny is a small manufacturing company bought by the current

MD, Jiri Svoboda from the state about a year before the project began. Jiri was the heart and soul of the organization. He had introduced a new product and was looking to both develop his management team and to achieve ISO 9000 registration by end 1995. Jiri Svoboda believes that the project:

- not only saved him 400 000 Kcs in quality consultancy fees but also significantly shortened the registration time, Lubenece received registration in March 1996;
- through the Business Development Programme, helped him to turn the management of the organization from a 'one man show' into a managing team. (He was able to prove the effectiveness of this during a six-week visit to Japan – everything went well whilst he was away.)

Mrs Klapolova's management team at PAS Zabreh has learnt that they will have to manage the business, no one else is going to do it for them. They have agreed their vision and values and had their 1996 Business Plan approved by the share holders in November. They have adopted a new management strategy which has involved them in completely restructuring the operation including starting two new lines of business. They have reduced the work force in the traditional business by one third using a payment by results approach designed to identify those who really wanted to work. The business has identified new markets and new customers, none of which was even envisaged before they started the project.

These results may not seem remarkable in Western terms but they must be seen in the context of:

1. The background of the managing directors and their teams. All but one of the MDs had held only middle management positions prior to 1992 and many members of the management teams had never held a senior managerial position.
2. The financial positions of some of the companies – PAS was very close to bankruptcy when Mrs Klapilova took over, indeed one of the companies did go into liquidation during the life-time of the project.
3. These people did it themselves. The consultants provided advice and facilitation but did none of the work – everything that was achieved was done by the managers and their people.

Overall the project has:

Empowered our clients

- focused on meeting the clients needs – for most it was the first time they had worked with consultants who were really committed to helping them to help themselves

- enabled clients to think of their organizations as complete, interactive entities, rather than separate parts
- helped them to understand and resolve the most significant organizational and performance problems
- demonstrated the value of team work and a participative style of managing in a practical way
- left behind the knowledge and expertise which will enable these managers to continue to solve the problems that they face.

Developed our counterparts

- provided exposure to new techniques and developed the skills to use them. Most had never heard of Action Learning and believe that the only way to help people was to tell them what to do
- demonstrated a 'holistic' approach to organizational restructuring
- shown that a 'pull' approach to consultancy / training can be effective
- broadened their OD experience
- enabled them to enhance their personal reputations
- provided them with products / skills that they can sell.

Improved ourselves

- the experience has provided invaluable learning opportunities
- demonstrated yet again the power of action learning to empower people
- been immensely rewarding and great fun.

The main factors which for us distinguish this project from the many we have run over the past twenty years has been the success of the learning process.

1. This is the first time in a Business Development Programme that we have worked with management teams from different companies at the same time. We had them together at the same workshop; we had five companies in the first workshop and six in the second, and all of the subsequent plenary sessions. We used common plenary sessions during the workshops, and the teams worked with their Czech facilitators to develop their individual vision, values, structure, roles and responsibilities, etc., sharing issues arising in the next plenary session. This process was so successful that in the second workshop, in which we had six company management teams – over fifty people – the managers themselves decided to set up a number of cross-company teams to review issues of common concern.
2. The in-company projects all delivered what was expected of them and provided a real development opportunity for functional managers and their teams.
3. The business clubs, which were really Action Learning sets by another

name, showed great success in sharing the learning. The clubs were all well attended and provided a very effective means of sharing scarce resources across all involved. Through the business clubs we created the opportunity for the managers responsible for specialist projects to share their experiences. We used this opportunity to actively encourage others to apply what the project companies were doing and to share the learning from this. By the end of the project over 50 per cent of managers from non-project companies applied some aspect of what they learnt in the clubs in their own companies. And it doesn't end here. We are now running a quality programme along the same lines and our monthly Saturday clinics are always attended by over twenty people. This means for many getting up at four in the morning and not arriving home before seven or eight in the evening.

How did we create these innovations? Basically through necessity. We were short of money and wanted to do our best for our clients. My Czech partner, who didn't know that these things were impossible, suggested them, I listened, we tried it and it worked.

For me the programme proves yet again the power of Action Learning and the 'rightness' of Reg's original idea.

10 An In-company Programme

Alec Lewis

This chapter deals with the initiation, running and evaluation of an in-company Action Learning programme. It reports the stages of building the group and the people involved in the preliminary discussions, and then goes on to describe the meetings of the group. This includes reference to the problem solving activity of the group members, to the way in which individual members contributed to the task and to the emergence of a team approach to the problem. The final two sections of the chapter deal with the assessment of the whole programme, and a consideration by myself of the role I played as set adviser during the life of the group.

INITIATION OF GROUP

The company from whose staff the Action Learning group was formed is in the textile industry, and the factory in which they work is in South Wales. The company is a large textile group with a wide representation of businesses in the industry. The South Wales factory was one of two factories still organized and managed as a relatively autonomous branch of the group operation. The second factory was in Wiltshire. The sponsor of the Action Learning group was the personnel and training manager of the group company, who had been introduced to the concept and practice of Action Learning at a seminar led by Professor Revans and organized by the South West Regional Management Centre in Bristol. The sponsor became convinced of the potential value of Action Learning and invited me to go to the Wiltshire and South Wales factories to familiarize myself with their operations and to discuss the possibility of establishing an Action Learning group within the business. These discussions further convinced him of the potential of Action Learning to his management and he then identified the client for the group as the production director, who after some questioning and discussion with myself and the sponsor agreed to get a team of people from *one* of the factories to look at a current problem. The identification of a problem

117

presented no difficulty, it was basically one of survival in the highly competitive textile market of today. This was highlighted by the agreement of the client to proceed on the basis of four group meetings only with a review by him of progress at that time before deciding on any further meetings.

The selection staff to form the Action Learning group was carried out by the sponsor and client in consultation with me and a team of eight participants emerged. They were all at a similar level of managerial reponsibility with the exception of the production manager who had been in his post for eighteen months and was senior in rank to the other members. He was directly responsible to the production director – the 'client' of the Action Learning group.

The rest of the members of the group included three forewomen each of whom had responsibility for managing individual production lines and were directly accountable to the production manager. They each had supervisors in their lines. Two managers representing the cutting room were in the group, and a progress manager and warehouse and despatch manageress completed the team.

Apart from the production manager and one of the cutting room managers, all group members had many years of experience with the company and had in fact worked in that factory under different ownership up to some eight years ago. This group therefore represented a cross-section of the production side of the business.

THE PROBLEM

Although the single word 'survival' would sum up the company's problem at the briefing meeting addressed by the production director, the problem which the group was to devote its attention to was described as:

> We need to improve overall performance. The order book is not healthy at the moment, we have to become more effective in order to keep our prices competitive. We are fine on quality but falling down on deliveries; our production flow is erratic. You are the people who can improve the productivity. How are you going to do it?

He then went on to introduce the concept of Action Learning and the set adviser who in turn explained his role as that of the 'external catalyst' and not the consultant with the magic formula to solve the company's problem.

At this stage there was very much the look of *déja-vu* on the faces of the prospective participants, and an impression of 'acceptance of the inevitable' was prevalent in the rather stilted discussion that followed the briefing. However, all participants finished this session with the commitment to 'give it a go'.

The first four meetings were scheduled as half-day meetings at fortnightly intervals to be held at the factory.

REFLECTIONS ON THE INITIATION OF THE GROUP

In this case, which is little different from my other Action Learning initiation experiences, it had taken over six months to get the group started, and this was with an enthusiastic sponsor! Without his enthusiasm the task would have been impossible. His keenness and interest in Action Learning had originated through contacts he had in two different Industrial Training Boards. They had attended various meetings at the South West Regional Management Centre, one of which had specifically been organized to discuss the concept and practice of Action Learning. The sponsor met me on two occasions to discuss the concept and how it might be applied to his company, then attended a seminar addressed by Professor Revans in Bristol. This finally convinced him that he should 'have a go'. Five visits later, including two with the client present, and several internal company meetings later the decision to try it on the basis of four meetings then a review was taken.

Looking back it is hard to see how any short cuts could have been taken. The sponsor had to identify the client, the client needed convincing that one of his problems might be capable of being treated in this rather different way, and both had to discuss at some length the composition of the group. In fact this preparatory work is almost as important as the actual group work. There is a lot of anxiety about at this stage and removing at least some from the sponsor and client is an important role for the set adviser. Some fundamental factors which helped to overcome the anxieties of the sponsor in this project were that (a) *he* retained 'control' of the process and (b) he had in fact an important part to play in the exercise. However, it may be more important to help them to 'live with their anxieties' because building false hopes of possible outcomes would be to totally defeat the objectives of the exercise.

THE FIRST FOUR MEETINGS

MEETING NO. 1

The first meeting started with a restatement of the principles of Action Learning; that this was an opportunity for these people to develop themselves in the context of the problem solving exercise on which they were about to embark. There was obvious anxiety around the table because of the novelty of the situation, and the breadth of the task which was facing them.

Each member of the group was invited to describe their own personal view

119

of the problem and to indicate whether or not they agreed that the difficulties outlined by the client in his brief were the major issues needing solution. In view of the fact that this was fairly obviously the first such opportunity to make such a statement any member of the group had experienced and furthermore were now being invited to express this view in public, it was surprising how honest and open the responses were. A sample of some of the actual statements used may serve to illustrate the nature of these responses and the attitudes held by the participants at this early stage of the exercise.

Forewoman (1):	There is nothing more frustrating than running out of trimmings, it's happening all the time.
Forewoman (2):	If we waited till all materials and trimmings were here we would never start.
Warehouse manager:	We are always short of a few garments at the end of an order.
Progress manager:	Other manufacturers let us down.
Cutting Room manager:	This is the wrong sort of work for this factory.
Forewoman (3):	Things aren't explained to us – orders are moved from our lines half way through.
Forewoman (1):	We've got all the worst work. (cf. other company factory in Wiltshire).
Forewoman (1):	There's a feeling out there that we cannot survive.
Production manager:	The current financial instability cannot go on.
Forewoman (2):	We get told this every week.
Forewoman (1) (about the Production manager):	He's so little I can never find him when I want him.

These selected statements from the set advisers scribbled *aide-mémoire* summarize in fairly clear terms the frustrations of the participants all of whom with the exception of the production manager, and one of the cutting room managers, had worked in the factory in the 'good years' when very large orders were the norm, facilitating long and therefore smooth production runs.

However, by the end of the first meeting it was recognized that small orders were a fact of life, and although all the evidence from this meeting suggested to the adviser that no one in the group admitted ownership of the problem, there was some agreement with the suggestions from the production manager at the end of the meeting that:

1. He would discuss with him individually their job descriptions. (Some lack of understanding of them had been revealed in the discussion.)
2. This might lead to a change in the current system which meant that seventeen people reported direct to the production manager.

3. An investigation into work flow in the cutting room – and the resources of that room.

He concluded his summary by asking members to think about how they might capitalize on the spirit engendered at this meeting.

MEETINGS 2, 3 AND 4

Although the second meeting started by picking up the specific points from the first which had required action, the discussion soon developed into a repeat of the first meeting with every individual providing anecdotal evidence of the inefficiences of those parts of the system for which he/she was not responsible. This prompted an intervention by the set adviser to look at the work that had been done on job descriptions since the last meeting. This did focus the attention of all participants who agreed that they needed to understand the responsibilities of each function, even if the recognition of the need was revealed through fairly basic observations, for example, the chiding remark from one of the forewomen to the cutting room manager who was supporting the case for a clear job description and for people to know the extent of their responsibilities. She said, 'Let's be fair, R . . ., I've seen you pulling a truck!' This summed up the difficulties in the factory with every member of the group going well outside the range of those activities which were central to their function in order to keep their function 'ticking over'.

By the start of the third meeting each participant had prepared a concise statement of their key roles in the organization and these were discussed in some depth. Inevitably perhaps, the next topic to appear on their agenda was the external factors to their system which could and did upset the smooth running of the factory. The question 'Who makes these promises?' in relation to delivery dates, highlighted the frustrations being felt on the factory floor where so many 'hiccups' were being experienced. One outcome of this discussion however was a recognition by the group that they each had individual responsibilities which were closely linked and even though external factors could sometimes be blamed for loss of production, there were several internal problems with which they should be concerned. This 'conscensus' appeared during the debate on the job descriptions for the three forewomen members. Although they described several instances of activities 'we do automatically' – which on reflection could be handled by the supervisors they were in broad agreement on the sections' objectives, namely,

1. To produce agreed quantity to agreed quality
2. To remain within cost limits
3. To meet delivery dates.

These objectives were used as the basis for a discussion on their individual job descriptions. No attempt was made to write them, but again, broad agreement was reached on the scope of their activities from discipline and wage queries to utilization of machinery, identification of problem, of make-up, and liaison with other functions, particularly cutting room, quality control and work study.

The last of the first four sessions was in some ways the most 'intensive' partly because the sponsor was due to meet the group at the end of the meeting to hear the progress reports, but partly because the group was beginning to function, working on current issues which were causing problems in the factory.

Thus, the first hour was devoted to the 'recent problem'. The cutting room came in for some sharp criticism from the forewomen because of an increase in the number of re-cuts and an apparent lack of urgency being given to this task in the cutting room. Interestingly, although the comments were critical and direct, they were accompanied by suggested solutions from the forewomen, for example, take all re-cuts back to original cutter rather than have all re-cuts done by one person. This, it was suggested, may have a psychological impact on the cutter and may help to improve his efforts. This led to a fairly heated discussion of the current general problems in the cutting area of the factory including resources, systems of bundling, checking delivery to production lines. The progress manager made an important contribution here as a dispassionate, neutral observer. The cutting room manager promised to change the current re-cut procedure, and to ensure that his team followed the agreed bundling and checking procedure.

The second part of the meeting was devoted to a debate on the latest production report with the latest financial report on the factory's performance in the previous month. This appeared to be a relatively new opportunity for some group members to comment on the figures. Inevitably, the question of relatively small batch productions was raised as an excuse for the poor overall performance. Two members of the group suggested representatives of the marketing function should be invited to the meetings.

GROUP REVIEW MEETING WITH SPONSOR AND CLIENT

At the end of the fourth meeting the sponsor and client joined the group to review its activities and to decide if a further four meetings should take place.

The set adviser had invited the group to consider the following questions to report on to the production director.

1. Identify any changes in individual behaviour or practice which the group discussions had set in motion.

2. Identify any changes in behaviour or practice which may still be needed but which requires further investigation and/or other people's authority.
3. Identify what this group might continue to do without the presence of an external set adviser.

The spontaneous remarks made by group members to the production director encouraged him to believe that the exercise was perhaps *beginning* to show some benefits in that: members were talking *positively* about actions that were starting as a result of the discussions – the *recut problem* was being resolved; changes in systems of bundling and recording at intermediate stages of production were under way, and the progress manager was involved in reintroducing a modified system of production control which had once seemed to be helpful to group members.

The group reported that having an 'outsider' as group adviser was important, because they felt that they could be more honest and critical, and because they felt 'different' from when they were in their normal production meetings. A further four half-day meetings were sanctioned.

SUMMARY OF THE REMAINDER OF THE MEETINGS

In fact, after the second group of four meetings a further three were held to complete the programme, which finished on the instructions of a newly-appointed finance director who decided to temporarily cut back on all 'non-essential' expenditure.

The second part of the proceedings of the group followed three phases: 1 frustration, 2 consolidation of the first four meetings, and 3 action.

The frustration phase is in part a description I give to the dominant attitude of some of the group members, but perhaps it is also a reflection of the feelings I had as set adviser at this stage of the proceedings. Several factors were contributing to my dissatisfaction with progress. As reported above, it was only at the seventh meeting that the contributions of members moved significantly away from the anecdotal towards the more constructive comments. Although the client had responded very favourably to their report at the end of the fourth meeting, the fifth and sixth sessions were characterized more by a resumption of individuals criticizing the rest of the organization rather than attempting to view the problem as one common to them all. Part of the reason may have been the presentation of another set of disappointing profitability figures at the fifth meeting.

My notes at the end of the sixth meeting may serve to illustrate my own impressions at that time, and also to explain what the group was doing which reflected its own frustration. I made these notes while travelling home from the meeting in order to clarify my own thoughts on what was happening. The heading for these notes was 'Impressions of the group after 6 sessions'.

A. Limited success

1. Some learning – in the form of getting to know the whole system and beginning to know the whole system and beginning to admit that 'others have problems'.
2. Another positive sign – showing signs of willingness to admit to own problems and to allow critical examination of reasons for these by other group members.
3. Another positive feature – some problems were actually being tackled – particularly the recent problem. Several group members suggesting practical ways of resolving this one.

B. Difficulties – 'failures'

1. Still more willing to talk than 'do'.
2. Some evidence of two individuals not feeling able or willing to contribute.
3. Still too prone to get sidetracked.
4. Feeling growing of fatal inevitability that 'the problems are beyond us'.

These summary notes reflect my anxieties and these are not peculiar to this Action Learning group. The set adviser is prone to get impatient, and to want to see action before a group is ready to move.

These feelings prompted me to talk over the progress of the group with the sponsor and together we decided that we should wait for the seventh meeting of the group where I would intervene on two counts. First, I should ask what specific progress had been made on a job description exercise, and second, I should direct some questions particularly at the two group members who had 'under-performed' in meetings five and six.

In fact the seventh meeting was much more encouraging. Following my introductory questions, all members of the group made positive contributions and within half an hour of the start all members of the group were initiating points of argument and discussion. Even the production manager who had sometimes in earlier meetings lapsed into a chairman's role, was willing and able to accept no more than a fair share of the discussion time. By the time of the eighth and ninth meetings the contributions were less anecdotal and more positively directed towards constructive criticism or suggestions as to how current systems needed amendment. One of the more positive results from this phase was the identification of the need to allow 'supervisors to supervise'.

The three forewomen in the group were taking definite steps to improve their supervisors' knowledge of what was going on, and to delegate to them certain tasks which they had tended to 'hold on to' during the current difficulties. One reported that 'they (the supervisors) are thinking better for themselves now'.

The 'action' phase began between the ninth and tenth meetings. Two significant events changed the course of the group, one external to the group and one intimately connected with it. The first was the successful bid by the company for a large contract to supply uniforms to a large public undertaking. This provided a very positive motivation to the whole group, who had in part blamed the absence of such large orders for the current poor productivity of the factory.

The second event was the resignation of the cutting floor manager who had been a member of the group, and who had been recruited only eight months earlier. Although this decision cannot be directly attributed to the work of the group, the examination of problems and bottlenecks in the factory had repeatedly focused on the cutting room. Group members had proffered several suggestions as to ways the cutting room might overcome some of its problems and the decision of the manager to resign may have indicated his unwillingness or inability to change procedures. The outcome was the appointment of an existing member of staff to the role of cutting floor manager and the ensuing meetings concentrated on accommodating the newly-won business within the changing systems which the group were initiating during this phase.

ASSESSMENT OF PROBLEM SOLVING ACTIVITY AND PERSONAL/ TEAM DEVELOPMENT

The diary of meetings summarized above may have indicated little that could be considered to have been problem solving activity. Certainly at the end of the first four meetings the set adviser's summary of progress which I prepared for my own purposes indicated that little real action was occurring between the fortnightly meetings. However, with hindsight, it was apparent that what was happening during this introductory phase was that the group was building itself into a team, albeit very gradually. The eventual acceptance by the group that the problem was one for which they had some responsibility, and for which they should be able to contribute at least a partial solution, was something of a breakthrough. Certainly by the end of the tenth meeting individuals in the group were displaying a willingness to contribute ideas, and practical suggestions for solving minor 'system' problems. They were also trying these out between meetings and reporting back on their progress. The tendency to use the meetings to provide more anecdotal evidence of where the system was failing did die hard. The production of a set of disappointing performance figures in the fifth meeting was all that was needed to push the group members back to their defensive positions, as was reported above. However, in their verbal report to the client, individual members attempted to describe the benefits of working in this group. They chose to do this by contrasting the Action Learning group meetings with their routine Monday production meetings.

The main difference appeared to be that at the latter most of them felt they were there to listen, whereas in the Action Learning group they had *eventually* believed that the production manager was listening to them. Certainly, improved communication between group members and particularly between individuals and the production manager was the major improvement recorded.

The second main difference was that eventually group members were accepting responsibility for action on matters they discussed during the Action Learning meetings, whereas at the regular Monday meetings they felt they were there to receive instructions. They were obviously more committed to taking action on those ideas which were their own or which they had accepted as a result of group meetings, than they were to accept instructions which did not always appear to them to be logical.

One of the benefits which individuals agreed on was that as a result of the lengthy discussions in group meetings on the theme of their individual responsibilities to the team was that they were much clearer on who the 'decision takers' were. There was scope they felt for widening this discussion to include managers who had not been in the group.

THE ROLE OF THE SET ADVISER

Planning and briefing One of the most important parts the set adviser has to play on in-company projects of this sort, is in the planning stages. Constant close contact with the sponsor and then with the client is vital in order to ensure that a complete understanding of the Action Learning process has been achieved among senior management. Then the advice which is needed on problem selection and on who should form the group is an essential contribution from the set adviser. Briefing group members is a vital pre-requisite to an effective group, both by the client, to ensure that the scope of the problem is understood, and by the set adviser to clarify his role and the Action Learning method.

Group meetings The role of set adviser appears to change quite significantly between different groups, and also between different meetings of the same group. In the case of the group described in this chapter, I operated sometimes as chairman, sometimes as catalyst and sometimes simply as observer.

Chairman In the early stages of the group I felt the need to 'set the agenda', using notes I had jotted down from the previous meetings. I also made efforts to include those who tended to be 'low contributors'. Another feature of this 'Chairman's' role was that had I not taken it, it would have naturally fallen on the shoulders of the production manager.

Catalyst Intervention under this heading tended to be more prevalent in the early stages, and was particularly aimed at moving people out of the anecdotal into the analytical mode of behaviour. Thus, regular questions of a factual nature I found were needed to get the group into the position where they could stand back from the daily routine problems and look at the overall situation.

Observer This is the important passive role of the adviser, where one concentrates on the group process as well as what is being said. It is from these observations that one decides whether or not to intervene as a 'chairman', 'catalyst' or some other role which may be appropriate.

REFLECTIONS ON THIS GROUP AND MY ROLE AS SET ADVISER

This neat subdivision of the role between chairman, catalyst and observer does suggest a fairly clear definition of the task of a set adviser. However, looking back at this group I can see that there were times when for example I adopted the role of chairman when it might have been of greater benefit for the group to find its own way. One fundamental question which I had in my mind at the end of the project was, 'Did I get the members of the Group to adequately reflect on their own learning?' My efforts in this connection were largely devoted to getting them each to describe how the group meetings varied from the other in-company meetings they attended. Their responses to this indicated a general awareness of a difference in attitude which they felt they brought to the group meetings. They believed that they could be open and critical with each other, and that their views were being seriously considered by the production manager (and sponsor). My informal contacts with the client in the ensuing twelve months suggested that one of the results of the project was to create a more participative and open style of management in the company, as far as this group of managers was concerned. As set adviser I should perhaps have attempted to arrange a follow-up meeting of the group some six months after it had stopped its formal meetings. This would have enabled the group to reflect on its own learning by critically examining any changes in style which may have occurred, with particular emphasis on whether any such change had had any impact on effectiveness.

This raises another question for a set adviser to an 'in-company' group. The follow-up should perhaps include discussions with the sponsor and the client on how the organization as a whole might assimilate the learning of the Action Learning group. In the group described in this chapter this was made virtually impossible because all the group members were closely related to the production function. There were special reasons for this, but the learning for the 'organization as a whole' was limited considerably by this design.

In summary, as set adviser to this group, I have confirmed to myself that the role is multi-faceted; that it requires a large degree of adaptability, that it provides a significant level of frustration, but that overall, the evidence of individual managers becoming more confident in their own capacity to manage, makes it a role that can be very rewarding.

11 Action Learning at Digital Equipment

Doris Adams and Nancy M. Dixon

Action Learning has been a component of a management development effort at Digital Equipment Corporation's manufacturing facility in Burlington, Vermont, for the past one and a half years. Approximately fifty people in management positions in the plant, from executive staff to supervisors, have been involved in the two cycles of the nine-month programme called World Class Leadership. Participants either entered the programme on a voluntary basis or were selected by their managers. The programme combined two-day and three-day workshops, usually one per month, spread over the nine months, with Action Learning sets which met on a weekly basis during the last four to five months. A variety of topics were included in the workshops, ranging from the history and future technologies of computers to the specifics of total quality control and coaching techniques. The sets provided an opportunity for participants to apply the techniques and ideas from the workshops to the solving of real organizational problems in the context of a small group.

DESIGN OF THE PROGRAMME

The goals of the Action Learning sets were as follows:

1. To learn problem-solving skills which are data driven and to concentrate on problem framing.
2. To discover and change rules which are taken for granted (underlying assumptions, stereotypes, norms, perceptions, and so on), and which impede effective group problem solving.
3. To develop the ability to reframe problems and situations.
4. To develop a high-performance team.
5. To develop coaching skills.

129

6. To learn consultation and project-management skills.

7. To resolve business issues.

Each Action Learning set had five to seven participants who represented different levels of management and various organizational functions. The heterogeneity was introduced to ensure that problems were approached from diverse viewpoints.

The organizational problems for potential set consideration were generated by the plant executive staff and the programme participants. Participants identified the problem they would like to work on and sets were formed around individual interest in the problem area.

In the second cycle of the programme a set adviser or coach for each Action Learning set was used. The self-managed sets in the first cycle in most cases proved ineffective in producing the level of learning desired and in developing implementable solutions to business problems. Participants had not developed, and were not supported in developing, the skills to be able to work through group conflict successfully and align around a common compelling goal. These steps seem to be critical to achieving the desired outcomes.

Coaches for the four sets in the second cycle of the programme were selected for the strength of their interpersonal skills. Argyris and Schon define the skills desirable for resolving organizational problems as Model II skills.[1] These include the need to spend time clarifying problems from diverse viewpoints and looking at the underlying assumptions which are operating in the situation. This involves the skills of inquiry, a willingness to suspend judgement until all ideas are considered, and openly confronting conflict or disagreement.

The designers of the programme chose these primarily interpersonal competences for coaches rather than a knowledge of the business, project management expertise or specific knowledge of the problem. Following Revans they believed that the coach who was naïve about the problem itself might ask the kind of difficult questions which would be useful in framing problems alternatively.[2] The role of the coaches was also to teach these interpersonal skills to programme participants. Since the perfection of these skills requires practice over time, the set and a skilled teacher/coach became keys to their development. The sets were encouraged to call in experts to obtain information useful for problem identification and solution.

The Action Learning set component of the second cycle of the World Class Leadership programme began as each set convened to determine meeting times and dates, establish operating rules, clarify roles of members and establish goals related to learning and the business problem. During the programme's three-day workshop on coaching, sets began clarifying the nature of their task or project. They obtained initial sponsorship from organizational representatives who were seen as the customer and person with the resources or authority to implement the change. The sets then identified the customer's requirements and standards for successful completion of the projects. Examples of rules (norms) developed for group operation were as follows:

- to determine if a leader is needed and what the leader's role will be;
- to challenge obstructive behaviour and process, and to find ways to redesign it;
- to obtain group consensus around the process to be followed;
- to build in a critical pause;
- to state your position and reasoning, and to be willing to have it disconfirmed;
- to listen to everyone equally;
- to bring people up to speed who miss part of the action;
- to raise difficult issues for discussion.

The sets then met weekly at the plant with their set coaches to implement the action planning process which they had developed. Full group meetings occurred at the mid-point and end of the Action Learning set experience. During these meetings, the groups shared progress and what they had learned and obtained comments and ideas from the larger group. The reflections of the four sets were presented and discussed in the final public forum of the programme.

The remainder of this chapter will discuss the nature of the learning and business results of the four Action Learning sets in the second cycle of the programme, and will review the revisions in the process which are being considered for future cycles. First, the experience of the sets.

EXPERIENCES OF ACTION LEARNING IN FOUR SETS

Set A solved a business issue related to waste elimination, particularly in terms of reducing unnecessary computer reports and person-hours required to produce the reports. They won a plant-wide contest for a poster supporting the elimination of waste (especially paper), and will extend their set activities until the last of their recommendations are implemented.

This set struggled for several weeks before they could answer the question: 'Why are we here?' Even though they had an area of focus when they formed – waste elimination – they took some time to arrive at a specific project that was compelling for the group and that had a clear sponsor. In the process they lost two group members who, in the face of more pressing work in their area of responsibility, chose not to persist in the effort to arrive at a common goal.

Pausing to work through the group conflict around member commitment and an unclear task led the members to disclose their thoughts on matters that they had not felt 'safe' in sharing earlier and which were preventing them from progressing on their project. They spent time reaching a good understanding of the group's process to date and the difficulties they faced related to the problem. Out of this discussion, the specific problem/task the group wanted to address emerged, a specific sponsor was located, and the group began practising the type of communication which would lead to collaborative action.

In their final reflections, they recognized many of Argyris and Schon's Model II skills as the key skills which led to their effectiveness. They asked questions to understand the other's view, bringing out for public discussion what they were thinking and not saying. They tested the assumptions that they were making about others' meanings, and stated their view with an invitation for feedback. One member said, 'It is more effective to say "this is what I think ..." and test it with others versus asking "what do we want".' The set found they had to slow down action considerably in order to develop the community of inquiry which led to having full information about the problem and the thinking of members of the group. They also adopted the view that members needed a free choice about set participation, and that varying levels of participation were acceptable; and they established a norm in which set members declared their commitment to action with the expectation of accountability by the group.

The coach and co-coach were invaluable to Set A's project and process accomplishments. The co-coach (a programme participant from the first cycle) brought effective project management skills. The coach introduced the issues that were blocking effective group action, provided the group members with 'online' feedback on whether their actions conformed to the new norms set by the group, and reinforced the emergent skills in communication and problem framing.

The cross-functional team was critical to solving the problem, as differing views were used in the process. In addition, implementing the solution across functions was facilitated.

It was important to the set's success that a sponsor be found who was clearly interested in the project and who would ask for information and check on progress. This sponsor also shared the activities of the set with the executive staff of the plant.

Set B developed a plan for improvement of the financial reporting process. Like Set A, they too identified as key elements to their effectiveness the struggle for defining a clear goal, and also the conflict that occurred prior to obtaining this direction. Their initial goal had been productivity improvement, and the specific project emerged from dealing with the conflict around the question:

'What is our goal?' This set also emphasized the importance of coaching to their learning and movement as a group.

The Action Learning set experience produced specific content knowledge for Set B in the area of finance and assessment of customer needs. The former learnings were made possible by tapping the expertise of one of the set members who assumed a teaching role in the set.

As the goal of the project became more and more specific, it became clear that accomplishing a number of small improvements was a valuable contribution to improving organizational effectiveness. Initially, this set's members thought that the outcome had to be of major significance. This belief created tension because of the competing pull of work responsibilities and the time it took to become an effectively functioning team.

The set experienced the tension between process and content (or task and maintenance activities) fairly constantly. Some set members argued strongly that the process must be effective to be able to produce the desired results, and they, therefore, wanted to spend time discussing how the process was going. Others wanted to spend time on the content, learning about the financial area, and identifying and solving the problem. This 'battle' was waged openly, and occasionally the set resolved the dichotomy using process techniques to act on content issues. The dilemma was not fully resolved in this set. However, members pointed out that they will return to their daily work groups with an appreciation of the tension, and some ideas about how to handle both group process and content issues more successfully.

There were differing levels of commitment among members of the set. A core group did most of the work on the problem. This core group developed the ability to be more open with one another, discussing undiscussables particularly related to the issues of content vs. process and commitment definition.

Set C addressed the most specific and initially compelling problem, developing a model for becoming competitive in the manufacture of one of the plant's products. The set formed around four members who were on the operations staff for this product, one of whom was the executive staff member and three who were in other businesses. Its pattern of development was somewhat different from that of Sets A and B.

Initially this set was goal-directed, had clear communication from its sponsor and was committed to developing the action plan necessary for implementation of the model for competitiveness in one product line. The group spent time pooling its information and establishing the additional sources of information it would need to address the problem.

As in Set B, a set member from finance helped the whole group develop the knowledge necessary to frame the issues involved in developing a plan to reduce the cost for producing the product. This was seen as a valuable lesson for the group.

About six weeks into the process, this set experienced the influence of external factors on a project team's goal and level of commitment. The first influence was felt as the set lost the member who was the executive level manager. He left the set when he assumed some additional responsibilities. This member had exerted strong leadership within the group and his leaving left members struggling with role definition. Secondly, the perception began to grow that the set's business focus was no longer going to be a priority in the Burlington plant. Based on this assumption, another set member who was most passionate about the initial set problem began looking for a position outside this business. After attendance at set meetings began to dwindle a core group of four members and the coach began to perceive what was happening and the next steps which the group needed to take to move forward.

The group members recognized they were in trouble – if they continued with the project and it was not valued by anyone then they would feel they were wasting their time; if they did not continue, they felt that they would be quitting and would be viewed as incompetent by their peers. Discussion of this problem led them to realize the importance of synthesizing where they were in terms of the project and of delivering what they had learned to the project sponsor in order to obtain direction regarding next steps. This would involve testing their assumption about shifting business priorities. In a meeting, the group synthesized what they had learned and prepared a report to be delivered to their sponsor as soon as possible. The group was thus able to reevaluate its goal and flexibly define new work in collaboration with the project sponsor.

In facing the breakdown, the group also began to recognize how their very goal-directedness had led them to suppress information which would have been helpful both in slowing down their process and in predicting and dealing with the changing business goals at an earlier point in the process. Several group members came to the realization that they were operating with underlying beliefs similar to those which led to the suppression of information. For example, one common thought pattern that guided behaviour was: 'When I am in situations where there are issues that are not being discussed and I fear there will be retribution if I share my view, I collude with the others by keeping my view private or contributing in a passive way.' In this situation the group avoided looking at their action, which prevented them from understanding and altering it.

In the end the group felt that they had achieved significant learning, about how to address projects and communicate effectively within groups, to take back to their work environment. For example, they became aware of the tendency of groups to use filler activities, such as presentations and reports, rather than deal with difficult issues, and of the strong tension between doing and planning, between acting and reflecting. The action often kept the group from spending time discussing and understanding its purpose, which led in turn to ineffective action. As the group began to raise issues, and members became willing to reveal what they were thinking, they became aware of powerful new tools for effecting business results.

Set D had the most difficult time with the Action Learning process. They eventually disbanded without even agreeing on a project goal. This group started with the aim of doing something with the customer integration programme. The set members identified several possibilities for action but did not agree on a project.

The project sponsor was not actively involved in assisting the set in establishing a specific project. Almost anything the set wanted to do was agreeable to this sponsor. Left to set up its own project, the group raised several possibilities, but no project achieved group consensus for moving forward. Without a clear goal, the group had no incentive to stay together, and the longer it took to arrive at a clear goal, the more difficult it became to maintain commitment to the group. Attendance diminished, and some members began taking action on their own to investigate or act on project ideas.

The set failed to suspend judgement in order to discuss each option openly, to bring up all the information about the potential project, and to assimilate each set member's reasoning related to the projects. Members who had an investment in a particular project maintained the position that their idea was the best one without testing its validity with the group. By the time they attempted alternate communication strategies, these win/lose dynamics had polarized the group, and members did not believe that alternative approaches could save the set. At the finish, members felt as though they had failed in the completion of the task and were concerned that they had not learned a sufficient number of skills to work through the group breakdown.

CONCLUSIONS

Significant issues facing Action Learning sets emerged from the experiences of the participants in the World Class Leadership programme at Digital Equipment Corporation in Burlington, Vermont. The successful sets, in terms of achieving business results for the organization and defining learning for themselves, developed an effective process of communication and a clear and compelling goal to which the group members were committed. Members were able to discuss openly the underlying assumptions they held about the problem, the group process and each other. They aired conflicting views and discovered a collaborative view through the process of consensus. Out of this emerged the group's goals. Working through intra-group conflict and the emotional response to task demands was essential if the group was to find effective ways to address the task, and to actualize what they had learned from this process. The process seemed to lead to the set members' commitment to the goals which emerged. At the same time, skilled coaching also seemed to be necessary if this outcome were to result. Unfortunately, in the course of conflict, some group members and one of the sets disengaged from the Action Learning process.

The pressure of the work environment was a powerful factor to deal with during this type of learning experience. The tasks of the sets were viewed as non-essential activity in comparison with the 'real' work evolving in the plant. Some members did not find support for their participation in the programme from their managers, peers and subordinates, and those members found it most difficult to remain active in the set activities. In the instance of the development of a competitive business model, the uncertain priorities of the plant led to a wavering commitment of set members around a problem which potentially was no longer significant.

Additional factors which contributed to set success were in the areas of sponsor support, team composition and expertise, and coaching relationships. Sponsors who monitored the set's progress and took an active interest in the set activities motivated the sets to persist in their activity. Effective solutions and implementation strategies emerged from cross-functional teams that shared different perspectives and had contacts in their organizations to support the implementation of cross-functional solutions. Set members learned from their expert members who had content or project-management skills. Co-coaching arrangements in two sets led to more effective coaching, as co-coaches assisted each other in reflecting on their practice and developing their coaching skills.

In general, each set participant found that much of the communication and problem-framing skills, as well as learning about group dynamics and content knowledge, was usable in their work environment. Also, the ineffective patterns of action demonstrated in the Action Learning set were not unlike those enacted in the work environment.

Currently, an evaluation of the programme is being conducted. Interviews of managers, peers, and subordinates of programme participants who were part of the core groups of the Action Learning sets in the second cycle have revealed that the participants have transferred behaviour learned in the sets to the work setting. Participants also recognized the expansion of their network of contacts. They described the programme as having supported their ability to span functional boundaries in their thinking and action.

The design and evaluation team is considering future alterations to the programme and its Action Learning set component. One of the changes contemplated is to integrate the theory and techniques of world class manufacturing (total quality control and just-in-time) and action science more specifically with the Action Learning set experience. The purpose of this change is to improve the relationship between real work and the Action Learning set process, by using these techniques to address actual business cases. Participants would come into the programme with business issues from their work area. The work of the sets would be to consult with each other to solve the business issues of set members, and in so doing, learn a new set of skills. In addition, an intact work team or project team might enter as a set to deal with the business issues they face and integrate this learning component into their work.

In the future, at the onset of the Action Learning set component of the programme, each group will be taken through an outward bound/ropes experience which will help break individual barriers to change and build the trust level in the team. Other individual work may be instituted to assess participant needs, support personal development during the set experience, and provide performance coaching and assessment as follow-up to the programme. A rigorous course will also be given to develop expert coaches for the sets. Several persons who have completed the World Class Leadership programme are candidates for this course. Finally, certification and credit for this programme are being explored.

The Action Learning sets at Digital Equipment Corporation in Burlington, Vermont, provided the participants in the second cycle of the programme with a rich learning experience which transferred to the work environment. The plant benefited from solved problems, and from a new level of skills in communication, problem framing and team development which was exhibited by its management-level employees.

ENDNOTE

Action Learning was a component of the management development effort at Digital Equipment Corporation's manufacturing facility in Burlington, Vermont for two years before the plant was closed. Some fifty managerial staff, from executives to supervisors were involved in two cycles of the 9-month programme called World Class Leadership.

REFERENCES

1 Argyris, C. & Schon, D. (1974), *Theory in Practice: Increasing Professional Effectiveness*, San Francisco: Jossey Bass.
2 Revans, R. W. (1983), *The ABC of Action Learning*, Bromley, UK: Chartwell-Bratt, p. 16.

12 Self-improvement in Chinese Joint Venture Companies

Zhou Jianhua

In July 1987, a self-improvement group of senior managers working in enterprises with foreign investment was set up in Wuxi, in the eastern part of China. The twenty-three members came from different joint ventures and each was a senior executive, such as chairman of board, managing director or general manager.

The group – called 'The Wuxi Association Of Chinese Managers In Enterprises With Foreign Investment' – has very clear purposes: the managers would be able to exchange information frequently; help each other to solve problems and work out right policies; and run the ventures successfully.

The co-operation group was sponsored by Shen Renyong, the first person to be appointed by the Chinese side as general manager of Sino-Swed Pharmaceutical Corp. Ltd (SSPC). SSPC is the first joint venture in China's pharmaceutical industry and comprises five Chinese corporations and five Swedish companies. Mr Shen was opening up a completely new business and, being short of experience, he had to learn by doing. Since he met so many difficulties he had to seek help. He called on his colleague, Meng Ke, the managing director of China Jianghai Wood Products Corp. Ltd, which is the first joint venture in Jiangsu province and was established a little earlier than SSPC, and wanted to discuss some problems with him. Instead of making a direct response Mr Meng described what had happened in his own firm and what measures had been taken. He told Mr Shen that he also was puzzled over many aspects. But both of them realized that the Chinese managers of joint ventures should be organized and help each other. Their proposal was sent to all their colleagues in Wuxi and they had soon got positive replies.

At that time there were 23 approved joint ventures in Wuxi. Of these, only seven had started production and very few had made a profit. Although most of the Chinese managers had long experience, they had similar troubles to Mr Shen and Mr Meng. It seems more difficult to run a joint venture.

At first the members of the group met once a month and took turns playing host. They worked out a two-step programme: The first step was to find out what problems or difficulties they really had, and the second step was to study what measures should be taken to solve the problems. They listed the major problems they met as:

1. *Cultural discrepancy* Partners come from different nations and have different cultures, traditions and customs. Foreign managers have different decision-making processes and estimating standards from Chinese managers. What culture should be formed in a joint venture?
2. *Cooperation with foreign managers* General managers are separately delegated by Chinese and foreign sides, and strive for their own employers' interests. It makes cooperation between managers very difficult.
3. *Control of investment* Price goes up dramatically and the costs of buildings, machines and materials always exceed budgets.
4. *Balance of foreign exchange* A joint venture must make balance of foreign exchange by itself so that it can buy materials and new machines abroad, and pay foreigners' salaries and profit; that is, firms cannot buy any foreign currency from banks.
5. *Export of products* The government requires the products of joint ventures to go towards exports. But production costs in China are so high, even over the sale prices of the international market, that foreign partners are not interested in export.
6. *Control of import channels* Most joint ventures import machines and materials through foreign partners. Some foreign partners are not very honest. They force up commodity prices and infringe upon the interests of joint ventures.
7. *Shortage of materials and energy* In China a lot of materials are supplied on the basis of the national plan, but the demands of new enterprises cannot be arranged at all. Another problem is the frequent power cuts.
8. *Recruitment of skilled workers* Many people hope to work for joint ventures since the firms pay higher wages. But it is very difficult for a new company to recruit skilled workers and engineers who are competent.
9. *Designing a salary and wage structure* The average wages of joint ventures can be 20 to 50 per cent higher than the state-owned firms and the ventures have more autonomy to decide what wage structure they take. But the traditional wage system based on the length of service and the trend of equal treatment have such deep and widespread influences that companies have not defined their wage policy.
10. *Low efficiency of officials* There are so many official barriers to get through before a new business begins that due dates often have to be delayed.

In October 1987, two lecturers of the National Centre For Management Develop-

140

ment at Wuxi took part in the group. They had just finished an MBA course and spent a half-year in Western companies. When one of the lecturers, Zhou Jianhua, was in Britain in the first half of 1987, he met Prof. R. W. Revans, the father of Action Learning. They discussed the possibility of introducing the theory into China and believed that it would be greatly beneficial. The other lecturer, Rong Zonghua, met Action Learning in Manchester Business School in 1984 while he was a member of a research group from China's management education circle, studying modern management education of western countries. After they came back, they tried to translate *ABC of Action Learning* into Chinese and introduce the theory to that business world.

ACTION LEARNING AND CHINESE PRACTICE

When the members of the Wuxi group understood the theory of Action Learning, they were very surprised that they felt so familiar with it. The managers thought that it should be taken up as a major approach of management education. There are three reasons to explain why the theory should play an important part in China's management education.

The first reason is that the former president of the People's Republic of China, Mao Tsetung, who was the founder of PRC and governed the country for several decades, had formed a similar theory. In 1936, Chairman Mao wrote a book titled *'The Strategy of China's Revolutional War'* which is very famous in China. The following paragraph on training of military officers is still impressed on most of Chinese:

> Not only reading is learning, but also doing. The latter is a more important way of learning. Learning warfare through warfare – it is our major method.

In the 1960s, Mao further summed up 'Learning to swim through swimming' as the major method to train officers.

The more important reason is that sharing experience is the traditional and popular method of learning in China. In order to improve management, leaders would organize a meeting to exchange experience. Normally, the participants of such a meeting work in similar positions. Perhaps they work in a trade and manage similar mills respectively, or they are in one large company as department managers. At a meeting several persons who are quite successful at their posts would describe what they have done and how they have been successful. Then the participants would be divided into several groups and introduce what problems they have met. Finally, a few points which are key factors in making the best results would be summarized. Before the Cultural Revolution, exchanging experience was the principal way of management education in China.

141

The most important reason, however, is that economic and political conditions in China are considerably different from those of developed countries and the principles of western management cannot be directly applied. Since 1979 China has started to carry out a new development programme. Meanwhile, the principles of modern management have been introduced from western countries. In the past ten years, management education has stressed the popularization of western management principles. Most universities have set up management departments and hundreds of business schools have emerged providing management courses for both students and managers.

In recent years, however, managers do not believe that they can find ready-made solutions for their problems from western management theories. They have to solve these problems by themselves. A number of management institutes have changed past educational programmes. The new programmes include more practical and less academic courses, and an increasing number of managers are invited to have lectures in institutes.

After the managers learnt of the theory of Action Learning, they were more confident that this method of self-improvement was very effective, and therefore made a new plan. From November 1987 to February 1988 they spent one day a week going through the programme in the following ways.

SHARING EXPERIENCES WITHIN THE GROUP

Each member of the group was in charge of a business and most of them had been on these management posts from the outset. At the group meeting managers described the development of their own ventures and the problems met. Everyone told the others what measures had been taken – maybe some were mistakes – and all had a strong desire to learn from the others. Individuals made helpful suggestions to their colleagues. Usually all of them concentrated on one main problem each time. The exchange brought an unexpected result: not only did the new managers learn from those with previous experiences in the same positions, but also the others drew on fresh ideas from new colleagues. Since then the managers meet monthly.

MAKING RESEARCH IN SMALL GROUPS

In order to design a new wage structure, they formed five groups and selected five companies to investigate. Each group entered a company and interviewed staff, workers, cooks, drivers, salesmen, and so on. They wanted to know, comparing it with the wage structure of state-owned enterprises, what wage structure joint ventures really should have. Then each group reported the results to all the managers. The association didn't make any decision on it and just provided a chance to learn. It expected managers to adjust their wage structure in terms of the internal situation of their own firms. For example, most joint ventures provide free lunch, but Allied Textiles Ltd has not taken up such policy although its business is very profitable. Since the company is in the area of its mother enterprise Wuxi No. 1 Textiles Company, Mr Gu Dingyuan, Chairman of the Board, was afraid that a big difference of remuneration or benefits between companies would influence the morale of the employees who worked in the state-owned company.

LEARNING PROFESSIONAL KNOWLEDGE FROM EXPERTS

The group invited some professionals to give lectures. These included China Bank's staff, the auditor of Accounting Affairs Office, a lawyer, a customs officer, the Industrial and Commercial Administration Bureau's officer, and so on. These persons introduced in discussion specific principles and procedures in which a joint venture would be concerned.

OPENING DIALOGUES WITH OFFICIALS

In China the establishment of a joint venture needs many official seals. The government either still controls the venture, or the venture needs the government's help in such matters as materials supply, power, employment, and export documentation. Since the planning system is still the major form of economic structure and most of the Chinese shareholders in joint ventures are the state-owned enterprises, the government controls almost every aspect of business development. Communication between joint ventures and officials is very important. The group invited officers of local government to talk face to face. The managers put forward proposals and requests, and the officials explained government policies. It greatly improved the relationship of joint ventures with local government and made the managers understand their business better.

EXCHANGING EXPERIENCES WITH FOREIGN PARTNERS

The association invited foreign managers to take part in the project and built up a close relationship with them. Foreigners were very interested in the project. Managers from various countries came together to discuss the difficulties that had been encountered and the measures that should be taken to resolve them. They shared a collective think tank. Kinya Iyi, the general manager of Wuxi Grand Hotel Limited, had forty years experience in hotel management. Under his control, the cost of construction of the hotel was a little below the budget. In contrast, the costs of new projects in other firms were all over budget by a big margin. Chinese managers therefore learnt much from Kinya Iyi. Foreigners also learnt from Chinese managers. Shan Yuhu, the general manager of World Interior Decoration Ltd, is a Hong Kong businessman and had had some trouble with employees. After communication was improved he had received sound advice from other managers.

Six months later the group had not yet planned to make any formal evaluation of the programme as the members felt they were still learning, but the appreciation started to come from the outside. In April 1988, the local government asked the group to train forty managers who worked in firms which intended to set up new ventures. In the training course, Shen Renyong introduced the results of the self-improvement programme systematically and stirred up great interest among the managers. In the end twelve managers became members of the group.

Now the programme is facing a problem in attempting further development. Bao Yongchang, the leader of the group, said: 'The members are not concerned about the same points, because the firms are at different stages of development.'

13 Action Learning in an Academic Context

Richard Thorpe, Maggie Taylor and Meg Elliott

The issues discussed in this chapter derive from our experience of using Action Learning approaches on postgraduate management programmes over the last fifteen years. Since our first programme – the MSc in Management by Action Learning – there have been significant changes in the modes of delivery we use and the markets we serve. These 'internal' changes are mirrored by wider changes taking place in the HE sector as it responds to the issues and practicalities of 'lifelong learning'. Roles and boundaries between places of working and learning are becoming increasingly blurred. The means of formally valuing or recognizing vocational and intellectual 'competence' are evolving and gaining acceptance.

What follows is an account of the evolution of an approach to management education and development based on Action Learning principles. We briefly describe the background to our original Masters programme which was considered to be 'ahead of its time'. We then go on to discuss the philosophy, structure and key processes of Action Learning on which the development of our portfolio of management education programmes is based. In conclusion, we reflect on how our philosophy and approach to management education, in an HE environment and the workplace, has moved forward.

AN MSc IN MANAGEMENT BY ACTION LEARNING

In 1982, our first Action Learning programme was drawn up in collaboration with the then Manchester Polytechnic and the North West Regional Management Centre. The aim was to devise a Masters programme that helped managers learn and develop whilst, at the same time, assisting their organizations to meet their strategic priorities. The result was the introduction of an MSc in Management by Action Learning which was unlike any of the traditional Management Masters programmes available at that time. With its greater emphasis on the practitioner's experience and perspective, the philosophy and principles of Action Learning had to be justified and articulated through rigorous academic quality assurance procedures. Today, such a process is less adversarial, though still challenging. This is partly because we now have a body of case experience to demonstrate the validity of an Action Learning approach in an academic context. But we can also draw on the wider Higher Education experience of work-based learning for academic credit and the shift towards competence-based management education, training and development through Higher Education–employer partnerships for delivery and accreditation.

By monitoring the progress and performance of the MSc curriculum, students and staff over the years, we have been able to demonstrate the tangible benefits of a paradigm shift from teaching to learning. For individuals, students and staff alike, there have been promotions, new appointments and new career directions. In terms of organizational development, notable successes to which the programme has contributed include the commissioning of a new hospital, the introduction of a new staff development policy, and the management of a reduction in staffing involving a £1.5 million budget cut.

ACTION LEARNING PROGRAMMES AT MANCHESTER METROPOLITAN UNIVERSITY

Since 1990, a range of other programmes have been launched, mainly as in-company development programmes at Certificate, Diploma and Masters level. All have Action Learning principles as their central philosophy and meet the requirements for academic rigour and scholarship one would expect from a university programme. They balance the theoretical with the practical, bringing practising manager and academic perspectives together.

Originally our market had an industrial base but this has now shifted as management development has become more pertinent in the public sector. We currently offer an open Masters level programme to managers in public, voluntary and private organizations. A more recent development is the single organization Masters programme, mainly operating in the public sector. At Diploma and Certificate level we have offered programmes only to organizations as part of their management and organization development strategy. All programmes have attracted both men and women, with a steady growth in the number of women participating in recent years.

The outcomes for participants and organizations have all been extremely encouraging. On the Masters programmes there is continuing evidence of rapid career development, both during and after completion of the programme. Across all programmes, a number of client organizations have confirmed their value to the success of divisional, regional or corporate initiatives. We are always encouraged by the 'repeat purchase' patterns of some employers, or requests for consultancy and research services from members of the course team.

Before describing the structure and operation of these programmes, it is appropriate to outline here some of the theories on which they are predicated.

MANAGEMENT LEARNING, STRATEGY FORMULATION AND ORGANIZATIONAL CHANGE

MANAGING – THE MEDIUM FOR MANAGER LEARNING AND DEVELOPMENT

We believe that effective management encompasses the whole complex process by which managers learn and enlarge their abilities. These include not only the components of knowledge and skills, but also the development of appropriate attitudes. Influential in our thinking here has been work by Hawrylyshyn and Burgoyne and Stuart, both of whom in our view offer an advisory insight into the nature of management competence.[1,2]

For total success in management development we argue that the relatively straightforward aspect of knowledge transfer needs to be supplemented and underpinned by the more complex process of attitudinal change and skill development without neglecting the integration of all three.

We feel strongly that managers need to be challenged with ideas that are different from their own and provided with frameworks to help them conceptualize their experience. We also believe that their management development can be improved substantially through actually managing. Here the work of Davies and Easterby-Smith has been influential showing as it does that managers develop most from experiences at work, not simply from specific education and training.[3] Stuart[4] has suggested the most valuable learning is natural learning and Davies and Easterby-Smith have highlighted 'shadow' tutoring where mentors move from the 'spotlight' into the 'shadow', helping managers to learn from their work as they go along.

We see management development occurring most effectively when managers learn on the job through experience, where the evaluation of a manager's activities lies in practical results and supplementary learning is practice-linked – in other words Action Learning. Action Learning in an academic context engages

147

the accumulation of a manager's experience and the nature of the problems brought to the programme.

Knowledge and information is fed into our programmes in a flexible way but the primary vehicle for developing skills and attitudes is through interaction in the 'learning set' and reflection on the experiences in tackling the work related problem or project.

STRATEGIES FOR DEVELOPING HIGHER-ORDER LEARNING SKILLS

EXPERIENTIAL Main Themes	SOCIAL CONSTRUCTION Main Themes
Managers learn from experience Managers need to reflect on this experience. Much significant management learning emanates from work-related events. Many aspects of management can only be addressed through action and involvement, e.g. skills, politics, power, moral dilemmas. The approach is learner centred, the individual can direct their own learning.	Manager as practical author. Reality is vague, only partially specified and unstable. Further specification is possible through negotiation and communication. Language is therefore important. Moral and ethical dimensions can be addressed and new meanings generated. Not doing science but making history.
Critique Individuals are viewed as prime focus. Relationships assume secondary importance. The individual is divorced from their social, historical and cultural context. Thinking is separate to action and knowledge (theory). Can managers always gain experience?	**Critique** Difficult to research, involves values, and individual views of the future. Could be a way forward.

Table 13.1 Two views of management education and development

One of the particular strengths of an academic programme based on Action Learning is its potential to develop managers' higher-order learning skills. In many academic programmes of this type Kolb has been cited as its theoretical underpinning.[5] As the antithesis of Behaviourism, Kolb bases his ideas on an experiential approach to learning, the main tenets of which are that managers learn from experience, and need therefore to learn to reflect on activities before they can conceptualize and re-formulate their plans and activities. The argument is that many aspects of management can only be addressed through action and involvement (e.g. skills, politics, attitudes and moral differences). The approach therefore is learner centred and individualized and the individual can direct their own learning.

But there is another learning theory or level of learning at which Action Learning works that we find equally attractive and strive to engender in the programmes we devise. This is the social constructionist approach. This posits that most managers achieve what they do both through the contribution and by the persuasion of others. Development activities need to recognize this in a way Kolb's theory does not.[6] Managers need to negotiate, to understand each others' perspectives and learn to argue for their ethical and moral positions. As such, management is not simply a scientific process of induction and deduction as Kolb suggests, but something that is socially constructed. Table 13.1 sets out in a simplified way the themes and critiques of the two views. In the words of Shotter a manager is also a practical author who recognizes that 'reality' is vague, unstable and only partially specified.[7] We believe that in this situation managers can create increased certainty in a situation through the way they negotiate and communicate with themselves and others. Language is the vehicle for this communication process and the language used in the persuasive 'utterances' is what can be practised in sets. As Wieck* remarks, we don't know what we think until we see what we say, and through language, meaning can be managed and subordinates persuaded, such is also the stuff of management and leadership.[8] Through this focus moral and ethical dimensions can be addressed and new meanings generated.

Much of what is written about strategic change and managing change is derived from a rational and positivistic perspective. This perspective makes certain assumptions about how organisations operate in relation to their environment and the future (i.e. they see the environment as something that can be analysed and the future a logical extension of the past). Other writers make the assumption that managers are seeking to maintain 'an equilibrium' and that managers can, through a variety of approaches adapt and reconfigure their organizations to new circumstances. But, we believe that, if managers can be encouraged to act, to recreate and reinterpret their circumstances by challenging the moral, ethical, social and economic bases on which a strategy was originally predicated then there is a far greater scope for learning and change becomes possible.

In our corporate programmes particularly we attempt to contribute to a climate which permits and acknowledges challenge by developing mechanisms within the organization that allows this to happen.

---

* The idea of communicating and arguing with yourself is a notion borrowed from Wieck – you don't know what you think until you see what you say – this can be done with yourself, before being tried out on others.

ORGANIZATIONAL CHANGE AND RESEARCH IN MANAGEMENT

Change in organizations is often handled inadequately. Organizations wait too long after recognizing a change in their environment before internal changes are made. When the organization responds, it often does so hastily, often auto-cratically and in ways that do not allow for the satisfactory resolution of dilemmas involving those concerned who have a contribution to make. We have known a great deal about organizational change processes for some time[9] – known, for example, that often the knowledge required to respond to change already exists within the organization itself, but no mechanisms or structures have been in place that could feed this vital information to those individuals in the organization who could act on it. The development of such mechanisms lies in the domain of those involved in the creation of learning organizations. We seek to identify individuals who, within the context of our structured programmes, are empow-ered to collect 'new knowledge' or work on a project associated with an organizational mentor or sponsor to ensure that the information they gain is transformed into practice or used to influence the decision-making processes in the organization. We see the establishment of an Action Learning set within an organization as the kind of communication mechanism conducive to successful change.

It is not only the ability to identify key individuals who may be appropriately positioned to intervene in change but the ability to encourage the development of learning mechanisms that will be able to focus on particular 'nodes' in the organization where individuals are free to move in or out – in this way acting as boundary scanners and in this role able to yield influence across the organization. Through this process the individual learns and the organization learns and develops and the change is realized.

RESEARCH

Our approach to research (defined as the collection of 'new knowledge') links those aspects of learning and change discussed above. Collecting information on a problem or opportunity also relates to debates about what actually constitutes legitimate research in management. One view of research often referred to as the positivistic approach/'scientific view' sees research as hypothesis testing where the hypothesis is a new theory or a deduction from existing theory and concerns the existence of phenomena under specific conditions. It is held that a properly tested theory is able to offer reliable knowledge which will allow behaviour to be predicted and, ideally brought about. The scientist/researcher would then 'turn over' the reliable knowledge thus acquired to the manager in charge or the academic community via an academic paper, or use it to improve their own practice of management.

A contrasting and many would say contradictory view of research, would take a phenomenological approach. Here researchers would argue against there being one 'objective truth' – particularly in the context of a social science like management. The focus for researchers would be on the view and perceptions of individuals not simply the observable. As a consequence importance would be placed on ways of uncovering the unobservable (e.g. views, attitudes and opinions). In doing so they would seek to understand the rationale for an individual's understanding of a situation or action rather than attempt to see everyone reaching the same conclusions. Such an approach makes multiple perspectives possible within the context of a specific situation, industry or context. The knowledge thus gained would not be seen as something for use only by managers to control or manipulate behaviour, but rather for use to bring about change though the stimulation of critical awareness by everyone involved in the 'research process' – i.e. those who work in the organization.

A further perspective is that of 'action research'. In many ways this is the perspective we use most often. Action research has a number of characteristics in common with Action Learning which, because of its stronger academic tradition, is useful in conferring respectability to the research process – particularly when used in our structured programmes in an academic environment – Action Learning is not so much a research approach, rather an educational process that makes extensive use of action research methods. As a process action research is complex, using both deductive (theory testing) and inductive (theory building) strategies, but it does have the advantage that it attempts to reconcile managerial and academic aims as a research approach for management and in a number of ways does involve an educational process.

'Action research' starts with the view that research should lead to change and that change should be incorporated into the research itself. Classical action research starts with the idea that if you want to understand something well you should try changing it and this is the focus of participants' projects on our action learning programmes.[10] From the relative success or failure of particular courses of action it is possible to formulate in a generalizable way what those courses of action were and what were the conditions for success or failure.

By challenging an individual's 'world view' we can begin to help managers think about the future and new possibilities rather than simply base their findings on historical data and move forward only incrementally. Helping managers re-frame their ideas or questions offers the potential for fundamental change. Action research offers the possibility of multiple outcomes and it also offers variety and choice for the manager. These choices are set out in the model overleaf.

151

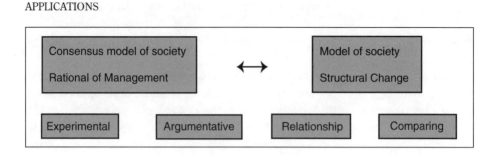

In the course of any one project the strategies adopted by the researcher may spiral from one type to another. Each offers a form of intervention and style of working which the individual perceives as most appropriate to a particular policy context and phase of development. It also offers a range of strategies and methods including taking account of power relationships which much more positivist approaches often ignore or discount or are less able to explore.

In all our programmes we ask our participants to focus on three aspects: their organization; their competence in managing the change process; and the literature in relation to the specific issue they are addressing. Learning and change is brought about through the emphasis placed on the collaborative nature of the process. This not only leads to the development of shared understandings between researcher and researched but also between the researcher and the mentor and managers who may well be involved in the implementation of the research findings. This sharing leads to greater ownership and consequently the increased likelihood that results of the research will be put into practice. In the context of the change model described earlier, our programme allows the researcher to bring new knowledge to organizational members who can act on it. Important therefore in action research is concern for contracting, diagnosis and evaluation.

Because of the collaborative features of action research, participants are likely to learn a lot from the process itself, rather than any formal account of the research findings. This we recognize, and encourage students on our programmes to write up their research as a narrative so that a record is produced of how understandings have changed and developed over time.

Now let us examine the structure and operation of Action Learning programmes at Manchester Metropolitan University in more detail.

THE STRUCTURE OF OUR PROGRAMMES

DURATION AND COMMON FEATURES

Our MSc programme takes two years and our Diploma and Certificate programmes, 18 months. Extensions of up to six months may be granted, subject to certain conditions, to participants facing disruption to their studies.

There are a number of areas of common philosophy that have practical manifestations. All our programmes involve:

- preparation, recruitment and contracting with the course participant and the client organization
- an induction programme which includes a compulsory programme for mentors, with key knowledge inputs and an evaluation of current competences using one, or a number, of the competency frameworks available
- supported learning sets where participants work on their managerial project
- assessment points.

All have an induction programme which includes a compulsory programme for mentors, certain key knowledge inputs and an evaluation of current competences using one or a number of the competency frameworks available.

Following this, all have supported sets where participants work on a managerial project with a facilitator – usually from the university. Unlike non-accredited programmes we build in a number of assessment points. The Masters programme is assessed on a project (an account of their action, research and change (9 months)) and a dissertation (an examination of the usefulness of the theory used and reflection on their competence as managers in bringing about change and their new understanding of their organization and its environment in attempting the change (12 months)). For many there is also an additional *viva voce* examination on their work.

The Diploma is assessed on an organizational simulation: a kind of case study that tests their abilities (on a case study of which they have no experience), a project (an account of the action, research and change) and a learning and development assignment (a reflective analysis of their learning).

The Certificate is assessed on four learning contracts specifically related to areas of management competence and a project (an account of their action and change).

PRIOR MANAGEMENT KNOWLEDGE

Each of the programmes outlined demand some prior knowledge of management theory but in different degrees. At Certificate level (aimed at junior/first line management) we assume little prior management knowledge although as a postgraduate/post experience qualification a degree or equivalent is normally required. The 'knowledge inputs' provided here cover the five areas of basic management competency, i.e. managing people, managing information, managing finance, managing resources and managing self. Our aim at this level is to offer a 'language' through which managers can begin to converse with each other and establish some common concepts.

At Postgraduate Diploma level, (aimed at middle managers in organizations) we expect graduate entry or equivalent (e.g. NCVQ level 5 or MCI level 1). The knowledge inputs we offer (in addition to the induction) are all conceptual. At this level we are interested in giving managers a critique in a range of management areas encouraging them to not only learn about new ideas but to challenge them. To do this we present them with ten two-day workshops which offer a critical perspective on a range of management topics. For example, managing change, strategy formulation.

At Masters level (aimed at relatively senior managers involved in strategic change) we are much more interested in the experience and level of awareness of management than their formal management qualifications.

In these matters of entry requirements and assessment academic imperatives appear to supersede client organization interests or concerns.

Much has been written on the subject of competence, who could argue to be against it, yet defining competence is far from simple and has caused much debate. In our Action Learning programmes we work with a range of management competency frameworks and are involved in helping organizations develop their own using either functional analysis or repertory grid approaches. In general we have steered away from being overly reductionist in our approach, seeing them as inflexible and problematic. That is not to say that we don't find them useful as a template for discussion with managers of their developmental needs, or of use as a basis for developing a common framework or language within an organization.

Whatever the level of programme in which we are involved some kind of competency audit is always undertaken as a basis for development.

PROJECTS

All our managers' projects are essentially practical. Theories and ideas introduced at this stage are developed to help managers conceptualize the problem and inform initial actions. All participants are expected to achieve some degree of implementation as we believe aspects of management such as power, politics and the ability to make and influence change can only be addressed following some action or intervention.

MENTORSHIP

When working with any organization involved in substantial change we find a need to intervene and engage with the organization at different levels. At the top there is clearly a need for senior management commitment and support – at the very least to ensure the resources participants will require are available.

However, if change is likely to have real impact there is also a need to ensure commitment in a number of additional ways:

- those involved as change agents are in appropriate positions in the organization
- the problem areas being investigated are important and not of merely short-term technical significance
- that maximum impact can be achieved within the life of the project – whilst recognizing the emotional nature and stress involved in managing change.

It is to ensure the above that we consider the role of mentoring as absolutely vital in both our open and corporate programmes. However we often find that the reality is that most organizations undertake the mentoring process in a very *ad hoc* way – in a way more often associated with recruitment and individual career development rather than a more holistic way – how an individual's learning can contribute and be related to overall organizational success.

COMPARISONS OF APPROACHES TO MENTORING[11]

Table 13.2 contrasts how, even when mentoring is systematic, it can offer a very partial approach when compared to a process view of mentoring.

As a consequence what we focus on is to begin to establish a recognition for

Systematic mentoring		Process mentoring
Attitude to structure	Specify roles and set boundaries. Make and follow specific plans.	Leave roles open, negotiate over time.
Value of mentoring	Useful but not central to learning or development programmes.	Central to learning and development.
Typical interactions	Occasional encounters.	Regular contacts.
Focus	Short-term, action centred.	Long-term personal.

Table 13.2 Two approaches to mentoring

155

and commitment to the process of mentoring which is not only about the development of individual participants but also the contribution to the overall learning climate within the organization, i.e. *organizational learning* at a number of interfaces both inside and outside the organization.

As a consequence in all our programmes, particularly if organizationally focused, we concentrate on aspects of the mentoring task and from the very start an emphasis is placed on encouraging individuals to reframe their roles. We have learnt that when organizations are faced with change senior managers are often reluctant to share their knowledge and experience as it can be seen as a loss of their formal power. The fact that their subordinates may be obtaining 'new knowledge' is itself threatening, often giving rise to fears of losing control and reinforcing insularity which in turn further inhibits learning. We attempt to encourage a different view of expertise amongst senior managers – one of mentoring which can be both personally enabling and powerful in organizational learning terms.

The objective of our initial work with mentors is therefore to encourage them to consider the phases of the change management process, i.e. from project problem conception and exploring ideas through to implementation and handing on. What is emphasized is the contribution they can make at each phase in the process.

Also emphasized is the question of roles and relationships between mentor and participant that might exist in the life cycle of any project.

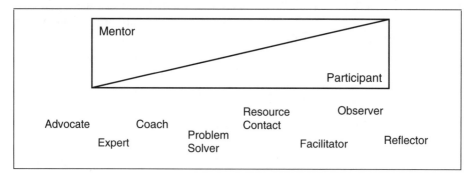

The skills involved are clearly complex and require the mentor being sufficiently sensitive to the levels of competence and confidence of the participant.

If appropriate time is invested, particularly in organization-based programmes, then the benefits for the participant, mentor and organization can be substantial.

Our experience with participants without this support suggests that:

● although there is individual development and learning and achievement of an award the journey can be frustrating and lonely

- the experience may actually result in learners becoming very cynical and disaffected with their organization
- the opportunity to effect change and capture the individual learning is dispersed or lost to the organization.

But what are the problems of introducing Action Learning in an academic environment? Can the problems and difficulties be overcome, and if so how can academic programmes employing this philosophy be made to work? In the following sections we address these issues using our experience, concluding with pointers to others in education considering the philosophy and approach.

PROBLEMS WITH ACTION LEARNING IN AN ACADEMIC INSTITUTION

FROM AN INSTITUTIONAL PERSPECTIVE

There is a tension in trying to deliver our type of programme within an academic institution which goes beyond the operational constraints of such issues as set size.

This tension relates to debates concerning what Higher Education is about. Although 'vocational' provision responds to a wider organizational environment, there is a requirement to recognize and develop knowledge in programmes such as the MSc. We appreciate that individuals have differing start-up points and can presumably regress as well as move forward or simply stop – for a while.

Our business however, is at one level about standards and awards. In the overall process we encounter a fundamental dilemma between ensuring that participants adhere to standards, and achieve their individual awards whilst at the same time working as a group and making appropriate change in the organizations in which they work.

These three objectives are illustrated below:

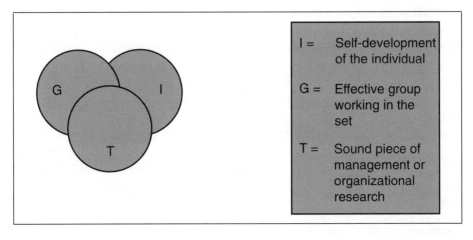

I =	Self-development of the individual
G =	Effective group working in the set
T =	Sound piece of management or organizational research

Educational institutions continue to adjust to pressures to deliver services efficiently and reduce high cost inputs. This has advanced the cause of traditional teaching, larger class sizes and distance learning rather than riskier, resource-rich, student centred approaches. Modularization, semesterization and credit accumulation and transfer schemes (CATS) need to be creatively adapted for 'development' rather than 'taught' programmes.

Tension between the need to deliver an 'academic' report to gain the award and the holistic nature of development may result in an over-concentration on delivering the task for the university which has specific requirements. This may not match the individual's development or enable the organization to 'capture' the learning.

The primary functions of the set are to support and encourage each participant through the project task and associated learning. Some sets are facilitated by the organization, some sets by staff from the university. During meetings members might outline programmes, indicate what they have discovered between meetings and outline what conclusions have been drawn. Colleagues then question how these conclusions were derived, what methods of analysis were used and, in the light of their own experience, check the validity of the assumptions made. One student represented the usefulness of the set to him in Figure 13.1 opposite.

Typically meetings take place fortnightly and after the initial sessions, increasing use is made of members' organizations or departments as the place to meet. This not only improves appreciation and understanding of that organization or department, but gives the organization member the chance to use the multiple skills of the set to help research the problem on site.

Action Learning as a vehicle for management and organization development at Manchester Metropolitan University has not been without its critics – not least some colleagues who see the method as challenging a hard-won discipline base. Those questioning the approach have claimed it is not sufficiently rigorous to warrant the award of a higher degree and is not in the 'academic tradition'. Advocates on the other hand have often not helped their case by claiming the method is more innovatory and all embracing than in fact it actually is.

Academic institutions exist for the development and dissemination of knowledge. Their value systems and career structures reward excellence and expertise in research and teaching, measured in terms of research, output and student numbers. The research output emanating from Action Learning makes it difficult to gain acceptance in 'top' academic journals and the resource-rich nature of the programmes often means that they either attract higher than average fees from organizations or contribute little towards improving the ever increasing staff/ student ratios.

In recent years pressures on educational institutions to deliver services

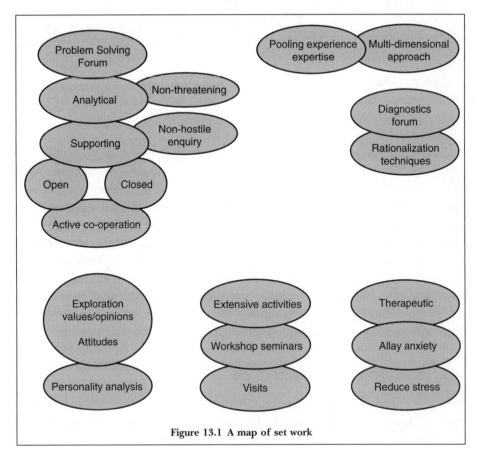

Figure 13.1 A map of set work

efficiently have often meant reducing inputs. This has advanced the cause of traditional teaching, larger class sizes and distance learning rather than riskier, resource-rich student-centred approaches.

The role of the 'expert' teacher or researcher is embodied in an institutional language emphasizing a dependency relationship, as in 'centres of excellence' or 'such and such a person, is a leading authority on . . .', and even 'reading for a degree'. In many institutions staff are noted for their preference for research rather than teaching – or helping students learning. Teaching has 'nuisance' value, as the financial and promotional rewards are derived from such activities as research contracts, publications, book chapters, royalties and consultancy.

In such a context, proponents of Action Learning are inevitably involved in attempts to establish credibility and acceptance within the institution on professional, intellectual and administrative grounds. At Manchester, the task has been to secure the recognition of Action Learning as a credible philosophy underpinning the whole of their in-company activity. Those involved have had

159

to accept the change in role that Action Learning brings, changes from 'teacher-expert' to 'learning facilitator', allowing students to make mistakes without this being seen as a 'fault' of the tutor – or seen as a loss of control in the learning process.

Changing the culture at an institutional and departmental level has probably been the most difficult task of all. However, over our fifteen years of experience there have been many measures of success at all levels – academic, participant and employer.

One measure of success is the calibre of the applicants who continue to enrol. For many, the choice of Action Learning is a conscious one – they like the style of development. The support and encouragement of our external examiners has been another. Student and client feedback and the promotions gained by participants have provided further confirmation of the value of the programme. Over the years we have undertaken close monitoring and evaluation and developed a strong academic justification for the components of the programmes we offer. We have also seen our ideas incorporated in other programmes nationally, seen our colleagues leave and set up Action Learning programmes elsewhere – often very similar to our own – and have been involved in workshops to help other institutions implement the approach. How has this been achieved?

FROM AN INDIVIDUAL/STAFF PERSPECTIVE

Part of the answer lies in recognizing the difficulties associated with a problem-centred, learner-centred approach to management development and finding strategies to address them. Some of these are outlined below:

1. *Loss or devaluing of skills* Management educators often have a genuine fear that involvement in such programmes devalues their skill and knowledge base. Given the current pressures in Higher Education this needs to be addressed by focusing on the value of the insights that can be gained into current practice and the opportunities for research and publications in contemporary areas of business and management.
2. *Fear of not being the expert* Tensions arise within educators when the role requires them not to put themselves forward as expert and allow other members of the group to come forward with their experience and expertise. Even going so far as on occasions leaving the formal academic 'presentations' to other members of the group. Fear of not being the expert relates to a problem of loss of control.
3. *New skills* Clearly the role of facilitator requires academics to acquire new skills. Preparation for classes is difficult and teachers often go into the situation with apprehension, fearful of the uncertainties which they

might find. It is common to find set advisors anxious in the face of a great deal of uncertainty.

4. *Changes in the student/client expectations* We have found that for certain types of managers the approach to learning we offer is well received. These managers search for relevance rather than knowledge for its own sake and enjoy the problem-centred/learner-centred approach. But there is also a high expectation that we will deliver, and any slippage in the process of sharing the responsibility for learning is often heavily criticized. The process they experience therefore is important in shaping their expectations.

The primary way in which we have addressed these problems has been through the development of an 'open' and cohesive course team. Changing the 'lecture culture' has involved a paradigm shift from teaching to learning, as shown in Figure 13.2 (adapted from a model developed by John Hughes – a previous course leader). This change necessitated a complete reappraisal of the role and skills required of the lecturer, together with the attendant risk and worry of being found wanting in the area of process, rather than content delivery. Developing confidence in staff did require major investments of time and energy resource and this could not have been without the support of senior members of the academic staff.

From	→	To
Teaching	→	Learning
Feeding	→	Finding out
Subject centred	→	Student centred
Content	→	Context and process
Talking	→	Listening
Expert	→	Examplar
Position of power over	→	Personal authority with

Figure 13.2 Changing the lecture culture

HOW CAN ACTION LEARNING BE MADE TO WORK?

PREPARATION, PUBLICITY AND RECRUITMENT

Over the years there has been a gradual shift from programmes having an institutional base to programmes that have an employer base. From our experience we have found that Action Learning will not work without shaping the expectations of course participants and clients in advance of joining the programme. In order to achieve this the teaching team have responsibilities beyond the class-contact hours allocated. The role needs, perhaps, to be more ambassadorial rather than evangelical. We ensure that all members of the team are involved in the recruitment process and this requires a complete awareness of pre-course requirements.

Advance publicity takes the form of course brochures, supplementary papers and any journal, articles or conference papers that we have currently written explaining what we are about. We recognize, as with the marketing of any service, that part of the key to success is to market ourselves, and to be seen as credible, knowing what we are about and experienced in delivery to our objectives. Notwithstanding the formal approaches to recruitment, we have found the most successful source of recruits to our open programme is through the personal recommendations of past and present course members and their experience of the institution.

INTERVIEWS

On all Action Learning programmes we interview all applicants. This is particularly important for in-company programmes where we are unsure of the experience and standing of the applicants. The general format of an interview is an explanation of the programme by a member of the course team followed by an explanation by the candidate of their management level, the extent to which they have already gained some formal management training and their individual career aspirations. As the project is crucial on all programmes, an exploration of this area by the participant is an essential part of this first meeting. This first meeting also gives the applicant plenty of food for thought about just what they might do and how they might tackle it.

For participants to work effectively in sets, applicants are required to be practising managers and for Diploma and Masters students to have a broad knowledge of management theories and concepts. Our expectation is that applicants to these programmes will have either completed a post-experience programme in management and business, or undertaken a relevant undergraduate course or professional qualification with a substantial management content. If managers do not have appropriate formal qualifications we often used an assignment as a means of assessing candidates' descriptive and analytical capabilities. Having jumped this hurdle and if the candidate appears to be able to benefit from the programme they are asked to write a project synopsis which provides the basis for discussion between the candidate and the organization client at a later date. It is true to say that we are increasingly giving credit for prior academic and work-based learning, and, given our intention to develop managers we are not averse to taking some risks.

CONTRACTING WITH CLIENTS

Client interviews are the second stage in the decision process. Normally, two course team members meet with the prospective student and their client. The philosophy and approach to the programme, the roles and processes involved and provisional broad development plans for the organization and participant are discussed. The intention is to establish a common understanding of the project area and gain agreement on organizational support that will be available for the participant. The value of this to us is an appreciation of the organization and its context, for the client it is a better understanding of the nature of the work to be undertaken through the project and the extent to which implementation is seen to be an important part of the programme. Only when a viable project is agreed with all parties is a person accepted onto the programme. More recently we have introduced a mentor programme which ensures that our tripartite nature of the programme is reinforced – student, university, employer.

THE PROCESS

BUILDING A LEARNING COMMUNITY: PARTICIPANTS AND MENTORS

All programmes consist of three interrelated phases:

1. an orientation phase
2. a problem-centred project (Action Learning phase)
3. a write-up and consolidation phase.

The intention of the orientation phase is to build a mature learning community as quickly as possible whilst generating appropriate knowledge, attitudes and skills for the action-centred project. Broadly, the objectives of this phase are:

1. to transfer certain information thought to be important for all participants

163

to successfully complete the programme (that is, the nature of the Action Learning, various approaches to research and aspects of project management and organizational change);

2. to allow participants to experience and value a mature approach to learning;
3. to create a supportive approach in the programme community;
4. to help participants examine their strengths and weaknesses (this is now done mainly through the process of audit);
5. to develop basic knowledge, attitudes and skills which will allow participants to analyse their own and their organizations' development needs with the aid of available resources.

In our approach participants are seen as major resources in the learning process. Initially, staff design and deliver the specific 'content' elements (P) [P = Programmed Knowledge][12] considered essential. Priority is quickly given to team building and the development and recognition of the significance of the pool of experiences and knowledge within the group. Our justification for this is that managers are used to having time pressures impose a structure on their day. We recognize that during the orientation phase any attempt to transfer to an unstructured learning too quickly would probably result in adverse reactions. Responsibility is increasingly shared with participants as a mature learning community develops.

We have found that course members benefit from initial training and exposure to participative learning approaches in order to appreciate the roles, responsibilities and processes involved in the programme. So a primary aim of the orientation phase is to undertake some task or small project usually related to the main project topic as a vehicle for this participative learning. This mini-project facilitates the development approaches and skills for diagnosing and analysing problems and implementing solutions, and often highlights important aspects of the main project that may require to be developed in more detail.

We have found that a wide variety of learning methods are appropriate during orientation. These include inputs, experiential exercises, self-directed study and discussions.

Broadly, the orientation phase is divided between the university, a residential venue and the participant's organization, as follows:

Week 1 Mentor's orientation.
Week 2 In college, deals primarily with 'hygiene' factors, initial introductions, the resources available and foundation knowledge, skills such as the Action Learning approach, models for internal consultancy, issues related to research and methods that might be employed.
Week 3 In a residential venue, the aim is to create and develop a supportive

climate, allowing participants to re-examine their development needs and to experiment with new skills and behaviour. Initially, indoor exercises are used to achieve this, culminating in an integrated outdoor exercise over two days. The use of the outdoors has proved a most successful medium for team building and providing the opportunity for members of the course simply to get to know each other better and begin to remove the protective layers of organizational status they often bring to the programmes.

Week 4 Each participant is based in their organization and begins set attendance either at work or at the university. They begin to work on their mini-project and develop insights into how best the main project might be approached and tackled. Learning contracts are developed.

Week 5 At this stage findings are presented to the set and project supervisor, and feedback received for the first time.

THE PROBLEM-CENTRED PROJECT (ACTION LEARNING) PHASE

By this stage in the programme, participants should have developed considerable freedom for direction and control of their own learning. This freedom, together with the support and encouragement from members of their learning set, their set advisor and their project tutor, will provide the conditions for much learning. At the Certificate and Diploma levels taught inputs provide new insights into aspects of management. For in-company programmes these are tailored to the organization's requirements and often delivered jointly, thereby offering both practical and academic insights.

During the early stages of the programme, each participant will have prepared a research proposal which, in essence, is a diagnosis of the organization's problem and an action plan for tackling it. The objective is not only to give focus to the first year's work, but also to provide a yardstick as to whether the proposed approach will satisfy the requirements of the clients.

As they tackle their organizational project, members are concerned with the identification, diagnosis, analysis and exploration of theories thought to be useful and the experimentation, implementation and evaluation of improvements related to their organization's problem and their own development needs.

It is normal practice throughout the project phase, for participants to keep an account of their experiences and insights, using a journal or log book. This is so that ideas and insights are captured and not lost for the reflective/consolidation phase.

LEARNING SETS

Action Learning sets are formed to provide as rich a diversity of talent, qualification, experience and organization as possible. Sets normally consist of up to eight participants together with a set adviser. More than this number would, we feel, prevent proper interaction taking place. We make no use of psychometrics to produce 'balanced' groups, but rely on a personal knowledge of our participants and their performance in the orientation phase. There are some rules. No two people from the same or competitor organizations go into the same set on the open programme. With in-company programmes, diversity comes from set members drawn from different parts of the organization. Another rule is that set members will not have their project supervisor as their set adviser.

If there are severe personality clashes, then the problem will be tackled. Harmony is important, for after the orientation phase the set becomes the course. Split sets and mergers between groups have always been problematic.

From our experience, we have learnt a number of lessons about set advising. Firstly, no two sets are the same, a flexible contingent approach often pays dividends, a set is not necessarily a team, and set advisors are not necessarily equal members. Finally, effective sets more often than not begin with an effective common experience and we have found the outdoor exercises ideal for this purpose.

A TYPICAL SET MEETING

Typically, meetings take place fortnightly. The first few meetings are normally held in college and thereafter increasingly at members' organizations. This not only improves appreciation and understanding of that organization but also gives the organization member the opportunity to use the multiple skills of the set to help research the problem on site.

During meetings members might outline progress, indicate what they have discovered between meetings and outline what conclusions have been drawn. Opportunity then exists for colleagues to question how those conclusions were derived, methods of analysis used and, in the light of their own experience, to check the validity of assumptions made.

WRITE-UP AND CONSOLIDATION PHASE

This phase is intended to further develop skills in reflection and conceptualization. Managers are often weak in these areas and many are apprehensive about the difficult demands this phase of the programme will make on them. A major requirement is for them to read more widely than perhaps they have ever done before and particularly their own journal and notes. Notwithstanding their initial reluctance most managers express a benefit from the process and confirm that strengthening conceptual skills is important in managing their own self-development.

During this phase, reflection often results in many project experiences being explained, new insights being achieved and concepts recognized and developed. At Masters level for example, the write-up takes the form of a dissertation: this reflective commentary records, analyses and evaluates the project experiences and the learning resulting from them at a variety of levels. At an instrumental level, reflection might show better approaches or techniques than those adopted on the project. At a higher level the whole nature of the project might be reconsidered in the light of a reflective assessment of the organization and its environment, and consideration given to management competencies displayed during the process and what implications there might be for development. Skills in analysing, evaluating, expressing and presentation are also developed in the dissertation. Before this phase, there will have been discussion on the requirements and assessment criteria for the dissertation. By this point in the programme, the ability to reflect and conceptualize should be well advanced and participants will have been encouraged to document each stage carefully as they progressed.

In all programmes sets meet regularly as do students and supervisors. The discussions between the participant and supervisor will probably now focus upon methods of analysis and presentation, and ensuring that the output progresses satisfactorily. They will also deal with the assessment criteria required of the award.

ADDITIONAL LEARNER SUPPORT

WORKSHOPS AND SPECIAL ARRANGEMENTS

The role of the project supervisor – the importance of contracting.
The role of the mentor (if not included in the earlier section on mentoring).
The pace of the programmes and personal commitment.

The most common sources of learning will be the experiences and knowledge of members of the learning set, the individual supervisors and the formal inputs and relevant reading. From time to time learning needs will be identified which are not adequately covered from these sources and for which other arrangements will be needed.

Alternatives that we regularly provide for students are as follows:

167

- Attending relevant lectures on other course programmes in the department.
- Learning programmes/programme packages.
- Visits to organizations to see and discuss particular developments or applications.
- Special workshops where sufficient interest has been identified in a particular topic.
- Distance-learning materials available on a variety of subjects at whatever level.

During the project phase of the programmes there are always a number of specialized inputs requested. Although we try to cover these in some way during induction by the very nature of the projects being undertaken we can anticipate a number of recurring themes. We are always being asked to elaborate upon:

- methods of data collection and analysis
- the marketing of services
- implementing change
- the role of the internal consultant
- financial management
- corporate objectives and the development of strategy.

ROLE OF THE PROJECT SUPERVISOR – THE IMPORTANCE OF CONTRACTING

Throughout the project and dissertation phases of the programme regular meetings take place between participants and their supervisor. Discussion centres around the participant's approach to their projects with a view to meeting the programme requirements and those of the client organization. The supervisor may also advise on technical or specialized aspects of the projects which the learning set does not have the resources to handle.

The term 'supervisor' is certainly at variance with an Action Learning philosophy. Its continued use in our vocabulary remains problematic in the expectations it creates. The result is a range of interpretations and models of the role. One model of the role involves the following responsibilities:

- helping each participant with the discipline of planning and progressing project work;
- helping each participant to reconcile any difference in interests or requirements between the programme and the client;
- helping to identify learning needs and to suggest relevant reading;
- liaising with set advisors, the course leader, workshop tutors and course committee, on the arrangements of workshops and other special events;
- helping each participant to evaluate the significance of problems or potential

problems, and to advise on approaches and sources of help for coping with
them. Any problem which is likely to affect the progress or quality of a
participant's submission should be reported to the course committee;

- advising each participant on the programme requirements and the presentation of their dissertation.

THE PACE OF THE PROGRAMMES AND PERSONAL COMMITMENT

Although there is a great importance placed on personal responsibility of the
learner in the programme, there are nevertheless certain mechanisms whereby
the pace and direction of an individual's progress will be monitored.

Firstly, the structure of the programme is quite explicit in terms of how long
the orientation phase lasts, how long the participant can expect to take over the
actual project work and exactly when the final assessments are to be handed in.
The programme structure therefore provides a basic timetabling framework for
the participant.

Secondly, each participant has their own personal supervisor. The role of
the supervisor includes not only providing guidance and advice on technical
methodological issues, but also on the very practical issues of time management.

Thirdly, the learning set also provides a context within which the relative
progress of each participant will be visible to every other participant. Should this
not provide sufficient motivation, it would be accepted, and indeed encouraged,
practice for set members to comment on the possible slow rate of progress of
one of their colleagues.

Individuals are also visible in their organizations as they undertake important
project and development work. Part of the progress is to seek and obtain top
management support, and continuing goodwill rather than resentment from
peers. At a personal level, then, the participant stands to gain relevant managerial
experience, together with a recognized higher degree.

Each of these factors tend to produce high levels of commitment from each
participant to completing the requirements of the programme.

MOVING FORWARD ON ACTION LEARNING IN AN ACADEMIC CONTEXT

Reflecting on the development of our portfolio of Action Learning programmes
at Manchester Metropolitan University, we can demonstrate the appropriateness
and flexibility of this approach to management and organizational development.
The core processes and methodologies are transferable to different levels of
management and different types of organization.

The area of significant growth in recent years has been that of in-company

169

programmes leading to Certificate, Diploma and Master's awards. This has prompted new development and partnerships for the delivery of these pro-grammes. Mentor training has been essential to developing a more receptive company culture not only to support individual managers and the implementation of their projects, but also to foster the growth of a learning organization.

Recognizing and valuing learning in the workplace is now 'common currency' in a society which is embracing competence-based approaches in education and employment. As a result, Action Learning in an academic context is becoming more acceptable and better understood. However, the case still needs to be reviewed and debated in the light of experience and new theoretical perspectives.

CONCLUSIONS

In this chapter we have set out the case for using work-related activities as the main vehicle for the development of managers. There is an initial discussion of recent research into the necessary competencies of successful managers. This research shows the complex nature of competence and how the acquisition of knowledge needs to be underpinned by the development of certain attitudes and skills, many of which are situationally and organizationally specific.

How these competencies might be developed is the next question addressed. The approach advocated is that of Action Learning, one where managers working in groups are set the task of solving a challenging organizational problem and learn from it at the same time.

To justify Action Learning further, the process is compared and contrasted with the methodology of Action Research and the similarity of approaches – at the stage of entry, contracting, diagnosis, action evaluation and withdrawal – are highlighted.

The strongest argument for Action Learning is that it makes for effective management development because it recognizes that in order to develop an organization there is a need to develop managers and the problem-centred strategy-driven approach to Action Learning is ideally suited to accomplish both.

By exploiting the power of learning on the job, it develops high-level manage-ment competencies in a social context that encourages both openness and a positive questioning attitude (what Revans calls the ability to develop 'Q') that leads to a true change experience. Managers are subjected to, and challenged with, a number of relative perspectives – probably in a way they have never been before – through other programme participants in set work. The strangeness of the situation and the process of reflection in which they indulge, undertaken in a college setting and with exposure to the wider frames of reference which academic staff and the management literature provide, offer a rich learning experience.

Action Learning overcomes some of the criticisms of management development which have arisen from the debate outlined at the beginning of this chapter. Action Learning uses the most effective situation for management learning – the manager's own job and the demands and experiences it offers. Because it uses the job as the learning vehicle, Action Learning enables managers to perceive more accurately their own context and that of their organization and, through 'set' work, to share this perception with others. They can also compare their 'theories in use' and learn from each other. The projects in which they are involved are developed to change the organization in the direction of greater effectiveness; they are confronted with the need to move from a passive to an active paradigm, to make changes, and to influence others to move from technique application to problem solving. At the same time they are encouraged to reflect, theorize and test out the effectiveness of their own actions in bringing about change and the competencies that underlie such actions. These can be related to the models of competencies discussed.

Because the structure of an Action Learning programme is based on a concept of learning style it can be tailored to the requirements of an individual manager or of a group of managers. Above all, through the process of Action Learning, managers experience 'learning how to learn' at a level beyond instrumental techniques, or procedural frameworks, or even theories. What they develop is a sound basis for their continued self-development – a competence particularly important, given the flux and challenges which they will face in the next decade.

In our experience managers who attend Action Learning programmes are never initially aware of the likely effect such a process will have on their personal development and attitude to management, but in most cases the effect is likely to be profound.

REFERENCES

1 Hawrylyshyn, B. (1979) 'Management Education, a conceptual framework' in *Management Education in the 1980's*, New York: American Management Association, pp. 85–99.
2 Burgoyne, J. and Stuart, R. (1976) The nature, use and acquisition of managerial skills and other attributes', *Personnel Review*, 5(4) pp. 19–29.
3 Davies, J. and Easterby-Smith, M. P. V. (1984) 'Learning and developing from managerial work experiences', *Journal of Management Studies*, 21(2), 169–98.
4 Stuart, R. (1983) 'Training and development: a natural everyday activity', *Management Education and Development*, 14(3).
5 Kolb, D. A. (1984) *Experiential Learning*, Englewood Cliffs, NJ: Prentice-Hall.
6 Holman, D., Pavlica, K. and Thorpe, R. (1996) 'Rethinking Kolb's theory of experiential learning

in management education: the contribution of social constructionism and activity theory', *Management Learning*, **27**(4), 489–504.

7 Shotter, J. (1994) *Conversational Realities: Constructing Life Through Language: Inquiries Through Social Construction*, London: Sage.

8 Wieck, K. E. (1979) *The Social Psychology of Organising*, 2nd edn, Reading, MA: Addison-Wesley.

9 Schein, E. (1980) *Organisational Psychology, Englewood Cliffs*; NJ: Prentice-Hall.

10 Lewin, K. (1952) '*Group decision and social change*' in Swanson, G. E., Hartley, E. L. and Newcomb, T. N. (eds), *Readings in Social Psychology*, New York: Holt.

11 Gibb, S. (1994) 'Inside corporate mentoring schemes: the development of a conceptual framework', *Personnel Review*, **23**(3) 47–60.

12 Revans, R. (1971) *Developing Effective Managers*, New York: Appleton Century Crofts.

14 Doctors as Managers

Tony Winkless

Within the National Health Service in Yorkshire there has been a long history of interest from doctors in exploring the nature and implications of management dating from the 'Griffith's Report'[1] of the early 1980s. This report sparked a series of reforms radically changing the nature of management in the NHS. In consequence, the doctor's role in the management of the complex and expensive resources of our health service has become increasingly important.

The NHS's training services had responded to this need by mounting a series of courses for senior registrars and consultants, largely based on the traditional format of lecture, discussion and management exercises. These had been attended by about 300 doctors. Arising from these programmes many of the doctors expressed a wish for further opportunities to examine the managerial changes taking place. They had also talked to colleagues with similar interests and encouraged them to sample what was on offer. This is an account of two Action Learning programmes designed to meet these needs.

It is important to bear in mind that, due to the nature of this evolution of interest, the doctors involved here were very likely to have been (and maybe still are) atypical of the majority of their colleagues in wishing to attend a management programme. And, although there was undoubtedly some degree of peer pressure, doctors of consultant status in particular have the freedom to choose whether to attend or not. It should also be appreciated that some of the doctors who attended the programmes were doing so in the face of criticism, and sometimes scorn, from their colleagues, who were suspicious of the motives of the organizers during these times of reform in the NHS.

Why then the interest? Participants were asked this question at the beginning of the programmes. One response from a senior consultant provides a good summary (it was subsequently labelled as 'The Manifesto' in the group):

- The NHS is promoting management training – the doctors are not.
- Doctors are probably the best people to manage clinical services.
- If doctors don't change, there will be increasing tension.

- Doctors are not an entirely happy group (the major discussion topic is retirement).
- To maintain the status of the profession.
- To help doctors in their fear of change.
- An opportunity to improve staff relationships, for example, nurses.
- No administrators now, therefore no scapegoat left?

ACTION LEARNING FOR DOCTORS

Two case studies are included here. The first is concerned with a group of newly appointed consultants. For hospital doctors, 'getting a job' means securing a consultant appointment. This is normally achieved in their mid-30s, and until this time doctors are considered to be in training. Only exceptionally do consultants move to other posts or to other hospitals. The second case concerns a group of established consultants, mostly of senior status in the profession.

Action Learning seemed to be an ideal approach to meet the needs of these doctors: an approach that would provide the flexibility needed to allow the participants to explore and experiment in a changing and undefined world of diversity and uncertainty. Revans had in fact pointed this way forward over 30 years before, and it is worth noting his observations which bear an uncanny similarity to many of the current issues in the NHS.

> How to run a hospital – indeed, how to run the National Health Service, or even how to run anything today in Britain – seems to have become of major concern. . . . The Hospital Internal Communication Project seems to suggest that there may be virtue in seeking escape from our grosser torments by Action Learning, rather than by the external advice of academic theorists or commercial consultants.
>
> . . . by working together, those who have to run complex organisms like hospitals, learning with and from each other as they go along, may achieve their ostensible goals more economically than hospitals which pursue more traditional and authoritarian policies.[2]

Since the consultants were being invited to join programmes which were based on a different design from that previously experienced during 'management courses' it was considered essential to make clear the nature of the programmes offered. Introductory sessions were mounted in both cases and the following description given for Action Learning:

1. Participants learn most effectively from tackling problems and generating meaningful activities from their lives and their work. In this respect, an important distinguishing feature is that the participants choose what they wish to work on, not the tutor.

2. All members of an Action Learning group are assumed to have the potential by way of experience, knowledge and skills to assist each other in their problem solving and development. That is, 'experts' are not routinely required.
3. The tutor's role is mainly one of facilitator, helping the programme run effectively, particularly in influencing the way participants contribute and relate to each other.

CASE 1   THE NEWLY APPOINTED CONSULTANTS

This programme evolved from one of the introductory management courses run for newly appointed consultants. At the end of this three-day course the participants (around 16) were invited to participate in an experimental Action Learning group. Eight consultants of the original group decided to join. The contract agreed with the participants was that the group would meet on four occasions, with a final meeting to evaluate collectively the content and outcomes. The meetings were to be arranged at about six-weekly intervals, between the hours of 3pm and 9pm. (In the event a further meeting was arranged at the participants' request.) The following is an account of the content and the evaluation outcomes of these meetings.

My previous experience of running Action Learning groups for a range of people (for example, NHS managers, unemployed executives, personnel practitioners) strongly suggested the need for an initial integrating event where participants could be helped to get to know each other, to share each others' concerns and needs, and to practise and test their skills of listening and confrontation. This latter aspect is particularly important since it profits no one in an Action Learning group if there is poor listening and feedback. Accordingly, the first part of our initial meeting was devoted to these aspects (a somewhat longer session would have been needed if the participants had not already known each other from the earlier programme).

The format for all later parts of the programme was the same, in that participants first listed the issues they wished to work on, followed by each individual taking turn in presenting and receiving ideas, challenge and feedback on their specific issue. These issues varied in nature and complexity, some being helped or solved quite quickly, while others were more intractable (a problem rather than a puzzle as Revans suggests) and spanned the life of the project. What was particularly striking was the openness and readiness the participants gave to addressing the issues raised during these meetings, a characteristic not always found in their managerial colleagues in similar circumstances. A summary of the types of issues which they addressed, collated under four main headings, is as follows:

1. SELF-MANAGEMENT/DEVELOPMENT

- coping with feelings of being threatened/isolated
- developing and practising assertiveness
- building self-confidence in dealing with management and colleagues
- reducing 'Type A' (briefly, susceptibility to heart-related diseases)[3] pressures from the working environment

2. COLLEAGUE RELATIONSHIPS

- introducing change in the face of opposition
- separating friendships from professional relationships
- negotiating in and between committees
- negotiating teaching sessions
- negotiating workload commitment
- managing approaches to research

3. MANAGEMENT RELATIONSHIPS

- managing the political and economic environment
- clarifying the roles of doctors *vis-à-vis* managers
- challenging a perceived undemocratic management decision
- negotiating the content of a job description
- role clarification in hospital reorganization

4. 'SMALL m' MANAGEMENT

- 'time and motion' study in clinic
- dealing with low staff morale
- balancing work priorities
- developing a working strategy
- managing the clinical and support team
- bed utilization and numbers
- apportionment of study leave
- design of wards

While this typology of learning needs, constructed on the basis of participants' declared issues, may be reasonably representative of newly appointed consultants, it should not be taken as a prescription for any standardized programme. Such an approach would run entirely counter to the philosophy of Action Learning, whereby participants generate their own agendas.

It may seem surprising that no clinical issues were raised. This, of course, might have been because the programme was seen as part of a 'management course' and alternative forums were available for discussing clinical issues. On the other hand, it might have been because, as more than one participant put it, 'Clinical work is the easy part of it.'

The term 'small m' management evolved in the group particularly to help the consultants distinguish between what they customarily viewed as 'big M' management (for example, Chief Executives, Finance Directors, Operations Managers) and those aspects of their job which although managerial in nature, were not normally described as such by those practising them. A clear exception to this distinction, however, may be found among those doctors who are responsible for large service functions such as radiology – a 'big M' responsibility by most standards. Perhaps, too, those interested in the practice of 'big M' management might discern some interesting similarities in all four of the areas given above with many of the models of management practice. In answer then to the often-raised question 'Do doctors have managerial responsibilities?', the simple answer is 'yes' – it is an inescapable fact.

What then about the outcomes and benefits of this programme as seen by the participants? First, participants were asked in the evaluation stage (a group-designed event) whether any changes had been made in the work place which could be attributed to the programme. The responses reflected the list of issues given above.

The self-management/development aspects were relatively highly represented in the area of developing increased levels of assertiveness; for example:

More assertive and looking at 'lateral' ways of achieving my aims
Self-assertion – reasons for lack of it were tackled successfully

Linked with this was the area of colleague relationships which was clearly an important issue for some participants, particularly in learning how to deal with more senior consultant colleagues; for example:

I have relaxed more, I realize others share my problems, and [I] find it easier to talk with more senior consultant colleagues.

The area of job management relationships was highlighted most frequently, with a variety of outcomes; for example:

177

> Much clearer contact with my managers, leading to a useful working relationship . . . I now actively seek them out . . .

> More vocal in my complaints to management
> More aware of the way managers want to deal with consultants
> Perhaps a more acute observation of the system and some insights into those within it. Hopefully an increasingly sophisticated view of how mechanisms are/can be manipulated

And finally, two participants referred to their 'small m' outcomes:

> Instituted a quality control study in Outpatient Clinic
> Taken on new responsibilities in controlling my team

The nature and usefulness of the Action Learning approach to this group of consultants were examined in the evaluation process by asking them whether there were any benefits from the programme that they had not envisaged. Their responses highlighted the learning community aspects of Action Learning; for example:

> Enjoyment of working with others and commonality of problems leading to increasing confidence in the work situation
> Being able to talk about difficulties and trust the participants to be neutral in their attitudes
> Learning from the difficulties and responses made by other consultants in the group. Realizing that we all have similar problems

Other comments focused on the problem-solving aspects:

> I gained more benefits than I had expected, that is, an analytical approach to problem solving
> I have learned to be more analytical of the motives of others

Action Learning groups vary in their length and in the frequency of meetings, and participants were accordingly asked for their thoughts for any future programmes. The popular view was that five to six meetings at a frequency of about six weeks was about right.

Perhaps most informative (and gratifying for the organizers), in response to the question 'If you knew at the beginning what you know now, would you still have joined the programme?', the unanimous response from these newly appointed consultants was 'Yes'. Linked with this were comments reporting more favourable responses to this form of training compared to the conventional, externally set repertoire of subjects experienced elsewhere in their careers.

178

CASE 2 THE ESTABLISHED CONSULTANTS

This second case study concerns a rather more ambitious programme, the fundamental aim of which was to provide a group of 18 established consultants with the necessary skills and experiences to carry out management training for their junior staff (senior registrars, registrars and house officers). In addition, the programme's objectives stressed the opportunities to explore both personal and more general managerial issues. As with the first case study Action Learning was at the core of the design.

In this case, though, two residential 'start-up' workshops, each of three days duration, were provided – one as an introduction to management (and getting started period), the second as an introduction to training methods and techniques. There followed six one-day Action Learning sessions at monthly intervals (three groups of six participants plus a facilitator). At each session during the first half of the day the participants worked on issues arising from their training project activities in their hospitals. In the afternoons there were group-designed sessions involving external experts who were directed and chosen by the participants. The issues raised during the Action Learning meetings and the subjects chosen for the afternoon session of the programme included the following:

- evaluation of training
- presentation methods
- assertiveness
- relaxation techniques
- programme design
- are doctors normal people?
- inter-personal skills
- persuasion
- time management
- career planning
- sharing progress reports
- trying out ideas on each other
- managing the department
- understanding the strategic and tactical issues
- personal presentation
- making deals with managers

These items were collected via facilitators' keynote recordings during Action Learning sets, and also by participants in their group-designed evaluation questionnaire and in their free account descriptions of their 'journeys' over the six months.

179

As with the newly appointed consultants, what emerged during the programme was a wide diversity of needs and gains from the programme. Again there is a similar pattern of issues. As illustrated below, the opportunities provided (a) to work on issues of personal development and (b) to explore roles outside the conventional consultant role were clearly valued (although these aspects were not envisaged as being the prime purpose of the programme). Greater diversity may be explained partly by reference to those participants who did not see their role (or their use of the programme) as to do with delivering management education and development (MED), and partly to do with the prevailing lack of clarity about the practice, nature and organizational place of the MED role for consultant staff. This is perhaps not surprising in view of the pioneering nature of the role.

In order to illustrate these points, extracts from the 'journey accounts' written by each participant at the end of the programme are given below. They are necessarily selective, but an attempt has been made to give a fair indication of outcomes. At a summary level they may broadly be classified as to do with the following issues:

1. An interest in management as an activity which is seen as an intrinsic part of the consultant's job ('big M' or 'little m').
2. An interest in relating the consultant role to that of management, and understanding the processes and practices involved.
3. An interest in training junior staff and/or peers in management skills, methods and techniques (it should be noted that the programme's objectives related to 'junior staff' as the target population).
4. An interest in personal development.

It is also worth noting that this group raised more strategic issues, perhaps reflecting their more senior status; for example:

I have run seven workshops for staff at my hospital and have seen all 16 members of the junior medical staff for discussions of progress/problems/training needs. . . . In a general way I don't think that the achievements of the programme can be overestimated. . . . I have personally encouraged and assisted about 30 doctors to develop their own management skills . . . we now have a small section on management topics in the library . . . members of staff frequently discuss their own further training, potential initiatives and problems with me on a regular basis.

The course gave me time to focus on the needs of junior doctors both in my department and the NHS generally . . . [to recognize] the importance of communication and workforce . . . the insights gained have helped me in my work as director and as consultant member of our hospital management group. . . . I hope to have the opportunity of passing on present skills to trainees and developing my own further . . . have had preliminary conversation about setting up some sort of management training for medical practitioners along these lines.

So against the advice of the Ivory Tower shouters, Red Riding Hood eventually met the Big Bad Wolf. Actually, other Red Riding Hoods had already told her that the Big Wolf was only as bad as you thought he was. . . . More than the little things Red Riding Hood learned, and they were many, she became more and more convinced to survive in the Forest where the Big Wolf ruled she had to know his ways [a reference to the management regime].

The programme was altogether helpful because it brought me to regard my project as a true and central part of my working life rather than a peripheral and extra one . . . it has been a frustrating, exhilarating, time consuming, educative experience for me. The project has got off the ground well, but it has taken a great deal of time and effort and continues to do so.

The main benefit I derived was through the Action Learning sets where I was able to obtain a lot of support completely unavailable elsewhere . . . some of the best advice was that I should stop 'owning' my entire project entirely on my own . . . with the help that I received we now have a firm programme for pursuing the issues of consultants in management. . . . I think we have obtained the best possible structure for any solution to emerge.

I agree 'the best answers' for me 'are within' and since I am usually able to find within the resources I need, I should be able to manage. Should needs arise not within me I feel I would know where to seek.

My project was targeted at my consultant colleagues rather than junior staff . . . [as] the group I most wished to influence . . . unexpected 'spin offs' from involvement in management training have led to a recognition of my role in training doctors in my unit . . . [and] an invitation to join a multi-disciplinary management development forum. . . . Without this course I should not be doing what I am doing in the management field now, and my hospital unit and my life would have been the poorer.

Now I am involved in the management think-tank looking at area-wide problems. I am close to the point of deciding whether to come off the fence and move further into management. . . . I would like to spend more time in management.

I am more aware of where the problems lie. . . . I am much more aware now that I can control my time . . . very difficult issues have been raised and aired . . . hearing the achievement of others gave me a clearer idea of where I should go.

SOME QUALIFYING THOUGHTS

In case it is thought that these programmes always ran smoothly and to the total satisfaction of all participants at all times, some indicators of the less satisfactory issues are necessary.

One participant referred to an initial 'destructive tendency' in testing out his work on self-assertion, another to being more aware of the frustrations of the work situation, while a third guardedly reported 'none which are as yet apparent'.

Another criticism concerned the lack of 'gel' in one of the Action Learning groups of the second programme, which was linked to the rotating-facilitator approach employed (the three facilitators shared the role across the three groups). With large programmes which form more than one Action Learning group the decision has to be made about how best to carry out the facilitator role. There are pros and cons for having the same person for each group, and for rotating the role. The former has the advantage of stability and greater knowledge of individual and group processes; the latter offers the possibility of a different style and the value of the 'naïve question'.

Some criticisms were made of colleagues who did not make regular appearances. Action Learning groups work best with five to seven people who are committed to attendance and involvement. The loss of a couple of people can be very disruptive.

Four participants expressed the view that the second programme lacked purpose and cohesiveness towards the end, and that a residential ending would have been useful. This point has been made on similar programmes where participants value the opportunity to bring the programme to a graceful end: residential events seem to help in this, particularly when the start-up is residential.

One participant referred to the lack of 'grass roots experience of the training staff' which, it was felt, handicapped them in their understanding and potential helpfulness in the realities of the consultant role and the demands of general management. This point is sometimes made by participants in Action Learning groups, although the facilitator role should not need to include content knowledge – indeed it could be argued that it is a distinct disadvantage to have such knowledge.

Some participants raised initial concerns and feelings of guilt over the self-indulgent use of their duties in the hospital. For example:

> Could I afford the time to attend? . . . Contrast between the loose free-flowing structure of the group with the hard realities of my management job, was it worth going on if I wasn't sure where we were going . . . in the end it was worth it.

THE ATTRACTION AND APPROPRIATENESS OF ACTION LEARNING FOR DOCTORS

What seems very clear from these accounts was the diversity of issues raised. No strictures were placed on the participants to confine themselves to the subject of managerial issues, yet this was perhaps not surprisingly the dominant theme. However, two further themes may also be discerned. One concerns issues relating to self-development, and this was explicitly referred to by over half the participants; for example: ' . . . recognizing the importance to identify action plans for personal needs and their development' . . . 'I am much more able to say "no, that is not for me" '; 'I have learned to be a better listener . . . '; ' . . . also helping to develop and grow as a person'; and ' . . . it has widened my horizons with regard to personal development'.

The other, and linked, theme concerned the attraction of Action Learning. All participants reported a favourable reaction to the programmes, perhaps because of the flexibility of the Action Learning approach which was specifically given favourable reports by half the respondents in their accounts. Key words used were 'addictiveness', 'supportive network', 'safety', 'listening and being listened to', 'stress reducing', 'respecting colleagues', 'group cohesion', 'trust', 'reassurance', 'kinship', and 'confidence'. Several participants referred to a sense of surprise that involvement with their group should prove so beneficial.

THE LONELINESS OF THE LONG DISTANCE DOCTOR?

A question remains: why did this form of learning design seem to be attractive to these doctors, who were perhaps atypical of the doctor 'body corporate' in volunteering to attend a course on management? They were atypical, too, in attending a management course designed in a way deviant from the norm of pre-set structured seminars.

Has it to do with the very rigid and strict training regime for doctors? This starts at around the age of 16 with a requirement for excellence in science subjects, followed by around 20 years of training, examinations and selection procedures with the final qualifying acceptance by peers, seniors and self not appearing until the mid-30s. The final struggle for appointment is won at the consultant grade – 'the light at the end of the tunnel', as more than one participant put it.

During this lengthy period, few opportunities for development of the self, as opposed to development of the role, are formally encouraged (or thought to be acceptable behaviour). Negative feedback rules supreme. Quitting the profession is frowned upon and a scary proposition. Perhaps as a consultant the doctor now has the legitimate basis to exercise personal power and autonomy, and to express awareness of and address some of these unfulfilled issues? A time which also coincides with a new and relatively unfettered freedom to explore new directions, both clinical and non-clinical. These are speculative thoughts, but they are also reinforced by my experience of over 300 personal counselling sessions with doctors, following (and stimulated by) personality questionnaire feedback.[4] The personal issues dominate with a force distinctly different from other occupational groups in my experience.

The following issues are typical:

I would like to do something else now, but I'm only trained for medicine

How do I assert myself in a functional/ helpful way?

They (the patients) want me to pop them a pill, but I know this is not the answer

How do I reconcile the pressures of my job with the rest of my world?

I'm looking forward to early retirement

How can I express my sensitivity with a clinic of 20 patients to get through?

If only someone had told me when I was doing 'A' levels that medicine was like this

It is salutary to note that, at the time programmes of this form became available to doctors following the 'Griffith's Report', Zigmund (a doctor) quoted Jonathan Swift in a revealing piece concerning the relative higher levels of psychological morbidity, suicide and marital breakdowns in the caring professions:

The stoical scheme of supplying our wants by lopping off our desires is like cutting off our feet, when we want shoes.[5]

Perhaps the hyper-expansionist programmes typical of this time, might just allow some space for the participants to express their full needs. At the very least, the accountant's bill for early retirement might reduce in size.

REFERENCES

1 Griffiths, R. (1983) *NHS Management Enquiry*, Letter to Secretary of State for Social Services, October.
2 Revans, R. (1982) 'Action Learning takes a health cure', in *The Origins and Growth of Action Learning*, Bronley: Chartwell-Bratt.
3 Friedman, M. and Rosenman, R. H. (1959) 'Association of specific overt behaviour patterns with blood and cardiovascular findings', *Journal of the American Medical Association*, **169**, 96–106.
4 Winkless, T. 'Personality characteristics: medical consultants and NHS general managers', in Brown, J. and Sanderson, D. (eds) (1997) *Progress in Medical Management*, London: Churchill Livingstone, September.
5 Zigmund, D. (1984) 'Physician heal thyself: the paradox of the wounded healer', *British Journal of Holistic Medicine*, **1**, 63–71.

15 Network Learning in an Austrian Hospital

Otmar Donnenberg

This chapter describes an effort to develop a hospital as a learning organization. The approach is based on Revans' principles of Action Learning. Action Learning is understood as learning to learn from real-life experiences within special settings of learning companions. In the management development programme for an Austrian hospital, described here, special attention has been given to thinking in terms of networks and in using the possibilities of network learning. Network learning appears to be an approach which is congruent with current interests in connectivity.

THE HOSPITAL

In 1994 the corrupt practices of top management, some professionals and staff officers of the local city hospital became known to the public. The hospital is part of the city administration and city politicians and top officials are responsible for what happens there. They set out to establish a clear direction and mission for the city administration and the hospital; internal and external control procedures were rigorously applied and a new top management was installed.

The hospital has 1000 beds and employs about 2000 people, 120 of whom perform managing tasks with responsibility for personnel. Schools for nursing and paramedical professions are part of the organizational complex which faces new financial arrangements in the near future, with a heavy impact on its policy and working structure. As the hospital is one of the many departments of the city administration, this greatly reduces the power of the hospital management at a time when competition between hospitals is increasing, and a strengthening of identity is needed in the face of numerous changes in the environment of the hospital.

THE NEEDS AND THE OBJECTIVES

A survey conducted among all employees reveals:

- very severe communication blocks between administration, doctors and nurses;
- 'forgotten groups' in the field of therapy and medical technical personnel;
- much anonymity and isolation, little identification with the organization as a whole;
- fighting and blaming as predominant ways of conflict handling;
- overcentralization and lack of transparency; seemingly endless decision processes, and frustration about what is felt as a very high degree of formality;
- dissatisfaction and rudeness among doctors and low discipline of some doctors participating in management;
- complaints about insufficient awareness of the city administration for the peculiarities of the hospital organization with unclarified rights and duties;
- strikingly less possibilities for operational personnel to attend training and seminars;
- not enough support from superiors with too little or no feedback in regard of actions and initiatives;
- ... but also: a lot of vitality and many proposals for improvements;
- a number of remarks were made about the relationship with patients: deficiencies in patient friendliness and also concerns about the increasing demands of patients and the ever growing complexity of patient treatments.

The new top management formulated a series of objectives as a basis for further personnel and organization development:

- awareness of the situation of the patient;
- satisfaction and sustained identification of personnel;
- effectively guided cost management;
- ongoing medical innovations;
- thorough communication.

They stated that a management development programme was to take place and indicated criteria for determining the character and the results of the programme:

- new knowledge must be work-related;
- promotion of interprofessional and interdisciplinary cooperation;
- contributing to the necessary organizational changes now and in the future;
- stimulating towards quality management.

They themselves participated in an intensive higher management course and made international contacts for the exchange of experiences. Their commitment

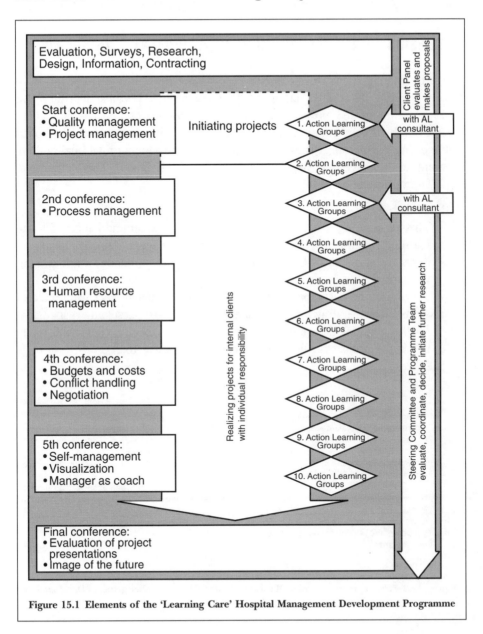

Figure 15.1 Elements of the 'Learning Care' Hospital Management Development Programme

to the necessary learning processes within the organization was great and they promoted the mood of 'We want to develop and perform on a high level with integrity', which existed among many of the employees, having been shown the good example.

THE DESIGN OF THE MANAGEMENT DEVELOPMENT PROGRAMME

The MD (Management Development)-programme described was chosen from several tenders. It appears attractive to management because learning and working are integrated; projects bringing about concrete and necessary change are 'part of the game', multiprofessional learning in self-directed learning groups and learning partnerships is heavily emphasized; introducing total quality management and management development are intimately linked. The elements of the MD-programme are (see Figure 15.1):

1. The project
   This is central as it serves as the vehicle and common focus for the learning of the participants, their project clients (mostly heads of departments) and their personal sponsors (mostly high-ranking managers).

   Programme participants choose the topic of their project from a list of strategic issues drawn up by management and are personally responsible for the negotiated results. Only projects with a specific client who really needs the project results are accepted (See Figure 15.2)

Project topics

- Patient-oriented layout of the department
- Optimalization of patient routing
- Patient transport within the hospital
- Internal Bulletin
- Introduction for doctors in training
- Adaptations of buildings for handicapped persons
- Nursing documentation
- Primary nursing
- Complication conferences
- Mission of the nursing school, of specific departments

- Employee satisfaction survey
- Remobilization of older patients
- Organization of day-care
- Telephone behaviours
- Manual for administrative procedures
- Waste reduction
- Communication between pharmacy and
- departments
- Organizational consequences of the new financial arrangements
- etc.

Figure 15.2 Project topics in the 'Learning Care' Hospital Management Development Programme

---

2. The conferences
   For each cohort of 22 participants there are six conferences of $2^1/_2$ days

spread over one year. They provide in a very compact form knowledge and skills geared to the needs and explicit wishes of the participants.

3. The Action Learning groups

Bring together up to six participants for 10 whole days' meetings between the first and the final conference. The group members coach each other as to the evalution and planning of their project activities. The groups practise systematically to manage their own learning processes.

4. Bilateral talks between the participants and their project clients and their personal sponsors

The participants and the project-clients negotiate about the assignment and monitor regularly the progress made. Every participant is entitled to choose a personal sponsor, this being a high-ranking manager who takes responsibility for helping the participant with 'helicopter views' and political support. They also meet regularly. Always both parties are expected to learn from the current experiences and to initiate improvements.

5. The steering committee

Top management, delegates from the workers' council, from the professional groups and the city government, as well as the quality manager and the human resource officer are members of the steering committee. They evaluate the course of the 3-year programme, which has now involved almost 70 participants. Decisions are made by top management.

6. Research and future search

During the programme some of the projects deal with surveys concerning specific topics (e.g. patient satisfaction regarding one of the departments). To a limited extent, data concerning certain indicators (e.g. absenteeism) are collected for the purposes of monitoring. Each time a group of 22 participants rounds up its programme activities they meet to look ahead, to describe scenarios and to develop options for the future.

BASIC ASSUMPTIONS OF THE APPROACH

There are several reasons why the concept of the learning network appears to be useful for MD-activities. Some of the reasons are presented below in the form of propositions.

1. INDIVIDUALISTIC LEARNING IS DETRIMENTAL TO CONNECTIVITY

Within the fragmented organization of a hospital with its many subcultures there is a great need for integrating the many efforts to the advantage of the patients.

189

Programme design. The group of participants consists – evenly distributed – of people from the field of nursing, medicine, medical technique and administration. In the learning groups members experience very intensively how rewarding it is to be able to gain admittance to the realms of other disciplines and units. From their sponsors the participants learn 'the great picture' (as they expressed it) which managers need in order to set priorities and make long-term decisions. The regular structured meetings with the client confront both the client and the project manager (the participant) with possibilities and limitations of the other party, and awaken the necessity to keep in touch with each other because much is changing while under way and what was defined at the beginning of the project has to be reconsidered again and again.

2. ATTITUDE OF POSITIVE INTEREST AND SOCIAL 'SAFETY-NET' ARRANGEMENTS ARE ESSENTIAL CONDITIONS FOR STIMULATING ENTREPRENEURAL QUALITIES OF LEARNERS

Without safety, warmth and recognition it is difficult for the learner to open up for new, unusual behaviours. Project managers by definition are faced with a lot of risks because they operate outside standard practices and put forward new proposals which can arouse anger and resistance from people who are afraid that their interests are at stake.

Programme design. The culture of the learning groups stimulates the participants to leave the zone of comfort to confront feedback and unusual questions. Risk-reduction is provided in a specific way by the personal sponsors and project clients of the participants and the steering committee in a general way.

3. PERSONAL ARTICULATION OF NEEDS BY CLIENTS AND ACTIVE CREATION OF SOCIAL SPACE BY SPONSORS ENCOURAGE LEARNERS TO TAKE RESPONSIBILITY

Tension is aroused by the discrepancy between the situation as it is experienced and the improvement as it is envisaged. People with positive energies who perceive the needs of the client in face-to-face contact and realize that there is a social space to engage in are able to embrace this tension as an intensive learning opportunity.

Programme design. The programme provides possibilities for participants to take initiatives and they can win substantial rewards for constructive actions: they enjoy learning facilities, have the possibility of making presentations, not only internally but also externally, are able to enlarge their personal network, become known, etc.

4. ORGANIZATIONAL STRUCTURES ENSURE THAT THE ONGOING CONCERN IS MAINTAINED, NETWORK RELATIONSHIPS ENABLE ACTORS TO UNDERTAKE UNUSUAL AND UNACQUAINTED INITIATIVES

A social network can be characterized as a system of transactions between persons, which are linked to each other on a voluntary and egalitarian basis with a limited amount of formality, offering each other a great spectrum of possibilities, which actors can make use of in direct contacts. An organization faced with a number of problems, for which there are no ready solutions, can create fewer limitations by tradition and habit, and more space for unusual dealings if a substantial number of the employees have learnt, not only to maintain the going concern in an organized way but also, how to enlarge and enrich networks.

Programme design. The programme invites those involved to active role-negotiations in many ways and promotes open solicitation for projects.

5. OFTEN QUALITY MANAGEMENT IS REALIZED IN THE STYLE AND STRUCTURE OF THE DIFFERENTIATION PHASE (BUREAUCRATIC MODE); MEASURES OF QUALITY MANAGEMENT DESIGNED ACCORDING TO PRINCIPLES OF LEARNING NETWORKS ARE CONGRUENT WITH THE STYLE AND STRUCTURE OF THE INTEGRATION AND ASSOCIATION PHASE (MODE OF HOLISTIC PERSONAL INTERACTIONS)

'Those who do not remember the past are condemned to relive it'. This reminder serves change-managers well: if they make a diagnosis of the developmental stage their organization is at and take account of the crises it is likely to face in passing from one developmental phase to another they are likely to be much better in choosing adequate interventions and an adequate style of intervening. They are less tempted to 'do more of the same' in order to solve the problem. Nowadays quality management is still very much – sometimes in an absurd way (the 'ISO-craziness'!) – tuned to the spirit of the differentiation phase of organizations. The differentiation phase is a stage of development which an organization gets into if it successfully survives the pioneer stage. The dominant features of the differentiation phase are standardization, automation and specialization. Accordingly, measures of quality assurance are sharply defined by specialists and elaborated in many procedures. Today many organizations are confronted with the shortcomings of the bureaucratic way of organizing and have integrated many aspects (client-centredness, multi-professional teams, programme management, etc.) and connected with each other in a very flexible way (virtual organization, strategic alliances, lean enterprise). The 'connecting stage' will be trapped very quickly in super-bureaucratic pitfalls if it is not integrated into the core business processes.

Programme design. The MD programme offers a bedding for 'life-oriented' quality assurance.

RESULTS OF THE MANAGEMENT DEVELOPMENT PROGRAMME

The objectives of the MD-programme were:

1. The development and the realization of solutions which are very much needed to overcome problems.
2. Increase in personal competence and a wider range of attitudes which are necessary to cope with future demands.
3. The emergence of new rules of cooperation and of behavioural patterns promoting a more productive learning climate ('culture of a learning organization').

The first results of the projects are seen at the presentations the participants deliver to their clients, mostly with their personal sponsors and with a couple of interested colleagues also present. A second participant also takes part for the purposes of observation: How does the satisfaction of the client with the results of the project manifest itself? How is the result delivered? What comes out of the discussion about the learning results of the participant – and his or her sponsor and clients – which they gathered during the realization of the project? Both participants then report the outcomes of this presentation at the final conference of the programme. Finally, the project results and learning results are shared with an external audience at a symposium organized by the hospital.

Increases in personal competence and the broadening of attitudes showed up in the first year of the programme:

- Self-organization of learning groups caught on well. After half a year of practice 'veteran' learning sets invited members of sets which had started later to share findings of their own about 'how to craft learning group sessions'.
- Top management returned from meetings with colleagues from other hospitals in Austria and southern Germany reporting that they encountered quite a lot of interest in the approach. It encouraged them to keep on going in their difficult task to increase morale in the hospital.
- The number of positive recordings in the media about developments in the hospital also contributed to the learning commitments. Deliberately a project about periodically gaining feedback from the patients was included

by hospital management in the list of programme projects in order to strengthen patient orientation.

- 'Questioning' is becoming a habit for me' said one of the participating nurses in a review of a learning group session.
- 'I realize that participants in the programme start looking at the broader context and think less fragmentarily' one of the medical department heads told his colleagues in a workshop for those who gave assignments to project-managers.
- 'We don't get lost so often in our discussions: The clarified objectives keep us on track' remarked one of the participating head nurses to a member of the steering committee of the MD-programme.
- 'A great number of issues which remained unresolved for a long time are effectively dealt with now thanks to project routines which we learned in this programme' (members of various sets).

Unwritten rules of the game and tacit convictions behind traditional behaviours are an ongoing concern of the participants. New rules which help bring about open communication and a new 'learning mood' are practised regularly in the learning sets and in the talks with sponsors and clients. Participants express progress in this field as follows:

- 'I now experience a lot of leeway – I had not expected we would gain so much liberty of action out of this programme' (head of purchasing department).
- 'The network relations which originate and develop in the sets and between members of sets which consult each other contribute a lot to conflict prevention' (medical head of one of the departments).
- 'It is a major task for our group of medical department heads to act as a kind of clearing house and to stimulate constructive discussions and patient orientation. We should do so on the basis of promoting consciousness of mission and goals and team development in our own departments' (medical head of one of the departments – not every one of his colleagues was enthusiastic about this statement).
- 'The "owner principle" ("owner of the meeting"; "owner of an agenda-item", "owner of an assignment") helps us to overcome diffuse and unclear arrangements which were customary in the field of organizational matters' (young medical doctor).
- 'I am looking forward to our colleagial consulting sessions where we coach each other; everytime I get glimpses of new worlds – the worlds of other departments and the working situations of colleagues from other professions' (an administrator).
- 'I am happy that I can get valid information now so quickly – the network

relations I got out of my own set and from other sets are a great help' (hospital technician).

NETWORK LEARNING

The various settings for interactive learning which the programme offers bring about organizational learning in a very concrete way. Participants experience that the 'learning organization' is not only an abstract notion and have practised to make it happen deliberately. In a couple of situations they have raised the question how patients and certain external stakeholders could also be included in this network of learning, and which conditions have to be created for doing so.

Part III
Questions of Practice

INTRODUCTION

There is only one way to get going with Action Learning and that is to go out and do it. Some of the best accounts in this book are written by people who are newly getting to grips with the idea, even trying Action Learning for the first time. Their learning enlivens their writing. However, even the most courageous of us can benefit from perhaps just a few words of sage advice. Here you will find plenty of that.

Part III starts with Alan Lawlor's chapter which has special personal value for it was he who introduced me to some of the magic of Action Learning in 1976. Amongst many other things he taught us Reg's three questions: 'Who knows (about the problem)?'; 'Who cares?' and 'Who can (do anything about the problem)?' David Casey has added a brief but powerful introduction to his two classic papers 'The Role of the Set Adviser' and 'The Shell of your Under-standing', surely some of the best writing on Action Learning by anyone.

Jean Lawrence's thoughts on how to keep 'Q' – the essence of Action Learning – alive in the face of the normalizing pressures of organization, also contains much wise advice. From the USA, Nancy Dixon, Larry Hales and Richard Baker discuss some of the difficulties within USA Human Resources people have with 'Q' and suggest how these can be overcome. Building on this Judy O'Neil's paper distinguishes set advising from the more common role of process consult-ancy with some interesting findings.

Finally two new chapters which redress some of the deficiencies in earlier editions of this book. Alan Mumford reminds us that the study of learning is a key part of Action Learning; he contributes some useful material here on how to bring the learning process to the surface for examination and improvement. Tom Bourner, Liz Beaty and Paul Frost have done us all a service by establishing their own Action Learning without the help of an external set adviser – something which Revans has frequently asserted as healthy and normal, but which is actually unusual. Their emphasis on the participant's – as opposed to the adviser's – skills is a genuine contribution to the development of Action Learning in practice.

16 The Components of Action Learning

Alan Lawlor

There is now a good deal of practical experience of Action Learning in its many forms. Moreover, there has been continual variation in its use, one programme benefiting from another – Action Learning has been learning about Action Learning. The purpose of this chapter is to describe the practical aspects of Action Learning and what is involved in actually running a programme.

MAIN PROGRAMME VARIANTS

Flexibility in programme design is endless but the following examples will give the reader some idea of how to choose the best model to suit their particular needs. All the programmes described are based upon the concept of combining the solution of real problems with individual/organizational development and each offers its own unique advantages. See Figure 16.1 for a model and Figure 16.2 for a description of programmes in output terms.

1. Part-time programmes. In these, participants continue with their own jobs while taking part in the programme. They are, therefore, cost-effective and enable people to learn as they work.
2. Full-time programmes. These are of the kind conducted by Revans in Belgium. They are obviously more expensive in terms of time and cost but also achieve more in individual development.
3. In-plant programmes. These have different advantages. They are a powerful medium for bringing about organizational change and though a higher cost per organization than external schemes, they are much lower per participant. On the other hand, external schemes inject fresh ideas into organizational thinking by bringing together people from very different backgrounds.
4. Combined schemes, which offer the advantages of the inplant and external programmes.

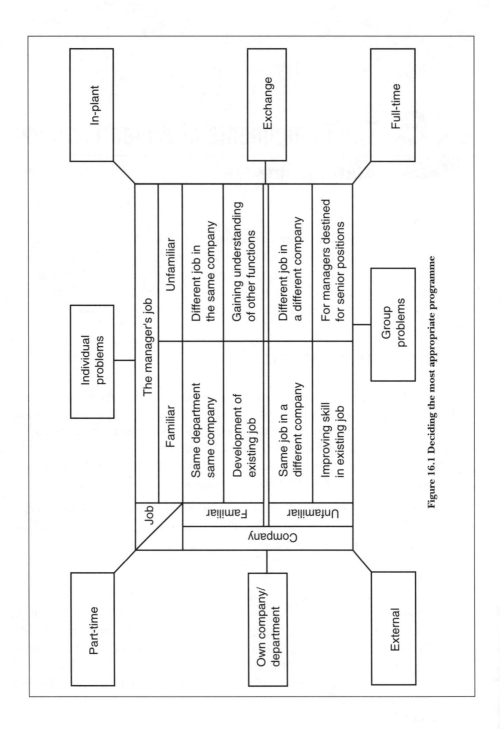

Figure 16.1 Deciding the most appropriate programme

The option chosen is obviously dependent on the needs to be met.

FULL-TIME OR PART-TIME?

By full-time is meant that fellows are released from their normal job to be engaged wholly on the Action Learning programme, whereas on part-time schemes the fellows continue to do their own jobs. The full-time approach is generally associated with the so called exchange scheme pioneered by Revans in Belgium.

Though extracting managers from their jobs for a period of six to twelve months and placing them in an unfamiliar organization is a powerful development tool it is an approach that forms a small percentage of Action Learning programmes. For this reason most of my attention will be directed to the part-time method. It clearly has many advantages including lower cost and the fact that the manager is not lost from the job. But there is another reason for adopting this 'learn as you work' approach. Managers are discovering that they can find the time to deal with their real problems and at the same time contend with the alligators that have been diverting their energies away from draining the swamp. Equally, they manage to attend set meetings where they critically discuss the interaction of their jobs with the problems they are trying to solve. In other words, work, problem solving and personal development all become part of one ongoing process; it is not a course which is separate and apart from work but a way of studying and learning from our day-to-day tasks. There is now little doubt that it is a cost effective method for developing managers and their organizations.

IN-PLANT OR EXTERNAL PROGRAMMES

In-plant schemes tend to focus mainly on organizational problem solving and development. They will generally involve larger numbers than external programmes, numbers of over 100 are common, consequently the programme has much more impact on the total environment. In fact the 'client group' actually take part in the Action Learning sets. In-plant schemes differ from Revans' original model in that the set focuses on one common problem. Set members are all volunteers and come from the same organization although not necessarily the same department. The client 'owns' the problem because it is part of his everyday line management responsibility. Set advisers are recruited from the middle management group and are trained to advise. In this way the whole management structure of the organization becomes an integral part of the

What options are available?	What will they do?	Expectations
1 Own job	1 Will develop the individual and improve performance in his current job	1 Individual development
2 Same job in a different place	2 Will broaden the individual	2 Will expect promotion
3 Different job in the same place	3 Will develop and broaden the individual	3 Will be looking for promotion and more general management
4 Different jobs in a different place	4 Very high level of personal development	4 MD or senior management within two years
5 Common problems tackled by a group	5 Will develop individuals, increase morale and commitment, and will develop the company itself	5 Individual and organizational development in tune with both groups of needs, organizationally very powerful

In-plant schemes have greater impact on the company and are far less costly per participant.

External programmes yield high individual development with a lower cost per company.

Figure 16.2 The effects of various programme options

problem solving process. In more recent programmes this involvement has been extended to include the shopfloor.

The in-plant approach also achieves another and more difficult objective sought after by managers and trainers, to create a learning environment that maintains itself. There are several examples of in-plant Action Learning in this book and indeed this is one of the fastest growing forms.

One example of the in-plant approach comes from Australia where Dr Roy Gilbert has introduced Action Learning as a way of running the Victorian State Housing Department. I said earlier that the aim of the part-time approach is to integrate work and learning into one process; however it is also possible for the whole organization to become involved – what Revans would describe as a learning community. If such conditions can be created programme length becomes irrelevant because learning is an ongoing process; a highly important aim when enterprises of all kinds are having to survive in a fast changing world.

The latest development has been to combine the advantages of in-plant and external schemes into one overall programme. Fellows on external sets get the benefit of the cross fertilization of ideas and at the same time help each other to launch their own internal schemes.

DESIGNING YOUR SCHEME

There are a number of issues to consider in designing your scheme:

1. How much time is needed?
2. What sort of preparation?
3. How big is an Action Learning set?
4. How often should the set meet?
5. Is the set adviser really necessary?
6. What is the role of the client?
7. How does learning occur?

I will now deal with these in turn.

TIME INVOLVEMENT

The first dozen or so part-time schemes were of a six month duration with set meetings about one half day per week. Throughout the time that these programmes were conducted we were continually questioning their design including their planned time. One important question if we are to be concerned with the productivity of Action Learning is 'can we achieve the same results in less than six months?' If we can then the part-time approach becomes even more cost-effective.

PREPARATION

Action Learning is based upon the simple and natural process of learning from doing. Once the right conditions are created it should become self-sustaining. However, there is still the task of getting things started. The following points are equally applicable whichever type of programme is chosen and experience has taught me that the preparation phase is crucial to success. It can be divided roughly into three parts:

(i) *Gaining organizational commitment and understanding*: this would include getting commitment from the sponsors (generally the senior manager who nominates the fellows on the programme) and the fellows themselves. They need to recognize that while significant benefits are possible equally it requires active participation by all concerned. At this stage consideration of the problem to be tackled is also necessary, emphasizing that they must be real here-and-now problems that already exist irrespective of the Action Learning programme. This kind of preparation can be obtained with a combination of visits to each organization plus one or two planning meetings attended by all of the sponsors and fellows. This stage is spread over about one to two months with a total time of approximately two days. The time spent on this kind of groundwork is well worthwhile, because of its effect on the Action Learning activity that it precedes.

(ii) *Introductory workshops*: Views vary, both in the length of seminars to start programmes and on their content. Moreover, we can also consider the other option of having no introduction and instead just start the Action Learning activity immediately after the 'getting commitment' stage. I have now experimented with the range of approaches from nothing at all to a two-and-a-half day residential workshop. As a general guide where a group of fellows, or at least some of them, have some understanding of the way people work effectively together as a team, then an introduction may not be so important, at least for the social skills aspect. In this case perhaps a one day meeting to explain the programme may be all that is necessary. But this kind of appreciation, in my experience, is not common, so some form of preparation is necessary for the group work that is to follow. This belief is perhaps supported by the often expressed view from fellows that it took them some six weeks to really get the open and frank climate which is essential for Action Learning. It is an insight that also gives us a clue to the length of programme – if we can reduce the six weeks perhaps we can reduce the programme.

Arising out of the above observations a team development workshop on a three day residential basis has now been developed which enables the fellows to gain a practical understanding of the interactive skills required for a group of people to solve problems. The main emphasis is on a simulated learning experience which involves real products or services and the employment of 'outside employees'. Through this approach the participants have to set up an organization, learn to work as a team and manage a group of 'employees' in very real conditions. During the workshop the first set meeting also takes place and the fellows arrange and conduct a meeting with their sponsors. Thus, at the end of the three days the fellows are more aware of their own influences on group processes and have a mature view of how to create and work in a climate of critical questioning.

(iii) The way problems are selected is important. It goes without saying that problems have to be genuine and in need of attention anyway. Everyone is wasting their time if the problem has been invented to put someone on the programme. Accepting this basic requirement, the following methods have been used to select problems.

1. Sponsors make the decision.
2. Jointly agreed by sponsor and fellow.
3. Obtained during introductory workshops.

Methods 2 and 3 support the principle of involvement and ownership which is essential to an effective Action Learning programme. The sorts of problem which can be tackled are:

Attitude change:	We need to change attitudes; to each other, to our work, our markets and the competition. In a fast changing world we must learn to adapt.
Business audits:	We need to know where we are now. Where do we want to be? What are the gaps in these two conditions? What are our values, attitudes, standards and beliefs? What are our strengths, weaknesses, opportunities and threats?
Product development:	What should we really be doing? How do we integrate work and development into one on-going process? How do we create an effective organization which can make profits?
Leadership/ management development:	Are our managers really providing effective leadership? Do they really own problems and their solutions? How can we motivate our people, persist with the solution of the real problems?

SET SIZE

How many fellows should comprise a set? Are there minimum and maximum set sizes? There are two factors which affect this decision. Firstly, the number of people necessary for effective social interaction and the necessary support to take place. Second, the time required to deal with the problems requiring attention. Experience suggests that a set of four is needed to meet the first requirement and that six is a maximum for the second. For instance, in a set of six, with six individual problems, where they meet one-half-day per week, on average the time per problem would be about half an hour. Consequently, any increase in set size beyond six will reduce the time to deal with problems. While for these reasons I have worked on the basis of sets of 4 to 5 fellows, innovations should be constantly in mind.

When Reg Revans and I visited India in 1979 to take part in the review stage of their third programme we were surprised and encouraged by their experimentation. The Calcutta group had only managed to get commitment from two companies and based upon my rough rule above this would have been insufficient to form a set. Instead we met a group of six very enthusiastic managers. The two fellows were busy senior line managers so to assist them in their investigations two young management trainees were assigned to them. In addition, a member of the client from each of the two companies attended set meetings. Hence what could have been a non-starter became a highly active set with the additional development benefits for the client and potential managers. Moreover, they had taken a further interesting step by running the first three months on a full-time basis for the fellows and the last three months part-time.

FREQUENCY OF MEETINGS

As a general rule sets should meet every one to two weeks for a duration of a half to one day each meeting. However, a better guide is the needs of the fellows and the progress of the problem solutions. It is unlikely that pressing problems can wait much more than 2 to 3 weeks before receiving some kind of attention. This point highlights the alligator/swamp dilemma; the set creates its own momentum of concentrating attention on the important issues and minimizes the distraction of the daily panic. But experience, as you would expect, has shown that problems do not want the same amount of treatment every week; sometimes it could be an hour and on other occasions only five minutes or no time at all. This blend of pressure and giving the time that is necessary is soon recognized by the set, perhaps with some guidance from the adviser.

An aspect of set effectiveness that cannot be emphasized too much is the importance of work between set meetings. If fellows do not get on with the investigation and implementation activities and therefore are unable to report progress, or even no progress, their meetings will soon become little more than discussion groups. If this happens momentum and commitment wane and the set will eventually disintegrate. This situation sometimes occurs when a fellow has an artificial problem or has no real willingness to learn. To prevent this the two previously mentioned prerequisites should be satisfied, that is prior commitment from sponsors and fellows; and selection of genuine problems.

Sponsors also play an indirect part in the frequency and quality of set meetings. As one sponsor said, 'fellows should be allocated one day per week to attend the Action Learning course!' Clearly though managers ought to be regarded as mature enough to make up their own minds if and when they go to set gatherings rather than be organized by the sponsor whose role is one of periodic interest in progress and support when it is needed.

A review at the halfway stage and the end of programmes, which necessitate a presentation to assembled fellows, sponsors and clients is another way of stimulating set activity and meeting regularity. While participants in Action Learning groups should plan and manage their own affairs, predetermined evaluation stages have the effect of motivating the principal people to get on with the inter-related tasks of problem solving and learning.

THE SET ADVISER ROLE

The set advisers are the mirrors which reflect the learning opportunities back to the participants. They question, confront, encourage and support. These are the facilitators who help the group know themselves, try out different approaches and become more aware of their own actions.

The continuity of meetings and how well those concerned help each other is especially enhanced by the set adviser. Their role is a combination of tea maker, project manager, scapegoat, process consultant and a motivator. Views vary on how important the adviser is to the success of a set. But except for a few managers who already have the social skills to make a group into a good problem solving team, experience shows that the set adviser is essential, at least for the first few weeks. This does not mean that organizations cannot provide their own advisers. Of course they can.

THE ROLE OF CLIENTS

I have already referred to clients and their importance to programmes. They can influence the development of fellows and if they desire the fellows can also help them to learn (what Reg Revans calls the social process of problem solving) and they can decide if the problem is to be resolved or stay as it is.

Furthermore, clients can be keepers of the status quo or catalysts for change. They also represent the political system, the coalition of power, which has to be motivated and worked through if any kind of change is to take place. In other words, the client, or 'structure d'acceuil' as it is called in Belgium, is a highly important part of change and learning. The problem in an Action Learning programme is how to get their continuing involvement and commitment. Though there is no simple answer to this question, experience has provided some guidelines. There are, in general, three means of involving the client:

1. The fellows, with the support of their set, seek out and try to persuade their client to solve the problem; over and over again, it is when the fellows endeavour to implement their solutions that clients' commitment is put to the test.
2. Fellows on external groups form key members of their client into internal Action Learning sets.
3. Set up an internal Action Learning programme which involves a significant proportion of managers and supervisors in dealing with the problems that concerned them. It has now been shown that this is a very powerful means of bringing about organizational change.

The latest developments are a combination of external/internal schemes and for external programmes to form sponsors sets in parallel with those of their fellows. Again the advice is experimental, there must be many other possibilities for involving the client.

FEEDBACK AND LEARNING

Insofar as the aims of Action Learning are in solving problems combined with personal/organizational development, learning how to learn is the real prize; it is one thing to solve the problems of the moment, whereas it is something quite different to learn how to deal with the unknown ones of tomorrow. Moreover, if what may be called a 'critical mass' of people know how to cope with what the future holds in store we could have that elusive animal the self-learning organization. Many have expressed views on what is 'learning how to learn'. I think it is a trial and error approach to problem solving with the important requirement to learn from our experiments. Indeed, the idea of deciding in advance how we intend tackling a problem, trying it out in the real world and then learning from the results has always been the basis of human progress. Some people, of course, have a natural feel for this process! They are probably not conscious of it but they reflect on their successes and failures, are aware of their own actions and do not let past ways of doing things influence how they tackle new situations. The clue is feedback from the results of our own actions; an Action Learning set, fellows and adviser, puts a forced draught under this inter-related process of declaring in advance what you intend doing, implementing your decision through the client and learning from these two stages; a process which in reality is rough and ready with many 'U' turns, reversals and full stops. The set is the real life laboratory where feedback about real here-and-now problems can be better understood.

Feedback comes from four main sources:

1. *The set*: the fellows are without question best qualified to remove the bandages from each other's eyes and to shatter illusions about problems. Furthermore, what fellows propose to do and when they actually try and do it is more effective if feedback is provided as it all happens.

2. *Set advisers*: they help fellows to give each other their own feedback, encouraging them throughout the programme to experiment with different approaches to their problems and the way they organize their set meetings; taking the personal risks associated with testing new ideas and behaviours in the real world is the essence of learning.

3. *Clients*: the client groups which often consist of superiors, peers, subordinates and may include suppliers and customers have always been a good on-going means of managerial learning. The Action Learning set causes the participants to reflect on their interactions with these key groups of people.

4. *Review points*: feedback can be a part of the programme through the device of review meetings. These generally take place midway and at the end of the programme. This approach provides the opportunity for fellows, sponsors and clients to evaluate individual learning; the impact on the problems and the influence of both on the organization. Current developments include establishing a sponsor's set with the task of how they can help their fellows to use Action Learning to solve their common problems – even experimenting with a fellow as their set adviser!

THE WAY AHEAD

In a world which is changing rapidly, survival is now uppermost in most people's minds. Not so long ago, annual growth was taken for granted and we could sell virtually everything we made. Now that has all changed, the developing world can make our traditional products as cheaply and as well as we can while at the same time the micro chip is eliminating work in our industries. Hence a leaner and highly competitive market combined with raw material suppliers in the third world now wanting a bigger share of the added value means all our underlying inefficiencies are exposed. In such conditions academic irrelevancies have no place, organizational development has got to concentrate on involving people in the means of their own survival and that of their businesses. Unless we learn fast how to change, we shall fail. Action Learning is providing a secure foundation on which to cope with an uncertain future.

I have tried to show that Action Learning is not so much about specific programmes such as full-time exchange schemes or part-time external programmes as about furnishing a basis for changing the behaviour of ourselves and our enterprises and to solve our problems. Experiment with it, try new approaches; it will involve risks but the rewards will be tremendous.

17 The Role of the Set Adviser*

David Casey

INTRODUCTION TO CHAPTERS 17 AND 18

The two pieces which follow (Chapters 17 and 18) were written eleven years apart; twenty years ago and nine years ago. There have to be some good reasons for republishing such old material and I believe each piece has a different justification.

'The Role of Set Adviser' is of interest as a record of where we all were in the mid-1970s – fired up by the personal leadership of Reg Revans. It is a simple statement of simple things, because that is what Revans taught us – simplicity above all else. That is his true strength; and it remains the true strength of Action Learning.

The second piece survives for a different reason. It attempts to capture something quite elusive – what Action Learning feels like. It talks of love and it speaks of pain. In this it reveals the second great strength of Action Learning – its capacity to help real flesh-and-blood people do difficult things.

Action Learning would not have survived if it were no more than a simple, rigorous intellectual thesis. It combines this profound simplicity of idea with the emotional answer to people's deepest needs. I believe the two pieces which follow have survived in the literature of Action Learning because in their different ways they reflect its two great strengths.

In Action Learning the prime source of help is the peer group – not the set adviser. The set adviser is a special member of the set, in some ways he is part of the set, in some ways not. His role, in Carl Rogers' terms,[1] is to facilitate learning. He is not a teacher in the sense of having a specific area of knowledge to impart but he is a teacher in the sense of helping others to learn. His locus is the set as a living community and not the projects as technical challenges.

---

* This chapter is adapted from Casey, D. 'The Emerging Role of Set Adviser in Action Learning Programmes', *Journal of European Training*, vol. 5, no. 3, 1976.

When we began, we called him a project adviser but this was misleading since his role is not directly related to the projects themselves, so we then referred to him as the project set adviser and finally we have come to think of him as the set adviser since his role focuses on the set.

Not all set advisers focus to the same extent on the set, some also contribute significantly to the projects themselves and we have yet fully to exchange experiences among the score or so facilitators who have worked on Action Learning programmes. These notes are written from a personal experience of facilitating eleven such sets and will, naturally, reflect my own view of the role. I try to behave consistently according to a set of assumptions about how experienced managers learn. These assumptions are mostly based on Rogers and Revans and no doubt now contain something of me as well. (Rogers would have it so since, if I have learned in any lasting way by being a set adviser, the learning must have been self-initiated and self-appropriated learning.) Before stating my assumptions, a word of warning – it is very easy to agree with any stated assumptions about learning, without facing up fully to the implications of these assumptions. I have found recently in talking to management teachers that almost without exception they identify at once with stated assumptions about learning, but a large number will immediately contradict by their behaviour one or more of them. This contradiction may be as learners or as teachers – as learners they may ask for the gospel from 'the expert' and as teachers they may become infatuated by their own ideas.

The power of Revans's idea, which lies behind every exchange programme of Action Learning, shows up with great clarity when an honest attempt is made to live through the implications of whatever assumptions one makes about how managers learn. In Action Learning these implications extend into two quite separate arenas – the project location, where the participant spends four days a week by himself, and the set, where he spends the remaining day with his colleagues and the set adviser. My own assumptions and some of the implications, in both arenas, which I try to face up to when working as a set adviser, are as follows:

Assumption 1: Experienced managers have a huge curiosity to know how other experienced managers work

This curiosity is the fuel which powers all Action Learning and it operates both in the project location and in the set. It is *not* matched by equal curiosity to know how management teachers think managers should work. Action Learning designs must therefore make *visible* and *accessible* the ways in which experienced managers actually work, so that the power of this curiosity can be tapped. These processes must be made visible and accessible in the set discussions as well as in the project locations.

Assumption 2: We learn not so much when we are motivated to learn, as when we are motivated to achieve something

The implication of this assumption in the project location is obvious – a difficult and worthwhile task must be presented. In the set too, a difficult and worthwhile task must be presented – it is the educational task of helping the others.

Assumption 3: Learning about oneself is threatening and is resisted if it tends to change one's self-image. However, it is possible to reduce the external threat to a level which no longer acts as a total barrier to learning about oneself

Left alone in the project location most individuals would react to opportunities to learn about themselves, by building instant defence systems to keep out any uncomfortable new information about themselves. The mechanism of providing a home base in a supportive set, one day each week, prevents these defence systems becoming too entrenched too soon – at least one day in five a participant can feel surrounded by support. However, this doesn't happen automatically, the set has to learn how to offer help in an unthreatening way.

Assumption 4: People only learn when they do something, and they learn more the more responsible they feel the task to be

The responsible nature of project work is well understood in management training circles, and Action Learning projects must be carefully selected, just as in any other form of project training, to keep the element of responsibility sufficiently high. In addition, the highly responsible element built into the set arena is the task of helping other participants with their projects and in deepening their self-perception. What could be more responsible than that?

Assumption 5: Learning is deepest when it involves the whole person, mind, values, body, emotions

The implications of this assumption will be clear enough in the project work, the whole person is inevitably fully involved in the project, which often takes a participant away from home to a strange location, with the daunting task of effecting some significant changes in an organization busily engaged in a business about which he demonstrably knows nothing. But he needs also to be involved as a whole person in the intimate working of the set, and the set adviser must use the dynamics of small group work to ensure that he is.

Assumption 6: The learner knows more than anyone else what he has learned. Nobody else has much chance of knowing

The assumption here is not that people always know what they have learned – but that the chance of anyone else knowing is very slim indeed. I find it very difficult to remain true to this assumption in spite of recurring evidence from Action Learning programmes and other activities. For instance, in one set recently one member found that he had learned profoundly about himself and about the processes of management, but after the programme was over he ascribed *all* this learning directly to his work in the field, doing his project. Another member said he learned much more of permanent value from the set discussions than from his project.

TASKS OF THE SET ADVISER

His assumptions about learning are not the only assumptions which determine the tasks of the set adviser. Since his main job is to facilitate, he will see his tasks differently depending on what he thinks he is trying to facilitate, in other words what he thinks the set members are trying to do, both in their separate projects and during set meetings. So his facilitating behaviour will be motivated by two forces – his perception of what set members are trying to do, and his assumptions about how experienced managers learn.

These two forces mould the job to a particular shape and it would be possible to start from very different beliefs and turn out a different task for the set adviser. One could, for example, assume 'each participant will need guidance from an expert in the discipline on which his problem rests': this would lead to a task of *expert adviser*. Another assumption, 'groups work more efficiently if properly led towards their objectives', would give a task of *leadership*, and so on.

In my own work as a set adviser four distinct tasks seem to be emerging. These are:

1. to facilitate giving;
2. to facilitate receiving;
3. to clarify the various processes of Action Learning; and
4. to help others take over tasks 1, 2 and 3.

In explaining what I mean by each of these tasks, I will try to illustrate where possible with recent examples, changing only the names of those involved.

TASK 1: TO FACILITATE GIVING

This comes first, because it helps set members to get better at the most rewarding part of their work – and the richest vein of learning for them – that is, giving to each other. The most effective set, I believe, is one in which this attitude of giving permeates every question, prompts every comment, motivates every silence, sparks every show of feeling. The questions asked in such a set, as each project is discussed in turn, are phrased to give maximum help to the person questioned and not to satisfy the needs of the questioner. When John asked why Mike had decided to circulate a particular piece of information in his project company, the question was designed to make Mike think of alternatives, not to help John decide whether he should do it in his own project company, useful though this might have been for him.

Generous questioning is only one way in which a set member gives. He gives his opinion too – sometimes it is good news for the receiver, sometimes it is bad news – both have to be delivered effectively. He gives his feelings of the moment more openly as the set matures and he learns the value of openness. Here the set adviser often has to break new ground for experienced managers, who may well have spent their growing years as managers learning to hide their feelings rather than express them in the working situation. Sentences which begin: 'I'm not sure . . .' are heard more and more in set meetings. Expressing his current learning as it takes place is also difficult for the set member, but helpful to others – to say: 'I learned a lot from listening to you struggling with that . . .' helps others to express similar feelings and more and more the person being helped is able to select what he wants, so that quite frequently he is able to say: 'I'm not finding this whole conversation useful at the moment . . .' or: 'Yes, I see . . . that's helpful, can you go on a bit, Bill?'

The set adviser encourages members to give support; emotional support is often badly needed – projects can seem impossibly complex, dauntingly diffuse and at some stage every member of the set needs massive support.

I find it difficult to help members to give freely of their technical experience, they are at first diffident, and make the judgement themselves about the usefulness of their own experiences. I see it as my task to encourage them to give it freely and in such a frame of mind that the judgement about its relevance lies wholly with the listener. This dialogue from my notes in a recent set meeting illustrates this kind of giving:

> . . . I don't believe, from my own experience at X, that you get commitment that easily

213

from shop stewards to looking at the terms of employment as a whole, I believe their commitment is confined to money!

Really? . . . I find that interesting . . . but if you don't mind I'll store it in the back of my mind for now . . .

Fine! I think I'm right, but it's your project!

TASK 2: TO FACILITATE RECEIVING

The ability to receive help from others is not distributed evenly among the management population and very competent, self-reliant men such as we have on these Action Learning programmes, often find it difficult. For this reason I like to emphasize the first task of giving – when the set members are skilful in providing help for one another they more easily accept the possibility of receiving help too. Eventually I expect the members of the set to go after help, searching diligently among the diverse experiences they recognize within the group. But this comes normally at a later stage; they learn first to give, then to receive, then to go looking for help.

The advantage of developing this kind of searching attitude is that it allows the searcher to probe deeply without any suspicion of dependency. The traditional teacher-student relationship is abandoned – instead of the teacher persuading the student to accept his ideas, the student is relentlessly searching the mind and experiences of the teacher. In an Action Learning set both 'teacher' and 'student' are experienced managers and the relationship described can be built up by the set adviser if he facilitates the ability first to give, then to receive and finally to search.

Accepting the view of himself which others have is also a field of great potential for the set member. Recently when someone was seeking help in framing his questions within his project company, he received a mini-lecture from a fellow set member who described in glowing terms how much effort he himself put into the questions he asked, ending with the statement: ' . . . I put a very great deal of thought into those questions'. This sparked an immediate retort: 'Well, you've got a more political situation!' Lots of things were going wrong here. The giver of help was satisfying his own needs, and doing it in such a way that resentment was building up in the supposed receiver, so that he totally rejected the help offered. The other set members were allowing this to happen. I quoted back to the set exactly what had been said and we discussed the incident fruitfully for ten minutes. The outcome was a declaration from a different member of the group that he frequently felt the first speaker to be 'speaking down' to others. This was said so sensitively that it was accepted with these words: ' . . . I'm horrified . . . do I do that? . . . thank you for telling me anyway . . . Painful, but useful to know. I'd like to know if I do that again . . .'

214

Another aspect of receiving is the ability to receive doubts expressed by others. Respecting the doubt expressed by another person is necessary if that person is to be encouraged to express his doubts more often, and here the set adviser who really is trying to reduce the external threat in the situation, in line with my third assumption, has to be able to express his own doubts too. I find there is a best time in the life of the set to begin to express one's own doubts and worries – too early retards the early growth of the group – too late and the opportunity to move from dependency to interdependency can be lost.

TASK 3: TO CLARIFY VARIOUS PROCESSES OF ACTION LEARNING

Action Learning is not simple, although based on simple ideas. The two tasks discussed so far – facilitating giving and receiving in a group – are by no means revolutionary and much has been written of them in therapy and sensitivity training. The extra dimension of an Action Learning programme lies in the fact that there are several unique and important processes taking place, which the set adviser must reveal to the set. He cannot do this until the set begins to understand group processes in general and this understanding is gained at set meetings, within their own learning cell. His task then becomes one of transferring this new understanding to illuminate at least four important processes taking place outside the set.

First there is the complex process of change, embedded in the web of relationships which we call the client system. This web comprises at least three separate networks, the power network, the information network and the motivational network (this is what Revans means by 'who can, who knows and who cares'). The forces for change which the visitor must identify and use to get his project implemented – not by him, but by his clients – are already there within the client system and it becomes the set adviser's role to point out the dynamics of this system as the work of diagnosis and implementation proceeds. If the participant can learn, with the help of his set peers, aided by his set adviser, how to work this system effectively he will not only achieve the implementation of his project, but will have enriched his managerial abilities significantly for all time. In addition, the organization in which a successful project is implemented will learn something of itself and how it goes about getting things done; there will be a new power released in such an organization for getting things done more effectively in the future.

The second process to be illuminated is the process of the project itself. Here the task of project management is no different in essence from managing any other greenfield project. The lifespan of the project must be contained within the timescale of the programme and the action leaner must control the whole project just as any project manager has to. This means deciding on the project objectives, planning resources, monitoring progress and all the other normal activities associated with a major finite project. This will be a familiar process to some participants, but many will find it new and challenging.

Thirdly, there are the processes of the total Action Learning programme which include the interaction of the managing body, the managing directors or other forces of power, the management development specialists within the companies, the participants, the tutors, the various sets, the nominating companies and the client companies, and the total learning community which often comes together at important points in the timetable. There will be interactions between sets as well as within those sets. There are often interfaces between one programme and another.

Finally, there is the process of this particular year of action learning within the total career context of the individual manager. Here is something which only he can manage and which will have been highlighted for him before he makes his decision to come on the programme. Included in this process is the constant awareness of his re-entry problem for which he must bear personal responsibility, although many resources are available to help him to reduce the difficulties of his eventual re-entry, whether or not he returns to his former job.

The set adviser must ensure that all these processes are identified, separated and illuminated as human processes for the participant, using his learning of group dynamics derived equally from the dynamics of the set meetings themselves and from the discussions taking place in those meetings.

TASK 4: TO HELP OTHERS TAKE OVER TASKS 1, 2 AND 3

This task, which I certainly give myself, may well be controversial among other set advisers. I aim to declare at the beginning what I see my tasks within the set to be, and try to involve the set in its own process work as early as I can. To establish in people's minds as quickly as possible that I wish control to be shared, I tend to use symptoms and symbols of control as examples. I will refuse to take minor decisions about where, when and how we meet, how we use our time, what we do about visitors, what administrative and domestic arrangements are necessary and so on. I then move on to encourage process comment from set members and point out when it happens, and, if it does not happen, I will ask why not.

My experience so far is mixed. Some individuals in each set do seem to grasp quite quickly what I am getting at, others see it as some level of abdication of the set adviser's responsibility. My justification for encouraging the set to share in the facilitating role is that I believe it is an important part of a top manager's job to work on the process of the work he undertakes with his groups, as well as on the content. I think I would go so far as to say that, for the chief executive, the ability to think out what the process should be and to see it through, is his greatest personal asset. The dilemma is that not all managers have the necessary interest, although I believe that those selected for a senior Action Learning exchange programme should certainly possess most of the required personal characteristics to do the job of facilitator.

Results are always encouraging and by the time the programme ends several members of any set are considering the process quite naturally and automatically.

WHAT MAKES AN EFFECTIVE SET ADVISER?

This question is being asked widely in management learning circles at the moment since Action Learning is making such headway. We do not yet know the answer, but some progress can be made by identifying a list of characteristics which seem to be valuable and a list of skills which seem to be needed and comparing these with some of the characteristics and skills needed for effective teaching in more traditional settings. My belief is that very many successful teachers could become excellent set advisers, since, by definition, they have what it takes. I am not so confident about the true academic. His commitment is to using his own mind; the real teacher's commitment is to using the minds of others.

I have described the tasks of the set adviser as I see them. It would be sensible now to move on from the tasks to consider what personal characteristics and skills seem to be needed to do the job.

CHARACTERISTICS REQUIRED

First the well known characteristics which all successful teachers have. Clearly sensitivity is needed – sensitivity to people and situations. Perception is needed and a quickness of mind. Conceptual ability too, to help others to conceptualize. But in addition to these qualities, which are widely distributed in the teaching population, we have come to recognize about five additional characteristics which may or may not be so widely distributed. These are:

1. Tolerance of ambiguity. Traditional teachers may like the security of a well prepared lesson given in a setting determined by themselves to a timetable which is known in advance so that their tolerance of ambiguity need not be high. The set adviser must live in a world of uncertainty and must be prepared to allow the learners to take control from him. Unless he enjoys this situation he is unlikely to enjoy the role of set adviser.
2. A quality of openness and frankness which is best described by Rogers

217

as 'realness in the facilitator of learning'; this implies an ability to recognize and express one's own feelings in the learning situation, as they arise.

3. Patience. Endless patience.

4. An overwhelming desire to see other people learn. Unless this is there to a high level the sheer frustration of the work in an Action Learning set would drive some traditional teachers to distraction. The rewards of set adviser must be in seeing incremental learning take place very slowly and very personally over long periods of time. This is what all teachers look for, of course, but in set work the teacher seems to be doing very little, although inside he is in turmoil, endlessly interpreting and modelling what is going on within the group, but only declaring to the group what he sees occasionally, for fear of upsetting the value of the process itself. To use so little of his hard-won interpretations is only possible in someone who has an overriding belief in the method and in the value of learning.

5. Empathy. This quality of 'operating through the mind of another person' is only enjoyed by those who can put themselves into other people's shoes and almost feel their feelings with them.

SKILLS REQUIRED AND NOT REQUIRED

In addition to the characteristics described above there is, of course, a range of skills. First, let us look at some traditional skills which teachers have invested many years to perfect, because they have been an important part of their professional repertoire, and which in the role of set adviser would no longer be of any value, while in the role. In that simple statement there lies a worrying threat to many a practising teacher. Not only does the statement make his hard-earned skills redundant, it raises the worrying question of whether he has, or can develop, the new skills needed for the role. Some of the skills he will no longer need are these:

Skills not required

1. Presentation skill. From the Assembly in ancient Athens to the House of Commons, hundreds of thousands of orators have ingrained deep in our culture the value of making a convincing presentation – and the expectation among students that it is appropriate for teachers to do this, is just as deeply ingrained. Add to that, the sheer pleasure most teachers get from making a well-polished presentation, and we have two very good reasons why it is difficult to let this skill lie fallow.

2. Structuring skills. It is no longer necessary to structure the sequence of lessons and the sequence of material within a lesson and the sequence

of lessons within a term to cover the material required by examinations. There is, of course, a design task to be performed but this refers to the whole programme and not to any one set. We normally have a steering group to discharge this role, for the programme as a whole.

3. Fluency. The ability to use the language in an oratorical sense. Excellence and clarity of delivery, the perfection of one-way communication.
4. The skill of preparation in advance of a teaching assignment. How much to prepare, how much to leave unprepared, when to ad lib, when to quote from authorities, and a host of other considerations.

Choosing to work in a new teaching role, which does not need these skills, built up painstakingly over the years, is not something that everyone can bring himself to do. Most teachers who work in a process way are young. This is no coincidence, it simply means they had much less to throw away. There is nothing to be gained by criticizing those conscientious teachers who have deeply-learned skills on which they have based their careers. I believe many of them, with help, can develop new skills quickly for the new role. Many of them want to, they are intellectually convinced that Revans and Rogers are right, but emotionally there is an understandable blockage. It is important to establish that we are concerned here with the demands of a particular role. The learning assumptions in this article were stated with reference to a particular learning setting, with experienced managers learning from each other, helped by a set adviser. There is no reason why the same set adviser should not deliver first class lectures, in settings where lecturing is appropriate – and there are many such settings. The management teacher who has highly developed skills as a lecturer need not feel threatened by the challenge of working in the new role of set adviser, his lecturing skills will have to be shelved while he is in the new role, but since he almost certainly has the necessary basic characteristics required for the role, he can quickly develop a new range of skills to add to the old, and powerfully extend his total capacity as a teacher. With this wider range of teaching skills at his disposal he will be in a position to adapt more effectively to the challenges presented by different teaching opportunities. What are these new skills?

Skills required

One meets a snag at once. The old skills, no longer needed, are familiar and easy to identify. The newer skills are emerging, unfamiliar and not easy to describe. They lie somewhere in these areas:

1. Skill in timing interventions. Too early and the intervention is not understood, too late and the opportunity has passed.
2. Skill in asking what must be exceptionally good questions which make

people think, but at the same time feel challenged and supported rather than criticized.
3. Skill in using the language of managers. To avoid speaking down, and resist the seduction of analysis and intellectualizing.
4. Selecting and applying the appropriate model to reflect processes taking place at a particular time. And skill in choosing the issue for examination which best relates processes within the set to processes within the projects.
5. The skill of saying nothing and being invisible.
6. Skill in hearing two or three processes at the same time, most of the time.
7. Skill in making statements truthfully whilst structuring the statements to be of maximum use.

The skills described are not very clearly differentiated from each other and ALP International is still working on compiling a better understanding of what various set advisers' skills are. Different set advisers work in different ways and there may well be several quite different roles which a set adviser can usefully play. These notes have emphasized the role of facilitator of learning because this is how I see it. Others add to this a further dimension of acting as environmental scanner for the set, encouraging the members to look outwards to an ever-changing world. Other set advisers contribute more than I do to the technical content of projects. By sharing our experiences we hope to learn too, in spite of the very real difficulty of ever being sure, from the outside, what is actually going on inside another set.

REFERENCE

1 Rogers, C., *Freedom to Learn*, Merrill, 1969.

18 The Shell of Your Understanding*
David Casey

SUFFERING AND LEARNING

It is a very old question. Is suffering necessary for learning? I have come to believe that suffering is sometimes necessary and sometimes not. In twelve Action Learning sets of five or six chief executives at Ashridge Management College over the past five years, I have watched half a dozen chief executives reach new heights of learning (for them) by crawling painfully through the most daunting jungle of pain and misery. On the other hand, in exactly the same setting I have seen an equal number of chief executives achieve what appeared to be equally significant learning for them, with no real effort – carried along on a light stream of joy and enlightenment, revelling in the sheer delight of their new insights. Learning is sometimes agony and learning is sometimes fun. Is it possible to identify which kind of learning demands suffering and which kind can be fun?

In my teens and twenties I was fortunate to experience at first hand two well tried systems of education – I was at school with the Jesuits and my first job was teaching with the Benedictines for three years. Here are two validated approaches to education, both ancient in their pedigree and accepted across Europe over several centuries. At school I learned through suffering:

> To give and not to count the cost,
> To fight and not to heed the wounds,
> To toil and not to seek for rest,
> To labour and to ask for no reward . . .

Ignatius Loyola founded the Jesuits in 1534 and the grammar school I attended based its education firmly on the principles he established more than 400 years ago, and in its way it worked. There are penalties of course (as with any system) – for example, the weight of guilt and self-denial which all graduates of the Jesuit

*First published in the *Journal of Management Development* (1987), **6**(2) pp.30–37.

system carry around for life. But also implanted for life are the joys of intellectual exercise, the springboard of self-discipline, the stimulus of competition, the urge to self-reliance.

Four years later I found myself appointed as a schoolmaster in a Benedictine school. Benedict and Ignatius were poles apart in their thinking about education. Benedict believed in the power of love: not just as we all believe in love – his trust in the power of love was so rock-steady and universal that in his schools no place was found for heavy discipline, no corner for punishment, no coercive external force (other than love) was allowed to impinge on the young people being educated.

If survival is any test of a system, then these two diametrically opposed systems of education are both successful – they survive side by side today; you can send your son to Stonyhurst or Ampleforth, exposing him to two very different sets of assumptions regarding what will help him to learn. In one system the assumption is that learning is a relentless fight against our sinful propensity to indolence, in the other system the assumption is that learning is enabled only in an atmosphere of love. McGregor's X and Y come pretty close.

The dilemma facing any set adviser is no different from that facing every teacher; do you make the student work or do you cradle the student in love? Do learners have to suffer or can they get there on a surfboard of effortless exhilaration? And, most difficult decision of all, when do you push and when do you stand well back?

My work at Ashridge has reinforced in me the certainty that the ambience of an Action Learning set must be an accepting, supporting cradle of love. I have no doubt at all that producing this environment is one of the most valuable roles of the set adviser. When the set consists of chief executives, it is even more important (and difficult) to make the set a place where people feel supported, liked, trusted and valued. However, in the last few years I have come gradually to understand that such an atmosphere of love is necessary but not sufficient. There is another task to be added to the four tasks I offered set advisers in a 1976 article called 'The Emerging Role of Set Adviser in Action Learning Programmes'.[1] In the ensuing ten years I have found very little to change in that article, but now I want to add something.

THE EMERGING ROLE OF SET ADVISER

In 1976 I identified these four tasks for the set adviser:

1. To facilitate giving.
2. To facilitate receiving.

3. To clarify the various processes of Action Learning.
4. To help others take over tasks 1, 2 and 3.

The broad 'Benedictine' assumption behind these four tasks is that set members can look after themselves and can facilitate each other's learning, with a little catalytic help from the set adviser. The set adviser's role is assumed to be transferable to them, and since the skills required in the set adviser's role are not particularly exotic (and are widely distributed among management teachers and among managers too) transfer of set adviser's tasks to set members is a fairly straightforward business. And for the most part I still believe that. But in addition, I now believe that there is a rather special bit of the set adviser's role which cannot be transferred to set members in a month of Sundays. There is a fifth task, which only the trained and experienced set adviser can do and it conforms more to the confronting Jesuit model than to the benign Benedictine model. The Benedictine doctrine of all-through-love will get set members so far and no further. There is a level of learning, particularly about oneself, which can be reached only through some level of pain. And set members are not willing, nor are they able, to push each other through very much pain.

Kahlil Gibran wrote 'Your pain is the breaking of the shell that encloses your understanding'.[2] In the Ashridge chief executive sets many participants believe that their ignorance is the shell which encloses their understanding, so they come hoping to dispel some of that ignorance. They see the other set members as intriguing sources of *knowledge* and they are aware that they themselves are valuable sources of knowledge for the others. And so it turns out to be. They probe each other's experiences and knowledge by increasingly skilful questioning. They do learn to give and to receive. And certainly many shells are broken – but often they are only the shells of ignorance.

These participants find the programme useful and go away satisfied, with their ignorance reduced. Hard-worn knowledge has been traded. But Kahlil Gibran wrote that *pain* is the breaking of the shell of your *understanding*, not your knowledge; these participants have suffered no pain, so their understanding remains where it was when we started. Knowledge can be gained by breaking into shells from the outside, understanding can be gained only by breaking out from your own shell, from the inside.

My own nagging doubts as set adviser started when first I realized that many participants actually want more than extra knowledge – they wish to gain in self-understanding. I began to see that my 1976 model of set advising was not always powerful enough to help them. If the set adviser restricts himself/herself to the four tasks identified in the 1976 'Emerging Role' article – the skill available within the group is limited to the skill of the set members and even when enriched by the tutoring of the set adviser, this may not be enough.

223

DEEP FEELINGS

In practice I often begin to feel that an individual needs to work things out at a deeper level than the set is able to accommodate. Sometimes it becomes clear that someone is about to express deep feelings which they dearly long to express and which they are finding very difficult to handle. Other set members may be aware of this but feel unable to help. Some may consciously or subconsciously contrive to stop the process going any further. They may have real worries about the group 'getting out of its depth' or they may be afraid that once a new level of exposure becomes a group norm, their turn will come sooner or later and the prospect may fill them with dread. So they abort the process. The skill exercised in aborting the process has to be seen to be believed – an innocent request to have a natural break, a throw-away flippant remark, an alliance formed by miniscule eye contact across the group – hundreds of tiny subterfuges like these are employed to break the spell and to sabotage a process which is just getting to the point of usefulness. Only when I twigged the subtlety of what was going on, did I realize that I, the set adviser, was the only person who could help. Simply uncovering the process itself was no use – the process would be denied and argued about – diverting attention even further away from the difficult work to be done.

Let us look at an example. Ted is a solid, competent 54. Proud to be running a £20 million division of a large industrial group. Also proud of having made his way to the top 'off the tools'. For ten years he has turned in more profit each year, on a rising turnover, so that his division has become a model, held up by the group main board as an example to the other divisions – most of which seem to be losing money. Without Ted's reliable performance year after year, the group would be in trouble. This was the picture Ted painted for us – a brilliantly successful career coming steadily to a satisfactory close. Ted talked of early retirement – he mentioned his age frequently. One day I took him on – partly because I could not believe in the perfect success story – mostly because I felt Ted did not believe in it either. Under challenge Ted was soon exposing himself as complacent – not shouldering his responsibility as a member of the main board – turning a blind eye to incompetence elsewhere, remaining safe in the success of his own division. I challenged him in a strong and straightforward way – was he prepared to accept incompetence at group level? Was it right that he should receive the accolade of a successful division managing director when he was clearly abdicating from his group responsibilities? Could he retire from the group without shouldering his responsibility to leave it in a healthy state? The questions all came from me. Every other member of the set sat quite still and silent as a dialogue between Ted and me continued for 20 minutes. He smouldered with anger.

At the next meeting Ted told us that he took the next two days off after this confrontation. He booked a hotel in Bournemouth with his wife and they talked for two whole days. He decided, with her enthusiastic backing, to stand up and be counted in the group. He told us, with a new glint in his eye, that he was the *only* person in a strong enough position and with the personal guts to put things to rights. It would be tough – but he felt young again. 'After all, I'm *only* 54!' he said. Every meeting after that Ted seemed to get younger. He has already achieved great progress (with some help from the set) and he is happier, full of energy and looking forward to the next ten years of hard, uphill fight. For me, the surprise came later – at the final dinner for this set Ted said he owed it all to me; not to the set, but to me. And in my heart of hearts I know he is right. I also know that such a significant breaking out from his own shell could never have happened if I had limited my role to group process work and denied the group my skill as a person-to-person consultant, within the group setting. So this is the fifth task I want to add to the four tasks in my 1976 article:

5. To act from time to time as personal consultant to set members, in the group setting.

THE SUCCESS OF FAILURE

Ted's example is one of many. In the past few years, every time I have worked this way with an individual chief executive, within the group setting, I have felt a failure. Because in the intensity of person-to-person work I would totally forget everybody else! What kind of a set adviser was this, totally oblivious to the group processes and stepping outside the classic role of catalyst? And yet, nearly every time I felt compelled to work in this mode, it worked. More importantly, I knew I had helped the individual do some work of importance for him and *that nobody else could have done it*. Typically, it has helped him break free from an imprisoning shell rather than break into other people's shells. Always, there has been pain. This is what Kahlil Gibran meant: 'Your pain is the breaking of the shell that encloses your understanding'. Self-understanding.

THE CHIEF EXECUTIVE TRAP

Are there some characteristics of chief executives, which make them different? Is there some special need that chief executives have in an Action Learning set, to work things out for themselves at a relatively deep level? Perhaps there is.

225

The chief executive role is acknowledged as a lonely role; is there anything else special about it? I think there is – the chief executive role is very special indeed.

A typical chief executive is a leader in his[3] organization, in his neighbourhood, in his clubs, in his professional bodies, in all his various activities. He is expected to exercise leadership everywhere he goes. And it becomes a self-fulfilling prophecy – no sooner is it known in the golf club that he is the managing director of Brown and Smith, then he gets elected to club captain. His skill at Speech Day prize-giving leads to a seat on the local Magistrates Bench and so on. All this has great benefits for him and his capacity for leadership grows as he gets pushed (however willingly) into various lead roles in different kinds of organizations, in different social settings. But there are great penalties too for the individual human being behind the 'great leader' exterior. It becomes increasingly difficult for him to say 'I don't know' or 'I'm afraid' or 'I need help'. As years go by, many chief executives find they have built up a survival kit which does not contain these phrases. They find another way to survive – and it is more likely to be based on knowing a lot, distributing their wisdom, giving advice, making decisions and telling other people what to do. And they find it works like magic.

Why it works like magic is because the rest of the world colludes in what can be a cruel way. People need to be led, managing directors need to be in place, decisions have to be made, magistrates have to be found and local authorities need to appoint chief executives – so the stage is set for a drama, some aspects of which contain the seeds of tragedy. Once they have a willing leader out front, clever followers can make almost any decision work (very often all that is needed is a decision because many options could be made to work) and when the decision is seen to work, the leader's belief in himself as a decision maker is bolstered falsely – reinforcing his self-image as a leader. The sardonic comment from one chief executive. 'When you are out in front, you are never quite sure whether they are following you or chasing you', is much more serious than at first appears.

And so, over many years, chief executives develop a belief in themselves. They learn to think of themselves as somehow different. People near them begin to flatter as they see opportunity for themselves in the chief executive's growing power and soon a chief executive can become cut off from any trustworthy feedback. That is a very dangerous position to be in. Some get pushed beyond the point where it is difficult to say 'I don't know', 'I'm afraid' and 'I need help' to the point of no return, when they begin to *believe* that they do know, they are not afraid and they do not need help. That is an even more dangerous position.

LITTLE UNDERSTANDING OF THEMSELVES

I have found on the Ashridge Programme that chief executives often have an insatiable thirst for knowledge and an impatience with ignorance. Most of them have an encyclopaedic knowledge of the world and a well developed forcefulness in projecting their opinions. In contrast, they have little understanding of themselves. They crack avidly the shells of ignorance and find only the rewards of more knowledge. To break out from their own shells and discover something of themselves is so terrifying that some of them cannot even begin to think of doing it. In my five years at Ashridge two such chief executives left the programme altogether – both at an early stage – as soon as they saw the awful dangers which might lie ahead if they once started to chip away at the strong protective shell inside which they had learned to feel safe. These two[4] were exceptions; most participants fully understand the nature of the programme and I believe most of them come because they want to find out something about themselves and see this strange programme as offering that possibility. Naturally enough, when the time comes to crack the shell of pain and come to an understanding of themselves, they are afraid.

They are afraid because their survival kit, carefully built up by themselves and by others over many years, is about to be whisked away at a time when they need it badly. Their colleagues feel afraid too, and hold back. Only the set adviser knows that it is now or never – and only the set adviser has the courage and the skill to sharpen the pick and tell the chief executive just where to tap, if he is to begin the painful process of learning who he really is.

Many chief executives decide to hold back. The opportunity for them may have arisen too late in the programme; they may decide that on balance they need their survival kit as it is; they may be near retirement age and judge that the potential pay-off for them is not worth the investment in pain ... there are countless valid reasons why chief executives decide not to break the shell of their understanding. For me, as set adviser, the important thing is that the opportunity should be there, if they want it.

THE CONSPIRACY OF LOVE WITH TRUTH

So, was Ignatius right or was Benedict right? In a strange way they were both right. Unless the atmosphere is one of trust and love, the chance for self-understanding would never arise, so sets of chief executives need a set adviser able to develop a 'Benedictine' environment. But unless the set adviser is also Jesuitical enough to hold on to his belief that the only way to help at the moment of truth is to push the learner through the shell of his own pain, no amount of supportive understanding will really do the trick. This conspiracy of love with truth is a formidable alliance and a potent source of help.

At this stage my conclusion is that (at least in chief executive sets) set advisers not only have the right to abandon process work from time to time and engage in personal therapy; they have the obligation to do so. Because if they do not, nobody else will.

Over the past ten years I have argued that the set adviser's role should be concerned more with group processes than with person-to-person consultancy. I still believe that. What I have learned from my work at Ashridge – and I thank Ashridge for it – is that to be dogmatic about excluding personal consultancy as one part of the set adviser's repertoire is wrong. As with any other skill used by the set adviser, it is simply a question of choosing when to use it. I also want to thank a good friend – Roger Gaunt knew many years ago what it has taken me ten years to learn.

REFERENCES AND FOOTNOTES

1 Casey, D. (1976), 'The Emerging Role of Set Adviser in Action Learning Programmes', *Journal of European Training*, 5 (3). An adapted version of this article appears as Chapter 17 of this book.
2 Gibran, K. (1926) *The Prophet*, Heinemann.
3 The Ashridge Programme is open to men and women chief executives but in practice all have so far been men. The masculine pronoun is used here only for convenience.
4 Both of these chief executives were 'sent' by their personnel directors. Most participants find the Programme for themselves by reading about it in general management journals or by word of mouth.

19 The Learning Process

Alan Mumford

Action Learning is a dual process. Participants tackle real work opportunities, problems, tasks, projects, in a context which specifically states learning as an objective. I describe this as a Double Value process – two achievements for the price of one.

However, as is always likely to be the case where real work and learning are explicitly associated, the excitement, significance and immediacy of the action element can often submerge the learning element, which may be perceived as lower priority, less connected with immediate organizational rewards, and 'something that happens anyway'.

Undoubtedly, as is the case with learning on and through normal work activities, people will learn from Action Learning programmes. The issue is really whether they extract the full potential for learning and development from their experiences. This chapter proposes that designers and facilitators ought to provide:

- a model of the learning process – what should happen when;
- assistance to individuals to increase their understanding of how they and others may learn differently from the same experience;
- help to individuals on how to build additional learning abilities which will enable them to learn more not just from the immediate Action Learning project, but from any future opportunities.

In my view these ought to be seen as requirements, not optional elements, since otherwise the duality of action and learning cannot effectively be sustained. The particular processes to be used to achieve this are of course debatable. This chapter suggests one approach:

- Changes are made to two of the Revans' statements about learning – system beta and the learning equation.
- The theory and practice of Action Learning is related to the influential theories of Malcolm Knowles and Peter Senge.

229

- A simple model of the task cycle and learning cycle demonstrates the conceptual and practical connection between task and learning.
- Individual preferences on how to learn as expressed through Honey and Mumford's learning styles shows the attractiveness or otherwise of different aspects of Action Learning for different individuals.
- It is suggested that Action Learning when properly delivered is a better basis than many other methods of development for enabling participants to 'learn how to learn'.
- Finally the chapter illustrates the implementation of these ideas.

LEARNING THEORY

REVANS

Revans' views about learning are expressed through a variety of statements, and clearly operate from the view that managers learn best from working on real problems, by working together on those problems. The most 'theoretical' elements of his philosophy are:

System beta

System beta derives from his view that learning is essentially the same as the scientific process. His model is a five-stage one, involving in a circular sequence:

Survey
Hypothesis
Action
Inspection
Incorporation

There are of course great similarities between this model and that of Kurt Lewin and David Kolb (suggestions that Kolb developed his cycle from Revans are inaccurate).

The learning equation

Revans' equation is:

$$L = P + Q$$

Learning Programmed   Questioning
Knowledge   Insight

Revans' view about 'P' has varied rather over the years. He has sometimes seemed to discount its value entirely, but his more balanced view is that he does not reject 'P' but wishes to put it in its appropriate place in the learning spectrum. He sees 'P' as traditional instruction which prepares for the treatment of puzzles or difficulties for which knowledge is already available to achieve a solution, in contrast to asking questions about the unknown.

This neat equation and the words describing it have been readily adopted by many Action Learning practitioners. My own experience with Action Learning caused me to offer a different formulation:

$$Q1 + P + Q2 = L$$

The case for this is that since the most effective learning is driven by the need to resolve a managerial problem, then the equation should start with the process of asking about the problem, issue or opportunity (Q1).

There will probably be relevant knowledge available for the resolution of that problem. So the second stage of the equation should deal with the acquisition of that knowledge (P), with the emphasis that it should be relevant knowledge, i.e. is actually directly associated with the problems or issues that have been revealed.

The combination of looking at and working on the issues (Q) and the acquisition of relevant knowledge (P) leads to a redefinition of the issue, a reinterpretation of experience, and the raising of issues of a different kind or at a different depth by the manager through the learning group (set).

This revised equation is a better description of the Action Learning process because:

- It immediately invokes the visual image necessary to encourage developers to get away from the idea that 'P' comes first. 'They must be introduced to marketing theories and methods before they try and tackle a marketing project'.
- It encourages the idea that learning is an iterative process not a single or simple-minded association of one type of learning called 'P' and another type of learning called 'Q'.

Arguably, the equation is still misleading, since it may still imply a finite period of learning, rather than a series of P and Q interactions.

OTHER THEORIES OF LEARNING

The common experience that managers learn by doing, and Malcolm Knowles' theory of adult learning[1], have sometimes been combined too readily to explain or justify simply getting managers 'to do things' as part of a development programme. As we have seen, the learning theory contained within Action Learning certainly emphasizes the 'doing' element. However, in its best form it also emphasizes an often disregarded element in Knowles theory, i.e. that people like working on problems and issues of direct relevance. (But the extent to which *all* managers are primarily driven by issues of practicality and relevance is examined below.)

More recently, Senge's[2] views on organizational learning, though not referring to Action Learning, are very consistent with it. Senge's particular emphasis on the significance of systems and system thinking, and the relevance of tackling organizational problems can be seen as the context within which Action Learning might often operate most successfully.

Proponents of Action Learning ought also to be aware of the theories of Chris Argyris.[3] His examination of the causes and processes involved in 'defensive routines' are especially significant. The fact that a particular issue might be seen as undiscussible could make it either a dangerous or ineffective element in an Action Learning programme. From another point of view it might be seen as precisely a virtue of Action Learning that it raises such issues for discussion. But then as Argyris shows, the fact that something is undiscussible might itself be undiscussible!

THE TASK CYCLE AND THE LEARNING CYCLE

The fact that they learn from the work they do is no surprise to managers and professionals. Convincing them that increased attention to learning from doing will produce additional learning outcomes is, however, not always accepted by them as a priority for action. Part of the problem is that while on the one hand we want to emphasize the association between doing real work and learning, on the other hand we want to underline also the importance of recognizing learning as a specific discrete activity, because otherwise it will get lost in the task. A further complication is that participants often see learning as being a quite different kind of process from the way in which they approach their normal work. One way of both causing a discussion about these issues, and removing some of the confusions and ambiguities, is actually to start with the way in which managers and professionals characteristically engage mentally in the work they do. The task cycle is my representation of this (Figure 19.1).

It is then possible to present the learning cycle – and of course to ask participants to identify the essential similarity between the mental approach they are used to employing for thinking their way through the work they do, and the mental model described in the learning cycle.

The Honey and Mumford version of the learning cycle (based of course on

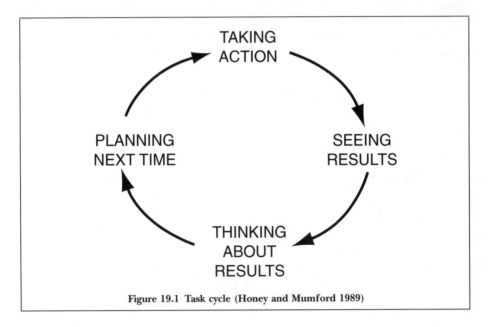

Figure 19.1 Task cycle (Honey and Mumford 1989)

Kolb and Lewin) differs from system beta in being a four-stage model (Figure 19.2).

The case made above for revising the equation to show that it starts with Q can be considered in relation to where Action Learning can be seen to start on the learning cycle. In the revised equation, 'Q' is clearly most strongly associated initially with the reviewing stage. Individuals and learning sets generate, consider, discuss, argue about the nature of the issues and problems.

They then reach some conclusions ('decisions') about what to do to tackle the issue. How much time? With whom? Who is the client?

Then individuals plan the action they are going to take as a result of the reviewing and concluding stages.

Finally they have the experience of actually carrying out the project.

But of course throughout this process a series of mini learning cycles are going on. Participants are having the experience of working with others in reviewing, concluding and planning. They are having the experience of defining the problem or project and getting the contribution of fellow set members on their definition. They have the experience of obtaining the commitment of a client to the carrying out of the project and to the likely implementation involved in it.

So the Action Learning process is potentially extremely rich because it contains within it opportunities for consistently going round the learning cycle and

233

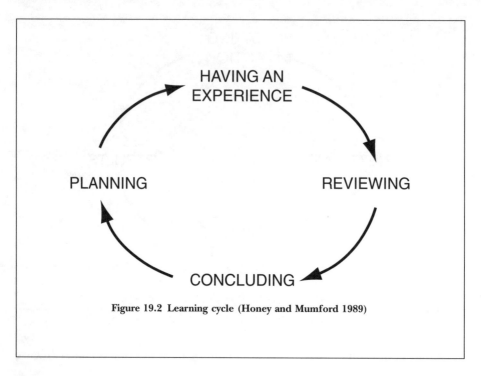

Figure 19.2 Learning cycle (Honey and Mumford 1989)

discovering more about yourself, more about the process, more about how to transfer particular experience to other situations.

LEARNING TO LEARN

Action Learning provides, as indicated above, not only a single opportunity to go round the learning cycle, but to engage in mini learning cycles at different times in various set meetings. If explicitly presented as a process to Action Learning participants, and if opportunities are created to review learning against the learning cycle, then individuals and groups can seize the opportunity to learn how to learn more effectively. A crucial word here however is 'explicit'. Some authors have claimed that Action Learning is a particularly effective process for facilitating learning to learn, but give no indication of how participants are supposed to achieve the potential involved. To suppose that individuals will either recognize or take advantage of the opportunity to understand and then perhaps to develop their learning to learn processes without explicit and direct encouragement is ill founded. Many participants will have had no previous acquaintance with the idea that learning is a process which can be looked at and which individuals can understand and develop for themselves.

234

The idea therefore that they will somehow pick this up for themselves without direct guidance, support and encouragement, probably from a set adviser, is optimistic, and will lead to a failure to achieve one of the important benefits.

There is very little explicitly in the literature about how learning to learn can most effectively be achieved. In addition to my own material there are occasional references to the use of the learning cycle and learning styles. Thorpe, in his important article[4] argues that Action Learning's most important contribution is 'as a means by which managers learn how to learn at the highest level of learning skills'. He goes on to identify the different levels of learning which might be achieved through the Action Learning process. In Thorpe's view participants achieve learning about the context of learning:

- As they confront and co-operate with each other in the group situation, providing a basis for comparisons, contrast and challenge which can unfreeze previous learning.
- In dealing with real problems they are engaging in the application of relevant knowledge and analysis as the result of that knowledge to more appropriate managerial action. The group provides a basis for building solutions on each other's experience and managers are encouraged to reflect and perhaps change their attitudes and beliefs.
- The essential part played by reflection is achieved in two ways. They reflect on the results of practical problem solving, but also on their learning processes and personal development. They become more conscious of their conceptions of the world in general, how these were formed and how they are changed.

Facilitation of learning to learn, whether at relatively basic levels of understanding of learning processes through the learning cycle or in the more complex form identified by Thorpe, can be stimulated by explicit discussion of theories, frameworks and practices. These must, however, be supported by aids such as learning logs, and explicitly created learning review sessions for full benefit to be obtained. International Management Centres provides as part of its MBA Programme a requirement that participants complete an Evaluative Assessment of Managerial Learning as part of the formal submission for which they obtain credits on the MBA. This covers the whole period of the MBA, and is drawn from the individual's learning logs.

LEARNING STYLES

Life would be wonderfully easy for us as designers and facilitators of learning experiences, and for learners, if everyone recognized the need to engage fully in each stage of the learning cycle to obtain full benefit from any learning experience. In fact, individuals may have different preferences about how they learn, and therefore about whether they are willing to learn through experiences related to particular stages of the learning cycle. David Kolb's[5] innovative work on how to identify such learning style differences was taken further by Honey and myself.[6]

We see a direct association between the learning cycle and learning style preferences as shown in Figure 19.3.

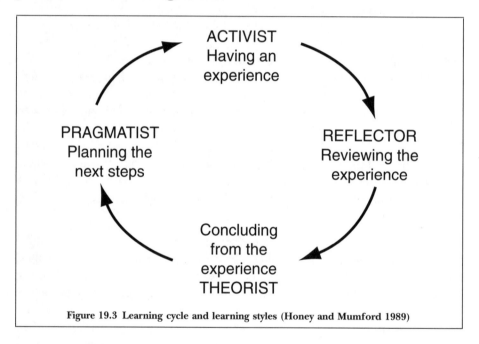

ACTIVIST
Having an
experience

REFLECTOR
Reviewing the
experience

Concluding
from the
experience
THEORIST

PRAGMATIST
Planning the
next steps

Figure 19.3 Learning cycle and learning styles (Honey and Mumford 1989)

Whereas with some management development methods there is a clear association between a strongly preferred learning style and the content of the method, this is much less likely to be true with Action Learning. As has been shown earlier, there is provision for participants to go round each stage of the learning cycle. However, individuals with strong learning style preferences will give more or less attention to particular stages of the learning cycle related to their learning styles. Well designed Action Learning programmes give exactly that balance which will ensure that there is no undue emphasis on any particular stage of the cycle, and therefore no need for any participant to be significantly turned off for any length of time during the Action Learning process.

The proviso 'a well designed Action Learning programme' is, however, very important. A programme which emphasizes the task and resolving problems, but does not give sufficient opportunities to reflect on what is going on, or which does not encourage the process of drawing conclusions from particular experiences will disappoint and perhaps frustrate those whose learning styles favour that kind of activity. The following analysis sets out to show how a strong learning style preference will impact on different aspects of an Action Learning experience. There are three especially significant points to remember about the following statements. The first is that our research showed that 35 per cent of managers have one strong preference – and this single strong preference is equally distributed across the four learning styles. So at any time on an Action Learning programme an individual with only one strong preference may be strongly inclined towards that experience, but be joined with others whose strong preference is in quite a different direction.

The second point is that we find only 20 per cent of managers with three strong preferences – indicating thereby the possibility of being drawn towards a much greater variety of learning.

A third point to be made is that participants will learn something from Action Learning activities whatever their strong or low preferences may be – there is a question of how much they will learn, and how keen they will be on that particular kind of learning, not that they will learn nothing.

The predicted response of strong learning style preferences are:

Activists

A sense of participating in something relatively new would be attractive to activists, as would the emphasis on attacking real problems. However they might be uncomfortable if the project or problem they were tackling extended over a long period of time. They are not likely to enjoy being reminded to get clarification of terms of reference, by attempts to provide structure, by encouragement to do detailed planning. Most of all they are not likely to favour what they would regard as too frequent or too lengthy attempts to review what has been done and what has been learned. They are quite likely to enjoy actually doing the project work. They would probably enjoy their own presentations in set discussion. They may well pick up ideas from other people. They are not likely to enjoy profound discussions about the meaning of what they or anyone else has done.

Reflectors

Reflectors would appreciate some major features of the Action Learning process, obviously in contrast with those likely to be enjoyed or not enjoyed by activists. They will, for example, relish the opportunity to produce carefully considered analyses, to collect data, to compare and contrast data and may find it difficult actually to start a project. They will bring additional information to the group and help the group to generate its own data. They will want their role in this respect to be recognized.

They will be particularly pleased to engage in the process of reviewing what has occurred within their own project and that of other people. They will appreciate the advantages of doing learning reviews and learning logs and discussing what has actually been learned within the group. They enjoy the process of thinking things over and the opportunity to give and receive feedback. They are perhaps unlikely to volunteer any of these initially, and therefore will be pleased to be supported by a process which encourages sharing of air time.

They are less likely to enjoy time limits in relation to a project.

Theorists

Theorists are likely to be attracted to some elements of Action Learning and repelled by others. They will like the opportunity of being stretched by a complex problem. They will probably appreciate, without necessarily agreeing with, the theory behind Action Learning. They may be uneasy about the concentration on a particular project. 'Is it right to spend so much time on a single managerial experience?' They may feel there are insufficient opportunities to generalize beyond the particular project. They will bring strong views (which they will not necessarily regard as theories) about the nature of a project, and what is actually involved in their own or other people's project.

Whatever the care with which the initial structure of the exercise is set up, it is likely to move into conditions of ambiguity and uncertainty; these conditions are especially difficult for theorists.

They are most likely of the four styles to want to have input -'P'.

Pragmatists

The high face validity of tackling real problems and the requirement to produce action plans, make this an attractive process for pragmatists. This is especially true where people work on problems for which they are accountable in their own organizations. Consultancy projects in a different organization may be less attractive, because of the potential difficulty of transferring learning from that situation to their own.

They may ask for 'P' input, but not dealing with theories and models as theorists might, but dealing with practical skills involved in the project, such as interviewing, planning or presenting.

Where sets can be created in which there is a balance of different learning style preferences, the result can be enhanced learning for individuals and the group.

MODIFYING THESE GENERALIZATIONS

The simplicity of Action Learning may cause participants initially to see it as 'a good thing', because it deals with real managerial issues. However, even those who are not strong on the theorist learning style may develop some concerns about the very specific nature of projects, how much transfer of learning there is going to be, and if there is not 'P' provided, whether there is sufficient testing content and opportunity in terms of knowledge built around the programme.

THE NEED FOR SUPPORT

The exposure and exchange which is a significant potential benefit can also provide concerns at both an individual and an organizational level. 'Do I really want to share this information about myself with my colleagues?' 'Is this organization really prepared to be challenged on its strategy, values, policies?' 'If I engage in either of these forms of challenge is the organization or is the group or are individuals really going to support me?'

A prime concern can be whether a client for a project, in those cases where participants are not fully autonomous in terms of carrying out action, will actually take action. There can be fears about projects being put on the shelf or being treated simply as interesting development exercises.

For those projects (almost certainly the majority) where the participant has no autonomous right to carry through the resolution of the problem or the implementation of the project, the identification of a client is absolutely crucial. Is there someone who is interested not only in having the project carried out, but in accepting responsibility for taking decisions on it?

Revans has talked about 'comrades in adversity' or 'fellows in adversity'. My colleague Joanna Kozubska produced the interesting insight that this sounded perhaps unduly negative. I agree with her that a more appropriate term is 'fellows in opportunity'.

The actual processes through which individuals learn in groups (as distinct from the general process involved in group behaviour) has been very little studied. One of the potential contributions especially in meeting the learning-to-learn objective is that groups should consider, reflect on and improve their behaviour as a group.

Unfortunately there has been insufficient recognition of the work context, i.e.

239

the sense in which the participant's environment encourages effective work on the project or problem, and encourages learning from that. Clear definitions of the nature of the help that might be offered by a boss or a mentor or colleague, how and when it will be provided, are very important.

In all these cases, there is a learning opportunity for those acting as supports for the participant on the Action Learning programme – one of the major potential benefits substantially understated so far in the Action Learning literature. The choice of Action Learning as a method might be significantly enhanced if this benefit was understood, and help was offered for 'supporters' to use the opportunity.

Very little has been written about the kind of support which ought to be provided for participants at work. (See, in contrast, the material available on the role of set advisers, for example, Chapter 17 in this book.) A research project I conducted on some Action Learning programmes run by International Management Centres in the UK showed how little either the participants, or those who should be supporting them at work, understood before the event about what needed to be done to create an effective learning relationship between them. Some of the issues were very basic – how and when were meetings between them to be set up. Other issues were at a rather deeper level – what kind of discussion about what kind of issues, managed through what kind of behaviour. Participants wanted behaviours such as effective listening, being interested, opening doors and providing information. Some things they did not want. 'I want to discuss my problems and the work given me on the MBA, not get answers to the problems'. The research seemed to me to show that much more could have been achieved if participants and supporters had been helped to a much clearer understanding of the potential in, and the opportunities and problems provided by, their relationship as required on the programme. But of course that could be seen as a micro example of what needs to be done generally to develop more successful developmental relationships between learners and their managers. This wider issue is addressed in one of my recent books.[7] Another, complementary, approach is suggested in some recent work I have done with Peter Honey, in which we look at the specific behaviours and practices managers need to engage in in order to produce a high quality learning environment.[8] Again this emphasizes the possible interaction between current concepts of the learning organization, and of Action Learning, and the shared behaviours and practices which will facilitate both.

Supporters of learning need to know and practice the same kind of understanding of the learning process and learning styles indicated for designers and participants earlier in this chapter. Particular questions which ought to be asked on how supporters provide helpful participants include:

- Has there been a discussion between the participator and the supporter on what the learning relationship on an Action Learning project is intended to achieve?
- Does the supporter understand the learning process, through being given some model, e.g. the learning cycle?
- Does the supporter use it in helping the learner, e.g. by providing quality time for reviewing, for encouraging learners to reach conclusions, and encouraging them to plan how to use what has been learned?
- Do participants and supporters understand the significance of a supporter having a different strong learning preference to that of the participant, e.g. one being a strong activist, the other a strong reflector, or strong theorist trying to relate to a strong pragmatist?

A detailed description of the application of learning styles within an Action Learning programme is given in my article 'Putting learning styles to work'.[9]

IMPLEMENTATION OF THESE IDEAS

The ideas presented above can be implemented in a relatively straightforward way. That implementation in my own case is directed by the view that sharing knowledge about, for example, learning style preferences is enabling rather than disabling – it can facilitate individuals learning one from another in any Action Learning set, rather than giving them an excuse not to learn from a programme, and not to recognize the strengths of others in the set.

The steps that can be taken are:

1. PREPARATION

- Send learning styles questionnaire to all participants, in advance of the programme.
- Collect copies of their score sheets in advance of the programme.
- Use that information to assess any preponderance of learning styles in the programme population.
- Decide whether to adjust any programme features, especially early on, better to meet any preponderant style. (Readers might like to consider whether and how they would change the early stages of a programme if they had preponderantly strong theorists, as compared with strong activists.)
- Use LSQ information in constructing groups and pairs.

2. PLENARY PROGRAMME SESSIONS

- Discuss the task cycle, learning cycle and learning style preferences with all participants.
- Encourage participants to review their own results in groups.
- Illustrate to participants how learning style preferences may affect their commitment to various stages of the programme.
- Suggest that the programme may enable them better to 'learn how to learn'.
- Give them the personal workbook *Using Your Learning Styles*.

3. IN GROUP OR SET DISCUSSIONS

- Encourage participants to review where they are at any stage of the programme in terms of the stages of the learning cycle.
- Encourage sets to use each other's strengths in learning style terms. (There are other strengths they ought to be calling on as well, but these comments focus on the learning aspects.)
- Encourage individuals to complete learning logs and/or written reviews.
- Ensure that these are shared and discussed.

All the above comments relate to direct participants on the programme. Other steps need to be taken for those described earlier as supporters.[10]

REFERENCES

1 Knowles, M. (1985) *Andragogy in Action*, San Francisco: Jossey-Bass.
2 Senge, P. (1990) *The Fifth Discipline: The Art and Practice of the Learning Organisation*, New York: Doubleday.
3 Argyris, C. (1985) *Strategy, Change and Defensive Routines*, Pitman.
4 Thorpe, R. (1990) 'An alternative theory of management education', *Journal of European Industrial Training*, **14** (2).
5 Kolb, D. (1984) *Experiential Learning*, Englewood Cliffs, NJ: Prentice Hall.
6 Honey, P. and Mumford, A. (1992) *Manual of Learning Styles*, 3rd edn, Honey.
7 Mumford, A. (1993) *How Managers Can Develop Managers*, Aldershot: Gower.
8 Honey, P. and Mumford, A. (1996) *How to Manage Your Learning Environment*, Honey.
9 Mumford, A. (1993) 'Putting learning styles to work', *Journal of European Industrial Training*, **17** (10).
10 Mumford, A. (1995) 'Managers develop others through action learning', *Industrial and Commercial Training*, **27** (2).

20 Set Advising: More than just Process Consultancy?

Judy O'Neil

One way that people try to make sense of something new to them is to relate it to something they already know. A role that people very often think of when hearing about what a set adviser does is the role of a process consultant. Reddy defines the role of a process consultant as 'reasoned and intentional interventions, into the ongoing events and dynamics of a group, with the purpose of helping that group effectively attain its agreed-upon objectives'.[1] Schein goes on to say that the relationship plays itself out through interventions that are made from an ambiguous power base, in the midst of ongoing work.[2] Through these interventions, the process consultant builds involvement and commitment, and gains acceptance for the importance of looking at the process.

Much of what has been written about Action Learning (AL) and the role of the set adviser could easily lead one to make a comparison to a process consultant.[3-6] AL takes place in a set, or group; a set adviser's activities are reasoned and intentional, and are intended to help the group attain its agreed objectives – learning through solving an actual problem; the interventions are made in the midst of ongoing work; and so on.

RESEARCH ON THE ROLE OF THE SET ADVISER

Much of the current literature on the role of the set adviser is presented as prescriptions, written from the personal experience of practitioners.[3,4,7,8] In 1995, I began to obtain some 'documented wisdom' of practitioners to try to better understand what set advisers do and why they do it; what set advisers say they do and what they actually do; and what they think is distinctive about their role as opposed to other similar practices.

The research is in the form of a modified phenomenological study that triangulates the results of interviews and observations. The subjects include 25

243

practising AL set advisers in the United States, Sweden and England. The observation sites are a multi-national food organization in the United States using an AL programme to help transform itself into a global organization; and a university in England using AL as a basis for its masters and doctoral programmes geared to people working within varied organizational settings. I have performed a deductive analysis of what these set advisers explicitly say about their practice, along with an inductive analysis of the interviews and observations, to begin to identify implicit themes.

How the role of the set adviser is similar to, and different from, that of a process consultant can begin to be answered from the data collected in this study. In order to examine the data, I would first like to look at the similarities and differences in backgrounds of the process consultant and set adviser; then discuss the explicit differences cited by the practitioners in the study; and finally compare the role, and activities, of the process consultant with that of the set adviser.

BACKGROUND OF THE SET ADVISER

An initial area for examination is the background of someone who is a set adviser. There is a wide range of views in the literature on the appropriate/ necessary background for a set adviser. In a group in Sweden, the advisers come from diverse backgrounds including doctors, lawyers, businessmen and psychologists.[9] A practitioner's group in the United States feels that the necessary background can include leadership positions, multicultural experience, teamwork, personal and organizational development, and knowledge of organizational learning.[10] Teaching experience also forms a good basis for being a set adviser.[3,11]

Harries also describes a number of activities that are useful, such as observing a set in action, being a member of a set, co-advising and just doing it, that is practise as a set adviser.[11] Finally, Pedler looks for experience in facilitating action and learning in groups.[8] A conclusion that could be drawn from what has been written is that there are many, and varied, backgrounds that a person could draw from in order to be a successful set adviser. This appears to be true in the process consultation literature as well.[1,2,12]

According to the data from my research, however, there are certain areas that appear in advisers' backgrounds with a degree of frequency. The most named experience is with training, and/or work with groups.

They obviously have to be interested in groups and how groups behave.

... experience in group and interpersonal skills ... managing group process. ...

244

Advisers frequently cite Tavistock experience, National Training Laboratory and Gestalt training as being influential in their current work. This earlier background of working with groups is very similar to the type of background advocated for process consultation[1,2,12] and would tend to reinforce a similarity between the role of a process consultant and that of a set adviser. Some of the advisers in the study have indicated, however, that they find the work with groups in AL a more meaningful way of working since they go 'below the process level, to the learning level'. This would appear to be an effort to differentiate what they are doing now from the kind of group work they have done in the past.

BUILDING ON THE ROLE OF THE PROCESS CONSULTANT

'I find that I go below the process level, to the learning level'. 'My work with the Action Learning set takes me further and deeper than when I used to work with groups'. These statements made by the practitioners in my study lead me to believe that the work they experienced earlier in their practice with groups has helped to form a basis for their current practice as set advisers. In order to examine this belief, I would like to first discuss some of the reactions of the set advisers in the study to the statement, 'The role of the set adviser isn't any different from that of a process consultant'.

There was a general consensus that the role was different. Many of the advisers see the role of the process consultant as one of the roles of the set adviser.

> They are not the same. I think clearly there are a number of skills which are germane to both.

> It's different. As a process consultant you are floating with the process. You are helping people to stay in it and be aware of what is happening. As a project adviser, if you make a chart now, you are on many more levels.

> I think it is different. I think it's one of the roles. But it is only one of them.

Helping a set to have an effective process for working together as a group is considered to be an important aspect of AL. The amount of time spent on it often is dependent on how the set is structured, that is, individuals focusing on their individual problems, or the group focusing on one, often organizational, problem. 'It is also different from facilitating with a group with a project than when they bring their own problems, because then you've got all sorts of other issues'.

Integral to an AL set, in addition to dealing with process however, is the focus on task and learning and task versus learning.

So for me, the set adviser is focusing very much on getting people to stop and reflect. And learn and reflect on what they've learned.

I think there is the important concern to make sure the learning is double loop learning.

A prime problem in AL sets is that people get – as I call it – seduced by the action. . . . you focus on the action and not on, well, what have you learned from that experience?

These additional explicit elements of the task/problem, and the learning that

Process consultant interventions[1,2]	Action Learning interventions – beyond those of process consultation
Diagnostic	
Cognitive	Ask 'naive' questions to help set make the implicit, explicit and the undiscussable, discussible
	Foster cycle of reflection, action, and reflection on action
	Foster critical reflection on organizational norms
	Foster critical self-reflection on assumptions
	Encourage reflection when set appears ready to act prematurely
Skills and activities (Coaching and counselling)	Provide 'P' – programmed knowledge
Behaviour description (Confrontive process altering)	Facilitate members 'giving' to one another
	Facilitate members receiving help from one another
	Make the way members work visible and accessible
Emotional/reflective (Confrontive through feedback)	Enable the helpful expression of emotions
Interpretation	
Structural	Help members to learn how to work changes in the system to effect implementation of project
	Release and enhance capacity for understanding and managing life and development
	Say nothing and be invisible
	Enabling learning

Table 20.1 Process consultantcy compared with Action Learning

should happen as a result of working on the problem with the support of the set and set adviser, appear to add dimensions to the role of the set adviser that are not necessarily present when working with a group as a process consultant.

'(The role of the set adviser in) . . . Action Learning is more holistic'. I'd next like to examine these added dimensions in more detail.

As a starting point for this examination, I'd like to refer to Table 20.1. This table compares a model for process consultation interventions drawn from the work of Schein[2] and Reddy[1], with AL interventions described in the literature and cited by the practitioners in my study. A further description of Schein's and Reddy's models, as illustrated in the left column of Table 20.1, are as follows. I have combined the two models in order to form a unified basis for comparing the kinds of interventions done by process consultants and set advisers.

Schein's intervention framework[2] can be used at any level of the organization, whereas Reddy's is oriented to small groups. Schein includes:

- diagnostic – any data gathering that impacts the organization; needs to be congruent with values underlying PC and the general goals of the PC project;
- confrontive process altering – making the group sensitive to internal processes and generating interest in analysing;
- confrontive through feedback – consensus that there is readiness and that it is a legitimate activity; ability to deal with defensiveness and facile acceptance;
- coaching and counselling – rarer so client needs to have a voice in use or process consultant needs to ensure client ready; encourage client to do themselves and then add;
- structural – helps manager to assess alternatives for changes and suggests alternatives not considered.

Reddy uses an intervention typology matrix to categorize the types of interventions that can be used in small groups.[1] The matrix categorizes the interventions according to type, focus, and intensity. The five types include:

- cognitive – abstract, intellectual or idea oriented; includes consultant questions;
- skills and activities – training or skill learning;
- behaviour description – process consultant describes what he/she has observed;
- emotional / reflective – reflecting the emotional or feeling component observed in the group;
- interpretation – hypothesis or understanding of what is occurring at a dynamic level.

According to the set advisers in my study, the interventions that Schein and Reddy describe are a part of the many roles of a set adviser. In the right column of Table 20.1, I've listed some of the additional kinds of interventions a set

247

adviser may use in his/her work with a set to support the set members in learning through work on their problem. These interventions come from a combination of what the literature describes as set adviser interventions and those described by the set advisers in my study. How these set advisers describe these interventions follows.

ACTION LEARNING INTERVENTIONS

ASK 'NAÏVE' QUESTIONS

Most of the advisers agree that questioning is the manner in which most AL interventions are undertaken. If a set is arranged so that each member has his/her own problem, then much of the questioning is done by other set members.[4,6] In this type of set, and when the set focuses on one problem, the set adviser is also involved in interventions that often take the form of questions.

> So it's sort of a series of questions asked and hopefully other people ask as well. . . . posing some questions at the beginning and the end has been very helpful.

> It's all questions really, isn't it? It's all asking questions.

Although almost any type of question is appropriate at different times in the life of the set, a particularly powerful kind of questioning can be referred to as 'naïve' questioning. AL programmes are often designed to ensure that these 'naïve' or fresh questions can be continually raised. Ways that this is done is through a design that ensures no experts in a set, having as much diversity as possible within set members, and having the set adviser play the role of a 'sophisticated barbarian' – one 'who by their very nature as an outsider, are intended to see the situation through fresh eyes and to use those insights to help raise critical questions that lead to the reframing of the participant's understandings'.[13]

REFLECTION

Interventions that can be categorized as reflection are described in many different ways in the literature and by the advisers in the study – a cycle of reflection, action, and reflection on action; critical reflection on an organization and its norms; critical self-reflection on assumptions; and reflection on the workings of the set.[5,6] Interventions that help create a cycle of reflection and action appear to be ones that are most used to help the set learn from their process, as well as their action, premature or otherwise, on the problem.

... if it means that you and the group, you ask the group to pause and reflect, yes, I certainly do that. Always at the end of a session ... and other times would be when they're getting into some sort of mess.

Let's take a round and see what do we see right now. And of course they are concerned about time, but now they have learned to trust that if we do this now we will save time.

Interventions to create opportunities for critical reflection are less common, but many set advisers look for them not only for the set, but for themselves as well.

I believe that in the end a lot of what people do in the set mirrors what they do back at work. If I can help them resolve, help people maybe look at what it is they're doing and it mirrors what they do outside, maybe that can help them with totally different things they get involved with outside.

It's actually not only trying to find out where they're coming from but it's actually trying to understand where I'm coming from too.

'P' KNOWLEDGE

Revans[14] emphasizes that one of the strengths of AL is recognized ignorance, which results in 'questioning insight – Q insight', and the previously discussed questioning interventions, not 'previously programmed, or "P"' knowledge. Some AL programmes are designed, however, with pre-set 'P' training modules built in, and/or the expectation that the set advisers will provide just in time learning as sets express or demonstrate needs. This design is often found in programmes that are intended to help bring about organizational change.[5,15] The design strongly influences the teaching role the adviser plays. Some advisers see this as a natural role, while others are discomforted by it as they see it as a contradiction to one of the basic principles of AL.

... I can act as a facilitator of information for them. More often than not direct it, but sometimes, particularly if it's a group of managers who are very scattered, to actually get it to them.

I need to be strongly convinced (about tutoring through just in time learning). ... I think that it's a trap, very seductive.

Those advisers who do see the role of a tutor for 'P' knowledge as something that they are involved with, try to be very explicit in differentiating the tutoring role from the other roles they play as a set adviser. Particularly when the knowledge is provided in a 'just in time learning' manner, the adviser will wait until the set has identified the need, and then only provides what is immediately needed, often trying to share the role with other set members.

249

You aren't a tutor when you're acting as a set adviser. . . . I was quite clear that I was shifting role.

I suppose in some ways, we do quite a lot of it. . . . the set has got stuck somewhere and a little bit of explanation or a little bit of something or other is actually going to ease that and help reveal to them some way forward which is not only of immediate use, but of long term use.

FACILITATE MEMBERS ABILITY TO GIVE AND RECEIVE HELP

In much of what has been written about the set adviser, an important role is to facilitate him/herself out of a job.[3,4,6] The way that this often happens is through the transfer of the needed 'facilitation' skills to the set members. This usually happens in small steps over an extended period of time with the set. Not all programmes are amenable to this transfer happening. Although both the litera- ture[4,8] and the advisers in the study suggest that AL works best when sets are able to meet regularly over an extended period of time, in many programmes within organizational settings, time is at a premium, and as a result this transfer does not always have time to take place.

I'm always stepping in when I see they are seduced into what I think is just one way of thinking. I throw some stones and they don't understand. . . . They're not in touch with it, so then I take some stones and throw them again. I mean it's not too nice to be that disturbance, but I know when they get it, I don't have to do anything.

To make the time out, to make them, to stop them when they are very resource oriented and if they are just by themselves, they should never take the opportunity to reflect. . . . it usually takes a long time to be able to do that by themselves. . . . I know that after a time they can do it without the set adviser, but it takes some time.

MAKING WORK VISIBLE

The idea of making a group's work 'visible' to them through interventions, mirroring or reflecting back what is happening in the group, is a type of inter- vention that is used in both process consultation and set advising. It can end up looking different in set advising due to the expressed need of the set adviser to try to avoid bringing the focus of the set to them, and being what I label later in this chapter as a 'mystery maker'.

The way I try to handle it – again to try and get focus away from myself, I would hope there's evidence in the group that I could comment on.

I might say, 'I'm not a significant person in this discussion, but I think I found this particularly difficult . . .' but that's dangerous because it really is beginning to impose your views.

HELPFUL EXPRESSION OF EMOTIONS

Just as the set adviser reflects back on what behaviour is happening in the group, he/she also helps the set to better understand what emotions might be coming into play through similar types of interventions. There continues to be the same concern, however, with trying to ensure that the intervention doesn't inappropriately create a situation where the focus of the set is on the adviser, rather than the set.

> Reflecting back to the set where it is. . . . Reflecting to them where they are in the process rather than the content. So I think the reflector role is a key role, probably the key role.

> So I felt anger and frustration with them, yeah, but what's that got to do with them? It's me, isn't it. So what I might do is ask slightly tougher questions.

LEARN TO WORK CHANGES IN THE SYSTEM

When looking at the background of set advisers, a second area that comes up with regularity is an interest in systems theory. For many advisers, this grounding helps them in the interventions they make to help set members understand how their project impacts, and is impacted by, the larger organizational system.

> I use a systems model when I work.
> I tend to think in systems and look upon the AL group as a system and then do systems interventions. . . . I use the triangle to try to help them focus on each other in relationship to each other and the system and the topic.

BEYOND THE ROLE OF THE PROCESS CONSULTANT

RELEASING AND ENHANCING CAPACITY

There appear to be some kinds of interventions that set advisers make that go beyond the purview of process consultants. One of these areas has to do with helping the set to use their learning beyond their set and project work, and impacting how the set members increase their life and development skills.

> And you really felt they had learned something, not only that is going to stand them in good stead with this particular exercise, but somehow it dawned on them that somewhere there is a truth that will be useful to me for a long time.

> . . . it's a critical situation, it's a crisis in the group . . . they have been like protecting mistakes or failure and they have fear and things look to go over the edge. To be a

set adviser in that situation, I like very much. Being there, trying to make the best of it for learning. . . .

SAY NOTHING AND BE INVISIBLE

Although it may be odd to think of this as being an intervention, set advisers talk of the value they feel they bring in just 'holding the place' for the set and 'giving them permission' by their presence to look at a problem in a different way. In my study, I also found set advisers who tended to do the opposite, that is, they appear to try to create a mystery about what they do. In doing so, they create a situation in which the focus is on themselves rather than the group. The group may be getting something out of the work, but the adviser is too, contrary to what should be happening in an AL programme. Some advisers are explicit in expressing this 'mystery'.

It's not possible to describe what I do.

That the group is not at all clear at the beginning what it is,
    why is this fellow here.

Others seem to be less aware that they mystify their role and sometimes struggle to be more explicit.

I can't explain how I decide (on an intervention).

I could say that it's intuitive (decision to make an intervention).
    But I suppose it isn't.

Being a mystery maker is the role most criticized by other learning advisers. It is one of the most frequently identified 'taboos' among advisers. In response to questions about taboos and obstacles in their work, advisers reply:

Bringing themselves (the advisers) in. 'I am important. Can you see me?'

. . . Revans' admonition about consultants . . . taking over the process and making it about them.

Although most learning advisers recognize the inappropriateness of the group focusing on the adviser rather than the participants, many struggle with trying to avoid being a mystery maker themselves. There appears to be a natural inclination to be more involved than is viewed as beneficial to the group, but most advisers recognize this as a problem and work to avoid it.

. . . a bit of showbiz . . . can get away with that because I'm the bloody adviser. It doesn't do you any good in the long run because it increases their dependency on you.

252

> I find that because I'm, one of my weaknesses, because I've been trained partly as a consultant, if I'm not careful, the role I get into is helping them solve problems.

Different advisers have different ways of 'saying nothing and being invisible'.

> ... we have some key words for being a set adviser that we are not going to 'steal the learning opportunities' from the participants. I have that very much in my mind and it has never been a difficult issue for me.

> ... Lead as little as possible. And if necessary accept the fact that they will tell you, 'well you could have said that 20 minutes ago'.

ENABLING LEARNING

Although there may certainly be an expectation the group members would learn when they work with a process consultant, there is a much more explicit 'contract' that learning will take place when set members work with a set adviser in an Action Learning set. Based on this explicit contract, one of the main ways that set advisers show up, and intervene, with the Action Learning set is to create the space and opportunity for learning to take place – which is probably the reason it's called Action *Learning*.

> ... it is squeezing learning out of anything and everything you do.

> Being there, trying to make the best of it for learning. Trying to have a good balance, not taking over, and just doing the very best you can for learning.

WE ARE ALL LEARNERS

Those of us who work as set advisers will probably see ourselves reflected in at least some of what the advisers in my study spoke about. Since many of us do have backgrounds similar to theirs, our intervention styles, our interventions, our views on Action Learning are probably similar as well. So what does that mean?

It is important that we continue to focus on, and develop, the kind of work and interventions that differentiate us from other types of practitioners who work with groups. We need to continue to ask questions, particularly 'naïve' questions; create the space for, demonstrate, and encourage the cycles of reflection, action, and reflection on that action; and ensure that any 'P' knowledge we provide is what the set has determined is needed.

We need to be sure that when we enter into work with a set, that, whenever possible, our goal is to transfer the skills that we bring to the set members, so they can continue their work and learning without us. We need to always

253

recognize that the learning the set members come to of their own accord is far more valuable than any we could hope to bring, and we can play a significant role by 'creating the space' for that learning to occur, and not do anything that could steal that opportunity from them. And we need to do all this while we 'say nothing and be invisible'.

Most of the advisers I spoke with also expressed the fact that they were continually learning. When asked to rate their abilities on a scale of 1–5, with 1 being low, most advisers rated themselves no higher than a 3 – and many of these were advisers with years of experience. What I think this reflects is the idea that all of us are always struggling with ways to do our work better. Hopefully hearing the views and voices of these many set advisers will enable us to realize we're not alone in this struggle and give us some thoughts for carrying on more successfully.

SELECTING AND DEVELOPING SET ADVISERS

As Action Learning continues to become more recognized as a way to help develop executives and managers, bring about organizational change, and begin to build learning organizations, organizations are increasingly interested in its use. As a result of this increased interest, one of the questions that needs to be addressed is how to build internal capacity for the role of set adviser. The data from my study has begun to provide some answers to that question.

Although individuals from almost any background have successfully worked as set advisers, it would make sense for an organization to begin by identifying people who match the most prevalent background – training or work with groups, with a secondary consideration of a background in systems theory. Second, many of the advisers spoke about the need to submerge their needs to that of the participant. 'First of all I would look for someone who is not too egotistical, somebody who is prepared to subordinate his needs to the needs of the group'. Several advisers mentioned that they came to the point in their life when they were able to turn the focus from themselves only after they had gained a certain maturity. While none said that the maturity could only come with age, many felt that the work would be difficult for someone quite young.

As stated in my introduction, the consensus is that the only way to fully understand Action Learning is to be involved in Action Learning. The same would hold true for learning about the role of a set adviser. In order to understand this important element of Action Learning, individuals chosen from an organization would need to work together in an Action Learning set.

A model that I have used with some success is for the individuals to choose as their problem, or problems, if they choose individual problems, one that would tie in with their issues around learning to be a set adviser within their organization. The action they would be involved with in solving their problem takes place in several venues. They work within the Action Learning sets in their organization, first by 'shadowing' an experienced set adviser, then being 'shadowed' by that adviser, and finally working on their own with the set. They also have the opportunity to practise within their own set using much the same process. Their cycle of reflection, action, and reflection on that action is around learning about and practising as a set adviser. In this way they go through the experience of Action Learning, while they are beginning to learn about their new role.

There is much more to be learned about the role of the set adviser. Some of the additional questions that I hope will be answered through my data are:

What is a set adviser's self-perception (espoused theory) of what he/she does?
What does a set adviser actually do in a set (theory-in-use)?
What are the differences between a set adviser's espoused theory and theory-in-use?
When does a set adviser engage in particular activities?
Why does a set adviser engage in particular activities?
How does a set adviser frame success for his/her role?

I look forward to sharing those answers with you.

REFERENCES

1 Reddy, W. B. (1994) *Intervention skills: Process consultation for small groups and teams*, San Diego, CA: Pfeiffer.
2 Schein, E. H. (1988) *Process Consultation*, Reading, MA: Addison-Wesley.
3 Casey, D. (1991) The role of the set adviser. In M. Pedler (ed.), *Action Learning in Practice*, Brookfield, VT: Gower, pp. 261–74.
4 McGill, I. and Beaty, L. (1995) *Action learning: A practitioner's guide*, London: Kogan Page.
5 O'Neil, J. and Marsick, V. J. (1994) Becoming critically reflective through Action Reflection Learning™. In A. Brooks and K. Watkins (eds), *Learning through action technologies, New directions for adult and continuing education*, **63**: 17–30, San Francisco: Jossey-Bass.
6 Weinstein, K. (1995) *Action learning: A journey in discovery and development*, London: Harper-Collins.
7 Mumford, A. (1993) *How managers can develop managers*, Brookfield, VT: Gower.
8 Pedler, M. (ed.). (1991) *Action learning in practice*, London: Gower.
9 Cederholm, L. (1994) Memo to LIM staff, Report of two MiL workshops on the role of the Project Team Advisor (PTA) and the Program Director.
10 Turner, E., Lotz, S. and Cederholm, L. (1993) *The ARL™ Project Team Advisor's Handbook*, Vol. 1, No 2, New York: Leadership In International Management.
11 Harries, J. M. (1991) Developing the set adviser. In M. Pedler (ed.) *Action Learning in Practice*, Brookfield, VT: Gower.
12 Parsons, R. D. and Meyers, J. (1984) *Developing Consulting Skills*, San Francisco: Jossey-Bass.
13 ARL™ Inquiry (1996) Boundary management in Action Reflection Learning™ research: taking the role of a 'sophisticated barbarian'. (Unpublished conference paper: to be published in *Human Resource Development Quarterly*, in 1997).

14 Revans, R. W. (1982) *The origins and growth of action learning*, London: Chartwell-Bratt.
15 ARL™ Inquiry (1995) Designing Action Reflection Learning™ research: balancing research needs against real-world constraints *Proceedings of the 1995 Academy of Human Resource Development Conference, pp. 2–3.*

21 US Human Resource Professionals and Action Learning

Nancy M. Dixon, Larry Hales and Richard Baker

General Motors has historically employed a cadre of human-resource development (HRD) professionals with the expertise to teach middle managers
competences identified with successful performance. Such competences are
represented by the 'P' in Revans's formula $L = P+Q$. However, in more recent
times, top Human Resource management at General Motors has come to recognize that to meet the new leadership challenges – continuous improvement,
customer satisfaction, teamwork, empowerment and personal responsibility – an
additional competence is required of middle managers. That competence is the
ability to think in new and fresh ways about existing problems. Such competence,
which is referred to here simply as 'Q', has been variously labelled critical
reflection, context shifting, reframing and paradigm shift. The essence of the
competence is 'the capacity to dig below the surface layer of perception to
examine taken-for-granted assumptions and values in order to determine whether
or not one is addressing the right problem'.[1] Thus, to meet the challenge of a
rapidly changing General Motors, top Human Resource management saw a need
for the 'P' competences which human-resource professionals had traditionally
taught to be balanced with the 'Q' ability managers could use to ask fresh
questions.

To respond to this need General Motors set up a development team of individuals from three organizations: a professor with a working knowledge of
Action Learning from The George Washington University; the president of a
management consulting firm, Baker & Company, with a reputation in the training
industry for innovative learning designs; and several General Motors HRD professionals with long-term experience consulting with and teaching middle
managers.

Action Learning was identified as one of the appropriate methodologies to develop 'Q' in middle managers. The initial vehicle for implementing Action Learning was three week-long leadership courses to be designed for newly promoted first and second level supervisors and third level managers. Specifically, the course objectives were as follows:

- to introduce managers to the ability to shift contexts, develop new perspectives and reframe assumptions within a challenging global environment;
- to facilitate the ongoing development of management knowledge, skills and insights; and
- to empower managers to utilize each other's cross-functional skills in action sets that would meet, following the initial training, for the purpose of solving complex real-world problems facing their business.

The development team was assigned two tasks: 1) to create the initial five-day courses for each level; and 2) to prepare the HRD professionals for their role as facilitators in both the initial classroom experience and later as set advisers.

The primary focus of this chapter is the second of those two tasks. In a sense this chapter is itself an instance of Action Learning. It is a reflection on the experiences of the development team as it attempted an unfamiliar task, that of assisting the HRD professionals at General Motors to gain the new skills, roles and attitudes necessary to model and facilitate 'Q'. We are sharing our experience in order that others who undertake to help HRD professionals switch from 'P' to 'Q' have the opportunity to learn from our reflection.

DIFFERENCE IN THE SKILLS NEEDED FOR 'P' AND 'Q'

The first task in the development of the facilitators was to delineate how the skill sets for the two learning processes, 'P' and 'Q', differed in order to plan the assessment and development process. These skills are as follows:

SKILLS AND KNOWLEDGE NEEDED TO TEACH 'P'

- Master the subject matter on which the instruction is based.
- Understand the task environment in which participants function in order to build connections between the content and their work.
- Explain the content in terms of practical guidelines or procedures which participants can employ when addressing problems they face on the job.
- Design and implement exercises that allow participants to gain proficiency in applying the guidelines or procedures.

- Ask questions that will lead participants to discover the 'correct' answer for themselves.
- Manage any resistance to the ideas off-line or in ways that are the least disruptive to the learning of others.
- Make the training a positive experience for participants:
  - keep things moving;
  - keep things light;
  - be seen as personable, likable, friendly;
  - 'save face' for participants by paraphrasing incorrect responses so that they more closely represent the correct answer;
  - reinforce correct responses;
- Avoid situations or topics in which lack of expertise might lessen instructor credibility.

SKILLS NEEDED TO FACILITATE 'Q'

- Design opportunities for participants to find their own answers to problems
- Design opportunities for participants to learn from each others' perspective, mistakes, and successes
- Encourage a climate where participants will both support and challenge each other
- Refrain from displaying one's own knowledge and understanding
- Challenge individual and group assumptions both about the back home environment and about the action that is on-line
- Give difficult feedback to participants
- Ask questions that assist participants in exploring the reasoning behind their assumptions
- Raise difficult issues even at the risk of participant's becoming annoyed with the facilitator
- Acknowledge facilitator mistakes publicly, framing them as learning experiences

In constructing such a list it became clear to the team that although the two skill sets varied greatly, the most striking contrast between 'P' and 'Q' was in the assumptions about learning and instructor responsibility that formed the basis for each.

The assumption on which traditional 'P' is based is that participants will be better managers if they learn and apply the skill and knowledge which management experts have developed. In the classroom it is the HRD professional's responsibility to see that participants understand and value those skills and ideas. Since HRD professionals have no line authority over the participants they must rely on their credibility as subject-matter experts and their skill in creating a positive classroom experience to accomplish these goals. If participants are resistant to the ideas which are proposed, HRD professionals are likely to see themselves as having failed in their task.

The assumption on which 'Q' is based is that managers learn best from working to resolve real problems. However, to do so they must get beyond the limits of their current assumptions. The facilitator's job, then, is not to provide answers but to assist in removing the 'blinkers'. Removing blinkers requires facilitators to challenge current assumptions and contexts. Even when accomplished with caring and concern, having one's current assumptions challenged is often a disconcerting experience. Facilitators must expect that at times participants will be angry or upset with them. With 'P,' facilitators credibility is based on their knowledge of the subject matter. By contrast, 'Q' credibility comes from facilitators being able to 'walk their talk', that is, being open to seeing their own limiting beliefs, contextual perspectives, and ineffective reasoning.

The development team hypothesized that facilitators, in attempting to facilitate 'Q' rather than 'P', would be faced with the same challenges as the managers they would be helping; that is, they would need to remove the blinkers of their current assumptions in order to act in new ways. The difficulties they would face in facilitating 'Q' would entail not only using different skill sets, but also modifying their assumptions about the role of expert knowledge in learning and about the nature of the responsibilities of the facilitator.

Further, the team hypothesized that, as with managers, the support and reward system within which the facilitators functioned would affect their success. For example, when teaching 'P', the HRD professionals had traditionally paid close attention to: the ratings on participant reaction forms completed at the end of the course; the number of participants that were attracted to the course; and the respect participants tend to bestow on those who display subject-matter expertise.

PREPARATION TO FACILITATE 'Q'

To test these hypotheses and to begin the facilitator assessment and development, a two-day meeting was designed for prospective facilitators. The objectives of the meeting were: 1) to model the facilitator skills; 2) to explore the concerns of prospective facilitators; and 3) to provide prospective facilitators an opportunity for self-assessment of their own skill level.

The meeting produced a mixed response from the prospective facilitators. They recognized that the 'Q' process was clearly going to bring to the surface uncertainty and paradox related to business issues. They acknowledged that they felt more immediate comfort leaving such issues alone. Yet at the same time, they felt that it was critical to General Motors for managers to be freed of their current assumptions in order to think in new and innovative ways about the business and its challenges. In addition, they welcomed the opportunity to exercise more facilitative skills than they were able to use in traditional courses.

The concerns which the prospective facilitators expressed about the 'Q' process are summarized here under three headings.

CONCERNS RELATED TO PROTECTING THE PARTICIPANTS FROM THEMSELVES

- Asking participants to deal with their own assumptions may cause them some pain – they may leave the workshop feeling badly.
- This feels like sensitivity training – a lot of people got hurt with that.
- How can we help participants save face in class if we are confronting their assumptions?
- If we teach participants to think in this way they may find themselves penalized when they go back to work and try to use these ideas.

CONCERNS ABOUT THE CONSEQUENCES TO FACILITATORS

- If we are confrontative our ratings on the participant reaction forms will go down. As HRD professionals we have traditionally set great store by those forms.
- People want answers, not questions, in the courses.
- People in the courses may not tolerate this kind of probing, they might just walk out.

CONCERNS ABOUT MAKING MISTAKES OR BEING SEEN AS LESS SKILFUL

- When we team-teach, one team member might turn out to be more skilful in this than another and hurt feelings might ensue.
- If we engage in lengthy discussions we will not cover all the material. We are likely to be criticized for that.
- It would not be fair to some of us to have to learn and practise these skills in front of our more adept colleagues. We should be given an opportunity to learn these skills in private, away from the organization.

In addition to the concerns listed above, the self-assessment revealed that the current skill set associated with 'P' was so automatic that prospective facilitators had difficulty setting it aside in order to use the new 'Q' skills. For example, they demonstrated:

1. a tendency to use questions to bring participants around to an answer the facilitator had already formed in his/her own mind rather than using questions to help participants explore their own ideas;
2. a tendency to try to persuade participants to the facilitator's point of view rather than attempt to understand the participants' reasoning and assumptions;
3. a tendency to avoid rather than confront difficult and contentious issues;
4. a tendency to act in ways that saved face for each other and the participants.

Finally, the self-assessment indicated that the prospective facilitators were often embedded in the same assumptions about the organization that the managers held. They were therefore unable to be helpful in identifying the manager's assumptions in order to raise them to a level at which they could be examined.

As a result of the assessment, the prospective facilitators devised a process to help each other gain the new skills by working together in teams, so that each could provide feedback for the other. There was, however, an unwillingness to commit fully to the 'Q' methodology as long as they felt it involved the risk of a negative consequence to themselves. In particular, the prospective facilitators wanted assurance by their own management that if the ratings on participant reaction forms were lower as a result of the 'Q' methodology they would not be held responsible. Realizing that traditional success indicators would need to be viewed differently for 'Q' learning to proceed, General Motors' HRD management offered the required assurance. The prospective facilitators, however, continued to express concern about how they would be judged.

The development team proceeded with the design of the initial courses and with plans to begin action sets following the courses. The first course, which was piloted at the supervisor level with externals facilitating, achieved mixed results. Before arriving, participants had talked with others who had attended earlier versions of the courses and therefore came expecting a very different kind of course from what was offered. They were, as well, new to their jobs and, as the prospective facilitators had anticipated, were 'looking for answers'. This need was particularly strong at the first-line supervisory level. Despite this, most participants achieved breakthroughs in their own thinking and left with a desire to continue the exploration. The course was seen as frustrating but beneficial.

As the process moved forward the internal HRD professionals took over the task of facilitation. Several activities were built into the design of the programmes to provide feedback to the facilitators about how the group was doing and how they felt about the facilitators. These activities, initially seen as high risk for the facilitators, came to be valued as a source of useful information. With the use of such tools and with strong management encouragement, the facilitators gained both skill and comfort. However, as expected, their existing assumptions and beliefs remained a hindrance to switching skill sets. In some instances the development team altered the facilitator tasks to provide more 'P' and less 'Q' to increase the comfort level of the facilitators.

ACTION SETS

As the time came closer to implement action sets, new issues arose. One related to the structure of Human Resources within US organizations. In most US organizations, 'Training' is responsible for providing 'P' through scheduled courses that often bring together participants from across the US. A separate branch of Human Resources, 'Organizational Development', is responsible for working with managers on-site through the use of small group activities that are problem solving oriented. Since Action Learning overlapped both 'Training' and 'Organizational Development', it was unclear which area should assume responsibility for the implementation of action sets.

A second issue, also related to the way many US decentralized organizations are structured, is that HRD typically does not have the authority to implement programmes in plants or divisions. At General Motors mechanisms were lacking to describe and promote the Action Learning concept to line management, whose support would be essential to the successful operation of Action Learning sets at the plant/office locations of the organization.

The Action Learning process is sufficiently attractive, and so greatly needed, that progress continues despite such formidable roadblocks. It remains to be seen whether Action Learning can enter an organization in the US through the Human Resources function; and further, whether it can be successfully facilitated by HRD professionals. In any case, from the lengthy experiment some lessons have been learned.

LESSONS LEARNED

HRD professionals experienced in leading 'P' learning often come to expect a well-thought-out instructional design complete with leader's guide. 'Q' processes, however, require a minimum amount of pre-design because of the situational nature of the learning event. The ambiguity and lack of explicit learning objectives associated with 'Q' requires HRD professionals to make a significant shift in skills as well as assumptions.

Because 'Q' facilitation demands considerable openness as well as a willingness to examine one's own mistakes publicly, not everyone should be encouraged to become a 'Q' facilitator. The selection process for identifying personnel for the 'Q' role should clarify what is required of a 'Q' facilitator in terms of both behaviour and values.

In the US, the traditional reward system for both the HRD professionals and the Human Resources department supports the use of 'P' rather than 'Q'. Human Resources departments are often budgeted according to the number of participants who have attended. HRD professionals are rewarded for the positive response they receive from participants. Major changes in the reward system for HRD are required to support 'Q'.

Through this experience with Action Learning, as well as with other learning efforts that are being implemented at General Motors, there is a growing realization that the distinction between 'Training' and 'Organizational Development' is in many ways artificial. Many at General Motors have come to understand that the typical US organizational structure which separates the roles of 'Training' and 'Organizational Development' may need to be redefined or abandoned for the full potential of Action Learning to be realized.

Having externals on the development team, in this case the professor and consultant, brings a perspective to those learning 'Q' that helps them to reframe their own assumptions about the new role of the HRD professional and the environment in which they are functioning.

The preparation of 'Q' facilitators who have been mostly involved in facilitating 'P' learning requires a very thoughtful process. This process is probably most successful when a master facilitator is assigned the tasks of teaching, coaching, and mentoring experienced 'P' facilitators as they learn the new skills.

Action Learning and the 'Q' learning process are difficult to promote or explain to action oriented managers in the US who have come to think of learning as separate from work. The 'Q' process, questioning insight, is often initially seen by managers as the stuff of philosophers or, worse, 'idle dreamers'.

Regardless of the ambiguity or situational nature of 'Q' learning, success indicators need to be identified by the facilitating team. Success indicators may be determined through discussion, consensus and critical reflection on the part of the HRD facilitation team.

Senior managers appear to value 'Q' more and to be more receptive to it, than supervisor-level managers. There appears to be a greater willingness on their part to reflect and to seek the perspective of others.

Although the act of challenging taken-for-granted assumptions of managers is a critical element in the learning process, it is helpful only if it is accomplished in a climate of support, trust, and openness. It is the combination of challenge and trust that facilitates 'Q' learning.

GLOBAL TASK TEAMS

The original Action Learning programme at General Motors was started in 1989 and was discontinued after two years, partly because of the problems described in this chapter. A subsequent Action Learning programme, called Global Task Teams (GTT) was developed in 1994. This section describes the GTT and contrasts it with the earlier programme, especially with regard to the roles and responsibilities of facilitators.

FROM AN INTERVIEW WITH GTT FACILITATORS JACK LAND AND JOE DOYLE

Global Task Teams (GTT) are an effort by General Motors (GM) to develop executive talent for the corporation. To do so 8–10 high potential GM employees from sites around the globe form an international team. The team addresses a significant operating challenge of a host unit over a three-month time-frame. The team is convened in the United States for the launch process. The team spends the next four weeks visiting pre-arranged companies that represent best practice in the task they have been assigned. The next eight weeks of the programme is spent at the host site putting together the realities of the site with what the team has learned through their benchmarking efforts. At the end of the three months, the team makes a set of recommendations to the site's senior management and in some cases begin the implementation process. A closure process helps team members reflect on lessons learned from the experience and anticipate their re-entry.

Since 1994 GM has assembled five Global Task Teams who have worked at sites around the globe:

Site	Task
1. India	To contribute to the design and implementation of a lean manufacturing system and related support systems.
2. Indonesia	To develop a template for integrating lean manufacturing systems into new operations.
3. North America	To develop a process to identify emerging market indicators that would point the way to potential new products.
4. Australia	To design a material flow process for a new body shop.
5. England	To review a preliminary market strategy designed to improve market and consumer satisfaction, making recommendations for changes and constructing an implementation plan.

According to the facilitators, for a task to be developmental it needs to have both a systemic element (requires taking the whole system into account) and a strategic element (includes the development of a strategy for implementing recommendations). As the teams begin to explore the challenge they have been

265

given, they frequently find themselves reframing or expanding the task as originally defined. The teams are made up of members from multiple functions which assists them in addressing the challenge systemically.

In putting together the GTT, GM makes a concerted effort to ensure that the teams are truly international, for example, the India team included members from Belgium, Egypt, Spain, Australia, Germany, and North America. Although GM's business language is English, some team members have considerably less English fluency than do others. Thus, one of the difficult challenges GTT team members face is how to achieve high performance with a multi-lingual team. This challenge mirrors the reality of GM as a corporation and thus serves team members as a learning laboratory for the future.

FACILITATOR'S ROLE

The facilitators meet with each team during the programme launch and then reconnect at critical junctions. One such junction occurs right before the team makes its first benchmarking visit. The facilitators help the team think through what they want to achieve through the visit and how they will approach the benchmarking site. After the visit they work with the team to debrief their experience and draw from it what they have learned for the challenge as well as applications to their home unit. These 'lessons' in reflective learning, team process and planning are representative of the philosophy of the facilitators, which is a 'just in time' approach to assistance. They wait until there is a need in the team before offering approaches or process help, for example, the facilitators would not introduce conflict management until the group actually encounters team conflict.

As the team continues its site visits the facilitators stay in contact through weekly updates and phone conversations with individual members. If these calls indicate that the team is in need of further process assistance, the facilitators may rejoin them for a few days, but excepting a special need, the facilitators do not meet with the team again until they are ready to leave for the host site. At that time, the facilitators work with the team to develop a strategy for entry into the site, again employing their assistance on an 'as needed' basis.

The final contact the facilitators have with the team is during the closure process where much of the learning in the GTT is crystallized. The facilitators assist the team around a number of important issues. They help the team think through, and when necessary revise, the strategy they have developed for the presentation they will make to the host site. The facilitators interview key people at the site to gain insight into how individual members and the team as a whole functioned, then use this data to enhance the design of the next GTT experience. Team members provide each other with in-depth feedback on a wide variety of leadership behaviours. Finally the re-entry issues are considered, both in regard to families, from whom they have been absent for three months, and their home site.

The issues facing facilitators of the GTT teams are considerably different from the issues described in this chapter. Both the participants and the facilitators themselves, view the facilitator's role differently in the GTT programme than in the earlier programme. The facilitators of the GTT come from an OD background rather than the training background which the earlier facilitators had. The GTT facilitators introduce themselves to the group as people who will assist with process issues and explain that upper level management hold the facilitators accountable for the team's process experience; for example, if the team were to have interpersonal conflict that prevented them from developing a useful product, the facilitators would be answerable for that failure. However, even given these caveats and differences, facilitation dilemmas still exist in the GTT.

Although the GTT facilitators make an effort to both clearly explain and demonstrate the process role they will play with the team, it sometimes remains ambiguous in the eyes of team members. Team members are likely to confuse the facilitator role with a more familiar administrative or even content expert role. A strictly process role, in a situation in which process often has low priority, is both difficult for team members to grasp and to hold on to. Although over the three-month period of the programme team members usually come to value this role, initially, it is confusing.

Because the facilitators are not full members of the team, leaving and re-entering as they are needed, they may be experienced as 'outsiders'. At each entry the facilitators may need to re-build relationships with the group, re-establishing their value to the group and their trustworthiness. Without such careful renewal team members may fear that facilitators are surreptitiously gathering information about individual team members which they would then report back to corporate.

Finally, although team members understand that the GTT is a vehicle for their development, they have a tendency to give precedence to the task they have been assigned and to see team or individual development issues as something to be addressed if there is time after their 'work' has been accomplished. Process issues are sometimes viewed as time taken away from work rather than being viewed as an integral part of work.

However, many of the issues that troubled facilitators in the earlier programme have not occurred with the GTT. One reason for these differences is that where the initial programme grew out of a training setting, the GTT was a variation of a developmental experience that centred around a job rotation programme developed for high potential employees from non-US countries. Thus the history of the two programmes, which has a strong influence on participant expectations,

267

were quite dissimilar. In addition the OD background of the facilitators may have better prepared them with the skills needed to facilitate 'Q'.

Five Global Task Teams have now provided documented assistance to host units around the globe which has earned them a growing reputation within General Motors for the quality of their work. GTT team members readily acknowledge the developmental gains they have accrued, including insights they have developed into different functions, skills they have gained for effective functioning within a multi-cultural team setting, experience in handling conflict, the importance of understanding other perspectives, and the systemic knowledge of General Motors.

Reference

[1] Marsick, V. J. (ed.) (1982) *Learning in the Workplace*, New York: Croom Helm, p. 5.

22 Continuity in Action Learning

Jean Lawrence

When Action Learning has been introduced in an organization what happens to it? Is it just the latest fad of a management development manager, or the chief executive? Is this first programme repeated appropriately? Do other areas of the organization become a new focus for Action Learning work? Do the managers involved in a first programme introduce new developmental ways of working with their own departments or divisions? Does 'implementation' remain a vital part of the work, or is it steadily diluted until Action Learning fades to some form of project work – or is there a complete reversion to taught programmes?

Other contributors to this volume have already drawn attention to the vital distinction Reg Revans made between 'P' and 'Q' – 'P' being the programmed knowledge that can be systematically taught and learned, with well-defined stages and outcomes, and 'Q' being the complex process of raising and working with fundamental questions that do not admit unequivocal answers.[1] Can 'P' and 'Q' live side by side in programmes or must 'P' precede 'Q' and be separate from it? Does 'P' always drive out 'Q'? What makes it possible to integrate them, and what breaks them apart?

Established courses – and the very word 'course' may indicate a large proportion of 'P' – attract participants over long periods; perhaps through general reputation or inertia? Organizational fathers and grandfathers seem to send their sons and grandsons, and even their granddaughters, to the institutions and to the very same programmes which seemed to help *them*. The programmes will be modified over time but their 'character' may well remain the same. Is this phenomenon based on loyalty to the institution, as for example, with sending undergraduates to colleges in Oxford, or, is it that practitioners in Action Learning are not presenting a variety of high-quality new opportunities persuasively enough to break a habit and generate the energy to accept a challenge.

Action Learning makes many demands on the organization, especially for those embarking on it for the first time. It may be that the complexity of these demands – these challenges – and the fact that they occur again in later programmes is largely unrecognized by those organizations and becomes one of the important factors threatening continuity. Action Learning encourages all those engaged in it to learn and change, and demands that they move forward; repetition, old answers to old questions, is not enough. Perhaps the continual challenge to old ideas, and the disruption and reorganization of established systems which may follow, is too uncomfortable. If the challenge comes from the middle of the organization and not only from the top, it may, sooner or later, prove intolerable.

THREE STORIES OF 'Q' AND 'P'

Let us look at three experiences:

1. An Action Learning programme closely related to taught modules, is well established at senior management level in a large organization. After three years, the head of management development moves to another appointment, a major change occurs in the environment of the company and new appointments are made at the top. Questions are asked, and answered, about the project work. New line managers are concerned about the way the disruption caused by enthusiastic project champions may affect their regular results. There is a move towards safety – the taught modules survive and are extended. There is a gesture towards project work in extended live case studies and group investigations, but implementation is dropped, in spite of the pleas of the training staff involved in the previous activities. New development staff may welcome the opportunity to change, rethink and promote new approaches.

2. A level of management in an organization is thought by trainers and top management to have deficiencies for which Action Learning may provide considerable benefits. A programme begins after careful preliminaries and is repeated three times in later phases alongside major organization changes. It is guided by a group of senior line managers and is seen to fulfil the objectives, regarded as highly successful, bringing additional unforeseen benefits. The line managers take up a new role in relation to management development in the whole organization. After three years the whole level of management has been through the programme; so, it is said, there is no further opportunity to pursue that way of working. The issues are compounded by the retirement of the person most involved with day-to-day work on the series of programmes.

3. A group of three top managers, each from a different small organization, take part in an introductory week and then embark on a series of six-weekly one-day meetings to support each other in their current problems.

They pay three meetings in advance for the meetings, including the help of the facilitator. A fourth manager joins them quite soon, and one of the originals leaves after two years. Now fifteen years later, they are still meeting regularly. Two more people have joined, one of whom has continued (with nine-month gaps) through two changes of organization, industry and location. Attempts, most of them successful, have been made to introduce Action Learning as a way of life in some areas of the organizations represented. There seems to be no reason for this continuous learning to end.

These experiences raise questions which go beyond the information presented, but, taking what is said at face value, we may conclude that there are particular difficulties with internal programmes. In the first of these two examples of internal programmes 'Q' declined and in the second the specific activities ended after about three years. Internal programmes inevitably have a higher component of organization development within them. If we concentrate on individual management development, the perceived difficulties in proposals for organization change may only appear as part of the 'unforeseen benefits', and not as purposive revolutionary activities. Isolating management development from organization change may be a way of reducing the threat to the continuity of programmes, and may help to explain the longer life of programmes where senior or top individuals work on their own development with others outside the organization.

Experience earlier with GEC and more recently with district managers in the Health Service before Regions disappeared, encourages me to believe that the variety within very large organizations may provide sufficient differentiation to develop continuity. If it is true that in some organizations, senior individuals must take their problems outside to gain new insights into what is happening and to work on the real issues, perhaps 'outside' can sometimes mean a fairly distant part of the same very large organization. A clearly bounded area of authority appears to be a prerequisite for participation in a successful programme of this kind.

My experience persuades me we should be particularly concerned about programmes within organizations or within parts of very large organizations. The difficulties seem greater but the benefits of success can be dramatic. Results may include a clear move in the culture of the whole organization towards a growth of leadership skills right down the system; developing a questioning innovative approach at all levels; and gaining confidence that whatever changes in the environment occur, the organization will be flexible enough to survive and prosper.

If the benefits can be so splendid and appropriate for today, how can we tackle the difficulties presented by introducing an Action Learning approach within organizations, so that the work is sustained to a point when it becomes 'a way of life'?

Let us take the example of an organization where influential people have come to believe that a commitment to Action Learning will bring important advantages, including improving the bottom line, providing much better service to customers, constituents, and so on. Given this ideal opportunity, what strategy can we adopt to ensure that we keep questioning alive?

AN ORGANIZATIONAL STRATEGY FOR MAKING 'Q' A WAY OF LIFE

An approach might be:

1. To work with the top management group to define their commitment to a specific approach, and to develop a programme for those senior managers immediately responsible to them. An outside consultant, probably engaged specifically for this role, continues to work with this group.
2. As the work is authorized, workshops are devised to develop the skills of those inside the organization who can work alongside the consultant at the senior management level.
3. Some months later the senior level have had the experience of set work and the achievement of projects, over a considerable period. They may now be helped to set up their own Action Learning activities in and between their own spheres of influence, involving those immediately responsible to them and those further down the system. The aim will be for line managers to facilitate groups of peers and those reporting to them as they tackle new work, new aspects of their work, or, indeed, as they develop ideas for new work.
4. Internal facilitators, consultants, developers, and trainers who have been involved in the workshops in 2 above, will be available to support this work in appropriate roles.
5. Programmes for developing (not 'training') staff, supervision, first level management, graduate intake, and so on, will be devised and developed on an Action Learning base. Projects ranging from simple quality circle tasks, through to operational and inter-departmental confusions will be tackled as part of the participants' normal roles, but supported by set work and the work of a facilitator. Facilitators will frequently be from among the work group involved, temporarily taking up a new role for this work.
6. A key to keeping 'Q' alive may be the regular, though possibly quite infrequent (one day in six to eight weeks perhaps), intervention of an outside consultant in the work of the top group. An extended board meeting without a regular agenda may be the form the meeting will take. The outsider's job is to work on the linkages within the group and to ensure that nothing is glossed over or taken for granted in the group.

Questions will be supported and always treated seriously, listening will be active and acute. Development projects and the development of individuals and the group as a whole will dominate the flow of work. If this top group is continually asking questions of itself others will feel more confident in taking this approach, which otherwise might seem dangerous. The process is liable to get everybody thinking and exploring and unsatisfied by the status quo. Greater demands will be made on management, leading to their development and again the subsequent development of their people.

Many attempts have been made to do most of these things, and it all sounds relatively straightforward as it is spelt out. However, we should remind ourselves that we started with an ideal opportunity. Achieving integration throughout the organization is, perhaps, the most demanding part. There must be some explanation for the degree of difficulty most of us have, and for the evidence all around us of the decline of 'Q' in organizations which courageously begin to work in a questioning way.

THREE PROCESSES IN ORGANIZATIONS WHICH INCREASE THE DIFFICULTIES

Let us now try to identify some of the processes which occur both in the organization and in those practitioners concerned to introduce and sustain it, to see how the interruption of the development of Action Learning occurs. There are, it seems, three groups which particularly influence the continuation or decline of 'Q', each of whom encounter problems and difficulties as the activities progress. There is the central powerful group in the organization, individual managers closely involved in the programme, and the practitioners who believe the approach is fundamentally effective and advantageous.

First the practitioners – what are the pressures on us from others and from our own backgrounds and attitudes as we try to introduce and establish Action Learning within an organization?

In Appendix 1 David Pearce has given a detailed account of the steps involved in starting up an Action Learning programme within an organization. These are still necessary steps but many of us find a great deal of difficulty as we follow that path. We may have learned to manage it better, but still we do not foresee all the consequences of early minor decisions and influences. The underlying processes are complex and these early steps may begin a story which is brought to an end after a very few chapters, by the very complexity it generates.

As we negotiate each stage in the development of an agreed programme, we have to remain open to change and modification. It is very unlikely that we will be satisfied with any previous design in these new circumstances. We will initially welcome the opportunity to work with those within the organization on a new joint proposal. But pressures are applied, commitments entered into, while politics and culture are little understood. It feels more like finding angles and loopholes,[2] than following a blue-print. We may well wish we could legitimately sell a product based in experience, and repeatable with only the slightest tinkering – but this would be a 'P' type programme!

As it is we recognize the need to gain commitment by top management before the work begins. Yet it often seems necessary, as the negotiations proceed, to modify the full acceptance of Action Learning, so that we risk losing its characteristic benefits. For example, implementation is not to be emphasized – recommendations will be considered, probably some ideas will be put into action, but the members of the programme may not be involved; or there must be some formal teaching in a, b or c at some point in the programme. If we can integrate the preparation for project work with the 'P' teaching, and ensure that the 'teaching' is as learner-centred as possible, will we keep 'Q' alive throughout the programme? Or will we find eventually that a rapidly moving management game overlaps the slow thoughtful preparation for, and choice of, a project? Inevitably then 'P' will drive out 'Q', as the need to compete and win against tight deadlines in a neat well-designed teaching vehicle takes priority.

At each stage it may all seem very reasonable – 'they need to have better financial skills so an accounting module is needed' and so forth. But at each point we may be allowing the results of the programme to be clouded by less definition of implementation, less clear increase in self-reliance as a taught module takes over, weaker work in the set because there is less at stake. These decisions about what we can afford to let go and on what aspects we must stand firm are very fine matters of judgement. Eventually those monitoring the activities may have considerable difficulty in seeing results, and wonder whether the effort they are making is worth-while. We may, unwittingly, have given away the essential benefits of Action Learning!

If, as is often the case, only a 'trial' set or a small group can work at first, assessment may rest on a very small sample activity and the reality of the experience inevitably includes many hazards – our judgement of the risks is crucial. The assessment may only be made at the end of this first limited programme (after, perhaps, six months) so that any second phase may start almost a year after the first. There is a very slow accumulation of experience, on which confidence can be based.

In addition to these difficulties we may experience conflicts about our own role. We may be basically academics, basing our strength in specialized knowledge and analysis. We may then feel that adapting to the roles required for Action Learning is comfortable in the investigation and report writing stage, but we have little experience in implementation. We approach it with little confidence: it seems nitty-gritty, endless, it is not something we want to be involved in. 'P', and variants on 'P', triumph. We can go only so far with 'Q'. So perhaps we are likely to collude with the client and agree too readily that implementation as such is not quite the cornerstone of Action Learning we thought it was. In later programmes 'project work' is included, reports are presented and tactfully praised, but the demanding nature of Action Learning has somehow withered away.

There is another process that may have a serious effect on the decay of 'Q', located in the second group – the managers taking part in the programme and those closely associated with their activities. Usually by the third meeting of the set, members are becoming enthusiastic, questioning and probing the work of the others, offering support, and listening to and questioning the responses they receive as they talk through their own ideas and activities. As the set progresses confusions of role can arise, as they try to balance their normal work role and their project role, working with both a 'boss' and a 'client' each having expectations and deadlines. The 'client' is hoping that the problem he or she has identified will be tackled and some contribution will be made to its solution. If the participant's boss *is* the client *that* confusion is minimized, but the variety of experience available to the participant is likely to be more limited, and the challenge may be reduced. Again, careful judgements at the design stage are required.

If we have all made good decisions at the selection stage we may have flexible enthusiastic participants who will, with the help of their fellows, turn each of these difficulties to advantage and learn from each hurdle as they cross it.

But clients also have their own anxieties. Processes which can stop the development of 'Q' can originate with them. They are seen by others to be committed to this strange activity. Perhaps they had a (secret) conviction about an expected solution and were disappointed when the analysis led the participant in a new direction. Or they may be concerned that if the project 'fails' it may reflect badly on the participant and/or the client. It may be difficult for them to be able to accept that as much – perhaps more – can be learned from an unsuccessful struggle in a demanding project, as from a highly successful, relatively straightforward project.

On the other hand success in a difficult project may mean the participant has tackled and dealt with a problem normally handled at the level of his boss. With renewed confidence has he become a competitor or, at the least, a more demanding member of the team for whom new opportunities have to be found? There might be expectations of promotion with the risk of loss of an experienced resource. Does the client (or the boss) want to support such developments repeatedly? Being good managers, they do, of course, want to develop their people but perhaps the decline of the programme after a while is not altogether surprising.

Thirdly, the most inimical process may be at work within the most powerful group. Influential managers may be in many different roles, and many ways to distort, divert or stop the work of Action Learning have been found. Some are quite conscious, for example, managers complain that their people are unlikely to meet their targets while they are working on the programme. Those who are taking no part in the programme may vary between ridiculing the work in the set, and envying what the members are so obviously learning, and the demanding experiences of clients. They may feel the programme is disrupting the managerial team, or it is too unstructured – the managers need to be more 'educated', they are not learning the latest techniques – 'now if we just put in time management . . .' – all conscious moves that may interrupt the development.

Some of the moves by these powerful people to stop such a programme may, however, be less conscious, and may originate in a desire to hold the organization steady, in fear of dilution or sharing of power. There is a strong need to uncouple, once again, the learning activity, so that learning can be kept safely within the confines of courses and training centres. Thus, the dominant culture, the way of life of those in power, rejects the more demanding aspects of Action Learning, and modifies and emasculates it until it is manageable without effort.[3] Gradually it becomes so structured and repeatable that it might as well be a course.

These are some of the processes at work as we try to establish continuity in Action Learning within an organization. If we are to succeed we must work to integrate the skills, understanding and commitments of these three groups.

SOME GUIDELINES FOR SAFEGUARDING 'Q'

Perhaps we have now some clues about keeping 'Q' alive.

First, if we have a bluechip opportunity to enter an organization with strong support from the very top, as discussed earlier, we can develop a full programme of activities as outlined. But we must take special care to protect the activities and, most importantly, should avoid expecting the idea to cascade – to flow down the organization under its own momentum. We will have to work at each level and in each area of operation to establish this new way of life.

Second, three ways to reduce risk and anxiety should be carefully evaluated. If the project is defined so that the client is the boss of the participant, there may be less role confusion for the set member. If clients (and perhaps colleagues of set members) are introduced to the programme very carefully so that their roles are fully understood, anxiety may be reduced. And if more than one set is initiated at the start of the programme there is less risk of quick assessment of the programme on little evidence and against a background of change and constructive disturbance of established habits. Anxieties can perhaps be contained.

Third, an understanding of the culture of the organization is necessary at the start. The rapid development of that understanding so that negative processes can be identified quickly, should be given priority as the programme begins.

Fourth, we can establish a steering group for the programme or activity. This steering group of senior managers at client level or above can take responsibility for the start and the progress of the programme. If such a group can be set up at an early stage in the negotiations, it is likely that problems of conflict with the organization culture, and of the roles of individual managers relating to the programme, can be well managed. The steering group will consist of line managers involved in activities recognized as central to organization success, joined by one or two developers, trainers or facilitators. There is an opportunity for development work in the group as they work on the new task of initiating and supporting an Action Learning programme. It will, initially, be concerned with the selection of participants and developing criteria for choice of projects, and arranging a process for matching participant and project.

It can continue throughout the programme picking up any difficulties in relating to the formal structure. The steering group also can, and usually does, ensure the interest of top management in the programmes. Its last role on any one programme may be to follow up an evaluation and to ensure continuity, if appropriate, by starting a second programme quite soon after the first. Ideally, the second should overlap the first to encourage learning one from the other.

Lastly, careful attention should be given to the structured part of any programme. Here I am referring to the administration in general, which must be watertight, and the timing, length, size, shape and cost of any programme. In both programmes and activities we need a clear understanding of relations with clients or sponsors, who have, themselves, gained a considerable understanding of the opportunities and perceived dangers of the approach. We are providing a boundary to protect the unfamiliar and unplanned activities so that those involved can feel relatively safe to question and criticize, explore their feelings and learn.

In particular, it is, I believe, important to 'end' a single activity or programme and to gain new commitment, a new contract, for further activities, if they are to follow. We should consider carefully, at the start, what we are to mean by 'ending' both the programme, and the projects within it.

With this early work completed we can arrange that participants leave the programme with a clear idea of how it has ended, and how they individually can take their learning further. They are no longer concerned with a programme but free to take full charge of their own futures. They may have completed a project and begun to think how that work can be developed, and by whom, for the benefit of the organization. A new version of 'who knows, who cares and who can'[4] is forming in their minds so that other colleagues may have an opportunity to contribute to a particular development and to learn from it. Or they may be considering how they can use their experience of learning powerfully in this way to develop the learning of their staff; they could start a process of continuous learning together, from the experience of their development activities. Or they may be looking specifically at their own roles, trying to see how to ensure that they individually learn from each task they tackle; and searching for ways to get and be given the support they will need when facing the challenges they can dimly see but are quite convinced lie ahead of them.

Thus, clarity about the structure at the start helps us to be able to work with members of the set with clarity about 'ending', which, paradoxically may mean continuity. They may, being completely released from the first experience, choose to promote another, providing themselves and others with particular opportunities to continue to learn.

I hope it is clear that in discussing the continuity of Action Learning I am considering a different set of issues from those involved in the continuity of successful courses. This continuity of successful courses is to continue to meet a development need of individual managers or groups of managers, who then have to take the responsibility of applying what they have learnt within their organizational roles. The continuity that we seek in Action Learning is to be a part of the actual life of organizations in a process of change, continuing because its contribution to organizational change is to sharpen awareness and to raise the levels of energy and effectiveness of managers in the company of fellow learners. Activities will change, systems will improve, people will do different things. We are required to provide a framework, an effectively managed boundary, and to continue to change and maintain it to protect the work.

This is not an exhaustive set of guidelines! The activities have inherent difficulties, but the level of effectiveness is well above any other form of development available now. If we can continue to learn from each other as we pursue these challenging tasks, 'Q' may be kept alive in many more organizations.

REFERENCES

1 Revans, R. (1983), *The ABC of Action Learning*, UK: Chartwell-Bratt.
2 Heller, J. (1979), *Good as Gold*, London: Jonathan Cape.
3 Morris, J. (1986), 'The Learning Spiral' in Mumford (Ed) *Handbook of Management Development*, (2nd Edn), UK: Gower.
4 Revans, R. (1983), op. cit.

23 Participating in Action Learning

Tom Bourner, Liz Beaty and Paul Frost

Much has been written about how to be an effective Action Learning set adviser but very little on how to be an effective set member. In this chapter we share our experience, as Action Learning set members and as set advisers, of what it means to become a more effective set member.

Most people join an Action Learning set with two aspirations: to 'solve' a real problem and to learn from so doing. Expressed in this way, it seems as though the learning is a by-product of solving the problem and thereby subsidiary to it. We believe that this is an illusion. The use of the term 'Action Learning' implies that the focus is on the *learning*. The attempted problem-resolution is the *vehicle* that is used to generate the learning. This is an important issue as it holds a key to the contributions of the other set members.

The core of Action Learning lies in *learning* rather than *solving the problem*. To see why, consider two situations. In situation one, a set member attempts to solve a problem and fails to do so but learns a great deal about themselves and their problem in the process. In situation two, a set member solves a problem but fails to learn anything of significance in so doing. It seems clear to us that situation one could still be termed Action Learning whereas situation two could not. Learning, therefore, is an essential ingredient of Action Learning whereas success in the problem-solving is not.

How does this help us to identify what makes for effectiveness in a set? It means that the primary role of the Action Learning set is *not to find a solution for the problem of each set member but to help each set member to learn from finding solutions to their problems.*

HELPING SET MEMBERS TO LEARN HOW TO FIND SOLUTIONS TO THEIR PROBLEMS

Some people come to an Action Learning set thinking 'the best way that I can help my fellow set members is to try to solve their problems for them'. This is natural and is normally well-intentioned – but it is misconceived. It can lead to their pressing advice on the other set members. What else can a set member do to help fellow set members discover solutions to their problems and learn from so doing? What other options are available?

LEARNING TO ASK GOOD QUESTIONS

Throughout life one is told by endless authorities what to do next, and one learns to obey. Much so picked up has already long existed, so it is here to be called programmed, *and denoted by P.... Yet much other learning also comes, neither from command nor example, but from one's own experience. Finding out for oneself may also be very mixed, like walking into a brick wall, making other mistakes, realising something does not work as expected ... or, occasionally, deliberately asking fresh questions – like Newton, inquiring whether the force keeping the moon close to the Earth was also that pulling the apple to the ground. Knowledge, ideas, attitudes, skills, new perceptions of what goes on are always turning up; what is so discovered, moreover, generally tells one something new about the self. 'Well! I must say! You do live and learn!' is so often said after the shock of finding out from one's own experience that some hallowed belief was long untrue.... Learning of this nature comes from* questioning *insight, and is denoted by Q.*[1]

Questioning insight (Q) is the goal when set members question their own experiences. What sort of question is likely to achieve this outcome? A 'good' question is selfless – it is not asked to illustrate the cleverness of the questioner or to generate information or an interesting response for the questioner. Rather it is asked as a way of opening up the problem owner's own view of their situation. There are a range of questions that can further this aim.

The 'open' question is one which cannot be answered in a word or two but requires discussion and explanation. Closed questions generally ask for one word responses, usually 'yes' or 'no'. Being asked closed questions can feel like an interrogation.

Didn't you feel foolish doing that?

Shouldn't you be more careful?

They tend to produce defensiveness and close down discussion. Open questions open up an area for discussion. Open questions ask the respondent to go deeper into their world in order to bring out an adequate answer. They include questions like:

How could you go about doing that?

What other options can you think of?

What resources do you have to do that?

Questions that ask for specifics can be helpful in putting the problem owner in touch with the realities of the problem. Questions such as 'can you give us an example of that?' are likely to generate specific instances which are richer in information content than the generalities which may be the product of earlier reflection. They are more likely to lead to new or revised generalities that constitute a further turn around the experiential learning cycle.

Another effective type of question is the one often used by interviewers that requires a reiteration and explanation of parts of the previous response. For example: 'When you say . . . what exactly do you mean?'

Yet another question that can be helpful if used sparingly is the question 'why?' 'Why do you want to do that?', 'Why do you think that?', 'Why do you expect that to happen?' and so on. In our experience, the 'why' question is more effective when applied to future actions than when applied to past actions. The former usually leads to exploration whereas the latter usually prompts *post hoc* rationalization.

You may wish to use a question to extend a person's range of perceived options in a situation. 'If I were in your situation I would do XYZ – what do you think about that for your own situation?'

Most statements contain various shades of meaning. Questions that start with 'Do you mean . . .' can be an effective way of discovering meanings that the speaker was unaware of. For example:

A: I believe that actually doing something is more important than just having good ideas.

B: Do you mean that you wish you'd stayed as a line manager rather than taking the job as in-house consultant?
Do you mean that you want us to tell you whether we agree with you or not?
Do you mean that you're sceptical of theoretical solutions that haven't been tried out in practice.

This form of questioning identifies the issues underlying the problem presented. Thinking of the problem as an onion with layers on layers can be a useful analogy. A group of people working collectively can bring about many different perspectives to help uncover the problem. A new angle can release a whole set of new possibilities.

LISTENING AND ATTENDING

If I want to help someone else to solve their problem (and to learn from so doing) then I need to know what kind of help they want: where they are with their thinking so far and what they feel about the issues. I can get this information mainly from two sources: listening to what they say and attending to the non-verbal cues they give which indicate the feelings and attitudes involved in what they are saying.

This is most unlike normal social intercourse where we take it in turns to be the focus in a conversation, where we often listen just enough to develop our own response and where we seek to relate what we hear to our own experience. In talking with others, our own agendas and our own thoughts often dominate while others are speaking and so we are not properly attending to what they say. Sometimes we are simply waiting for an opportunity to speak ourselves. Listening properly means having the right purpose in listening and much more than just leaving a silence for the other to speak. This type of listening is often called active listening because it involves paying close attention to what the other is saying and letting them know that you are doing so.

Much can be gleaned from active observation as well as active listening. People often reveal their feelings in the way they look as they speak and in their body language. An observation like 'when you said that you frowned' can provide feedback that helps them to articulate their feelings and therefore helps them to uncover important aspects to the problem they are describing that can otherwise remain hidden.

LEARNING NOT TO INTERRUPT

In most human conversation a convention of reciprocity prevails. When I say 'good morning' I expect a similar reply. I talk a bit about my ideas then you talk a bit about your ideas. Sometimes this convention is broken by mutual consent: perhaps I have had an interesting experience that I want to tell you about and you encourage me to talk more than usual. Sometimes, however, the conversational transaction is uneven just because I talk too much and you 'can't get a word in edgeways'. In this case, you are unlikely to find the conversation rewarding.

In a group context the situation is more complicated. This is presumably one reason for some of the elaborate rules of committee such as speaking 'through the chair'. An Action Learning set meeting provides plenty of opportunity for interrupting for those who are so inclined. Some people are so inclined because they fear that they will forget their important point or important question or that the conversation will move on and it will become inappropriate later. A simple solution to this problem is to be prepared with a paper and pen so that these ideas can be jotted down and contributed at a later time when interruption will be unnecessary.

LEARNING TO CONVEY EMPATHY

Developing empathy will help you to make the best contributions; when it is right to confront rather than offering a shoulder to lean on. However, there is another dimension to empathy. Empathy *conveyed* is more powerful than empathy *concealed*. Only if you convey your empathy can the problem owner know that you are 'on their side'. With this knowledge, the problem owner can allow themselves to share with you (and themselves) less palatable aspects of the problem and your contributions (even those that confront) will be more welcome. How can you convey empathy? One way is to check with the problem owner your understanding of the way that they are thinking and feeling about aspects of their problem:

> So you feel anxious that if you don't get the system installed you might lose your own job? Is that right?

> It sounds to me as if you're pleased with the progress that you've made to date but you're concerned that the real test will be how you deal with the Finance Director.

SUPPORTING

There will be times when it is appropriate to offer a shoulder to lean on; times when you want to express how much you hope that a fellow set member succeeds or that you share their disappointment with a failed action; times when you want to remind a fellow set member of the personal resources that s/he possesses.

> Your infectious sense of fun should help you in that situation.

Useful support enables the recipient to move forward through areas where their feelings are blocking their progress.

> Is there anything that we (the other set members) can do to help you to handle that?

Support can take place outside of set meetings too. For example, a telephone call from a set member to check the outcome of a difficult interview; perhaps a posted clipping from a trade journal that you feel would be useful.

CHALLENGING

There will be times when you want to convey your scepticism that a proposed outcome will produce the results required, or when you want to confront a fellow set member with your anger at a proposed line of action which you believe is unethical. Useful challenges are made when the recipient of the challenge is helped to think through their problem and come to clearer understanding as a result. A challenge made when I am feeling insecure may simply lead me to cave in under the extra strain. However, when I am confident and clear about my issues a challenge can help me succeed and find the learning in an outcome:

Just what did you learn from that experience?

How would you handle that differently next time?

What other options do you have?

Exactly how do you intend to do that?

The key question here is: how do you know when to support and when to challenge? Our answer to this question lies in *empathy*. If you have a good sense about how the problem owner is feeling and thinking then you'll have a good idea how to respond. And if you're not sure, you could always ask something like: 'Are you looking for support here or do you want us to try to find obstacles to what you are proposing?'

PROVIDING INFORMATION

Sometimes you may be able to provide the information that a fellow set member is seeking or you can provide the source of the information. For example, you may wish to offer help such as a reference to some statistics that a set member will find helpful.

OFFERING ADVICE

We have suggested that advice isn't necessarily the best way of helping fellow set members to solve their problems and learn from so doing. Are there any times when it is appropriate?

If your intention is to extend the range of options available for consideration by the problem owner then offering advice can be a valuable thing to do. Much depends upon how the advice is proffered. We would say that it is almost invariably counterproductive to *press* advice. Once the problem owner has heard the advice s/he will know if s/he can do anything useful with it. If you are operating from the attitude that 'each person is the world expert on their own problem' then you will have little difficulty in recognizing this. If you are operating from a belief that you understand the situation better than the problem owner you will have more difficulty recognizing this. You will also have difficulty appreciating this if you are interested in demonstrating your powers of percep-tiveness, analysis or persuasiveness to the rest of the group.

How do you know whether it will be productive or counterproductive to offer advice in a particular situation? Our answer to this question is to refer you back to our discussion of empathy. If you have managed to get in touch with the feelings and thoughts of the problem owner then your judgement about whether or not your advice will be helpful is likely to be sound.

HELPING TO GENERATE ACTION POINTS

There can be as many good questions asked about proposed actions as there can be in exploring the problem. Check whether an action will be appropriate. Some good questions at this stage include:

And who is likely to be affected if you do that?

What would happen if you did nothing at all?

What would be the result if this works to its most ideal?

What other options have you got?

Other questions at this stage can raise issues of feasibility of the proposed action – time available, resources required, power and influence needed, etc.

THE PROBLEM OWNER

So far in this chapter we have concentrated on how to help a fellow set member. At some stage in a set meeting each set member will take on the role of problem owner when the focus of the set will be on that person with their own problem. In this section we look briefly at ways by which the problem owner can gain most from the set in terms of solving their problem and acquiring as much learning as possible in the process.

LEARNING TO STRUCTURE YOUR TIME IN MEETINGS

Your time slot in a set meeting is there for you to use as effectively as you can. It is your responsibility to use your time slot in the way(s) that are most productive to you. What is most productive to you may be different from that which is most productive to others in your set. You may want to consider the different ways that different people in the set use their time slots and then treat this as a range of options available to you.

Here are some examples of ways that people have used their 'time slots' in our experience of set meetings. You can:

- ask the set to stay quiet while you give a brief presentation and then ask for comments
- take questions and comments as you proceed
- flip-chart an *agenda* for your time slot
- use a flip chart to illustrate the issues
- use a flip chart to structure the discussion or you may want a completely unstructured discussion
- specifically ask for information
- ask for suggestions for dealing with a situation where you feel bereft of options
- ask the set to brainstorm possible ways of dealing with an issue that you face
- ask the set to focus on the consequences of your actions (or inactions!) since the last set meeting
- ask the set to focus on the possible consequences of some action(s) that you intend to take
- ask the set to discuss an issue while you sit saying nothing but just taking notes of any useful ideas that emerge
- structure your time slot around the questions:
  What action points have I completed since the last meeting?
  What were the outcomes?
  What do I want to achieve by the next meeting?
  How can I do that?
- tape record your time slot when you are the problem owner. You can then replay the tape when you are driving to work in your car. We know set members who have done this and claim that they hear much more when they are replaying the tape than during the session when they recorded it.

You may want to use your time in different ways according to what type of issue you are bringing to the set and what stage of development your thinking is.

LEARNING HOW TO PREPARE FOR SET MEETINGS

Learning to be clear what you want to discuss at the set meeting is valuable preparation. This doesn't mean that you have to be clear about what you want to say. That is the role of the set – to help you to explore your concerns. But you will benefit more from the session if you are clear about the problems or issues and are ready to explore them with the set.

LEARNING TO ASK FOR WHAT YOU WANT

Explaining to the set how you want to use your time slot at the outset will give them the greatest opportunity to help you to do so. There are many different ways to use your time slot (see above) and if you think through the process that you want before the set meeting then you are likely to enhance your learning in the time available. Help the set to help you.

LEARNING HOW TO ELICIT AN EMPATHIC RESPONSE

The other set members can't really appreciate how you feel about your problem if you don't communicate your feelings. Without that information they will not be able to make accurate judgements about when to support and when to confront. If no-one in the set asks you about how you feel about the issues that you take to the set then tell them anyway.

LEARNING HOW TO TAKE CONTROL OF THE PROCESS

It is no good spending time discussing something that is unlikely to generate your next action points even if you find it interesting – keep the attention on *your* issues. Express yourself clearly and firmly on this; be assertive. Useful phrases here include:

What I really need is . . .

That's interesting and now I'd rather move on.

If someone offers you some advice or makes a suggestion that you disagree with you don't *have* to argue the point. That will just sustain discussion of the topic. A good solution here is just say 'Thanks very much for that idea. Now my next concern is . . .' This will move the conversation on to the areas that are more productive for you. You don't have to *defend*. You can *absorb* and then use that which is useful from what you have absorbed and ignore the rest. Learning to do this is a valuable skill outside of set meetings as well as within them. People who have to win arguments, score debating points and generally have to be seen to be right tend to have less productive sessions within Action Learning set meetings.

LEARNING HOW TO RECEIVE

We have suggested that a precondition to being an effective set member is learning how to actively listen. During your own time slot as problem owner the need to listen is no less important. Listen properly to the questions that are asked and the comments that are made. If you decide to reject the ideas you hear then your own ideas will have been strengthened by having considered alternatives.

We mentioned above the experience of some set members tape recording their time slots when they are the problem owner. Why do people who do this report that they hear more when they replay the tape in their car than they did in the set meeting? Is it because they then can allow their defences to fall away and listen properly to the contributions of the other set members?

Learning to receive also involves receiving support. Sometimes we feel that it is a weakness to admit that we need help. Sets can be truly supportive only if allowed to be so. Learning to give in to the support that is offered to you can be a most valuable lesson for both inside and outside of the set.

LEARNING WHAT TO REPORT BACK

If you are like us then you'll start most of your sessions by reporting back on the outcomes of your action points generated at the last meeting. Articulating the outcomes and subsequent events can be a useful way of making sense of them.

There will be other times when you want to move swiftly on to consider future actions. Don't feel that you need to provide detailed accounts of the subsequent events for the benefit of the rest of the set fellows. When your issue is under discussion your role is not to entertain them by telling them a story but to help them to help you to try to develop action points to solve your problem and learn by so doing.

You certainly shouldn't feel that you have to talk to fill in your time slot. If things are not going well with your project then talking can be a means of avoiding awkward issues. While you are talking, no-one can ask you any difficult or challenging questions. If your inclination is to talk for the sake of safety then that is the time to stop and invite comments and questions.

LEARNING HOW TO GENERATE ACTION POINTS

A most important dimension of the work of an Action Learning set is to generate action points to be worked on before the next set meeting. Good action points have a number of characteristics. They are clear, specific and measurable. They are also feasible to complete by the time of the next set meeting. It is easier to be clear and specific after the issues have been well explored and alternative actions discussed. You should ensure that they are expressed in a form that enables you to know whether you have been successful or not.

LEARNING TO ACT ON ACTION POINTS

The most important preparation is to have completed the action points from the previous set meeting. Someone at an evaluation session following an Action Learning programme said: 'One of the first things I learned, is that in an Action Learning programme if there's no action then there's no learning'. This may not always be the case; the third time you return to a set meeting with the same action point outstanding can be an occasion for significant learning about yourself. But action generates feedback and feedback is important to learning. A good definition of feedback is: 'information from any source that lets you know how you're doing or being perceived'. In our experience, it is those set members who undertake the most action that receive most feedback and gain most from the Action Learning process.

SUMMARY AND CONCLUSIONS

Much has been written about the role of the set adviser and little has been written about the role of the set member. In this chapter we have attempted to redress the balance. A reasonable conclusion would be: act as selflessly as you're able during other participants' sessions at a set meeting and act selfishly during your own session (i.e. during the period of the set meeting when the spotlight is on your problem).

What is written in this chapter is the product of our reflection on our experience in sets. You, however, might have developed or observed ways of being effective in sets that we haven't noticed. Moreover, having read our remarks, reflecting on your own experience might lead you to different conclusions. If that is the case, then follow the guidance of your own experience. We urge you to trust your own judgement, on the basis of what does and doesn't work for *you*.

REFERENCE

1 Revans, R. (1987) 'The learning equation: an introduction in "Action Learning",' *Journal of Management Development*, **6**(2).

Part IV
Evaluating Action Learning

INTRODUCTION

This new Part reflects the increasing attention being given to the evaluation of Action Learning, which is itself a sign of the maturing and widening acceptability of the idea in various settings. It is also, as noted earlier, in part a by-product of increasing academic interest.

Picking up from Tom Bourner and his colleagues in the last Part of the book, Krystyna Weinstein puts participants' voices at the centre of her valuing of the process. This is something so obvious and fundamental that it may often be overlooked. Ian Cunningham's impressive qualitative study of chief executives and their learning also makes much use of the participants' voices to create an evaluation which tells us a great deal about what works and what doesn't.

Nancy Dixon reporting on experience in General Electric in the USA points out that Action Learning is more than just a task force. She questions aspects of practice which rely on recommendations to action, rather than participants being given the discretion to act and learn directly. Judy O'Neil and her colleagues report on 'action reflection learning' – a variation which emphasizes and formalizes reflection processes in the group setting. They discuss various tensions which are relevant to all Action Learning.

Completing this section are Mark Easterby-Smith, Alison Johns and John Burgoyne who provide a comprehensively revised version of their primer on how to evaluate Action Learning. For those thinking about evaluating their efforts (and shouldn't that mean all of us?) this is a good place to start.

24 Participants' Voices

Krystyna Weinstein

What do participants gain – and learn – by taking part in Action Learning programmes? The best way to discover is to let them recount, and tell their own stories, in their own words.

In the summer of 1993 I undertook a study to ask participants what they had gained from Action Learning.* I interviewed some 70 people on sixteen different programmes. Nine of the programmes were in-company programmes, seven were mixed-company, and five had academic links. In addition I spoke informally to many people currently on programmes; included the insights from sets I had worked with over the years; and used comments from colleagues' experiences.

The programmes were differently designed, depending on their varying purposes: leadership and team development, individual management development, graduate development. The projects thus also varied: from set projects to individual projects.

As I talked to participants, it emerged that each of the six elements in an Action Learning programme – the set; the project i.e., the focus on a real task or action; the processes in the set; the set adviser; the time allocated to the whole programme; and the focus on learning – offers participants something valuable. The participants' responses – which I quote below – recall what they gained from each one. But first, the 'magic' that people spoke of.

THE 'MAGIC' OF ACTION LEARNING

What struck me was the general enthusiasm of participants for Action Learning. Of course there were dissenting voices, and I will give them their voice later.

---

* I incorporated these participants' voices into my book which introduces Action Learning to the 'uninitiated': *Action Learning: A Journey in Discovery and Development*, in the Successful Manager Series (paperback, HarperCollins, 1995). Only available from the author.

But some of those who found it to be 'magical', as one participant put it, had this to say:

> You become aware of yourself and others. You become aware of your qualities and skills.

> You learn to value good productive communication and you want to transfer it back to work.

> It gives you space for you – it values and respects the individual, and hence gives you confidence.

> It's like putting together your own programme. . . . You find that in addition to your project, the ostensible learning vehicle, you're simultaneously working on time management, empowerment, presentation skills, assertiveness. . . .

A chief executive in a local authority:

> . . . there's nothing else like it. . . . It's a holistic approach – you bring the whole person to it, not just the person in a role, and it encourages you to be a whole person wherever you are, so you use not just your knowledge but your whole experience and your emotions. It can be draining but it's powerful. You come and talk of a 'disaster' at work and you go away feeling the confidence to deal with it.

A senior manager:

> I always come away revitalized and re-energized . . . it gives you time and space to stand back and reflect . . . unfreeze your thoughts, rise above everyday problems . . . brings things into perspective in a non-judgemental, supportive yet challenging way, . . . which makes you take responsibility and ownership. It's very exciting but at times daunting. But you get a great sense of achievement.

And a sales manager said simply 'It's the best programme I've ever been on'.

What became apparent was that in addition to the 'anticipated' learning that participants were able to list, i.e. what they had planned to focus on and learn while on their programmes, was a vast array of 'unanticipated' learning, i.e. insights, awareness and knowledge that emerged as participants worked *in the set*, hearing each others' stories, helping each other, and reflecting on what they were doing, and learning; and as they pursued, *away from the set*, either their project, or just their everyday work.

So, what – in an Action Learning programme – gives participants such a buzz, such a feeling of energy and achievement?

WHAT YOU GAIN BY WORKING IN A SET

Participants gained quite specific benefits and learning from working in a set, on a regular basis, with the same small group of people all committed to working on real work issues – as well as themselves – and learning. The set itself turned out to be, I realized, a microcosm of what a 'learning company' could be.

REALIZING THE VALUE OF MIXING/WORKING CLOSELY WITH COLLEAGUES FROM OTHER FUNCTIONS AND/OR ORGANIZATIONS

Whether the sets were mixed-company ones or from the same organization, the comments were similar.

> You come [to the set] with assumptions about people and the different parts of the organisation they work in . . . you label them, but then you see the different constraints they work under . . . and begin to understand them better.

In many instances they learnt about other parts of the organization they'd never heard of – which gave them a better picture of the organization they were working for.

From those on mixed-company sets came comments such as: 'I thought our way of doing things was the only, the best, way. . . . I've learnt that there are many other ways of tackling the issue I'm working on. Ours isn't necessarily the best.'

RESPECTING AND VALUING EVERYONE

One of the premises of Action Learning is that a group of like-minded people – not necessarily experts (except in their own work) – can help each other. But getting people to believe this is often a different matter! So, several commented that it was often people in different functions and fields who challenged them the most effectively.

> I was amazed at how the non-experts in a given field can help you by asking intelligent questions – often very simple ones . . . their lack of familiarity with my issue caused me to explain it from basics, and often made me think more laterally.

THE VALUE OF WORKING IN A 'SUPPORT' GROUP: SHARING AND HELPING OTHERS

One of the main emphases in Action Learning is on sharing – experiences, thoughts . . . and feelings (which can be difficult, even scary, for some people). This sharing, out aloud, said participants, enables others to hear different ways of tackling issues and problems – ones they could learn from. The sharing also brings out the differences and diversity in the set.

> It's the diversity [in the set] which is the richness. . . . One of the most fundamental discoveries for me was the valuable resources that existed in our set . . . an eye-opener for what exists in other groups.

295

Many talked about the power of simply telling their story and thinking out aloud, '... saying things you didn't know were in your mind.... The same doesn't happen if you're merely thinking quietly to yourself.' And an engineer remarked: 'No matter how we defined our projects, we all landed up with the same fundamental problem – of how to relate to and work with other people!'

INCREASED SELF-CONFIDENCE

As everyone's stories and dilemmas emerge in a set, members realized that '... we all share similar problems, regardless of organization, function or even project' which gave them confidence. 'You realize you're not alone with your worries and concerns, or alone to resolve them'. This, in turn, meant that asking for help and admitting to not knowing, became OK. 'I now have the confidence to say I don't know or don't feel confident.' But confidence grew also out of having their views listened to and considered by others. A research scientist admitted: 'I'm quite timid.... As I saw I was able to help others, I realized I couldn't be talking complete rubbish.' Another said, 'Hearing your ideas accepted and valued by others gives you confidence.'

HAVING TO TAKE RESPONSIBILITY

Because the notion of Action Learning is that you return, at each set meeting, to tell the others what you have achieved – or not – since the last set meeting, there is 'pressure' on you to act.

> The set forces you to take responsibility. They have expectations of you at every meeting ...'. Or as another put it: 'We're often in life tempted to avoid the heat, to avoid thinking of certain things ... but the set won't let you.'
> 'You're made to face up to things because the set asks you and pushes you gently. You're forced to face your weaknesses – maybe it's just giving presentations, which you're avoiding.

REALIZING THE VALUE OF BEING HONEST

Being honest – at work – is not something that comes easily for many people. Action Learning helped many drop their masks.

> The set helped me be more honest with myself – particularly admitting to my emotions, and seeing them as a valid part of the picture. So, if I feel frightened, threatened or hassled, that's part of the equation that I need to look at – either alone or with others.

One training manager said it had been a risk – but was now a relief – to admit to colleagues that he was unsure of how to proceed on a particular matter he was working on. Admitting to uncertainty made him feel much more relaxed and open. And the ideas he gained from colleagues were, he assured them, helpful.

BUT A WORD OF CAUTION

Those participants who were unhappy, and cited the set as being one source of unhappiness, mentioned set members not keeping to the groundrules, unhelpful set members and – in one or two instances – set members not coming regularly to set meetings. One or two others mentioned set meetings being too far apart, i.e. more than a month between meetings.

WHAT YOU GAIN BY WORKING ON PROJECTS OR WORK-FOCUSED TASKS

Most participants stressed that choosing an appropriate project was very important. From their experiences – either because they had chosen 'badly' or had seen others floundering – the following criteria for a project emerged. It should be something:

- important for your organization/department/section
- for which you are responsible
- over which you have authority
- you have to implement, ideally
- that has your manager's and/or a senior manager's support and commitment.

Most commented on how useful it was to be working on real live projects – and in particular ones that were linked to their own work, or that offered them opportunities for development.

'Implementation' was highlighted by several: 'I learnt what was practical, what was bearable and what was acceptable . . . next time I make proposals I need to consider those on the receiving end much more.' Another pointed out that ' . . . it's taught me to be flexible and to have various strategies, not just one, for implementing proposals.'

So, what did participants say they gained from working on projects?

IT BROADENS YOUR HORIZONS, OPENS YOUR EYES

Most participants said that 'Hearing others' projects broadens your horizons, gives you the bigger picture.' They gained, they said, knowledge, insights, and understanding.

297

Projects which involved meeting and talking to people never spoken to before – particularly senior managers – revealed to junior staff that people behind those doors ' . . . are approachable human beings!' They expressed amazement at how helpful they were. 'I had always thought they would think I was wasting their time.'

And a young manager commented, 'I realized that just a little bit of knowledge and research can give you enough to approach others to ask for help.'

IT INSTILS A DISCIPLINED WAY OF WORKING

One sales manager put his finger on what had been important for him.

> It gave me some methods and systems . . . a structured approach to any assignment: how and where to look for help and resources, collecting evidence, being clear about the problem, making sure you have criteria for measuring or evaluating what you're doing, having strategies for coping and managing. Before, I'd be running at 90mph and getting nowhere.

Many alluded to the fact that this 'discipline' was an amalgam of having, in their mind's eye, or on paper, a 'learning cycle', which they adapted into a working cycle. Thus rather than rushing from idea to action, they built in extra stages, considered more options, worked out different scenarios and allowed for frequent assessment. Many also talked of building in thinking and reflection time. But as one ruefully commented, ' . . . there is no place for thinking and reflecting on our time sheets!'

IT OFFERS THE OPPORTUNITY OF COMPLETING A PROJECT

Participants holding junior positions had often not been given responsibility for managing a project until the programme. The experience proved beneficial in various ways. Several commented that their managers now had more confidence in them and had given them more responsible work to tackle. Another laughed as she remembered how her manager told her he was also learning as she tackled her project, using him as a sounding board!

Staff in an engineering workshop, working as a set to 'improve our team-working', chose as their project to increase the efficiency of their workshop – which they achieved, with amazing results! One of them commented:

> The result of working together is that people are now more willing to co-operate with one another, to share their expertise . . . morale has definitely improved. There's more understanding that we survive collectively and not individually . . .

BUT A WORD OF CAUTION

Those who mentioned the projects as being the source of their unhappiness with the programme, singled out some main factors:

● Working on a project that was totally unrelated to their work, and not being given the time to do both the project and their everyday work.
● Not having individual 'mini-projects' within the larger set project. Where, as happened in one programme, the set focused on one set member's problem only, the others felt totally uninvolved in the project – and hence the programme.
● A project suggested by senior managers, to resolve some larger organizational issue, but with no forethought given to what, or how, the set members, either individually or collectively, might benefit and learn from it.
● Being given a project which was purely advisory in nature, but with no responsibility to implement recommendations; and becoming aware that their project was likely to be shelved – like so many others before.

WHAT YOU GAIN BY USING – AND STICKING TO – THE PROCESSES

The way the set works, i.e. the processes it adopts, proved to be a fundamental 'learning' for most participants. A set works differently from other groups and meetings. The airspace accorded to each member, the stress on questioning, avoiding giving advice, even turning suggestions into questions, the giving of honest feedback, the time for reflection and silence – these gave participants an insight into a new way of working.

THE BENEFIT OF AIRSPACE

Having their own time, when everyone's attention and energy was focused on them and their 'issue', being listened to, attended to, with no 'hijacking' into others' stories and experiences – this was a 'luxury', something they'd never experienced before. 'I don't think I've ever been really listened to before', was what struck one participant. 'I didn't realize how powerful that was ... it was wonderful!'

Hearing themselves talk out loud was not only a novelty, but a benefit for many.

As you talk you resolve your own problems – if you're honest about what you say ... as you explain things to the set you hear your own inconsistencies, the missing elements, the illogicalities. But you need to do it out loud.

299

LEARNING TO LISTEN

Listening proved to be a new experience for many. As several participants reflected:

> Listening is not easy . . . it requires a lot of practice. . . . Complete listening is about comprehension, not just recall . . . and comprehension is also about empathy and being non-judgemental . . . and trying to understand what the other person is saying, and why, and burying your biases.

Being listened to also built confidence and self-esteem in those listened to. 'Listening to others is one way of showing that you respect them . . .'. 'Listening', mused one, 'is one of the most important management skills.'

THE POWER AND IMPORTANCE OF QUESTIONS

Asking questions has, as most participants quickly realized, several major benefits.

> Good questions tease out the real issues. They make you think. Often they're questions you haven't thought of, or ones you wouldn't dream – or want – to ask yourself.

Questions proved, for many, more valuable than advice.

> The advice is often impractical and I get frustrated hearing too much about others' experiences – they're not mine, and they work in different situations.

Yet asking helpful questions was not easy. 'It was more difficult than I had imagined . . . you realize how often we fall into the trap of giving advice . . . you feel you've offered something concrete by suggesting a solution.' Others realized that asking questions was not a sign of stupidity or ignorance – simply of a need for clarity.

THINKING MORE CLEARLY

The questioning processes of Action Learning made participants think more deeply: 'It makes your brain work at a different level and speed'; 'It brings you face to face with your assumptions and prejudices . . . and if you're pushed you have to explain them, not justify them. That's much harder.'

Participants also distinguished between being challenged and being confronted. The former was both intellectually and emotionally acceptable; the latter smacked of aggression. 'Challenging can be developmental – both as you challenge others and they challenge you.'

Ultimately, most participants recognized, a set might not always be available for such challenges; they needed to internalize the process for themselves.

STOPPING TO REFLECT

Busy-ness and action are often taken as signs that people are working, and achieving something. Sitting quietly, by contrast, may be interpreted as being unproductive, even lazy. For more 'active' participants, the emphasis on reflection in Action Learning proved frustrating in the early stages of a programme. Most subsequently learnt to value such 'quiet' time.

> I've learnt that rushing into action isn't the way to move forward . . . in the set we can legitimately look at the reverse of this: the thinking that is needed for any activity to be ultimately effective.

> Stopping to reflect, with the help of the set, had many benefits.

> The set gets you to try and look objectively at what you're doing or thinking . . . and you often find that you are part of the problem you have described. We're all so good at blaming others.

HAVING THE OPPORTUNITY TO STUDY A GROUP WORKING PRODUCTIVELY

The processes in the set opened up a different way of working with others. One 'top' team of a small company, after just one Action Learning day, changed how they worked in their managers' meetings because: ' . . . we'd been so much more productive in the set'.

So, as many said 'I've learnt transferable skills by working in the set: how to listen and focus on questions, how to facilitate, how to act as a mentor and how to present – you find you're presenting to the set all the time.'

Many discovered the important distinction between task and process: 'I now feel it's legitimate – in other meetings – to comment on the processes I see happening, and not just to work on the task.

BUT A WORD OF CAUTION

Although most participants were full of praise for the processes, a few worried that the questioning was not challenging enough, and that there was too much emphasis on positive feedback and support, with set members being too nice to one another – which was comforting but unrealistic, and even unhelpful.

Many participants admitted that in the first set meeting they felt at a loss to know what would be helpful to others: what were good questions to ask, how to avoid giving advice, how to rephrase their suggestions into questions, how to give feedback that would be helpful and not hurtful, and so on.

WHAT YOU GAIN BY HAVING A SET ADVISER WORKING WITH THE SET

It gave some participants insights into how they, as managers, managed . . . and could change.

> I used the set adviser and his way of 'managing' us as a model for managing. I see my role as being a 'set adviser' to my team back at work, I try and adopt the way our set adviser worked, using questions in a quiet way. . . . I try to avoid telling people what to do, and thereby doing their thinking for them, but let them work it out for themselves. It's a way to empower them.

Others commented on how their set adviser's frequent question of 'So what did you learn from that?' had now become 'like an ever-present echo' for them, no matter what they were doing: a true impulse to learn from whatever situation they found themselves in.

BUT A WORD OF CAUTION

The role of the set adviser is a delicate one and several set advisers were criticized by participants for:

- becoming too involved and talking too much!
- being critical and judgemental of set members during meetings
- not observing the groundrule of confidentiality.

Two sets commented that their set advisers were managers from their own organizations who had been given just half a day's 'tuition' on being a set adviser, and patently didn't understand the role they were playing.

WHAT YOU GAIN BY SPENDING TIME ON THE PROGRAMME

A number of participants commented, at the outset, about how long action programmes last: could it be done in a shorter time? How could they convince their managers that it was time well spent? By the end of the programmes they were clear about why time was crucial. 'Don't give up early', was the advice of one manager.

> Time is crucial. You become like a sponge – gradually saturated – and then you need more time before it begins to drip out, and you realize what's been happening and what you're learning.

REFLECTION TAKES TIME

'Reflection isn't the instant thoughts you have. It's a longer, deeper process'. Or, as another participant put it: 'Action learning sows seeds that take time to germinate.'

LEARNING TO LEARN TAKES TIME

Revans himself has said that Action Learning is simple, which is why it is so difficult to explain. One manager commented that although the concepts had been quite easy to grasp early on, ' . . . it took time to see the real benefits, and to know how to do it. Much of that was because, early on, I kept wanting books and experts to be around, and it takes time to get used to doing all the questioning and learning yourself.'

So, the value of action learning is in ' . . . the repetition and the constant building on what you've tried out once, to get it better.' Another added: 'Going round the learning cycle once isn't sufficient. We meet monthly and feel – and can see – that we've matured over time.'

LEARNING TO TRUST TAKES TIME

The trust that is required in the set for truth to begin to emerge also takes time. 'Real honesty was a long time coming, but when it did the progress was incredible.'

LEARNING TO THINK TAKES TIME

Another participant pointed out that 'Action Learning makes you think – but that doesn't happen quickly. It takes time. The questions often dam up old routes of thinking, and it takes time to go down the new ones.'

One manager summed up what time now meant for her:

> I see time as an ally – it gives me a sense of perspective. It's no longer a foe or enemy. Instead of 'I must' or 'I should' I now find myself saying 'I will' which has a longer-term and a more thoughtful ring to it. . . . We always have time; we simply choose to use it in different ways. It depends on what we value.

BUT A WORD OF CAUTION

The benefits of Action Learning don't accrue overnight, nor within the space of one set meeting. Trying to cut back on the time spent in set meetings, as some sets did, and having, say, two hours for six people, resulted in no real work being accomplished. As one set put it, 'you have to wait for five meetings before your turn for your "airspace"'. Two or three sets adopted a practice of "bidding" for airspace but this again meant that those who held back received less space and help than the more vociferous ones. As several participants said: 'it's only Action Learning if you have to come to each meeting and face the set with what you've done – or not done. Otherwise, where's the "action"?'

WHAT YOU GAIN BY FOCUSING ON THE LEARNING

The two key words in Action Learning are: action, and learning. Most participants understood 'action'; they had more trouble initially with 'learning', having spent much of their education being taught! Learning, they realized, isn't simply a product that grows in the mind, to be regurgitated verbally. It is also a process. It is about 'how': how to gain knowledge and insights, and how to apply them; and so it is also about changing – and doing things differently – and what difference that is making.

So, what were participants now doing differently? what had they learnt in a more general sense?

I'VE LEARNT THERE'S A LOT TO BE LEARNT

Since one purpose of Action Learning is for participants to become aware of how and when they learn, most participants commented on this, often quite novel for them, notion.

One woman commented that she now realized that 'everything is data from which I can learn'. Another that: 'I've learnt that I learn best when challenged by others. I have a tendency to dismiss things quickly.'

Another realized that 'I've made the jump from magnifying things, to seeing a bad experience as simply that . . . it needs to be reflected on, but not colour your subsequent beliefs or actions.'

I'M MUCH MORE AWARE – OF MYSELF AND OTHERS

One manager summed up what was different for him: 'It's generally heightened my sensitivity back at work . . . to everything: memos, interviews, group discussions. I begin to recognize what is happening and it helps my responses and reactions.'

Other typical comments included: 'I've learnt to be my natural self – to be direct, friendly, blunt when necessary'; and 'I'm more aware of the effect I have on others.'

I'M MORE FORTHRIGHT AND CHALLENGING

The confidence people had gained through working with the set had benefits back at work. It increased their effectiveness, and gave them more energy and commitment to their work. 'I'm prepared to be controversial . . . I know I don't have to accept blindly what I'm told to do – I can go back and redefine issues.' Another said 'I'm more forthright . . . It's given me the confidence to disagree constructively.'

Another said: 'I can now admit to having made a mistake – to be honest. . . . From that I've also gained the confidence not to be overly diplomatic, conciliatory or accepting.'

With this increased confidence often went what many referred to as a change in thinking. 'The mind set changes – and your thinking becomes more positive.'

IT'S TAUGHT ME TO THINK

With some confidence several said: 'I'm better now at challenging myself, asking those awkward questions.' Others talked of 'thinking more laterally'.

Some had begun to seek a similar level of intellectual and emotional stimulus and support back at work. 'Exposure to constructive criticism in the set makes you aware of its absence at work. I [now] seek it, encourage it, and try to give it myself.'

'Action Learning', said one young woman, 'gives you a detachment, a tool for analysis. You identify where you went wrong, you learn from your mistakes . . . and it's applicable not just at work.'

I THINK I WORK MORE EFFECTIVELY WITH OTHERS

Working more effectively with others came, participants realized, from valuing them, being tolerant, and respecting differences. 'I've learnt there are good ideas out there . . . even someone you've mentally dismissed has them.'

Another said: 'I'm normally frustrated when I'm not in control in a group. I've learnt that I don't have to "own" and control everything. I'm more tolerant of others and they are then better able to work with me . . . Being a perfectionist is a problem!'

And a young manager remarked that 'I've learnt not to jump in so quickly with responses and suggestions, comments or criticisms.'

I'M A MORE EFFECTIVE MANAGER: I LET GO AND DELEGATE

A young, first-time manager realized that 'managing is much more than being good at the work of my department – and simply talking loudly. I have so much to learn, and it isn't to do with the "tasks" we tackle but with the processes we adopt when working together.'

One departmental head at a university remarked that 'I now don't feel threatened by having my staff question me and give me their opinions. Before, I feared I'd find that threatening, so resorted to being autocratic'.

Another manager told how he was taking Action Learning back into the workplace: 'Before, if my staff asked me how to do something I'd have told them. Now I say; 'what do you think?'

BUT A WORD OF CAUTION

Learning doesn't come easily or instantaneously. Several participants talked of their initial impressions and fears.

One described the shock and horror he felt at the beginning of the programme, and what he called the 'middle-class head banging':

> I thought, I'm not going to express my doubts and feelings to someone I don't know. It was all slow and tedious, and I saw the set adviser as being 'manipulative', constantly asking questions, prying. . . . Then suddenly it was my airspace. I began to talk about the issue I'd decided to bring . . . and next I knew an hour and a half had gone by. Others were saying 'that was interesting' and I began to feel valued . . .

Another, older manager admitted he came ' . . . in fear and trepidation,' convinced he'd be out of his depth, having had no formal education. But, he continued, he soon realized it was about experience and common sense, and that he could easily hold his own.

For another it was the opposite: 'no books, no lectures; you have to find things out for yourself. . . . But then you realize that the answers are in yourself, and you begin to bring them out with the help of others. It changes the way you work and approach tasks.'

'You must persist,' was the message. 'It's later that the penny begins to drop' was a thought echoed by many. 'Hang in, don't give up. The longer you're there, the greater the benefits.'

AND THE RESERVATIONS ABOUT ACTION LEARNING?

Several of the people I interviewed were unhappy about the programme they had participated in. Their reasons were varied:

- no confidentiality in the set
- incompetent and unhelpful set advising
- irrelevance of the group's project to the individual's work and needs
- unhelpful set members
- lack of interest and 'empathy' of certain individuals with the Action Learning process.

The last point was echoed by many who were happy with the whole process, but who had had in their sets individuals who had left the programme. Several participants felt that there are indeed people who will have no empathy with the Action Learning way of working. This may be, they said, because they are afraid; but it may be because they are genuinely better suited to working alone. There are yet others who have an individualistic and/or aggressive streak in them, and who may not wish to change their way of working: maybe that's how they achieve their best work?

But there were other reasons why some participants felt they would not take part in another Action Learning programme if it were offered. And their reasons were:

- It's too time-consuming.

Several participants felt this. Those who commented tended to have worked on a project which was not directly related to their own work, nor did they play an active role in the project itself.

- It's too nice and cosy; not challenging enough.

True, it does encourage respect for others, and not being judgemental or aggressive. But a good set adviser would ensure that it was challenging.

- It's a feminine process.

A number of participants – mostly men – called Action Learning a 'feminine' process, because it advocates respect for and consideration of others; and because it is non-aggressive and non-competitive. For this reason they felt it would not take hold in many of today's organizations. Their own experiences on a programme, while interesting, could not be applied in the wider context of their organization.

- It's too vague for money-minded managers. Its benefits are not specific enough; too hit and miss.

Action Learning, because it focuses on learning, can never guarantee what participants in any programme are going to gain and learn. They will set out with aims, but in the end participants – as on any other programme – learn what it is they want to learn, and are open to.

- It needs some 'P' (taught input).

Agreed, and any good programme – or set adviser – will ensure there is some, as and when the participants feel they need it.

- It doesn't seem to help with the politics which infest organizations.

Not directly, but it gives participants a better understanding of the politics, and the opportunity of exploring, with the set, some strategies for dealing with those politics.

- It creates a working environment within the set which is unlike our real-life work situations.

Yes, it probably does, but those who have experienced the benefits of this 'new' and different way of working can begin, particularly if they themselves are managers, to change even in small ways what happens back at work.

WHY HASN'T IT TAKEN HOLD MORE WIDELY?

Action Learning is in fact being widely used – but in forms that are not always the real McCoy. It's worth making this point since participants on programmes which were dilutions of the real thing simply gained less from the programmes.

More interesting, however, are the comments from those who participated in effective and well-managed programmes. These can be summed up in the following three statements:

It's too soft for the rigours of business today. It can be seen by more macho, autocratic managers – who are often those in senior positions – as being namby-pamby, and a crutch for the weak.

For it to take hold, the culture of the company is important. If it's authoritarian, fragmented and structured, with egoistic managers, where someone is always blamed and where mistakes are pushed under the carpet, then the programme is likely to ruffle feathers and expose people who prefer to hide.

It's too revolutionary for many companies; it teaches you to ask questions.

25 Action Learning for Chief Executives: An Evaluation

Ian Cunningham

This chapter is based on research I carried out in 1986. A fuller version with greater detail of the views of participants and the research methodology can be found in Cunningham (1986).[1] The programme was the 'Action Learning for chief executives' course at Ashridge Management College. (The title is abbreviated in Ashridge as 'ALCE' and I shall use that designation here.)

Revisiting this material ten years later it still seems valid. Nothing in subsequent research on management development seems to undermine the support for Revans' basic ideas that this research provides. However having said that the basics are fine the research does challenge two of Reg Revans' notions. Firstly it does suggest that integrating 'P' and 'Q' often does not seem to work out well in Action Learning programmes as practised. The people involved in setting up the programme covered by this research have been close to Revans and know his work well. Yet it could be argued that their emphasis was almost solely on 'Q'. Also personal experience of a wide range of Action Learning programmes over the last 23 years prompts me to suggest that this is a common issue.

The second area of concern is that Revans has been critical of the role of consultants and developers, often stating, for instance, that set advisers are not needed – and indeed may get in the way or be driven by base desires merely to line their own pockets. The evidence of this research supports earlier studies I carried out that effective set advising is crucial in making sets work.[2] I should say that I had no personal involvement in this programme and wrote up my research for initial publication when I was chief executive of an institution that could if anything be viewed as a competitor of Ashridge. (It is to Ashridge's credit that they have in no way wished to influence the content of my report on the programme.) Hence I hope that it can be seen as a balanced piece of work whilst it does not claim detached objectivity – only because there is no such thing as wholly detached objective research. (See, for instance, Reason, 1989).[3]

THE PROGRAMME

The ALCE programme has been operating at Ashridge since late 1980. Superficially it is similar to other Action Learning courses. For example, participants meet in sets of about five persons, each with a set adviser. The sets meet for one day at a time at intervals of about one per month for six months or more. I shall comment later on the extent to which this programme differs from other Action Learning courses. Fuller details of the ALCE programme are contained in Braddick and Casey (1981)[4], Casey and Hastings (1983)[5], Casey (1984),[6] and Hodgson and Brown (1995).[7]

THE RESEARCH

In the spring and summer of 1986 I interviewed 32 out of the 41 participants who had made up the eight sets run at Ashridge by that time. The remaining nine people were unavailable for various reasons; no one refused to be interviewed. My research assumptions are close to those associated with New Paradigm Research or Post Positivist Research[8,3]. Central to this stance is the recognition of the limited and partial nature of my analysis and the emphasis that I was not trying to identify some absolute, objective truths. More detail can be found in Appendix II of Cunningham (1986).[9]

I wrote a draft report in September 1986 and circulated it to all the participating CEOs for their comments. I specifically asked them to check that the report reflected the programme, and to tell me if I should change it in any way. Sixteen CEOs replied: 14 said that it was fine as it stood and that I should not change it; one suggested a minor addition (which I have made); and one felt I could reduce the length of it. The latter point was countered by others who said that it should not be reduced. For example, one CEO wrote, 'The report caused me to live through every facet of my experience; don't change it.'

The research was stimulating and enjoyable to carry out, despite the serious logistical and travelling problems it created. All the people I met were helpful, prepared to talk and generally keen to contribute to the research.

THE PEOPLE

Of the 41 CEOs who participated in the ALCE the following is an analysis of their organizational bases:

Public sector	8
Family business	8
Part of larger organization (private sector)	23
Own business	2
Total	**41**

There was no CEO from a large corporation. All participants were male. Their ages ranged from the late 30s to 60. Within the apparent similarities there were also great differences, for example in terms of:

- home circumstances
- place of work (which varied from Belfast, Newcastle and Perth in the north to Bristol, Winchester and Croydon in the south)
- social class
- education
- personality

MAIN ISSUES

The following is a summary of the main points identified in the research, some of which are elaborated later.

1. Most participants benefited greatly from the programme.
2. Such benefits were often expressed in general or personal terms, rather than about specific things learned.
3. However, there were specific organizational pay-offs for some people (though these were often seen as secondary to personal learning).
4. Self-analysis and personal re-appraisal were central issues for many.
5. One set was significantly less successful than the other seven studied. A number of design and logistical problems were identified by this set.
6. There was a wide variety of sources of recruitment to the programme, and range of reasons why people joined it.
7. The initial set meetings were often felt to be confusing and frustrating. However, this phase was worked through as sets realized how to use the programme to best effect. The process of the set was described in rich detail by participants. For many it was a new experience (and a positive one for most).
8. A number of sets continued to meet after the formal programme concluded.
9. Four factors in the programme were considered important: management, design, face-to-face activity and theory.

311

10. The overall design was liked, but there were specific concerns about the mix of participants in a set and the timing and timetabling of meetings.
11. The role of set adviser was regarded as important.

BENEFITS OF THE PROGRAMME

Overall the benefits and pay-offs from the programme were clearly very great. However, in many cases people found it difficult to be precise about *specific* things they had learned. One interpretation is that the ALCE programme provides mainly for the development of what could be labelled more personal learning as opposed to the learning of specific techniques of management. At the same time, people did indicate some specific payoffs, and before going back to elaborate the more personal learning, I will quote here some examples of organizationally oriented benefits:

> It helped me a lot. It helped me to have a very close relationship with customers. They are interested in what we think. They felt that something was being done to make me a better senior manager of a business they had a stake in.

> Certainly the ability of myself and my chief executive to communicate has dramatically improved since I went to Ashridge. I don't lose my temper as much as I used to. I try to keep the discussion sensible and constructive.

> I suppose that is really one of the principle things I have learned in terms of a 'skill'. The art is how to ask questions rather than give answers.

> What I got out of it was some real help and guidance during a very, very difficult transitional process which enabled me, frankly, to make better decisions in running the business. That is a true statement. That's all I can say about it.

> It really does bring home to you the problems that you have. The real ones, not the superficial ones.

> I must say that since I have come back I have often, consciously, quite consciously, done a bit of that with my own people. They have had a problem and because one of the things I learned was to listen I was able to stand back from all the problems (and not problems which required an answer now). And the 'phone goes and I pick it up now. Before I would offer solutions straight away. Now you see I say 'Oh dear. I wonder what do you think?' ... because not all problems are things which require me to decide today. If somebody rings up and says we have got to take a decision 'now', then I take the decision now – right or wrongly – I don't want to ask anybody. But if it is something that is going to hit us in a day's time or two days' time or four days' time, when there is time, you can alter your approach to the problem and the person who has got the problem. And I find more and more I don't find a solution at all – what I do is manoeuvre the people so they find their own solution. And it leads to a somewhat more pleasant working situation.

Other specific pay-offs mentioned included:

- one person re-structured his organization as a result of discussions in the set;
- people talked of 'broadened horizons', 'making me more aware and keener to do things', 'made me question more things';
- some CEOs did 'collect tools and techniques from other members of the set'. For example, a local authority CEO decided to use ideas from marketing and market research for the first time;
- two people commented that they had been prompted to go and read more as a result of the influence of the set.

In some cases people commented on their colleagues in the set, for example:

X talked a lot about the value he got from it for himself, and of course the promotion which he has now got which he did feel was assisted by his involvement within the set.

He certainly said that he had changed and, I think, felt more relaxed – I can't remember the words he used. I don't know whether it was relaxed but certainly gave the impression that he had thought about a lot of the things that had come up in the set.

RE-BALANCING

For many people, the development seemed only to come after self analysis and re-appraisal of their situation. This then gave them an opportunity to re-balance their lives, for example in dealing with both the rational/thinking aspects of their work and the emotional/value based dimensions.

As one person commented:

I was able I think to keep a very balanced view of that which I might not have otherwise done. I would have been very – I think – potentially depressed about it and it would have shown through more than it actually did. The other evidence is the fact that my wife used to say to me: 'Are you going on your course? Are you going for your group therapy this week?' and I would say: 'yes' or 'no', as the case may be and she would make the comment: 'Well I think you had better go and have your group therapy because it enables you to be a far better human being and get all the pressures and problems off your shoulders.' So, yes, I think it did make a difference.

Well, I'd say that I know it was totally unique to me. Totally outside my experience and it was a lot more than group therapy but frankly it was an opportunity to air things, concerns, problems and issues with other people and get their input, which enabled me then to make practical decisions and better decisions than I might otherwise have made. That's what I got out of it. The added benefit was that it was a real opportunity to get it off your chest. So all right it helped me. It was a group therapy in that sense and if that's group therapy I don't give a stuff.

313

Others commented on the supportive value of the set, for example:

> It helped me enormously. I owe my sanity to the set.

> It helped me over a hole.

> A boost to flagging morale.

> It put the whole thing in perspective and I stopped worrying about it then and just got on with the job and focused on what I should have been doing all the time.

> Helped me through difficult personal circumstances.

> You go for a day and come back revitalized and feel you have learned something. And maybe that faded after a while and then you sit back and think: 'Well, did it actually help me?' Perhaps my wife has commented more than anyone... she found that it was very good for me, that I came back... really more enthusiastic and feeling invigorated, I think really. Particularly some of the sessions more than others. I think it is traumatic for most people in some way or other because it usually makes you face up to some fairly large problem.

> The people here have not said 'Oh, Ashridge has made a difference to you'. They don't see any real difference. I probably find a difference. I remember once ringing one of the lads up [in the set] because I felt particularly depressed and fed up and was dying to talk to him about why I felt depressed. And he told me about his problem and I talked to him about his problem for quite a while and didn't talk about mine at all. And I thought 'Mine wasn't such a big problem after all'.

> I keep struggling with the word 'self-realization', which is awful really, but it is probably the nearest I can get. I think it changed me from being put in a job where I didn't know how to do it and being a little bit worried that I not only didn't know how to do it but that the devils had got their knives out ready to carve us into little bits. I think it helped to get me through a period where I certainly realized that probably nobody ever knew what to do anyway – you make it up as you go along. The fact that you get a title like MD shouldn't actually mean that all the answers are there.

There are a variety of further quotes which indicate the richness and value of the programme:

> You are actually not learning how to manage or about a specific subject, you are actually learning about yourself. Not really about the theory of management or accounts or whatever course you are on. You are actually there analysing yourself. It was interesting from my point of view to see these different types of people, different areas, different backgrounds, we all have the same problem. Basically the problem is always the same... ourselves. Our not understanding the problem.

> I don't think there is any doubt [there is a pay-off], but I feel it is entirely subjective. One of the things I have got out of it was it helped make me a general manager rather than just a guy who had been put in the seat. Now it could have been that the company could have done ten other things to do that. I rub shoulders and have become part of a group of people called managing directors; I got great personal kudos out of saying to the guys who worked for me: 'yesterday I spent the day with the guy who runs the

X Group . . .' etc. Now I got a lot out. What it did to my ego to find that those guys didn't have magical answers to everything and that my views on some of those things seemed to be as important to them as theirs were to me. Not on their own, but when one of those was seeking views or comments they were looking to four people. They never said to me 'we are not interested in your views' so I was able to feel I was contributing to a group of people that I respected because they ran successful businesses.

You really question 'was I doing the right thing?' 'do I really want to do it any more?' 'should I be doing something entirely different?' So I came to the conclusion that this job, considering I have been here 14 years, was not really giving me self-satisfaction and I got to the stage where I was coasting to some extent because there was, perhaps, a lack of challenge or even, perhaps, a lack of involvement because the more efficient you make the organization and the better you can make the people, the more you can pass the decision-making. In actual fact the less you become involved yourself. The conclusion I had come to was that the job wasn't fulfilling any longer. Some of the problems of the business here and some of the problems was that I wasn't able to think like that and that's something Ashridge has done for me. But there again it takes you away from the work. If you sit in an environment every day you never actually think about it. You have got to be taken away from just sitting there and listening to other people's problems. They are all actually similar and the conclusion we came to was most of our problems were more than 50 per cent self-created by not facing up to something or whatever.

It's mainly finding out about yourself. Once you can handle yourself then, for the most part, you can handle the rest. Because things start to become fairly obvious if you once understand how you're reacting to it.

I don't think there is any question of that. I found it a tremendous benefit. The hard part is actually saying where, how and why. It is very difficult to specify what do I do differently now? What change have I made? It had a tangible effect. I find that extremely difficult to put forward. I think the others find it equally so. Some of the others have even asked 'what's it done for you?' Nobody can actually answer the question though. One of the surprising things is the very strong group loyalty. A very close bond. I mean my wife had difficulty in understanding why I have such a strong affinity to this group of people I didn't know five months ago. They are from all round the country and I only see them once in a blue moon. And why, for instance, we had to rearrange our holiday last year, at considerable inconvenience, because there was a meeting. That's very difficult to understand.

LACK OF PAY-OFF?

One set was markedly less successful than the others, and I want to comment on that group separately. However, even in successful sets there was a minority of people who felt that they had not benefited greatly. In two cases people left the programme before its completion; in others people stayed to the end. However, in *all* cases the CEOs concerned could see the value of this approach to learning.

THE SET THAT DIDN'T WORK SO WELL

Here are some quotes from people in this set in order to give some background:

I think my immediate feeling at the end of the series was that it was a bit of a waste of time, but I knew I would revise that feeling after a bit and sure enough I have, after a couple of months, and it was worth the time spent, but it could have been a lot more worth it. I think it is a combination of things, including getting the atmosphere right, including getting everybody there. But just as importantly the chance combination of people concerned, where I don't think we hit it off in the way other groups did, which was a pity because I think they have got a considerable amount more out of it than we did.

I am terribly aware now that all of the potential that I saw in the technique I have done almost nothing to benefit from since the end of that – it's how long ago now? It must be getting on for a year.

I don't think it was really fulfilling a need. Maybe there was a need that I had not recognized. But I certainly didn't find that when I attended the course that it was very stimulating.

I asked most people in the set if they would recommend the programme to other CEOs or not. They indicated that, with provisos, they would. For example:

I think my approach would be two ways. I think I would only want to recommend him to go on it if I thought he was going to actually be a positive part of that group. So that I would be interested to try and find out what it was he thought he was going to get out of it and what he was going to put into it. But yes, I mean unless I interpret him as being negative in terms of the effect he would have, and therefore somebody who would feel it was a failure because he wasn't prepared to accept the basic discipline of the thing. Then yes, I would recommend it.

Despite the problems with this set, some people did get positive things out of it. One person reorganized his management structure, commenting:

It emerged. I couldn't say I left the last meeting saying 'Eureka I have it!' I began to realize there was something I could do.

Others positive comments were:

I think I have definitely made some improvement actually in the way I use my time. I think in a sense I have got more determined to make certain I spend more of my time on what I think is important.

What did I get out of it? I got several things. First of all a commonality of problems. An awareness that at chief executive level you do run out of places to go for, not necessarily specific advice, but for an exchange of views with your peers and that I came away from the set with the feeling that my problems were really not entirely different from those of other people.

The reasons offered by participants in this set as to why it had been less successful included:

1. Not everyone attended each meeting (and one person left the set completely). Attendance by everyone at each meeting was seen as desirable.
2. The day meetings were usually not a full day because of travel problems for some people – this didn't give the set time to gell.
3. The set, unlike some others, didn't meet up the night before. Other sets have commented on the value of a night-before get together to unwind and re-connect to colleagues.
4. Some felt that the mix of people wasn't right: that somehow the 'chemistry' didn't work. This may have contributed to a feeling that there wasn't a high enough commitment to the set. This also meant that people didn't open up as much as in the other sets.
5. The gaps between meetings were seen as too long (they went longer than 4 weeks often). This didn't give enough continuity to the set.
6. Some felt the set might have worked given longer, and given that logistical problems could have been sorted out. The rigid six meeting format was seen as a disadvantage.

DESIGN ISSUES

To quote one CEO:

> The design is superbly simple. When you look at what we actually did, all we did to start with was agree some dates and send one another information about the businesses we ran and a little bit about ourselves. The set adviser talked for about ten minutes worth of what it was all about and we took it from there.

In broad-brush terms this statement is valid. However, when one looks at the detail there are some complex issues to consider.

1. PREPARATORY WORK

This varied from people who had thoroughly checked out the idea and felt enthusiastic about it to those who were pushed into the programme by someone in their organization. A number of CEOs expressed specific concerns that they came to address, for example: 'I wanted to broaden my horizons'; 'my business wasn't going how I wanted it to'. Others felt that their preparatory thinking was inadequate or shallow, and that they made the decision to attend on poor information. In some cases they felt that better briefing from Ashridge would

317

help. In other cases CEOs blamed themselves for not checking out the programme more.

Participants usually saw written material before attending (for example, Ashridge prospectus, articles about ALCE). Such written material was generally seen as helpful, though often participants felt it did not give a full enough picture of the programme. Many participants spoke to someone from Ashridge before they signed up. In some cases these were telephone conversations, in others, someone had visited the CEO in his office. Some who had only spoken on the phone said they would have preferred a visit from someone from Ashridge.

In general, because of the unusual nature of ALCE (to many CEOs) there was a feeling that the college might invest more on pre-programme contact, though people recognized the time and cost factors in this. By and large they saw that this would need to be one-to-one contact (presentations were not particularly favoured).

2. INITIAL SET MEETINGS

Comments about the initial set meetings varied from the practical and factual to the more critical. For example:

> I didn't understand, or didn't recognize it as I should, that it was very much about me. It is, it's me as a person. . . . Get to know me as a person. Get to know my strengths and weaknesses. What I want is some help as a person rather than a business. One tended to come and talk about the business. But it's me really . . . and it took me, certainly a couple of, you know, visits to really get to understand that. And that may be me. I don't necessarily blame the course.

A number of CEOs commented that the initial meetings were 'tense' and 'uncertain' and some felt that this early less-productive phase could have been moved through more rapidly with more assistance from set advisers. Others were not sure and felt that the early struggles to get to know each other and understand the process were inevitable. A positive suggestion from some was that perhaps the first meeting, which was mainly around fixing dates, could have been extended to include an overnight stay (so that more ice-breaking could occur).

3. GETTING GOING

In moving from the initial meetings to making the set work people sometimes expressed concerns about how the course was turning out. It was 'a bit of a shock' (to quote one CEO who had expected a taught course). Others felt frustrated because they did not know where it was going and what (if anything) they were learning. However, such views usually changed after a time. Comments from participants included the following:

I think we might have got a lot more out of it if what we were trying to do had been better explained. I went in, I read the literature when I went in but I was really groping . . . I was tending to flounder a bit over the first two meetings until the set adviser gradually, as his catalyst role was, caused us to stop and think a little bit more about what was happening. I think if we had been briefed on that a little better I think that might have helped to get us on the road a bit quicker. Yet, here again when I say that, for me personally, the others may not have felt the same because some of them had already had some background to this. Some had some experience of group work in this field; I hadn't. So for me, while they weren't floundering, maybe over the first couple of meetings I was.

At the beginning of the course, we found it very difficult to accept views, or even suggestions. All we were particularly interested in was telling people our problems. And I think most of us had fairly fixed ideas how we would solve them. And it was only later on in the course, and subsequent meetings, where, certainly I for one have been quite noticeably impressed by the change of attitude of the others over the progression of time. As you become more familiar with the individuals and begin to realize that, yes, they can brainstorm . . . and can give you a number of other ideas that you may well have kicked out. I think Ashridge for me taught me to listen a lot more; you know, rather than talk.

I think it is a funny sensation because the first day we were there we got pretty concerned with a person who doesn't like to talk about his problems. And he also keeps his business life and personal life completely separate if possible. When I went there on the first day not having any idea what they expect and got involved in another chap's very personal life on day one I thought, God, this is not for me! On the way back, I drove back in the evening, I sat for two and a half hours in the car. I had time to think about it and I thought it is not so silly. Your personal and business problems are interwoven and you probably do not realize it unless you sit down and actually think about it. So I decided to go back for the second day and the second day worked pretty well. It was fairly intense and tiring and then when I was due to go for the third day I had been at X Co and had a fairly difficult day and almost got to the stage of packing up there and then, so I had arranged to stay overnight to go on the Ashridge course and I did, in fact, consider not going. I thought I would go home and forget all about it. However, I went on the course and told my fellow colleagues what had happened the day before. That was very interesting to hear the different reactions from the other four individuals.

After the first meeting I came away from I didn't feel any relationship really with anyone else in the group, because they were from different backgrounds. And I thought: What do I really have in common with these people? And it took, I think, about two meetings to really establish that we all had problems. They were all different. I really don't know how that happened. How the group sort of welded together but by about the third meeting people were being very open and very frank and very positive. They were all contributing. No one sat back as a passenger. People wanted to participate. People were very honest. Now what the magic ingredient was I don't know. I can only put it down to the chemistry and the maturity, the commitment. And the fact that the people wanted to be there. They all wanted to learn. They wanted to participate.

4. THE SET IN OPERATION

Again quotes from course participants illustrate some of the richness, power and excitement of the process:

> The big thing about it I think, from the point of view of somebody who is Chief Executive of a company, is that in a group like that you are actually able to talk and talk honestly about your problems and feelings. I think it is virtually impossible to do that with anybody else. You can't do it with people you know in the company because you're always defensive or you are always maintaining your position in relation to . . . directors and . . . board members. You are not as honest to them I think as within a group of people outside . . . I don't think the same course would work really with people for example from within the same group of companies. I would be very sceptical.

> That's the main thing I think, opening up. Yes. People are not used to doing it are they? . . . Men in this society particularly are not used to doing it.

> Listening to the way that they tackled those problems, telling them about mine, comparing notes in a very free atmosphere after the first two sessions we were able to talk about things that I wouldn't dream about talking to a colleague and, frankly, I would even hesitate to talk about to my wife in some cases because a very strange relationship developed in that set. And I expect this is so with all the sets, where you haven't actually got any close inter-relationship at all and that enabled you to be very open and free in what you said to one another. Also indiscreet furthermore.

> I think the greatest thing you have, with this group of four other guys, who are in the same sort of scrapes I am in every day of their lives. Some of them have been in scrapes I have not been in and there are some scrapes they are going into that I have been in and they haven't. And that's what helped. I think that is the thing that the group has to sell. I don't think it teaches you an awful lot – it's not like going on a course – like to learn about VAT or something. It is just not like that. The group gives you this support group that you can use or find comfort in and I think if you are the head of a substantial patch in any business it's a good thing to have. A place to go to. A place where you know you are not going to get beaten up. I mean that is the thing it gave me more than anything else. This sort of comfort. And the fact that you could honestly feel that you had helped other people with things you may or may not have said. And also that feeling of privilege that other people talk to you as an individual or as part of the group about their problems and allowed you into their problems and to express your views and to question their views. This helped me greatly.

5. SUPPORTING AND CONFRONTING

Part of the value of sets clearly comes from the 'supportive confronting' environment, where participants are cared about sufficiently for them to be challenged in quite a powerful way. People talked of the set being 'brutal' at times, and experienced themselves being 'nailed'. Yet this was balanced by the support provided.

Comments exemplifying this factor included:

I think one of the values of taking five or six total strangers with no business relationship whatsoever has a lot of merit because you can actually talk fairly openly. We came quite close on a couple of times to falling out . . .

We did a lot of that right back to the bare bones of soul stripping. We didn't hold back anything.

You get a lot of pretty clear observations as long as you are prepared to open yourself up.

It's a sign of weakness (in my company) to seek advice . . . you could store up problems to bring to the table because you know you could get a truly honest view.

A progress meeting . . . if you hadn't implemented (what you said you would do) by the time you got back to the next meeting you had better have a good reason why. Because otherwise you go through the whole rack again.

Now, in the work situation one of the Chief Executive's problems is too often he can solve things by power rather than technique. I think because of the pace of things very often he has to solve them by power . . . But it can become addictive – I think is one of the dangers, and I think one of the important things about that group as an Action Learning Set is it actually does most Chief Executives good I would think. Certainly I felt it did me good to be in a situation where you weren't God. You know, you were facing problems with people who would actually disagree with you and you would have to accept they had every right to a different view. Whereas there is a danger in a line management situation, that you assume when people disagree with you it's because they are wrong. I don't mean it quite as strongly as that but you can always solve it by rank if you are not careful.

That really I think probably sums up the nature of the set really; that you feel it is supportive. It may be very critical and absolutely stop you in your tracks but it is supportive in the end . . . in a way that you probably would never get within your own organization.

And again we eventually pinned him down. Actually nailed him and it took us some time to nail him.

And he was a very difficult guy to get through to. Every time one put up a suggestion, X would knock it down by saying: 'Yes, we thought about that.' I personally didn't feel I was getting through to the guy because every time I said something, he said: 'Yes, yes, we thought about that. That's a good idea but we have thought about it' or 'we have tried it'. And again it took – it was about the fourth meeting with this particular guy. Then he came clean and what he had been worried about essentially was the fact that the overall business in which he was a part . . . was getting into some difficulty, and the guy running it wasn't really sort of aware of it and no one else seemed to be too concerned about making him aware of it and making him do something about it. He had got sufficiently wound up by one of the group meetings where we all had a go at him. About what he should be doing, etc, etc, etc. And he came back the following month and said: 'Well thanks for your advice. I did what you said and these are the changes that are going to happen, I think.' So we are all watching now to see what happens. So I think we really helped that guy. But again he was going through a personal crisis as well as a business crisis and he didn't know quite how to handle it. He was able, I think, despite the fact that he said 'Yes, well we tried that and we tried this.' I think we were registering with him in his sub-conscious to the extent that he was able to get guidance and went away and did it.

This latter point is an important addition to earlier comments. It seems that people for all sorts of reasons don't recognize at the time what needs doing. And the group might feel it's failed. However, the message may well get through at a more unconscious level, helping the person to take action at a later date.

6. AFTER THE FORMAL COURSE HAS ENDED

A number of sets continued to meet after the formal course ended. This was more a facet of later sets (the early sets did not continue to meet). In some cases people felt that their set went better afterwards than it did when it was under Ashridge's wing. It's as if the first six meetings helped the set to bond in such a way as to allow them to go further. In other cases people were less sure of the value of continued meetings, or they saw the set becoming more of a social gathering than a learning event.

Some comments include:

Well he [the set adviser] is not there now but I think we have got through the process of knowing each other. Of being able to say to each other precisely what we think at any point in time and we tend – now obviously we listen a lot more than we did before. And we are more prepared I think to accept suggestions than we were before and really the set adviser's role isn't needed now.

When we have met we have had good sessions, but it has to be said that I don't think we have had a complete session which everybody has turned up to. I think people felt the formality of it was over and it was more of a social gathering.

Where we have all got together and out of six of us I think there has always been at least four of us there, sometimes five sometimes six. It was more difficult I think to get us all together when we were trying to organize a date after the formal dates that we had fixed than obviously it was when we had the formal dates fixed. But we do talk to each other ... there is still quite a lot of discussion goes on backwards and forwards. So we try to keep ourselves up to date with what's going on out of interest.

We have meetings – we have had one meeting since and are due to have another one this week. And the meeting that we had worked very well. In fact I think, that is having had all the sessions at Ashridge, that worked very well. It wouldn't have worked in the early days; it wouldn't have got anywhere without a catalyst really. And I think the nature of that catalyst is very important.

THE ROLE OF THE ADVISER

A key argument about the set adviser role is whether one needs one at all. The views of ALCE participants concur with my own research evidence[10] in supporting the need for such a person. The quotes that follow below are very clear on this. One CEO commented:

> I clearly think the group at the outset needs a focus. So it has got to be there at the outset. You have got to have someone to set it up, run it, who can sort of act as moderator, if you like, and be the stimulus for questions and also to bring people back to order and to guide people. Without those two guys there I don't think it would have got off the ground. I think there is no question about that.

The most used metaphor for the set adviser role was that of catalyst. For example:

> The set adviser played a very minor role. He played the perfect role for whatever he was supposed to be, a lead, a catalyst, I don't know what. But what he said was well worth listening to.

> It would be totally impossible to do that without a set adviser to start with. And it was a very necessary ingredient certainly for four or five meetings. Perhaps if X had been able to come consistently from the beginning we might have got to a sort of self-reliance point a little quicker. But we couldn't have done it for less than four. Basically because you are finding out about people and you're finding out things about people that people don't admit to themselves. So there's little chance of them admitting something to a total stranger unless there's a catalyst to do so. We admitted things to each other but there are not other people in this world who actually know that. Things we would never dream of telling our friends, our business colleagues or even our wives. Another thing is – it's a lot to do with the sort of common bond. We know things which are very, very personal. Or very, very private, I probably think would be [more appropriate]. But without that catalyst, as I say, you couldn't have done it.

'Catalyst' is perhaps too limiting a description. One role he did fulfil was that of an 'infill', that is he filled in and did what nobody else was doing; for example:

> I mean he obviously did quite of lot of filling in of gaps when silences descended because I suppose in effect we'd lost our way. We'd run out of steam or – and occasionally when people were pushing a bit too hard. Yes, for all of us there came a time when you reach a sort of breaking point, when you feel like standing up and walking out. And generally he managed to sort of pull it back from doing damage to somebody.

> He came in at times – I think when he thought there was an element of confusion. Then he joined in. He then joined in because I think he had always got something tracking at the back of his mind and he wanted to feel that the consumers, us, were getting value for money and he didn't want us trailing off into things which possibly were wasting time and weren't sort of moving the experience on. So he would come in then but he was quite unobtrusive. You know, he seemed content to sit around. I

mean he used to have to guide it. I mean the way the process worked in there was that each one of us would talk about something. Talk about ourselves, about problems. And he used to have to prod that. But after the first two meetings, by the time it came to the third and fourth meetings, we were deciding what we were – who was going to talk, and who we would allow to talk and sort of developed a sense of fairness.

The use of the term 'guide' in the above correlates with another person's comment that the set adviser would 'guide and steer'. Here are some relevant quotes:

So the set adviser steered it and he didn't want the conversation to degenerate. Some of the things he pointed out in the early stages were when you know somebody would talk about a problem he had got and other people didn't question to enable the person who had got the problem to question himself. They question for themselves only and then started suggesting specific answers for the guy. We soon learned that that wasn't the way to help the other fellow.

I think the most fundamental aspect would be that he taught us to ask questions. When we stopped asking questions and started proffering solutions, he would stop us and bring everything back down to earth, and get it pointed in the right direction. Because all that's happening when you start offering advice – I mean I know nothing really about those other people's work. I don't know their mode of operation. I don't begin to understand the types of customers they have and so on. I don't really know – well not really enough to be able to go and say: 'You should be doing this.' And that's what was tending to happen. It would be; 'Well, why don't you do such and such? If you do such and such – ' it started trying to get detailed solutions . . . from people who really weren't in a position to know and understand. So he'd bring it back and he'd turn it into a question sort of – it's difficult to describe actually.

It is useful to have somebody there who actually intervened. He wasn't just sort of an observer who took pressure off people when they were under pressure. It's sort of a responsive way and the way he played it was actually to intervene in a positive sense and say: 'Hang on, that's not the way to do it. What you need to do is not to give opinions but to ask questions.' And he kept on reminding us that the way in which we were going about our work wasn't very productive.

This description of the set adviser's role implies that he was 'directive about attention' but not 'directive about action'. He clearly, according to the CEOs, didn't just make comments about the process of the set; he confronted issues in order to direct people's attention to what they were doing and what they (in his opinion) should be doing. However, what I did not get from CEOs was any hint that he was teaching people (in the way in which that term has come to be used).

This directiveness element links to what some CEOs saw as the ground rules for working. For example:

Firstly the ground rules which the set adviser established that – the first one was that . . . when you start with one person's problem everybody else wants to chip and get their oar in. And he said from the very beginning that you must let one person ask a question and then develop that idea before the next person will ask his question. Otherwise . . . you are all trying to score a point . . . Develop ideas and see where they get to. And the other ground rule he said was that you must not make suggestions on how the problem's going to be resolved. You can ask questions. I presume other people have identified those two points? Because they were clearly stated at the beginning.

Interestingly, some people saw that once they had worked through the early problems in the set, they would get into advice giving (and see it as useful). One set that was carrying on after the programme was clear that it disagreed with their set adviser on this.

THEORY ISSUES

I want initially to make the simple point that the theoretical assumptions under-pinning ALCE seem vindicated from my research.

A quote from someone who left the programme after one meeting is interesting here:

> I actually think it is a better method at all levels. I don't really believe that taught courses do a fantastic amount of good at the end of the day regardless of the content. I am not totally happy with the effect they have on other people within the company . . . we send some to Ashridge and they all come back determined to get things moving but I think that any course done in isolation for an individual or even a group of individuals, cannot really work unless the environment is already receptive. But I think far too many people come off courses and are not about to apply what it is they have learned. But I also believe that on many of the courses that the case studies or actual teaching itself is in itself a little bit divorced from reality.

Others made similar comments. The value of this approach is also confirmed in a Local Government Training Board report. They studied the ALCE programme and other programmes that provide for CEOs. Their conclusion was:

> It is apparent that the Action Learning programme had the greatest impact on the participants and, even more significantly, these were permanent changes in behaviour applied directly to their work and which are still continuing.

It is interesting to counterpose this with some of the earlier quotes about the benefits of the programme. People could identify a change, but often found it difficult to articulate why this was so. My interpretation is that they were trying to make conscious learning that was often unconscious and trying to comment in linear, linguistic form about learning that hadn't taken place in a linear, sequential mode. If you ask someone how they learned a subject in a classroom they can usually tell you the sequence by which they were instructed. If the teacher is a skilled presenter such an analysis by the learner will correlate reasonably well with the syllabus the teacher was working to. In Action Learning there is no syllabus and no teacher (in the sense of a skilled presenter). More importantly it seems that people learn different things from Action Learning than they do from a taught course.

A distinction I have found useful is between the concept of 'competence' and the concept of 'capability'. Competence has become a favoured notion in recent years. However, the research in this programme does not support the kinds of competence lists generated both by companies and by the NCVQ and MCI. A typical quote from a participant was

> I recognized that if I was ever in an environment that was quite different I could probably survive. Which I hadn't previously had . . . It gave me confidence . . . that I could open out a bit more. I could pursue other courses of action for career development.

If you take this kind of language with other quotes I have cited you have a way of thinking which does not correlate with typical competence statements.[11] I would regard the way this CEO expressed himself as describing more an aspect of capability – something broader and more sophisticated than a competence.

One can take the example of 'listening' which appears on some company competence lists. A competence approach might look to drilling managers in listening competence through, say, listening exercises on a course, so that the manager could demonstrate that they could 'listen' to someone else. This typically comes over as different from the kinds of comments made by participants on the ALCE programme, such as:

> It developed quite a good attitude in myself, listening to other people rather than trying to jump in and solve – give the answers. Which is what I had always tended to do in the environment I was in. I hadn't got the time to bother to listen to the other guy. We had to take action and the best action to take was *my* action because I hadn't got the time to think about anybody else's.

> I hadn't realised how little I actually listen to people who were trying their very best to contribute. I always felt I listened a hell of a lot to people coming in here asking me questions and so on. Yet, because I was asking questions of the bits that I wanted to know I wasn't really giving them an opportunity to contribute, other than what I wanted them to contribute. In other words: 'Answer the question please; I don't want your views on anything else, I just want the question answered.' And I think that was the big benefit to me and I think we all tumbled to that at various stages; and once we had tumbled if we asked a question and they went off onto something else, we tended not to say: 'Oh, the hell, I don't want to know about that.' We let it go. And I think we all found that at different times.

A key element of the Action Learning approach is also to address problems participants bring rather than offer pre-packaged solutions, and this again correlates with a 'capability' model. This links to points made by some CEOs that the problems were eventually seen as themselves. Thus the set, if it works well, causes people to face their own beliefs, values and feelings. This makes the process quite different from a solely competence model. However, for some people working on problems wasn't enough. For example:

> I think perhaps I would very much like to learn more how to actually deal with those problems identified; how to solve them as well as realizing I've got them. I'm not sure I actually found that out at the end of the day. If you like, I'm still struggling with the problem.

The basic notion of working on problems before working on solutions seems valid. Yet if solutions are not eventually addressed perhaps the course is missing something. In the early days of its inception there was the idea that participants would use the set as a base from which to access other learning resources in Ashridge (academic staff, books, sessions on other courses, and so on). This does not seem to have happened. Yet it could be added back into the programme.

This returns us to the issue of integrating 'P' and 'Q'. There is no doubt that the key value of the programme has been in the 'Q' domain. Given that this is the neglected dimension of most education and training activity, there is ample justification for seeing programmes like this as a necessary balance to standard taught courses. However, it is possible that the ALCE programme could have been enriched by a design which met the original objectives. It is also interesting to speculate as to whether the minority who failed to benefit from the programme might not have gained more through a design that integrated 'P' and 'Q'. A 'capability' approach suggests that you need both.

A worry I have in commenting on the above is that some might see my remarks as justifying adding a taught element to such a programme. The research study discussed here provides no support for such a position. Of the CEOs interviewed none wanted such a move. What seems to be needed is to give freedom to programme participants to access learning resources *as they choose*. But in order to do this they needed assistance in knowing what is available. That does not mean teaching people – rather it means helping them to map out ways of meeting their needs in their own ways.

Allowing for these caveats there is no doubt that the programme justifies Revans basic position on the development of managers. As Revans has found, though, this research will largely be ignored and management developers will continue to use approaches that have not been tested in this way. The reasons for this vary but the most common seems to be that Action Learning and related approaches appear threatening to those who see their role as maintaining authoritarian control over learners on courses.

REFERENCES

1 Cunningham, I. (1986) *Developing Chief Executives*, Ashridge Management College.
2 Cunningham, I. (1984) *Teaching Styles in Learner Centred Management Development Programmes*, University of Lancaster PhD.
3 Reason, P. (ed.) (1989) *Human Inquiry in Action*, Sage.
4 Braddick, W. and Casey, D. (1981) 'Developing the forgotten army', *Management Education and Development*, **12**(3), pp. 169–80.
5 Casey, D. and Hastings, C. (1983) 'Day release for chief executives', *Personnel Management*, June.
6 Casey, D. (1984) 'Lifeline for lonely bosses', *Chief Executive*, September.
7 Hodgson, P. and Brown, M. (1995) 'Learning at the top', in *Directions* (The Ashridge Journal), July, pp 12–14.
8 Cunningham, I. (1989) 'Interactive holistic research', in Reason, P. (ed.) *Human Inquiry in Action*, Sage.
9 Cunningham, I. (1986) op.cit.
10 Cunningham, I. (1984) op.cit.
11 Cunningham, I. (1994) *The Wisdom of Strategic Learning*, McGraw-Hill.

26 More Than Just a Task Force

Nancy M. Dixon

Action Learning has gained popularity among large multi-national companies in the United States as a method for executive development. It is seen as a considerable improvement over more traditional lecture-based programmes. A typical Action Learning programme, as it is implemented in these organizations, begins with a large group workshop of 3–5 days length. During the workshop, teams of 5–12 executives are formed to address specific organizational problems which have been identified by top level management as critical organizational issues. In the weeks following the workshop, each team sets about collecting information on the issue they have been assigned. Often information is gathered both inside the company and from external sources. Each team meets periodically to discuss the information they have collected, sometimes in face-to-face meetings, but more frequently through conference calls. In some cases, an interim large group meeting is held at a half-way point. Each team develops a recommendation for the issue it has been assigned. At the end of the specified time period, usually several weeks, the large group again meets for several days and each team presents its recommendations to the executives who have assembled to hear and respond to the ideas.

Action Learning, implemented in this way, produces several positive outcomes. One important outcome is that participants deepen their understanding of teamwork. Through Action Learning as described above, team members also learn a great deal about the organizational problem they have been asked to address, particularly when it necessitates understanding a part of the business members have had little exposure to before. Thirdly, the organization gains some outstanding thinking on an issue that is of great importance, thinking which can result in 'out of the box' recommendations. Finally, the colleagueship that develops between team members is a worthwhile organizational benefit, one that facilitates future interdependent work.

With minor variations (the length of time, whether teams compete with each other, the number of members on each team) this description typifies the way Action Learning is being implemented in the United States in its most recent and popularized form. However, this form of Action Learning is difficult to distinguish from a typical cross-functional task force that is well known to most US managers. Its seeming familiarity induces US corporations to make use of those factors which are similar to cross-functional task forces and to overlook those factors associated with Action Learning that are dissimilar, but which carry the greatest potential for the development of participants.

Moreover, this protocol does not characterize the way Action Learning was designed and implemented by its originator, Reg Revans. Rather it could be thought of as a modified or perhaps Americanized version of Action Learning. The modifications being:

Revans model	American model
● participants address a real problem	● participants address a real problem
● 9–12 months in length	● 3 weeks – 3 months in length
● participants are involved in problem identification, solution generation, and implementation	● participants provide recommendations only and are not involved in implementation
● participants volunteer for the programme	● participation is required or proscribed
● team meetings are primarily face to face	● team meetings are primarily electronic

To examine these differences more thoroughly it is helpful to look at one US company which implemented an Action Learning programme in 1994–5 along with the results they obtained.

UNISYS EXECUTIVE DEVELOPMENT ACTION FORUM

Unisys, a world-wide supplier of information services and systems, had recently announced a major strategy shift intended to reverse its loss of market share and restore the corporation to a competitive position in the world-wide market. The new strategy, which required radical change in all sectors of the corporation, necessitated that employees become more team centred, customer focused, and fast cycle. The existing executive development programme, aimed at the top 200 executives, had consistently been well received, but appeared to produce little change in the behaviour of this critical group. Thus, the need for immediate and radical change to the current executive development programme that would prepare the executives to model the new behaviours in their everyday actions.

The Director of Executive Development sought out other Fortune 500 companies in the US to identify innovative management development approaches. The Director found that Action Learning had been gaining popularity in the US and was being heralded as a development approach that could achieve greater behaviour change than traditional management development. To implement Action Learning through the executive development programme the director put together a design team made up of internal and external consultants which created the Executive Development Action Forum (EDAF), an Americanized version of Action Learning, with the following characteristics:

- 25–30 participants were selected and assigned by their supervisors to attend the EDAF; many of the participants had attended previous executive development sessions.
- Participants were selected from differing business units with the aim of building relationships across units.
- Participants completed pre-work which included collecting 360° feedback on themselves, reading articles, constructing a vision statement for their unit, and completing a wellness inventory.
- A system-wide issue was identified by a top level executive who became the Action Learning client. The issue selected was to find ways to improve and speed the product development cycle from idea generation to the phase out of a product.
- Participants were divided into four teams, each of which was assigned a different phase of this problem.
- Each team was provided a process facilitator as well as a senior level manager who was to serve as a resource.
- The programme length was established at four months during which time participants would continue their normal responsibilities as well as working on their Action Learning task.
- Participants began the programme with a one-week session, then were asked to meet in teams over the next four months to work on their task, and to come together again as a total group for a final two and a half days.
- The first week of the programme was a mix of content sessions, sessions designed to build interpersonal skills, and time set aside for the teams to meet. Also during that week each participant met with a coach to review the 360° feedback they had received and to create a development plan to improve those areas where the feedback had revealed weaknesses. Wellness sessions provided exercise and a focus on health and nutrition.
- Lotus notes were made available to share documents and reports during the interval.
- In the final two and a half day meeting teams were to present their recommendations to upper level management and report on their own learning.

The resulting programme bore a strong resemblance to a typical cross-functional task force. Most of the EDAF participants had many past experiences working

331

on or chairing task forces. Their understanding of the political realities of such work was:

- Although task forces provide an opportunity for visibility with top management, there are also potential downsides of task force work. If, for example, the task force makes recommendations that are not in keeping with top management opinion, team members can be viewed as incompetent or as resisters to change.
- Even when task forces make recommendations that are popular with top management, team members receive little personal credit for the outcomes, therefore, members often see it as sensible to hold task force work to a minimum, putting their energy into areas for which they are being measured.
- Task forces are an opportunity to build relationships with peers in other parts of the organization which can prove useful in the future. It is important, however, to avoid earning a reputation for being 'difficult to get along with', thus conflict, even around substantive issues, is often avoided. Recognizing that the task force experience is time limited, members often choose to wait out conflict rather than addressing it.
- It is a truism of organizational life that few recommendations made by task forces are ever actually implemented. When recommendations are made by one group and handed off to others to implement, the likelihood of the recommendations being carried out is slim. Understandably those charged with implementation always need to study the problem for themselves in order to gain enough knowledge to do their task – and since there are many possible solutions to any problem, it is likely that their study will lead them to a somewhat different solution. Given that task force members understand that their recommendations are unlikely to be implemented, their focus is easily redirected toward creating solutions that will bring the team members some recognition while keeping them out of political trouble.
- It is widely acknowledged that being a member of a task force is part of the 'dues' one pays to move ahead in an organization.

Participants in the EDAF were willing to work on the Action Learning teams, but their way of working and the amount of energy expended tended to reflect the realities of their past task force experiences. They saw the Action Learning teams as task forces and acted in keeping with their understanding of how one functions effectively on a task force. Predictably, the Action Learning teams minimized their face-to-face time, focused on task over process issues, and were primarily concerned with how top management would view their work.

During the four months the Action Learning teams met mostly by telephone rather than in person. Several factors influenced this more limited way of meeting. First, each of the teams had one or more member from a non-US country, greatly increasing the travel time it took to meet in person as well as the cost of meeting. In addition, the four months occurred during the last quarter of the year when many participants felt considerable pressure to focus on issues within their own area of responsibility. Limiting meetings to telephone conference calls reduced the amount of personal development that team members could experience. Over the phone it was easier for team members to be unaware of others' reactions, to 'tune out' difficult or boring exchanges, and to 'put up with' rather than 'deal with' recalcitrant members.

During conference call meetings participants tended to stick to task issues and to only address issues related to their own self-development or team development when task issues had been satisfied, which frequently meant not at all. Team members had concluded they would be judged by the task outcomes they presented to upper level management – not by how much they had developed as a team or changed as individuals. That interpretation led them to give priority to task issues over development issues.

The upward focus of the teams was also evident in the interactions between team members. For example, each team tended to have at least one member who frequently absented him or herself from the telephone conferences or failed to complete agreed assignments. However, there was little discussion of these problems in the team meetings. Team members did not see it as their responsibility to contact missing team members nor to confront them about broken agreements.

Much of the conversation in team meetings was focused on the client; what the client *really* wanted and what others had heard about his reactions. The client unknowingly exacerbated this focus by comparing the four teams noting, for example, that one group seemed to be farther along than another or that one team was more thorough in their analysis than another. There was a related tendency for the teams to focus on the presentation that would be made to top management, that is, the way the transparencies would look, the wording used, and who would present what part.

Even given these limitations the EDAF achieved substantial benefits in four areas; (1) organizational understanding, (2) individual development, (3) development of teamwork and (4) organizational outcomes.

ORGANIZATIONAL UNDERSTANDING

Team members interviewed employees from across the organization as well as analysing many documents related to product development. They also bench-

333

marked Unisys against other companies and learned a great deal from the comparison. These activities served to broaden the company-wide perspective of the team members. It also gave team members a new appreciation for the wealth of talent within the company. Team members developed a sense of urgency about the changes that needed to be made within Unisys which enhanced their own commitment to those changes. Over the four months, participants began to see themselves as being able to have a powerful influence on top management, and moreover, as having responsibility for using that influence to assist Unisys in making the needed changes. This sense of responsibility has proved to be one of the most impactful and long-lasting changes to result from the EDAF.

INDIVIDUAL DEVELOPMENT

A number of factors led to individual development. In some cases the 360° feedback created a readiness for examining individual development issues. Team members could see the same problems reflected in the team as had been reported in their own feedback. Team meetings, although limited in the ways already described, still afforded a medium through which some members were able to increase their awareness of their impact on others. Finally, the wellness activities served as an analogy for the difficulties participants faced in making developmental changes.

TEAMWORK

It was evident that some of the Action Learning teams functioned more effectively than others, and thus the realization that there were skills and norms that were necessary for effective functioning of a peer team, which many participants conceded were lacking in themselves. Some participants recognized the need to develop these skills within their own sectors if Unisys was to reach its goal of being 'team centered'. They began to view their Action Learning experience as a useful model for Unisys' future way of working.

ORGANIZATIONAL OUTCOMES

The recommendations for changes in the product development process which were made by the Action Learning teams exceeded the expectations of the executive team. They viewed the recommendations as insightful and candid.

334

Although the Action Learning teams were not charged with responsibility beyond making recommendations, a number of the team members felt so strongly about the need for the changes they had recommended that they joined a subsequent group who implemented many of the recommendations. In a separate initiative the team members from Europe put into place a number of the specific recommendations.

One of the most beneficial organizational outcomes was the relationships that developed between team members. The ability to pick up the phone and ask another for information or help was seen as invaluable. Even during the four months of the programme, participants resolved a number of issues between functions that could not have been addressed without a personal relationship having been built.

LEARNING LOST

The limitations of task forces outlined here would not be unfamiliar to most managers. Nor would the realization that, even given such limitations, task teams do benefit both the members involved and the organization as a whole. The issue then, is not that team members cannot learn on Action Learning teams that model themselves on task teams, but that a great deal of potential learning is lost.

At the heart of this loss is the separation between work and learning that exists in task force teams. Typically, task force teams view something that occurs as preparation for work, not as integral to it. Moreover, learning is seen as taking time away from work rather than informing it. By contrast, there are two intended outcomes from Action Learning: solving an organizational problem and the development of the participants who are involved in that resolution. The two are, however, intertwined. Team members learn about themselves, and thus change themselves, when they are engaged in problems that matter to them, and team members cannot solve organizational problems unless they change themselves since all organizational change must necessarily involve individuals within the organization themselves changing. It may be that organizational members have, for so long, segregated work and learning in organizations, that it is difficult to conceive of the two as coupled. There may be a tendency to label any activity organizational members engage in as one or the other. At the least, it may be tempting to regard one of the outcomes as primary and the other as simply facilitative – but it is the interplay between the two that produce both individual and organizational learning. One is sacrificed to the other only at the risk of forfeiting both.

In task force teams members make recommendations but do not themselves *act* on the solutions they have constructed. By contrast, learning occurs when an Action Learning team engages in a cycle that involves: (1) actively working to make sense of a situation, (2) acting on what they have concluded, (3) experiencing the results of their actions, (4) rethinking the situation based on the results, and (5) acting again. The 'learning' in Action Learning occurs when participants reflect on the action they have taken, not on just their planning. If team members cannot experience the outcome of their plan, their learning is aborted. An analogy would be a tennis beginner trying to learn how to serve the ball by making a serving plan – but never actually hitting the ball and consequently never knowing where the ball would have landed. Action Learning is most effective when team members create a plan to solve a problem and then, in collaboration with those impacted, implement the plan. It is this ability to learn from one's actions that is lost when Action Learning mimics task force teams. As illustrated in the Unisys example, members who have put time and effort into understanding an issue are strongly motivated to carry it through.

Perhaps the most critical element that is lost when Action Learning takes on the characteristics of a task force, is individual development, that is, the opportunity for team members to learn more about themselves in a way that allows them to modify their own behaviour. However, the development of individuals is a long-range goal while the resolution of a problem is more immediate – and it is always tempting to forgo the long term for the sake of the immediate. The kind of development that individuals are able to achieve through Action Learning is unique to organizational settings. Action Learning can develop individuals who are more self-aware, more cognizant of their impact, and who have a more differentiated frame from which to view the organization and its future issues. Ultimately the most significant benefit of Action Learning may be that it can prepare organizational members to better resolve future problems.

Individual development requires time – often more so than organizations tend to want to allocate to it. Since all organizational members are to some extent blind to their faults, and since they receive little real feedback on them, working in an Action Learning team can become a very pivotal developmental experience, but only, of course, if there is time for team members to see each other in action. As team members struggle with the issues inherent both in their own team's functioning and in their interactions with the problem owners and implementers, team members can lend insight to each other to understand both the positive and negative aspects of their impact. It is a very human characteristic for people who are working together on an issue they care about, to also come to care about each other. Out of that caring they can offer support and equally important they are often more willing to talk openly and frankly with each other – having developed some investment in the others' well being. Development requires both support and challenge and requires both over time. Action Learning is one of the few vehicles that offers both attributes in a work setting.

Having named the problems an abbreviated form of Action Learning engenders, it is important to again acknowledge that even in its Americanized form, team members **do** learn and the teams **do** assist organizations in addressing difficult problems – it is just that they fall far short of their potential. It is as if many US companies have grasped the outward form of Action Learning, that is, teams working on problems, without, however, attending to its essence.

27 Life on the Seesaw: Tensions in Action Reflection Learning™

Judy O'Neil, Victoria Marsick,
Lyle Yorks, Glenn Nilson and
Robert Kolodny
ARL™ INQUIRY

To help bring about the continuous learning required in organizations in the 1990s, educators are interested in ways of learning from the experience of actual work. One result is an increased use of the adult education method called Action Reflection Learning™ (ARL™).* ARL is an approach to Action Learning as a management development strategy that places participants in teams to work on strategic projects sponsored by senior executives from their company. Each ARL programme is structured to accomplish management development needs in support of the company's business development goals and objectives. The general structure of these programmes is described in more detail below. ARL enables people to learn from projects that address actual organizational strategic issues. The literature on learning suggests that people learn better when they address issues that are important to them. Actual strategic issues, however, have deadlines and constraints. What are the tensions created between learning, the explicitly stated purpose of an ARL programme, and the need of the participants to resolve the strategic business issue? What is the relationship between learning and task accomplishment?

In this chapter based on the results of research conducted in an ARL programme we begin to explore the answer to these questions. We start by defining ARL and discussing how the tension between action and learning is inherent in the definition, a tension which we describe with the metaphor of a seesaw. Next we provide information on the general structure of an ARL programme as well

* Action Reflection Learning™ and ARL™ used throughout this chapter are registered trademarks of Leadership in International Management, Ltd (LIM) and are used in this chapter by permission.

339

as the specific programme that is the study site. This provides the context for discussing our research. We then explain the methods used in the research, discuss our findings to date, and look at tentative conclusions and implications for adult learning.

ACTION REFLECTION LEARNING PROGRAMMES

Action Reflection Learning is a form of Action Learning (AL) practised by Leadership in International Management Ltd (LIM). AL draws its theoretical base from Reg Revans, a British physicist, considered to be the father of AL.[1] The relationships, and potential tensions, between task and learning begin to be framed by examining some of the definitions of ARL and AL. Pedler relates learning to action, and stipulates that one cannot take place without the other:

> Action learning is an approach to the development of people in organizations which takes the task as the vehicle for learning. It is based on the premise that there is no learning without action and no sober and deliberate action without learning. . . . The method has been pioneered in work organizations and has three main components people, who accept the responsibility for taking action on a particular issue; problems, or the tasks that people set themselves; and a set of six or so colleagues who support and challenge each other to make progress on problems.[2]

ARL is a variant of Action Learning that places significant emphasis on the role of reflection in the learning process. A range of methods for facilitating reflection on the experience participants are having during an ARL programme are utilized including 'stop and reflect' periods in project teams and reflection and dialogue sessions involving all programme participants as a learning community. (Stop and reflect periods are a regular feature of ARL programmes. Participants stop the work they are doing to reflect, individually and as a group, on what they are learning about themselves, the project work, and their interaction as a learning group.) An important focus of this method is on helping participants to learn through critical reflection and the reframing of the strategic problems faced by the team. As participants work their problem, they learn to learn and think critically. Using the help of a project team adviser (PTA), and their teammates, they begin to reframe the problem and see the situation in new ways. This type of learning may begin to create tensions between task and learning, since as the team learns, members are likely to begin questioning some of the fundamental assumptions that underlie the way in which strategic problems are typically framed in their organizations.

ARL programmes usually take place over a six to nine month period during which project teams meet as a group four times in week-long residential sessions. Participants work on, and learn from, their projects with the intervention assistance of the PTA; attend appropriate seminars; and engage in other activities that fit the programme's focus. Between these residential sessions, participants return to their jobs, but continue to work on their projects.

The programme that is the subject of the research reported here is being run in a large international food company that has decided to function as a global company. The ARL programme was co-developed with the company to establish a global perspective among the senior operating managers in its geographically based divisions and to address seven key issues identified in a customized corporate culture survey; teamwork, employee development, trust, leadership, communications, conflict management, and innovation and change.

Three ARL programmes were conducted over a period of two years. Each programme consisted of four six-day meetings, spaced approximately five to six weeks apart. Twenty managers from various parts of the organization participated in each iteration of the programme. Within each programme the participants formed four project teams of five people each. Each project team was assigned a project that was relevant to the globalization strategy of the company and sponsored by a member of the corporate executive committee. The projects had been selected by the executive committee based on their strategic importance to the company. A LIM project team adviser facilitated each project, helping participants to critically reflect, question assumptions, and reframe their team tasks. In between the formal meetings of the programme, participants balanced their work on team project related tasks with the demands of their jobs, much as a manager might do as a part time member of a task force. Project team members would periodically communicate long distance using electronic mail and conference calls. It was typical for teams to arrive a few days ahead of the formal start of a programme meeting to work on their projects. The project teams would also communicate with their project sponsor on an ongoing basis. At times meetings were scheduled with their sponsor during the programme sessions. Requests for funds for completing project-related tasks (e.g. visits to other sites or companies for benchmarking, conducting surveys, etc.) were negotiated between the teams and their sponsors.

RESEARCH METHODOLOGY

This has been an ongoing ethnographic study using a participant observer at each programme session. This role has allowed close contact with the participants while being unobtrusive. The observer has collected data via observations, note taking, and opportunistic interviews. Overt participation was minimal. Initial interviews, directed toward assessing the programme's impact within the company, were also initiated. After each programme session, the data were

341

jointly analysed by ARL Inquiry, a five-member research team. This kitchen cabinet helped analyse the data by identifying developmental themes, provided a point of triangulation, and helped structure the participant observer role for the next session. The data reported in this chapter were gathered during the second of the three ARL programmes. The tensions described were evident throughout the programmes.

TENSIONS BETWEEN TASK FOCUS AND LEARNING FOCUS

There are always tensions in any learning experience between performance that demonstrates existing capabilities, and entrance into a vulnerable space where one tries out new knowledge and skill. ARL programmes, however, increase tension because people work in real situations, and as a result, get real-time feedback from internal organizational clients and peers. In this section, we discuss some of the tensions between learning and resolving the strategic business problems that lead us to describe ARL programmes with the metaphor, life on a seesaw.

TENSIONS BETWEEN EXPECTATIONS OF LEARNING AND DELIVERING TANGIBLE, VISIBLE PROJECT RESULTS

The first set of tensions results from the fact that the projects were real and highly visible. The corporation is task oriented and expects tangible results. Given that significant development resources were being spent on these programmes, and people in the company not selected for participation were not yet sure that the programme created tangible results, participants felt a tension between expectations for clear project team results, versus expectations that they learn, which involved outcomes that could not be as clearly articulated and that were not as easily understood by those not in the programme. Some teams felt this same tension from their sponsors who were pressuring them for results.

Participants were aware of the visibility of the programme and the need to produce results. During the first week, participants commented that they felt guilty spending time in the programme because their peers were not yet clear that time spent in this programme was worth the investment. Questions were being raised about the cost of the programme in a downsizing mode. The programme director pointed out, ' . . . we're in financial pain in this company . . . it's only been within the last couple of quarters, we're spending a lot of money on this programme, we're trying to assess how well this programme is working.

People are curious, they ask questions.' Interviews with non-programme-partici-
pants in the company suggest that people were watching to see the extent to
which projects were implemented and results achieved, as illustrated by the
following comment: 'A major risk is that people throughout (the company) will
make judgments if this approach works. If management can't follow through if
they don't implement the recommendations people will lose confidence.'

The issue of evaluation was raised explicitly by one participant:

> I never expected it to be like a primal scream therapy, where we roll on the floor,
> explore our souls and inner self. This is a management development programme and
> I expected that how I perform might affect my career. I expect that how our project
> comes out may affect my career. I always speak out at these things, but someone told
> me that they are intimidated by the silence of some who used to speak out.

The programme places participants in situations in which they must take responsibility for determining how much risk they are willing to take. We hypothesize
that they experience a dilemma in that avoidance of risk is itself a risky alternative, and certainly detrimental to learning.

TENSIONS BETWEEN TIME REQUIRED FOR LEARNING AND TASK

The second set of tensions is between the time required for learning and the
time required for attention to the task. Early in the programme, when under time
stress, groups tended not to take time to reflect. However, those groups which
did reflect, once they got past the deadline, could begin to see what they learned
from the experience. When people took the time to reflect, despite time pressure,
the quality of their learning at times seemed higher.

In the first week, the participant observer reflected that 'individuals are
experiencing various insights'. He inferred that these insights had not yet been
translated through reflection into action because he did not yet see new
behaviours. One participant stated, 'I've gained a lot of new insights, but not yet
learned.'

By week two, one group experienced conflict and took time off-line, including
a specially scheduled dinner, to address this conflict. During a team reflection
at the end of the week they went around the table and responded to the question
posed by a member of the team 'Are we still a team?' One person said, 'We had
an up and down week. We reformed well . . . bonding again. Then we got ahead
of ourselves, had conflict, and had to go back and reform, still norming.' Another
member said 'We're all different personalities, [and have] different needs, and
we agreed we would continue by consensus.' A third member of the group said:

> In regard to [the forming-storming-norming model] . . . depending on what we are

343

doing, we are all three things at one time. We are most aware of the process, stopping ourselves. We raise awareness about ourselves, and there's a different level of comfort learning about that. Communication is the glue that keeps us together.

Another said, 'We are most vulnerable in trying to meet deadlines. [Person X] and I are very different; I am unimpressed by deadlines. [Person X] wants to meet deadlines under pressure. [when] we are out of control. That's the only danger for us.'

Late one night in the third weekly seminar, one group was preparing to participate in an audit process in which groups critique one another's work. One member felt that when he tried to make contributions, others would override him in order to complete the task. When the group did the stop-reflect, they recognized what they had done and commented that their process had fallen apart.

TENSIONS BETWEEN GROUP CONFLICT AND HARMONY

The third set of tensions has to do with maintaining harmony in order to perform the group task as opposed to surfacing and dealing with the conflict that might be needed for deeper learning to take place. One participant observed, 'if no conflict, you get nothing'. The groups that were most open in dealing with their conflicts and disagreements also had the most innovative outcomes. In two groups, for example, when power was assumed by someone in the group, others in the group confronted this. By contrast, in a third group, members were reticent to assume power, and as a result, they were continually dependent on the skills of the ARL PTA. In the fourth group, the issue of power was raised, but the group consensually ignored the power issue, choosing instead to replicate the hierarchical relationships extant in the organizational culture.

We hypothesize that groups that could surface and deal with conflict would be able to think in new ways about the task, and as a result, could learn at deeper levels.

IMPLICATIONS FOR LEARNING THEORY

The theoretical base of ARL is not clearly defined, but we believe that the model contains elements of two, somewhat contrasting, learning theories: the scientific problem-solving model or the American pragmatic school, embodied in the work of John Dewey; and the life-world model, that holds various interpretations depending upon the school of phenomenology with which it might be associated.

Yorks summarizes the roots and essence of Dewey's theory of learning from experience:

> In Dewey's pragmatism how one learns from his or her experience is couched in concepts derived from the scientific method. Darwinism had influenced Pierce and James and had a strong direct influence on Dewey (1910)[3] as well. The empirical methods of new objective psychology were also influential on his thinking. In education he called for the controlled type of learning exemplified in science (Elias and Merriam, 1980).[4] Mezirow (1991)[5] writes that for Dewey reflection meant validity testing in the sense of rational problem solving.[6]

By contrast, the phenomenological focus is more oriented to what Husserl called the life-world 'i.e. the world in which we are immersed in the natural attitude that never becomes an object as such for us'.[7] At the risk of oversimplifying, we can identify several assumptions of the continental school of phenomenology *vis-a-vis* learning from experience:

> All meaning is intersubjective, contingent on social construction on the part of humans who are immersed in a structurally pre-given life-world. Objective science is part of this life-world. Human actors make sense of their daily life through a dialogic relationship. The meaning of a theoretical proposition comes into being only in the context of a particular application or individual history.[8]

Learning from experience in the phenomenological tradition is often uncomfortable. Learning takes place when something in one's taken-for-granted life-world becomes problematic and is therefore disorienting. From a hermeneutic phenomenological perspective, learning is an act of interpretation. It involves a fusion of horizons between the horizon of the person [who is immersed in his or her life world] and the horizon of the lived experience that is the object of attention.[9] New meaning emerges from that fusion of horizons.

For the purpose of examining the interplay of these polarities in the ARL approach to learning, we have cast these models in terms of polarities that are purer than can be sustained in either theory. We use the data in this case to raise questions about the contrast between these two models, even though the data and the inferences drawn from them are preliminary.

We believe that these two underlying theoretical perspectives, a strong emphasis on problem solving and the additional orientation of the life-world concept, capture a source of the tension that appears to exist between task and learning in an ARL programme and that evokes the idea of life on a seesaw. Participants come into the programme with a strong pragmatic, problem solving focus. This focus fits well with the pragmatic part of the base of the programme. Participants are quickly introduced, however, to concepts such as stop-reflect, that cause them to begin to question their taken-for-granted life-world. Early in the programme, participants do not always understand the value of this type of

345

learning, so they begin to experience tension between the need to meet expectations and produce results, and the need to take time to work through what, for some, is an uncomfortable experience.

As the programme progresses, many participants and groups begin to better understand the important relationship between the learning that comes from the examination of the meanings and assumptions they hold about themselves, their group and their task; and the successful completion of the task itself. There is evidence in this programme that participants who become aware of this different learning frequently pushed away from a narrow focus on solving the project problem toward examining events in their life-world that were uncomfortable for them, and that therefore became problematic. We believe that such examination could result in a deeper level of learning that goes beyond the immediate project and requisite task-related skills. Although tension continues to exist, these participants and groups recognize the value, and have the skills, to be able to manage it.

ACKNOWLEDGEMENT

ARL™ Inquiry is a research group affiliated with Leadership in International Management Ltd. Data were collected by Lyle Yorks. Analysis and ideas were jointly developed with Yorks and the following people (alphebetical order): Robert Kolodny, Victoria Marsick, Glenn Nilson, and Judy O'Neil. O'Neil and Marsick took the lead in writing up the jointly developed analysis.

REFERENCES

1 Revans, R. (1982) *The origin and growth of action learning*, London: Chartwell Bratt.
2 Pedler, M. (ed.) (1991) *Action learning in practice*, London: Gower.
3 Dewey, J. (1910) *How we think*, Lexington, MA: Heath.
4 Elias, J. & Merriam, S. (1980) *Philosophical foundations of adult education*, Malabar, FL: Robert Krieger.
5 Mezirow, J. (1991) *Transformative dimensions of adult learning*, San Francisco: Jossey-Bass.
6 Yorks, L. (1994) Understanding how learning is experienced through collaborative inquiry: A phenomenological study. Unpublished dissertation, Teachers College, Columbia University, pp. 23–4.
7 Yorks, L. op. cit. pp. 28–9.
8 Yorks, L. op. cit. pp. 34.
9 Yorks, L. op. cit. pp. 35.

28 Evaluating Action Learning

Mark Easterby-Smith, Alison Johns and John Burgoyne

There is no common agreement about what constitutes a valid evaluation. But from a welter of definitions and viewpoints[1-4], we might distinguish for our present purpose two distinct definitions: evaluation as *judgement*, and evaluation as *development*. The former definition implies an attempt to assess the value, or worth, of an activity or programme against certain explicit or implicit criteria – usually in order to decide whether to continue funding and resourcing the activity in question. The latter definition tends to assume the continued existence of the programme, and therefore implies adoption of various procedures and processes to enable the programme to become better.

The next problem is to decide just what is to be evaluated. The extraordinarily wide dissemination of Action Learning causes some difficulty here since it is evident from this book, and elsewhere[5-7], that its nature can vary greatly with the context in which it is applied and according to the different approaches of those who initiate it. Each may bear a greater, or lesser, resemblance to the forms and nature of Action Learning as developed and propounded by Professor Revans. Indeed, Revans' own approach to Action Learning varied somewhat over time according to the different constraints of the context within which he was operating. Apart from variations according to context, one may also view any particular Action Learning intervention from a number of different perspectives, in simplified form, these are illustrated as a hierarchical 'tree' (see Figure 28.1).

The figure indicates that there are a number of alternative structures and designs which may be used to facilitate Action Learning; that on one hand they are based on a fairly consistent body of ideas regarding its essence, and on the other hand these structures and designs may be experienced in a whole variety of ways by those who participate in Action Learning. At the two higher levels it is possible to identify theories which have influenced Action Learning practices. Thus, the central ideas of Action Learning are related closely to the views of John Dewey and his associates about the need to establish a linkage between

347

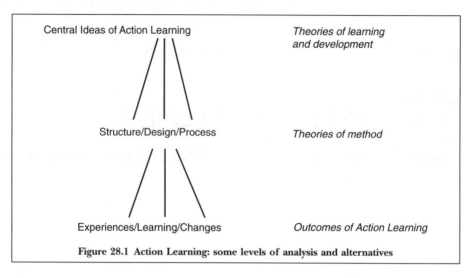

Figure 28.1 Action Learning: some levels of analysis and alternatives

thinking and acting; similarly Revans (1971) argues that the desirable processes within Action Learning rely heavily upon scientific methodology.[8]

Those readers who have worked through the book so far will appreciate that 'development' is a concept central to the theory and practice of Action Learning – at least in the sense of improving situations and increasing the capacities of those who manage these situations. Thus the notion of evaluation as development is very close to the central philosophy of Action Learning, and we shall therefore comment in the following section upon how evaluation may be seen as an integral part of any design. This does not, of course, negate the value of, and the need to make, some wider judgements about Action Learning. Indeed, judgement (or audit, as Revans calls it) is an important feature of the Action Learning cycle (system beta), and we shall therefore discuss in the final part of this chapter the various attempts that have been made to assess the impact, and value, of Action Learning.

DEVELOPMENTAL EVALUATION: MAKING IT BETTER

Many of the central ideas of Action Learning have been discussed in the first part of this book. It would appear that there is rather less diversity of opinion amongst writers and practitioners at this level if only because those approaches which deviate markedly from the central tenets are rarely accepted as being 'genuine' Action Learning. Nevertheless there is still a certain amount of divergence, and despite being rather abstract, some of the ideas may be examined empirically. For example, Revans discusses a number of theoretical questions about the way learning takes place within an Action Learning framework.[9] Does learning occur suddenly or in small increments? Is learning a single factor or a multi-factor process? And so on. These are questions about the nature of Action Learning and of the theories underlying it. Based on his own experience, Revans has his own view about the answers. Another view comes from Mumford in this book (Chapter 19) where he offers a restatement of Revans' L=P+Q as Q+P+Q= L, thus laying greater stress on the circularity of the process and the importance of starting with the questions of the learners. At this level, there may therefore be some role for evaluation, either in examining the validity of some of these theoretical ideas, or in attempting to refine and develop such concepts. Either way, Revans probably has a marked advantage in these areas, since his book[8] represents one of the first attempts to think through some of these issues in relation to managerial learning.

At the next level, the *structures/designs/process* whereby Action Learning ideas may be implemented within a particular context, there is an enormous amount of variation. The breadth of possibilities may be deduced from the range of applications described in Part II of this book, and some of the relevant variations are summarized in Chapter 16 by Alan Lawlor. There are many points in a programme where it is worth reviewing whether the particular procedures adopted are appropriate at that point in its life, and to enable adjustments to facilitate individual and group learning. For example, in Action Learning based programmes run at Lancaster the ideal 'set' size varies greatly. When members of the set are engaged in exploring and developing ideas about their future action, it is often beneficial to have at least five or six members within a set; once they get involved in implementing specific actions in their work, the ideal set size may be little more than two or three members; but when they come to review their experiences, far larger groupings may be appropriate (ten to twelve). Some participants appear to have marked preferences for smaller sets; others prefer larger sets. Similarly, the particular teaching style for the set adviser may lend itself to larger or smaller groups.

The primary role of evaluation when looking at the structural and design aspects of Action Learning processes must therefore surely be to assist with the right adaptation to the particular needs of the people involved at that point in the history of the Action Learning intervention. It implies that evaluation should be seen in development terms, or as 'short-cycle' evaluation. Clearly it is consistent with the philosophy of Action Learning to place the problem and responsibility for conducting this evaluation with the participant involved in the exercise. But this is more than a 'process review' being conducted at the end of each session; it requires some detailed thinking about wider design and structural issues and may require clear decisions and action to be taken as a result of this. There are a number of ways of organizing this kind of do-it-yourself evaluation. For example, buzz groups might be asked to develop lists of issues concerning the operation of the set, and these are then reported back to the rest of the group in order to collate feelings about particular issues raised; alternatively the task might be delegated to one or two individuals who would take on the responsibility of interviewing the other members of the group in a fairly unstructured way before reporting back to the group as a whole. Naturally it would be unwise to prescribe ideal procedures in cases such as this; all we are implying is that the Action Learning processes should be deliberately designed in such a way that the people involved can learn about how they might operate more effectively.

But it is also possible to generalize beyond a particular context. Weinstein concluded after studying a range of programmes that a number of common factors influenced learning outcomes.[10] The main ones were: (i) the adoption of work-focused projects; (ii) the composition of sets; (iii) the process within the sets; (iv) the style and skills of the set adviser; and (v) the 'time' factor (in the sense that Action Learning programmes are typically spread over a longer period than most other courses and programmes). She found that key to the learning process, particularly in the early stages of Action Learning, was a competent set adviser. Lewis, who conducted a 'developmental' evaluation in the Prudential Assurance Society, found that it could not only highlight issues of content and process, but perhaps more importantly, organizational features and support which either need to be in place or to change in order to assist both individual learning and organizational development.[11] Conclusions drawn from the evaluation of an Action Learning programme provided for senior management at the University of Plymouth also stressed the importance of the visible involvement and active support of the vice-chancellor, the need for clear project criteria to be established and the importance of providing wide publicity for the programme within the institution so that there could be general awareness and support of what is going on.[12]

This leads to the third level at which Action Learning might be considered: that of the *experiences, learning or changes* that take place within, and as a result of, an intervention. In effect, the preceding paragraph has suggested that through understanding the experiences of participants in Action Learning processes, it may be more possible to take decisions leading to the improvement of the structure or design of Action Learning. It is in terms of learning and change that a *judgmental* evaluation must primarily be formulated; but there is still room for *developmental* evaluation at this level too. Since the former is rather a large topic, we shall consider it in the subsequent section of this chapter, and confine our comments at this stage to the developmental evaluation.

In some respects, Action Learning is concerned less with the experiences of individuals than with the learning and change that results from these experiences. The structural considerations that we have discussed above are intended to promote more effective learning and change in general, but they are seen primarily as the responsibility of set advisers (if any) and of group members. Learning and change must be seen primarily as an individual responsibility, and the concern of developmental evaluation should therefore be to help individuals become more aware of their own learning and change processes in order that this might be facilitated. Personal learning diaries are now used quite frequently on post-experience courses, and some companies have initiated developmental diaries in which managers are expected to record their own processes of change and development. There is a range of other techniques available whereby individuals may examine their own learning progress and process. Weinstein[10] found that some of her groups would hold a review at the end of each set meeting. This often became institutionalized within a group. Set advisers would start the process by asking repeatedly: 'So what have we learned from that?', and this would then become something of a mantra that set members would frequently mutter to themselves, and to colleagues and staff back at work.

JUDGMENTAL EVALUATION: THE IMPACT OF ACTION LEARNING

The impact of Action Learning may be assessed at the level of its effect on individuals, on the organization (more readily apparent as outcomes from specific projects and programmes and less easily apparent in terms of building a 'learning organization'), and in wider terms, upon management education as a whole. The notion of 'scientific' evaluations where an experimental group of participants is compared to a control group has been strongly criticized by Parlett and Hamilton[13] on the grounds that the methods of physical science are not appropriate to educational settings where people are active participants rather than inanimate objects. However, a few useful studies are starting to emerge. Enderby and Phelan[14] provide an example of this type where they compare customer perceptions of service in bank branches where staff had been involved in Action Learning with those of branches where staff had not had the Action Learning experience. Naturally the former became more positive after the programme.

Despite this it is clear that some people do not relish their encounter with Action Learning: this may be to do with themselves, with the particular variant involved, or with the general philosophy of Action Learning. However, the majority of people who encounter Action Learning and allied educational methods do accept it enthusiastically and subsequently adopt many of the underlying ideas within their normal working lives. We suspect that this is not merely a matter of following the latest cult: these ideas have roots which can be traced

351

back to the Socratic method, with its underlying principle that the answer lies within the individual.

There have been a number of specific Action Learning evaluations that have taken place over the last three decades. Early studies that are widely quoted include the Hospital Internal Communications Project (HIC)[15], the Inter-Universities Project[8] and the GEC Project[16]. Some recent studies include Weinstein[10], Lewis[11] and Johns[12].

With the exception of the HIC project and Weinstein's evaluation, most of these studies have been conducted and written up by people who played a major role in them, and there is thus a somewhat uncritical flavour to some of the literature. In extreme cases this borders on the evangelical. This is not to say that it is not of value, because much of it is penetrating and absorbing, but it is still possible for outsiders to question the objectivity of these accounts.

Weiland and Leigh's study[15] is therefore unusual in that after a rigorous and exhaustive data collection exercise they concluded that the project had had very little effect on the hospitals involved. Changes were observed amongst scattered individuals, but not in the more important organizational variables. No changes in patient care could be detected with the measures used, nor was there any general increase in morale as indicated by absenteeism and turnover figures – in fact absenteeism increased slightly over the periods of the project. Curiously enough, they revised their views several years later, commenting more favourably on the impact of the programme, particularly with regard to reduction in the average length of patient stay in comparison with other hospitals in the area. This was explained on the grounds that it had taken a number of years for the impact of the Action Learning programme to work through to the basic performance criteria by which the effectiveness of the hospitals were then measured.

Weinstein's study of Action Learning programmes[10] included in-company, mixed company, and those linked to study for further degrees in both public and private sector organizations. She concentrated on individual learning and describes both anticipated and unanticipated outcomes. Her findings mirror those of Johns who found that the most significant outcomes were better teamworking, more open relationships, greater individual confidence and self-awareness, and greater awareness of the importance of 'process' when attempting to achieve tasks.[12]

ACTION LEARNING AND THE LEARNING ORGANIZATION

Despite the positive results at an individual level, Weinstein's participants doubted that their newly acquired learning skills would be sufficient in themselves to transform their organizations into learning organizations. They doubted that they would be able to affect their wider work environments so that these skills would become recognized and valued.[10] Lewis comments that whilst it was the training budget that was the driver for such activity it raised the question of how the transformation to learning organizations could ever be possible.[11] What he did find though, was that where all five ingredients specified by Garvin[17] were present: 'Noticeable and measurable improvements in individuals, sections, districts and divisions of the field staff occurred'. Although these commentators agree that Action Learning programmes might make small contributions to the development of broader learning cultures, Lewis sums up neatly the missing link when he acknowledges that the Action Learning activities in the company were not part of any grand strategy: the missing link between Action Learning and the creation of a learning organization was integration at the strategic level.[11]

At the wider level of management education as a whole, one is tempted to speculate about what the state of management education in the UK would be like if there had been neither Revans nor Action Learning. McLaughlin and Thorpe claim that Action Learning represents a new paradigm.[18] Unfortunately its direct impact on Higher Education has been limited. Only a handful of universities have established programmes with specific Action Learning labels, even though ideas such as group work and project methods has been incorporated extensively, especially in the case of post-experience courses. Even in companies there are many more examples of the label 'Action Learning' being applied to educational interventions, yet in most cases these programmes have been regarded as rather experimental, and they have rarely become institutionalized into the mainstream of corporate practice. One notable exception is the Prudential Assurance Company where Action Learning became the major vehicle for management development within one of its divisions, with over 300 sets involving over 2000 staff being run over a period of eight years.[11]

So the prime impact of Action Learning has, so far, been indirect. And it has operated through incorporating ideas piecemeal into the mainstream of management education and development – both in companies and educational establishments. On occasion this has no doubt led to mis-application of the central principles, but it would be churlish to reject a certain amount of eclecticism and experimentation as being 'non-genuine'. Indeed if the method and philosophy is to progress it is necessary that it will depart from some of the principles that have been laid down by Revans and early pioneers.

Finally, however, one might judge the impact of Action Learning by observing how some of its basic terms have found their way into the everyday language of trainers and developers – to the extent that Action Learning is no longer seen as anything odd or unusual.

REFERENCES

1 Cronbach, L. J. (1963) 'Course improvement through evaluation', *Teachers' College Records*, **64**, 672–83.
2 Scriven, M. (1967) *'The Methodology of Evaluation'*, *AREA Monograph on Curriculum Evaluation No. 1*, Chicago: Rand McNally, pp. 38–89.
3 Easterby-Smith, M. (1994) *Evaluating Management Development, Training and Education*, Farnborough: Gower.
4 Guba, E. G. and Lincoln Y. S. (1989) *Fourth generation evaluation*, London: Sage.
5 Revans, R. W. (1979) 'The nature of action learning', *Management Education and Development*, **10**(1), 3–23.
6 Precious, B. (1982) 'Flush doors to the 80's: A case study of action learning', *Management Education and Development*, **13**(2), 89–97.
7 McAdam, J. (1995) 'Joint action learning: a collaborative paradigm for the management of change in unionised organisations', *Journal of Managerial Psychology*, **10**(6), 31–40.
8 Revans, R. W. (1971) *Developing Effective Managers*, New York: Praeger.
9 Revans, R. W. (1971) op. cit. pp. 117–18.
10 Weinstein, K. (1994) 'Experiences of action learning: a dialogue with participants', *Management Bibliographies and Reviews*, **20**(6/7).
11 Lewis, A. (1994) 'Action learning in Prudential Assurance', *Management Bibliographies and Reviews*, **20**(6/7).
12 Johns, A. H. (1996) 'Evaluating the outcomes of action learning: an evaluation study of the University of Plymouth's action learning programme for the senior management group'. Unpublished project for MA in Management Learning, Lancaster University, May.
13 Parlett, M. and Hamilton D. (1972) 'Evaluation as illumination: A new approach to the study of innovatory programmes', *Occasional Paper 9*, Centre for Research in Educational Sciences, University of Edinburgh, Edinburgh.
14 Enderby, J. E. and Phelan D. R. (1994) 'Action learning as the foundation for cultural change', *The Quality Magazine*, February.
15 Weiland, G. F. and Leigh H. (eds) (1971) *Changing Hospitals*, London: Tavistock.
16 Casey, D and Pearce, D. (1977) *More than Management Development*, Aldershot: Gower.
17 Garvin, D. A. (1993) 'Building a learning organisation', *Harvard Business Review*, July–August.
18 McLaughlin, H. and Thorpe R. (1993) 'Action learning: a paradigm in emergence', *British Journal of Management*, **4**(1).

Appendix 1 Getting Started: An Action Manual

David Pearce

IS ACTION LEARNING WHAT YOU NEED?

This manual is intended:

1. to help you recognize some situations where Action Learning would be appropriate
2. to help you set about getting it started
3. to give you some ideas about how to manage it once it is started.

Action Learning is a well-tried way of accelerating people's learning so that they can handle difficult situations more effectively. It does this by creating a situation where relevant people get together to solve the problems of today in such a way that everyone learns explicitly and powerfully from the experience – building capabilities while making considerable progress on the problems being treated.

So, how is it different from everyday life in most organizations? Surprisingly it isn't very different. Yet people who have experienced Action Learning will tell you it is. It is mainly to do with the facts that:

1. problem areas and potential opportunities are highlighted
2. conditions are created where people really want to see results
3. a new mixture of people are brought together to work on the problems and opportunities
4. at least one adviser usually works with the group to help it function best in its job of doing relevant work to achieve the necessary output, while accelerating each person's learning of how to be more effective
5. it is allowable to admit ignorance
6. people learn that problems are solved by asking the right questions rather than trying to impose favoured solutions
7. the Action Learning situation is more demanding and testing than many day-

to-day situations, but it is also more supportive in a tough but realistic way.

You will recognize elements of day-to-day management, strategy management, project teams, group dynamics, problem solving and decision taking, and so on. They are all part of it.

Action Learning's uniqueness lies in the fact that it does not prescribe any one solution as best, or any one way as the correct way. It creates the conditions where people can learn the best way to achieve results within the constraints which are imposed. In doing so each person discovers and tests out his strengths and develops new ones.

Action Learning creates favourable conditions to enable people to 'learn best with and from each other by tackling real problems'.

Action Learning is unnecessary if solutions have already been found and tested. It is also of no help if some powerful individual or group is presenting a solution and has the weight to implement it.

Action Learning is of use if:

1. no one knows the solution to the problem
2. no one knows the way out of the complex situation (of course there will be different opinions about the best way)
3. there aren't enough people who can pose the right questions in situations of uncertainty
4. there aren't enough people who will take the risk in difficult situations, and will produce good results

One thing is certain, you won't get a feel for Action Learning or understand it until you try it – just like golf.

Forget Action Learning when:

1. answers are already known
2. the learning is programmable
3. it can be done more cheaply by other means
4. the conditions are stable and are likely to remain so
5. systematic analysis can give the solution
6. the top man, or a group of top people, is determined to go their own way regardless of the outcomes.

Deciding whether Action Learning is applicable

Ask yourself the two questions in Figure A1.1 simultaneously, and follow the arrow directions from there.

356

HOW TO BEGIN

Starting Action Learning is similar to starting training activities, but there are some significant differences:

1. the programme participants will need real problems/opportunities to work on
2. important people will need to be prepared intellectually and emotionally to accept that the programme will bring about changes to the ways things are done
3. people who do not consider themselves as participants on the programme will be involved, i.e.
    (a) the person(s) who own(s) the problem/opportunity
    (b) individuals and groups who are significant in the problem/opportunity
    (c) departments which have a bearing on the problem/opportunity
4. line management will need to be involved in deciding the forms of the programme because it involves them and their business. It cannot be left to functional experts.

TYPES OF ACTION LEARNING PROGRAMMES

Because Action Learning is concerned at one and the same time with people and problems/opportunities, programmes can be aimed at differing levels of complexity.

Least complex

People		Problems/opportunities
Individual	M	Own Job
Pair	O	Highlighted project at same
	R	level
Small team	E	Highlighted project at higher level
Large team/department		Team project in one department
More than one department	C	Team project in more than
	O	one department
The whole organization	M	Project involving the whole
	P	organization
More than one organization	L	Project involving the whole organization
	E	plus its suppliers, its customers, the full-
	X	time trade unions, the government, etc.

Most complex

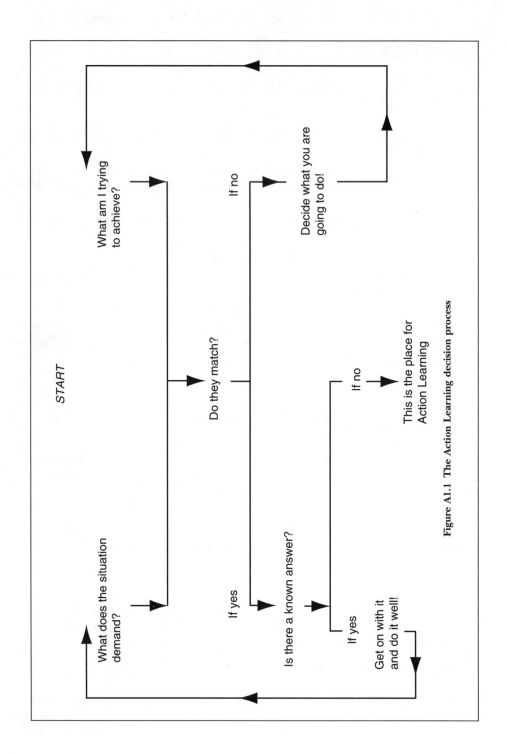

Figure A1.1 The Action Learning decision process

Most Action Learning management development programmes start with the people. A simple matrix can show the types of situations that can be created for the learners (see Figure A1.2).

Type I *Own job* tends to be useful for developing an individual's current competence and future capabilities. It also clarifies his role and problems related to the job.

Type II *Highlighted projects* These can be valuable for increasing a person's vision and abilities in a bigger organizational context, and can achieve progress on a problem/opportunity.

Type III *Same job* done elsewhere. This tends to be the least effective in developing managerial problem solving because of its overconcentration on technical puzzle solving.

Type IV *Project in a stranger organization* tends to be highly effective for significant personal development and helping the client organization to learn to value different experiences and views.

	TASK—known		TASK—unknown	
S I T U A T I O N Known	Own job	I	Highlighted projects	II
Unknown	Same job in another part of the organization or in a different organization	III	Project in another part of organization, or in a different organization	IV

Figure A1.2 The learning matrix

All sorts of possibilities for personal and organizational development can be produced using the options in the matrix. Combinations of types I to IV can be incorporated into one programme. On the other hand, if you are a senior manager looking for quick significant results on an important problem/opportunity, you may wish to consider team based management development activities.

DECIDING THE TYPE OF ACTION LEARNING PROGRAMME

See Figure A1.3. Start by asking the question, What is the problem/opportunity? and follow the appropriate arrows to guide you through the appropriate action path.

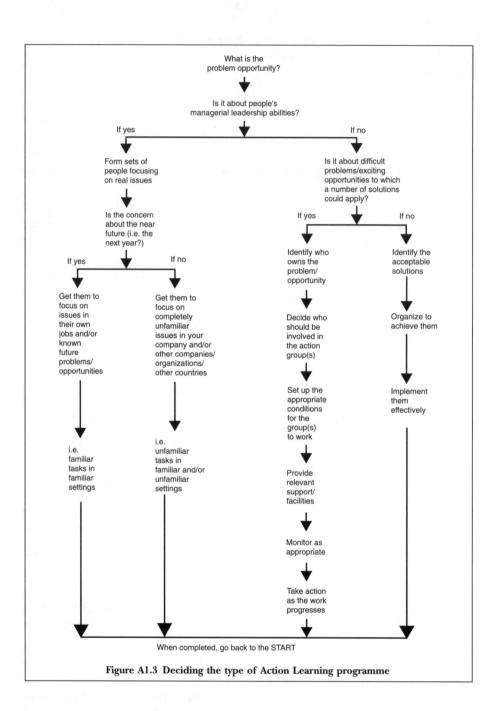

What is the
problem opportunity?

Is it about people's
managerial leadership abilities?

If yes

If no

Form sets of
people focusing
on real issues

Is it about difficult
problems/exciting
opportunities to which
a number of solutions
could apply?

Is the concern
about the near
future (i.e. the
next year?)

If yes

If no

If yes

If no

Get them to
focus on
issues in
their own
jobs and/or
known
future
problems/
opportunities

Get them to
focus on
completely
unfamiliar
issues in your
company and/or
other companies/
organizations/
other countries

Identify who
owns the
problem/
opportunity

Identify the
acceptable
solutions

Decide who
should be
involved in
the action
group(s)

Organize to
achieve them

i.e.
familiar
tasks in
familiar
settings

i.e.
unfamiliar
tasks in
familiar and/or
unfamiliar
settings

Set up the
appropriate
conditions
for the
group(s)
to work

Implement
them
effectively

Provide
relevant
support/
facilities

Monitor as
appropriate

Take action
as the work
progresses

When completed, go back to the START

Figure A1.3 Deciding the type of Action Learning programme

STEPS IN SETTING UP AN ACTION LEARNING PROGRAMME

Decide you really want to do it

↓

Start explaining why and what you are doing

↓

Gain some support and commitment

↓

Agree the people and problems/opportunities that it is aimed at

↓

Produce a basic outline of the programme, i.e. objectives, estimated (or fixed) timings, costs, resources, activities, etc.

↓

Try to produce a cost/benefit analysis (in operational terms and as far as possible in financial terms)

↓

In some cases produce a prospectus explaining the programme

↓

Agree a budget (try to get an allowance which the participants can manage)

↓

Recruit resources internally and/or externally, i.e. set advisers, etc.

↓

Get participants and problems

↓

It is particularly important that you spend lots of time and energy briefing *everyone* you possibly can, but particularly: participants, the problem/opportunity owners, participants' bosses, your personnel/training colleagues, and your boss(es)

↓

Bring the appropriate people together for a start-up activity. Involve participants' advisers and try to involve problem/opportunity owners, and participants' bosses.

↓

GO!

THE SET

In most Action Learning programmes participants work in small groups of 4–6 participants plus one or two advisers. This group has become known as the set. (See Figure A1.4)

Each participant brings to the set:

1. a problem/opportunity
2. which is owned by a client
3. the problem/opportunity is in an organizational context
4. the participant brings himself (i.e. his own particular experiences and mental frameworks, etc.)

The adviser has the general role of helping the set to work on the projects and on the learning.

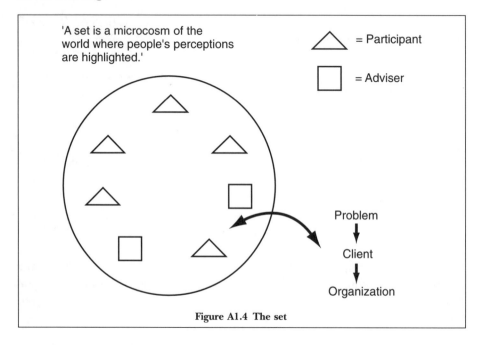

'A set is a microcosm of the world where people's perceptions are highlighted.'

△ = Participant

□ = Adviser

Problem
↓
Client
↓
Organization

Figure A1.4 The set

Sets tend to meet regularly. The frequency and duration varies with the circumstances. A typical way is for the set to meet for a whole day once a week, a fortnight, or sometimes once a month. All sorts of other variations are possible.

> a project set is a temporary system with a strong problem orientation, and it results in cohesion, shared involvement, and a sense of purpose, which are similar phenomena in a task force. . . . Adherents say an action learning set is not a task force because a task force seldom has a learning objective.[1]

WHAT HAPPENS IN A SET

There is no one way for a set to operate. It depends upon the mix of the particular adviser(s) and the delegates.

In practice the early stages are often dictated by the set adviser's preferences. This can vary from high structure (chairmanship) to virtual abdication (laissez-faire). If you are an adviser, you need to decide what you are likely to do best while taking account of the needs and expectations of the set members.

If the set is to become mature it will need to work through a process which is common to all new groups.

Forming	Dependence
↓	↓
Storming	Counterdependence
↓	↓
Norming	Independence
↓	↓
Performing	Interdependence
↓	↓

Typically, each participant in turn presents the problem/opportunities he is grappling with while the other set members and adviser(s) listen, pose questions and offer advice and suggestions. This process tends to cause the presenter to rethink his position and approach. This leads to further thoughts and ideas to be tested in action during the intervening periods between set meetings. The results are then presented and discussed at a later set meeting.

The presentation in the set of organization problems/opportunities leads the discussion and action into the full range of managerial activities, e.g. strategy and tactics, finance, negotiations, getting things done through others, marketing, internal and external politics, organization, managing change, etc.

The set's reason for existence is to improve work performance. Once that is established, it releases the legitimacy to talk about anything and everything else from metaphysics to high technology. But it is always anchored in the reality of action; because each client is expecting results from his participant.

Each set and each individual takes a different path depending on previous experience and current pressures. This is one of the most difficult things for people who have not tried it to come to terms with – particularly trainers who have been steeped in systematic training principles, and personnel people who are accustomed to the tight control of industrial relations.

There is a tendency to believe that there is a common core that can be given to everyone and is right for everyone. At the level of skill and knowledge for doing certain tasks it is true. At the level of managerial action in conditions of uncertainty, it is patently not true. Each person must find his own way of being successful in difficult situations.

At various stages, relevant people can be invited to join the set. These can be clients; people who have a potentially useful expertise; people who have expressed an interest, etc. But the set tends to become very protective of its territory creating a series of strong norms in the early bonding stage of its life. The set adviser can help to prevent the set becoming too inward looking. It is useful to get sets to visit each other's place of work. Most sets like to draw a lot of flip charts. But a number of set advisers have commented on the reluctance of typical members to produce effective written material. Also getting sets to read things, even newspapers, is often quite a challenge.

Like all human activities which are dealing with difficult problems, the pace varies a great deal from frenetic excitement to abject dejection – but rarely boredom.

OUTLINE OF A TYPICAL OWN JOB (TYPE 1) PROGRAMME

SETTING UP THE PROGRAMME

Time likely to be taken 2–6 months

1. Getting delegates (usually quite time-consuming).
2. Course organizer/set adviser interviewing each delegate and his sponsor (usually his boss), plus any other interested parties, such as personnel specialists, training managers or management development advisers.
3. Agreeing the project the delegate will treat on the programme, i.e.
   (a) current job
   (b) selected parts of job, that is, an area which requires special attention because it is a problem or because it has never been properly tackled for whatever reason
   (c) a special part-time project devised by more senior management. With this option it is vital to ensure that the project is real and sufficiently important.
4. It is useful if each delegate is asked to do a simple write-up to create a benchmark of where he is. It can help later to judge progress.

DURING MEETING

1st Meeting
Preferably dinner on the first evening and a short session afterwards. It is useful if sponsors can attend this session. Next day the set works a full day with the set adviser(s).

At this first meeting the business is:

a. The set adviser describes Action Learning, the aims of the programme, the format of the programme, the role of the set adviser, the facilities available, i.e. budgets, and so on.

b. Each delegate describes his job/project as he sees it, what he is trying to achieve, and how he hopes to achieve it.

Professor Revans's questions are useful at this stage: What am I trying to do? What is preventing me from doing it? What action am I going to take?

2nd to 5th Meeting
1 day every fortnight (i.e. months 1 to 3):

1. Working on projects
2. Working on delegates' needs/skills; supporting and criticizing
3. Visiting one another's companies – as a set and individually
4. Dealing with whatever arises

6th or 7th Meeting
(i.e. months 3 or 4)

1. Invite clients and/or sponsors to the set for lunch and an afternoon meeting:
   (a) to explain what has happened
   (b) to answer their queries
   (c) to show progress
   (d) to learn from one another

7th/8th/9th Meeting
(i.e. months $3^{1}/_{2}$ to 5)

1. Continue working on projects, particularly on action
2. Continue working on members' needs of skill/knowledge development, support and critiques
3. Visits as appropriate

10th Meeting
(5th month)

1. Review activity $<$ programme successes and low-spots
                     personal progress

2. Decide how to handle unfinished business, that is, how to continue with activities which still need handling, by working pairs, and so on.

PEOPLE AND PROJECTS

PARTICIPANTS

Participants on Action Learning programmes have been very diverse. What they have had in common is that they have wanted to improve the situation they found themselves in. Are there some guidelines to follow? Perhaps the following points may be of some help:

People who have jobs with one or more of the following:

a large amount of discretion
a lot of ambiguity
a great deal of problem solving
a co-ordinating role
a need to innovate
a complex reorganization to handle
technological change; including computers
introducing new systems
complex politics within the company and/or in relation to suppliers, customers, trade unions, government agencies, the community.

When is an appropriate time?

at the very start of a completely new job
in preparation for a promotion
in the early stages of a first managerial appointment
when complex change (as outlined above) needs to be handled
at the crucial point in a high-flier's career
when a good man has lost some impetus
when there is uncertainty about the way a good performer's career should develop
when it is vital for two or more significant people to have to work together
during reorganizations
during and after takeovers
during business crises

It is an advantage if each of the prospective participants wants to develop significantly as a risk-taking achiever.

PROJECTS

Throughout these notes the term 'project' implies a real management task/ problem/issue on which action must be taken. Any academic interpretation of 'project' must be avoided.

The first thing about an Action Learning project is that it must be a piece of demanding work. Also, at least one significant person must want results from the work. In order not to waste time tackling purely technical or relatively simple aspects of work, it has been found useful to keep in mind the difference between puzzles and problems.

PROBLEM

Where there are a number of possible solutions on which reasonable men can disagree.

PUZZLE

Where there is a right answer provided the right resources are applied to find them.

The following areas may present Action Learning problems/opportunities:

  a complex managerial job
  introducing change
  a problem which concerns more than one department
  a new business opportunity
  motivation and productivity
  problems of relationships with suppliers, customers, trade
  unions, government, the community
  handling a foreign culture
  reorganization
  introducing a new technology
  expansion or contraction

For an individual, action projects can be:

  coming to grips with a new job
  delegating current responsibilities while preparing for a new one

367

pairing with a manager in another department and both helping each
other   to improve the situation

doing an action project in addition to one's own job either in your own part
of the business

or in a different part of the business

or at a higher level

or in a different company

doing a full time action project (like those above)

CLIENTS

A client is someone who owns the problem and wants the participant to work
on it.

Gaining a client's support is essential in effecting change. Programme organizers need to be very sensitive in their handling of clients during the setting-up
stages, otherwise they may store up problems for the participants.

Clients should also be built formally into the programme wherever possible,
i.e. at the first meeting of the programme, at the mid point and at the end.

During the programme a participant may decide that his original client is not
the right person, and may negotiate a change.

In own-job projects the client is sometimes difficult to decide. At one and the
same time, it can be the participant, his boss, all sorts of other people who are
involved in part of his job.

SPONSOR

The person who puts forward a participant for the programme, and who feels
responsible for his progress.

THE SET ADVISER

At its simplest, the set adviser's role is to help the set and its members to work
on the problems and on their own learning. His secondary objective should also
be either to make himself redundant as quickly as possible, or to become a full,
equal member of the set with his own declared project.

The set adviser's first job may be to brief the participants, their bosses and
their clients as a preparatory stage before the programme starts. This is a
crucial phase that needs to be done well. However, it does not necessarily have
to be done by the set adviser.

The set adviser needs to start working with the set from its very first meeting.

This is the time that the bonding of the set takes place, and the important norms are established.

Each set adviser will need to decide his own preferred way of operating. Each set adviser does things differently as a result of personal preference and previous experience. It has often been found useful to gain practice in the role *either*:

> by being a set participant before trying the set adviser's role,
> *or*
> work with an experienced set adviser, *or*
> take your courage in both hands and try it.

It is useful to remember the things you are *not* there to do:

> provide solutions
> be an expert on everything – omniscient
> control everything – omnipotent
> be a teacher/chairman/leader/tutor

but you can do all of the above at certain times – just like every other set member can.

You are there to:

> help the set work effectively
> help the set to work on the projects
> help create the conditions where participants can learn to be more effective
> *either* become redundant as quickly as possible
> *or* become a completely equal interdependent member of the set.

I try to do the following when I act as a set adviser:

1. Act as I really am, bringing into the set all my limited but rich experience.
2. Try to respond honestly and openly at all times – very difficult!
3. Work with the set on the problems/opportunities and to find ways to meet skills and knowledge needs.
4. Work on the group processes.
5. Try to get each set member to understand and face up to himself – all that he is in his many roles, of which being a worker/manager/superior/shop steward is only part.
6. Work on Action Learning processes, that is, posing questions, gaining an overall view of the problem, stages in a project, gaining support, risk, and so on.
7. Introduce ideas.
8. Try to get people to see the connections between ideas, people, events,

problems, the environment, etc. Try to get something appropriate done about the realizations and perceptions.

9. Work with individual set members, if it seems natural and appropriate to their needs and the situation.

10. Work on organizing specific formal or informal learning experiences to meet needs.

By its very composition, the set will create the conditions where each individual will be pushed fairly forcibly towards a search for a greater understanding of himself – but it is possible to resist if one wishes. After all, each participant (and the set adviser) is trying to be effective in a series of difficult tasks. Each set member is in the same boat and is probably trying desperately to help each of the others. The fear of failure creates sufficient conditions for each person to try their hardest.

PERSONNEL AND TRAINING SPECIALISTS

The steering of an Action Learning programme is a complex online activity in its own right. The personnel and training function often acts as the initiator, but not always. Line management itself can, and does, run Action Learning.

The personnel/trainer who decides to introduce Action Learning is leaving the safety of courses where there is total control in a classroom environment. One becomes involved in the real dynamics and politics of running the enterprise. There are risks, but the rewards can be high. Skilful use of appropriate Action Learning activities can lead to improved performance at all levels, and to a shift in the way the organization operates. Your task is to help management, at all levels, see the possibilities which can ensue from involving their people in the real problems and opportunities of the organization. This may not be easy for some managers to accept. They may need support in learning to do things differently. The Action Learning approach of high support and high critique is helpful.

THE ACTION LEARNING WEB

The instigators of Action Learning programmes are inevitably caught up in a web of activities which involve a large part of the organization. Once an Action Learning programme is started all sorts of people are involved, and the interaction between different functions and systems are highlighted and affected.

It is vital to be aware of Action Learning's interactions in the web of organizational interests (see Figure A1.5). Managing the situation is a mini general management role.

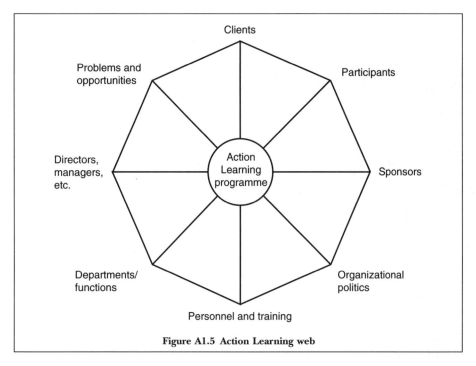

Figure A1.5 Action Learning web

Appendix 2 A Review of the Literature

Alan Mumford

This literature review is a selective commentary rather than a full and comprehensive list of all the material published on Action Learning. The literature really starts with Reg Revans, and with his book *Developing Effective Managers*[1]. When I first reviewed the literature[2] it was not difficult to identify all the articles that had been published, and in 1985 no-one else had produced a book dedicated to Action Learning. By 1994 my review[3] had to be more selective partly because of a substantial amount of repetition in the content of articles, partly because it seemed much more helpful to identify issues rather than simply to list articles. Not only were there more people practising Action Learning and writing about it, but more issues had emerged for discussion, and more experiences were available particularly now outside the UK. This chapter is a revision and updating of my two previous reviews.

WHAT IS ACTION LEARNING?

We start with Reg Revans, acknowledged, except sometimes in the United States, as the founder of Action Learning. In the UK Action Learning first came to prominence paradoxically because of work done by Revans in Belgium, reported in *Developing Effective Managers*[1]. Although as he has reported frequently in other books a number of earlier activities particularly in the National Coal Board and the National Health Service contributed to the structure and development of his ideas, it was the Belgian experience and his report on it which generated publicity, interest, growth and activity by others who followed Revans' philosophy. The word philosophy is carefully chosen – it has been for others to develop experience of and provide detailed help on the structure and processes of Action Learning programmes. His ideas, although essentially practical in nature, are clothed often in conceptual and structural statements and though by no means devoid of practical illumination, his writings usually avoid any simplistic cook book illustration. This first book, however, does provide substantial description of the processes involved, and particularly he gives here more than in his other books a fuller analysis of the learning process itself. Though long out of print this is an important book to access for anyone who wants to test his or her understanding of learning against some very specific Revans initiated and run Action Learning programmes.

Otherwise there are problems about which of Revans' books to read. *Action Learning*[4] contains the fullest though as always with Revans by no means a complete statement of his views on Action Learning. An alternative is *The ABC of Action Learning*[5]. In addition there is a fascinating collection of his published and unpublished papers, *The Origins and Growth of Action Learning*[6]. This covers more than 40 years in the development of his ideas. At over 800 pages, it is like so many other aspects of Revans, grand in scale. It has a breadth of vision, perceptiveness and a special use of language which is somewhat reminiscent of the monumental biography of Churchill by Martin Gilbert. My comparison is deliberate; Revans dominates the field of Action Learning in the way that Churchill dominated the UK during World War II. However, while the book is required reading for anyone interested in the phenomenon which is Revans, and contains some of his thinking, for example, on learning organizations not available elsewhere, it is not a good introduction to Action Learning. Since so much has been written about experiences in the UK, the detailed chapter here on the Nile Project, full of specifics, insights, large-scale issues and small details is especially interesting. Similarly, there is detail on his work in hospitals and schools, as well as chapters of more general and conceptual interest.

One warning about anyone reading Revans, who has previously heard him speak. Much of his writing is rich and dense in texture, not always easily assimilated at first reading. In that sense it is quite different from his easy and direct speaking style, still to be experienced at the time of writing, though Revans is in his 90th year. In this regard, it is appropriate to mention something, although it is not a book or article, namely a video by Revans[7] which as a professional production has considerable advantages over other videos of filmed conversations with Revans.

Although there were collections of articles and books, until 1992 no single author perhaps had the temerity to offer a comprehensive book on Action Learning. Perhaps it was significant that in fact the first book involved two authors, who could bear the burden between them. McGill and Beaty have gone into a second edition, which suggests that the book has found a market.[8] They describe how Action Learning works, different types of sets and the differences between sets wholly sponsored by organizations contrasted with independently formed sets.

Most significantly they describe differences between sets focused on the organization and its needs, and those focused primarily on personal development. Their emphasis is on Action Learning as a vehicle for personal growth and relationships. Valuable though this can be (discussed further below), it is rather too exclusive as a prime cause of Action Learning. No doubt in consequence they give great emphasis to the discussion of the importance of group process. In their second edition they remedy a previous weakness by discussing the learning and development process; unfortunately the issues and ideas have not been integrated in the actual practice covered earlier in the book.

Inglis[9] was the next in the field, and amongst other worthwhile features gives more emphasis than some authors to the issue of implementation, and indeed adds I for Implementation to the familiar Revans equation of $L = P + Q$. The book is particularly strong in the use of practical cases and detailed statements about the design of programmes, workshops, the role of clients and set advisers. Uniquely he comments on fees, presentations and do's and don'ts for clients. Weinstein[10] concentrates on participants, not done in a lot of other articles or books on Action Learning. She saw 69 participants from 16 different programmes and follows in consequence a line which Revans might well find sympathetic. Revans talked about 'The inveterate hankering of the tutor to be the centre of attention'. Weinstein's book provides us with the views of those who matter more – the people in Action Learning sets. Two other aspects of the book make it particularly valuable. She emphasizes the use of the learning cycle and learning styles and the value of support provided by logs and report back processes as prime reasons for completed learning. Since most of the material about Action Learning so far has been written by those convinced of its value, as indeed Weinstein is, she is particularly significant in providing a section explaining why Action Learning has not been accepted as widely as its fans would hope. This is a very important contribution for anyone moving into this area or suggesting that another organization takes on Action Learning.

Pedler[11] says that his book is designed to provide a practical introduction to Action Learning that is friendly, lively and encouraging and it meets this objective. It is particularly good in relating to meeting the needs of managers rather than management development specialists. In some respects it is comparable to Revans' ABC, and to the chapter by Jean Lawrence referred to below.[12] The chapter setting out the kind of context in which Action Learning would work and not work is helpfully different from anything else I have seen in print. There is a good chapter on the range of things that people have learned, and a very actionable checklist on 'my problem' as a way of understanding Action Learning. These are particularly worthwhile features in a book which otherwise helpfully sets out many of the basic features of Action Learning.

Of course much useful guidance is to be found in individual articles or chapters. Pedler offers his definition – and Revans' gloss on it in this volume, as does the introductory chapter in McGill and Beaty[8]. Two other particularly noteworthy descriptions are given by two of the UK's longest standing practitioners, Jean Lawrence and John Morris. Jean Lawrence's piece[12] is particularly appropriate because it is written as a dialogue between questions from people wanting to know about Action Learning and answers offered from her own experience. Since the whole basis of Action Learning is the issue of Q – the Questioning approach – Lawrence's chapter is fundamental at several levels of understanding. The chapter by John Morris[13] is particularly helpful in reviewing three pitfalls. He describes these as the tendency of action and task to become over-dominant, the potential to retreat into discussion groups, and the possibility of generating projects which are essentially internal consultancy rather than directly managerial in form.

The original Revans equation $L = P+Q$ is constantly repeated in articles about Action Learning. Sutton[14] thought this too restrictive. Only Mumford[15] has offered a restatement. He argues that it should read $Q + P + Q^2 = L$. In his view Action Learning must start with questions which then generate appropriate P, i.e. inputs and programmed knowledge relevant to resolving problems, which in turn leads to further more extensive or deeper questions. This revision has not yet been widely accepted.

Wallace[16] has provided the most substantial review of the Action Learning approach. While he does not himself fully answer his own questions about the coherence of its principles, the absence of evaluation, or evidence from elsewhere about how professionals learn to improve their job performance, his article is essential reading. Two especially important issues raised by him are whether a defined project, as distinct from an ongoing problem is a necessary feature of Action Learning. He is especially concerned with the unreality of projects in unfamiliar settings – a point on which he differs from some other authors, not least Revans with the original Belgian experience.

That original experience is a particular demonstration of a continuing area of debate. This concerns the associated issues of the location for the Action Learning project or problem, and the likelihood of implementation. Boddy[17] set out first the now familiar figure describing possible locations:

		TASK	
		Familiar	*Unfamiliar*
SETTING	*Familiar*		
	Unfamiliar		

The Belgian projects were all unfamiliar tasks in unfamiliar environments, and this has been an acceptable and in some cases desired form of Action Learning since. There is a paradox here because of course Revans' original work in for example the Coal Board and the Health Service was of familiar projects in familiar settings. Implementation becomes an issue where individuals are essentially carrying out consultancy assignments. Where learners recommend actions to others rather than being responsible for eventual implementation themselves, Mumford argues that the Action Learning experience is fundamentally different.[18]

THE LEARNING PROCESSES INVOLVED

Since managers are always likely to be seduced by the demands and rewards associated with completing a task, as compared with working on process or learning, we perhaps should not be surprised that a similar disjunction often happens in material about Action Learning. Specifically, the balance between Action and Learning seems to have tilted towards the former because of the excitement generated in both educators and managers by the idea that a learning programme can involve effective action.

TYPES OF PROGRAMMES

Sutton in the previous (second) edition of this book provides a brisk survey of different kinds of programme.[19] They range from examples clearly related to Revans' original idea of an individual working on a project, to programmes built with some combination of P and Q and directed at an academic qualification. As well as the examples presented within this volume, others may be found in Peters[20], Mumford[21] and Lawlor[22].

Preston and Biddell[23] illustrate a rather different kind of programme, through which issues about individual management of careers were raised in an initial workshop and then carried through by an Action Learning set process.

Q OR P + Q?

Revans provides the fascinating paradox of a man who has either invented or discovered Q, yet has to describe it through a constant outpouring of P through his articles and books, as illustrated in earlier references.

The issues of P and Q are well ventilated in this present volume. Other contributions include Morris[24] who surveys the general significance of the balance between P and Q. Smith[25] thought that what he called 'purist' Action

Learning disregarded P and argued that Q could not stand on its own. Sutton[14] thought some of Smith's statements extreme and invalid. There seem in fact to be very few examples of what Smith called 'pure' Action Learning, except Casey's work with Chief Executives[26]. Q without P may exist in the practice of trainers and consultants but if so they have not written about it. Sutton[27] argued that P was necessary at least to have an Action Learning set understand what was happening within the set.

Otherwise P seems an inevitable and necessary feature of Action Learning programmes associated with an academic qualification though there are substantial differences in how and when it is delivered. For example Harrison *et al.*[28] shows that P delivered at a time neither valid nor relevant in terms of the real concerns of participants on the programme is ineffective. The mistakes honestly revealed in her article are the more ironic in that this kind of error could have been avoided by reading the literature, i.e. P! Whether by circumstance or design, the literature on American experience is almost entirely on non-qualification programmes with little emphasis on P.

SETTING UP ACTION LEARNING PROGRAMMES

The appendix by Pearce in this volume remains essential reading. It is the neatest and most comprehensive summary although other chapters in this current volume and the books by McGill and Beaty[8] and Inglis[9] have useful additional information. Pedler's short book[11] already referred to, provides a questionnaire to test readiness for an Action Learning programme which would not only meet that need, but also help to draw out indications about what needs to be built into such a programme for a particular organization.

PROJECTS AND PROBLEMS

The literature remains massively dedicated to the concept of using defined projects with a beginning and an end. Wallace[16] has challenged this as an invariable requirement. Mumford[15] also says that he has changed his mind, similarly moving away from an exclusive requirement for projects towards working on ongoing problems which may have no clearly defined beginning or terms of reference.

Prideaux[29] contains a very important review of individual project statements, what arose from them and how difficulties were overcome. The article also, by implication, raises the issue of the extent to which these projects were more geared to Action Research than to Action Learning, a phenomenon always likely to be encouraged within programmes directed as these were towards an academic qualification.

378

STARTING THE PROGRAMME

The question of P input is especially significant in relation to how a programme is started. Guidance on this is available in this volume and in McGill and Beaty[8], Inglis[9]. The latter provides detailed design for a Start Up Workshop.

There are two associated but separate issues. There is a natural and proper assumption that you have to say something about the nature of Action Learning, as mentioned briefly above. McGill[8], Sutton[14] and Inglis[9] help with this. However, the complexities and difficulties involved have not been fully debated in print. On the one hand participants need to know as early as possible what Action Learning is and what they will be doing. On the other hand they cannot really understand it until they have experienced it.

A further issue is whether you provide processes which are designed to support Action Learning through a different, though action-oriented, method. So some programmes contain so-called 'team building' exercises early on, and others provide 'outdoor' experiences. This seems particularly to be the case in some of the American programmes[30], but the outdoor element especially has been criticized in[31]. The issues here seem partly to be about the relevance of creating special events to 'explain' Action Learning processes rather than using Action Learning experiences themselves. There are also more generalized issues about the effectiveness of team building events or outdoor experiences as development in their own right – or wrong. The use of simulations as an introduction to Action Learning would perhaps be more easily accepted if the authors involved described the bridges they thought the simulations were building in learning as well as metaphorical terms.

One argument for simulations is that the relative unreality of the task enables participants to focus on what they are learning. Since in Action Learning the task is genuine, there is a greater likelihood that action will overwhelm the learning process.

LEARNING ABOUT LEARNING

It is altogether too clear from the books and articles reviewed here that very few authors have thought it necessary to discuss the learning process as distinct from task achievement or group process. Some authors, McGill and Beaty[8] perhaps to an undue extent, have focused on process issues. Authors within this current and other volumes of Action Learning experiences certainly frequently talk about what individuals or groups have learned. However, the way in which they have learned seems in many cases not to have advanced far beyond accepting the admittedly crucial Revans point that people with similar problems drawn together will learn with and from each other. There are occasional refer-

379

ences to the Kolb Learning Cycle, which surely in some form or other ought to be a constant element in all Action Learning programmes. Action Learning provides a marvellous illustration of the potential completeness of the cycle – much more so than many other forms of management development. Mumford's case for this is developed in Chapter 19 of this book. He argues that as much explicit attention needs to be paid to the learning process and to individual preferences about how people learn, as to the construction of relevant and effective projects. (See also Reference 32.)

Coates[33] showed how he builds the learning cycle and learning styles into one of his programmes. Two other significant contributions are made by Marsick et al.[34] whose emphasis on the requirement for effective reflection explains the amended title which she and her colleagues use 'Action Reflection Learning'. Her experience, and that of her colleagues is in Sweden and the USA; Prideaux from Australia offers fascinating ideas about creating a learning community to give real meaning to a learning set.[35] In addition he offers helpful ideas about the use of learning diaries, and possibly uniquely in Action Learning literature, the use of learning contracts. This could well be selected as one of ten 'must read' articles.

Although Chris Argyris has not, I believe, written about Action Learning, a great deal of his work could be strongly associated with it. Since Action Learning projects often challenge the present, and sometimes seek to redefine the future, his ideas about espoused theory versus theory in use, 'single loop' compared with 'double loop' learning, and defensive 'routines' could help people understand better the kind of learning which potentially could be achieved. An article which conveniently collects all three of these, recommended for those who may not see any of his main books as high priority reading for Action Learning, is Reference 36.

An article by Lee[37], though starting from experience with Action Learning in central Europe, raises fundamental issues about who is making what choices to learn what within Action Learning programmes.

PARTICIPANT LEARNERS AND ADVISERS

Since Action Learning has as one of its crucial elements 'fellows in adversity' as Revans called them (or 'fellows in opportunity' as Mumford suggests[15]), the ways in which they help one another to resolve problems and especially to learn from one another in resolving problems is an important issue. Unfortunately the literature on this is amazingly thin. The focus in most books and articles is on projects, processes, programmes in the procedures and policies necessary to implement Action Learning. All P! Very little has been written on what the other

P – the participants – actually should do especially in their sets. McGill and Beaty do provide a chapter in their book[8]. Unfortunately this does not include anything on the learning process as such or on the individual styles and skills of learning used by different individuals.

Mumford's article[32] highlights the importance of being able to put and respond to good questions and more unusually illustrates how to facilitate learning to learn.

Lewis[38] gives some views on how individuals responded to the Action Learning process. Weinstein's book[10], concentrating on individual's views, sets out not only what individuals thought they learned, but to some extent how they learned it.

Another view of the different characteristics of set members is given by Bunning[38] who makes some interesting comments about the creativity involved in sets and set members and the ability to grow by reducing defensive self-esteem. (See also Argyris[36] on this.) The power of the set as an enclosed learning vehicle can, like other management processes, produce negative consequences by its exclusion of other managers. The disturbance created by a group positively pursuing significant projects affects not only more senior executives in the organization but also those colleagues not participating on the programme. Reid[40] shows how other managers can be brought in for particular stages of set discussions, thereby reducing both feelings of exclusion and the likelihood of wider commitment to implementation.

Most writing has centred on the development of managers. A different aspect of exclusion is covered in articles by McAdam[41], and Meehan and Jarvis[42]. The former describes a collective collaborative process he calls 'joint Action Learning' involving competing interest groups in unionized organizations. Meehan and Jarvis describe the results of applying Action Learning at different levels in their organization including the shop floor workers. Froiland[43] gives some examples of the extension of Action Learning sets beyond the managerial population, and shows some of the advantages and some of the defensiveness that might be created in jobs below managerial level.

Of course most books and articles are written by people whose interest and to some extent profession is to write – the consultant initiators and implementors of Action Learning programmes. There is remarkably little output by participants describing for themselves their experiences. This is particularly interesting because one of the early books on Action Learning by Casey and Pearce[44] did have contributions from participants. While this book is no longer prescribed reading for Action Learning adherents in relation to the design and processes involved in the programme in GEC, it has more than historical interest precisely because it is unusual in offering detailed comments by some of the participants. Weinstein's book is primarily focused on the views of participants[10].

I can find only three articles by participants. The first by Caiae[45] not only described what it was like to be a set member, but also related those experiences to the learning cycle and the Honey and Mumford 'learning styles'. Mercer[46] provides a fascinating account of a relatively elderly small firm managing director working on his problems through a Masters Programme in Action Learning. Mead[47], like the other two describing qualification based though different programmes, reviewed the experiences of himself and colleagues in enabling one another to learn and specifically in drawing a colleague back from the brink of departing from the set. The process and results of set members helping each other learn is reviewed in a detailed article which is not only helpful in itself, but indicates what a rich field of research has yet to be tilled[47]. The authors studied the 'absorption and implementation of ideas resulting from interaction with other associates on one's own programme', which they described as cross-fertilization.

Another article by Mumford[49] also opens up a new field of study. He questioned both participants and their managers and mentors about the relationship between them. It seemed clear that neither participants nor those supposed to be helping them at work properly understood what was necessary to generate an effective helping relationship. The only reason for expressing surprise and disappointment on the absence of participant views, which after all is common to most articles and books on management development, is that Action Learning does, in its philosophy and supposed practice, depend so much on what participants provide for each other, rather than on what tutors provide.

The views of participants in one organization, MCB University Press, are presented in two articles[50,51].

SET ADVISERS

The paucity of information direct from participants contrasts in one sense extremely unfavourably with the volume of material on the role of set advisers. Cynics might claim this is a demonstration of Revans' dictum of 'The inveterate hankering of the tutor to be the centre of attention'. There is nothing wrong with the amount of information available in itself, it is just out of proportion, in relation to attention to participants.

In this volume I would personally choose the chapters by Casey, supplemented elsewhere by Bennett[52] and Kozubska[53]. Casey added to the advice in this volume the single most helpful piece of advice about when a facilitator should intervene. Intervention should be guided by remembering that the purpose is always for participants to learn 'so you often bite your lip'[25]. A good overall summary of many of these contributions is available in Donaghue[53] which would serve as an excellent starting point though not a sufficient finish for this subject. The McGill and Beaty book[8] emphasizes the help a set adviser can bring to a group process, while Inglis[9] ranges over a wider field, from administration to the learning process.

ACTION LEARNING AND MANAGEMENT EDUCATION

Academics have increasingly become first interested in, and then involved in, Action Learning. Thorpe[55] criticizes some traditional management education processes, especially the lack of reality. He supports the more holistic approach offered by Action Learning compared with discrete competences and argues that Action Learning's most important contribution is 'as a means by which managers learn how to learn at the highest level of learning skills'. (But see my earlier comments on the extent to which this is actually achieved.)

An important article by MacLaughlin and Thorpe[56] extends the idea in even more academic language, to claim that Action Learning represents a new paradigm. This latter article is perhaps more relevant to educators looking for philosophical contributions to dissertations than to practitioners, but is no doubt an encouraging discovery at a philosophical level.

Wilmott[57] is not convinced about the need to associate Action Learning with traditional teaching in, for example, organizational behaviour or problem solving. He argues, however, for an association with what he calls critical management theory, dealing with the contradictory forces playing on managerial work, and facilitating social as well as personal transformations.

Gregory[58] discusses the significant educational issue of how an individual's learning can be accredited within an Action Learning process. The clearest conclusion is that a final dissertation is assessed. They also say that students 'will be encouraged to keep a journal which can be used to measure progress against original objectives'. It is not clear whether this is assessed – unlike IMC's Evaluative Assessment of Managerial Learning[59]. The significant issue raised by Gregory, exactly what can be assessed, is not really fully addressed by him. In fact the issue of what is assessed, and how, is actually discussed more, perhaps to the surprise of some readers, in the collection of articles about the experience of International Management Centres[59,60]. Perhaps this issue is particularly difficult for management educators, a point further illustrated by Gosling and Ashton[61] who do not address the substantial issues proposed in the title of their article which describes neither the Action Learning elements in their programme nor the processes of academic assessment for these.

Raelin[62] contrasts professional education and Action Learning and actually says more about the issues of assessment, though it is not clear if he is speaking from experience.

In Australia a boost has been given to Action Learning sometimes through the university system, but even more through the Technical and Further Education System. The National Staff Development Committee for TAFE has published material on the theoretical background for Action Learning[63] which gives an extensive survey of many of the basic issues about Action Learning and a useful bibliography; they have also produced some videos of Action Learning sets in action. These are particularly significant for management educators, since the sets are discussing educational problems. Peattie[64] describes experiences in four members of the Teaching Company Scheme, which is a partnership between businesses and business schools in order to achieve organizational change. He describes the opportunities and limitations offered through this particular partnership.

Another experience in Australia is particularly relevant in this area. Kable writes about a programme he ran for senior administrators in two universities[65]. The article implies that the university setting made the acceptance of Action Learning more problematical.

ORGANIZATIONAL OR PERSONAL OBJECTIVES?

The attractiveness of Action Learning to many management development practitioners and management educators is that it is a good development process for individuals and for groups.[8] Organizations may have a different sense of priority, focusing more on the ability of this process to secure answers to significant problems, some of which they have not in fact recognized before they start the Action Learning process. Is Action Learning seen, and by whom, as the best way of learning to be a manager? Or is it the best way of contributing to business performance? Some authors exemplified in this book would emphasize that it is the best route to personal growth. Most proponents look for some combination of these, but the largest weight of evidence offered about utility seems to be in the area of organizational improvement.

Some writers are now bringing out the connection between the power of Action Learning and the development of organizational learning. Perhaps significantly, explicit material on this so far has been produced by Dixon[66], Watkins and Marsick[67] in the United States; Mumford[68] has tried to bring together his various experiences with senior managers including Action Learning and the impact of these on the creation of a learning organization. Zuber-Skerritt[69] deals with some of the more conceptual issues.

Cases in the collection by Peters[20] are organization centred. The experiences of an organization totally devoted to Action Learning as its preferred learning methodology is reviewed by three internal authors[50], and by an external appraiser[51]. In both cases the issues of implicit and sometimes explicit conflict between personal and organizational needs are reviewed. In contrast, Casey describes some of the issues of personal development among chief executives in his book[26]. Perhaps not surprisingly Braddick, also using experiences from Ashridge Management College, discusses the contribution of senior level Action Learning programmes to personal development[70]. Contributions which some might see as more extreme in the areas of personal analysis are offered by Cederholme who uses Gestalt and Buddhist concepts together with Ericsson and Jung as support for his work on his programmes[71]. Vince and Martin[72] discuss a number of issues about personal growth. They start with concerns about emotional resistance or avoidance of learning, the role of Action Learning in breaking dependence on a teacher and placing emphasis on responsibility for the learner. Finally they comment on the political, i.e. power issues which are likely to arise in Action Learning groups.

The issue of power returns us to the set adviser. However much the set adviser tries to reduce it, that role is one of power – even if only to declare that it is the group that has the power and not the set adviser! So the propositions made by McGill and Beaty about self-facilitated Action Learning sets[8] are note-worthy. On the face of it self-facilitated sets place the responsibility and therefore the power for growth on set members. Revans has occasionally been quoted as being against the employment of set advisers though it is not clear exactly when in the process he would do away with them. The difficulty of the proposition advanced by McGill and his colleagues, which certainly seemed geared to issues of personal development, is that they are writing purely from their own experience, and offered no evidence of others using their ideas and practices.

CULTURAL ISSUES

Unique as Action Learning is in its direct association of real work action and learning, and powerful in its consequent attraction to managers, is it appropriate in all circumstances?

If we look first at issues of organizational culture we note the wide variety of organizations in which it is claimed Action Learning is being successfully employed. Not just in manufacturing, commerce, finance or indeed even central or local government but also in health, management education and not-for-profit organizations. All these are tested in the literature review so far. What we do not have are any articles describing failure (with the honourable and partial exception of Harrison[28]). Even in that illustration it seems to have been the P element that failed rather than Q. So although we have statements about the nature of organizations which are likely to facilitate the effective introduction of Action Learning and indeed the specific circumstances for this, see for instance

Pedler[11] and Lawrence[12], no case studies have been published on failed Action Learning interventions. Therefore we have no rigorous case support evidence on which to assess the likelihood of the success of an Action Learning approach in any particular organization or type of organization.

Nor do we have evidence justifying any mass cultural assertions about the acceptability of Action Learning. We know it has been successfully introduced in a number of countries. Initially an almost entirely UK phenomenon with, for many years, no success of substance in the USA, even that massively business school culture is beginning to succumb. In addition to two articles substantially based on General Electric experience,[73,74] articles quoting more widespread use in the USA have begun to appear.[75-77] The USA was preceded by Australia, and individual authors there, as already indicated in this review, made significant contributions. Prideaux and Ford in two articles bring together the components of Action Learning with associated work on competences, teams and careers.[78,79] Enderby and Phelan not only describe an Australian project but also give one of the few illustrations of evaluation.[80] The material produced by the National Staff Development Committee in Australia has already been referred to.[63]

Chapters in this book review other experience in Australia, the USA and China, the latter actually written by a Chinese national. Also about Chinese experience but by a European, Boisot has written two articles.[81,82] The particular features of ancient Chinese culture with modern Chinese authority might be thought particularly antipathetic to the non-authoritarian and questioning approach of Action Learning, but the article suggests not.

Articles on Hong Kong[83] and Sri Lanka[84] explicitly discuss the issue of the extent to which learners expect authoritative teacher-led training, yet responded well to Action Learning.

Apart from the original Belgian experience there seems to have been few articles covering experience in other European countries except Sweden[85,86] and Finland.[87] The article by Lee[37] raises issues of general application but is specifically focused on the different kinds of expectation of participants in central European countries.

IMPLEMENTATION AND EVALUATION

Management development is notoriously lacking substantial material which evaluates the effect of particular development interventions. Evaluation could answer the question of whether Action Learning is more suited to the achievement of some objectives but not others as a method of development. Is Action Learning more effective, and if so to what purposes and in what context, than well prepared and conducted case studies, or the stimulating experiences available on outdoor/adventure training? Is it more effective as a group process than T Groups, or other unstructured experiential learning groups? Nor has there been any substantial comparison between the effectiveness of different management development methods, until Mumford[88]. In this resource he compares the effectiveness of different management development methods to meet different needs, and reviews the special kind of contribution which Action Learning could make.

Nor are comparisons made easier when there is disagreement about what particular words embrace. For some people simulation is a form of Action Learning simply because it is action and people are learning from it. The differences between Action Learning and Action Research are more difficult to explain because they have much more in common. Those differences are, however well explained in Zuber-Skerritt[89] and by implication in the article by Prideaux.[90] Dixon[91] embraces a slightly wider field by discussing similarities and differences between Action Science and Action Learning. Codori[92] in her description of a particular project within a Masters programme illustrates an Action Research rather than Action Learning project, because although students carried out a real piece of work it was not one selected by them nor was it one for which they held any management responsibility, nor were they involved in implementation.

While to some extent therefore the absence of evaluation can be explained as a characteristic phenomenon in management development, and the attribution of particular virtues to Action Learning is confused by association with other processes, explanation is not the same as an acceptable reason. Mumford[68] suggested that one reason for the absence of evaluation was that for many clients the results of Action Learning were so clearly beneficial that they had no interest in conducting rigorous evaluation. The few attempts at evaluation therefore glow more brightly in the dark. Easterby-Smith and Burgoyne in this volume provide an excellent academic review demonstrating the difficulties of evaluation as much as they do the potential. Prideaux and Ford[78,79] similarly from an academic background review a lengthy programme.

Cunningham's chapter in this volume gives an interview-based review, especially significant because the programme was for chief executives. Enderby and Phelan[80] provide the most startlingly concrete illustration and the only one which begins to meet the question about the particular virtues of Action Learning compared with other methods. Their evaluation took groups who had participated in Action Learning and groups who had not and showed that the perceptions of service by customers in bank branches affected by Action Learning were better than those in branches not affected by Action Learning. Of course a tough bank manager might still argue that perceptions of service did not necessarily mean more profitable business, but we should be grateful for at least this level of evaluation.

Reg Revans has always been particularly pleased by the evaluation carried out by Wieland[93], not least because a perception of initial failure was followed subsequently by a declaration of success. The article by Reeves[51], while not strictly evaluation, presents some very interesting assessments of the effectiveness of Action Learning programmes; Weinstein[10] similarly in a more anecdotal account presents the case for success – and also illustrates some failures. The article by Wills and Oliver[9], while not fully meeting the attractiveness of the title 'Measuring the ROI from Management Action Learning' does actually mention some specific financial figures. Howell[95] reports a more traditional review, using respondents' answers based on a programme in Australia against the stated objectives of the programme.

Lamond,[96] reviewing problems of setting up and then assessing projects within a formal management education context, brings us to a crucial issue. What results are we actually trying to evaluate? Do we intend to look at how much more effective managers are at creating and learning from projects? Or are we trying to evaluate the significance to an organization of the projects that have been implemented? (See Wills and Oliver[94].) Which brings us to the issue of how central implementation is to Action Learning philosophy and practice. The original Revans work in the Coal Board and hospitals seemed directly focused on implementation – managers responsible for carrying through the results of their discussions. Yet his Belgian experience in at least some cases involved no direct implementation; here managers were advising others on what to do.

Mumford has argued that the inclusion of implementation is a fundamental feature of the most rounded form of Action Learning – no doubt because of his addiction to the learning cycle.[18] He proposes a continuum, representing the difference between a project wholly suitably described as a consultancy project, with no responsibility for action after the project, through a project involving recommendation, approval by a higher authority and then action, through to direct responsibility for implementation. Others have argued that implementation is not feasible as an absolute requirement for many participants – they simply do not have the authority to carry through the results of a project. Chapters in this book present implicitly or explicitly the different types of involvement or lack of involvement in implementation.

It seems appropriate to finish this review on the issue of implementation. Clearly Action Learning can and does involve projects and problem solving which substantially address recommendations for action by others. If to accept this is in some sense to diminish the original power of Action Learning involving implementation, then we should look for more experiences and more articles describing processes through which participants address how they implemented the design and carrying through of their project proposal, even if they were not involved in a final act of creative action on it.

REFERENCES

1 Revans, R. W. (1971) *Developing Effective Managers*, London: Longmans.
2 Mumford, A. (1985) 'A review of action learning', *Management Bibliographies and Reviews*, **11**(2).
3 Mumford, A. (1994) 'A review of action learning literature', *Management Bibliographies and Reviews*, **20**(6 & 7).
4 Revans, R. W. (1980) *Action Learning*, London: Blond & Briggs.
5 Revans, R. W. (1983) *The ABC of Action Learning*, Bromley: Chartwell-Bratt.
6 Revans, R. W. (1982) *The Origins and Growth of Action Learning*, Bromley: Chartwell-Bratt.
7 Revans, R. W. (1984) *Revans on Video*, Bradford: MCB University Press.
8 McGill, I. and Beaty, L. (1995) *Action Learning*, 2nd edn., London: Kogan Page.
9 Inglis, S. (1994) *Making the Most of Action Learning*, Aldershot: Gower.
10 Weinstein, K. (1995) *Action Learning*, London: HarperCollins.
11 Pedler, M. (1996) *Action Learning for Managers*, London: Lemos and Crane.
12 Lawrence, J. (1994) 'Action learning: a questioning approach', in Mumford, A., (ed.), *Handbook of Management Development*, 4th edn, Aldershot: Gower.
13 Morris, J. (1991) 'Action learning: the long haul', in Prior, J. (ed.), *Gower Handbook of Training and Development*, Aldershot: Gower.
14 Sutton, D. (1989) 'Further thoughts on Action Learning', *Journal of European Industrial Training*, **12**(3).
15 Mumford, A. (1991) 'Learning in action', *Personnel Management*, **23**(7), July.
16 Wallace, M. (1990) 'Can action learning live up to its reputation?' *Management Education and Development*, **14**(2).
17 Boddy, D. (1981) 'Putting Action Learning into action', *Journal of European Industrial Training*, **5**(5).
18 Mumford, A., (1997) 'Action Learning as a vehicle for learning', in Mumford, A., (ed.), *Action Learning at Work*, Aldershot: Gower.
19 Sutton, D. (1991) 'A range of applications', in *Action Learning in Practice*, M. Pedler (ed.), Aldershot: Gower, Chapter 8.
20 Peters, J., (1988) 'Customer first – the independent answer', *Business Education*, **9**(3/4).
21 Mumford, A., (1987) 'Action learning special issue', *Journal of Management Development*, **6**(2).
22 Lawlor, A. (1985) *Productivity Improvement Manual*, Aldershot: Gower.
23 Preston, A. P. and Biddle, G. (1994) 'To be or not to be?' *International Journal of Career Management*, **6**(1).
24 Morris, J. (1991) 'Minding our Ps and Qs', in Pedler, M. (ed.), *Action Learning in Practice*, 2nd edn, Aldershot: Gower.
25 Smith, P. (1988) 'Second Thought on Action Learning', *Journal of European Industrial Training*, Vol. 12, No. 6.
26 Casey, D. (1993) *Managing Learning in Organizations*, Open University Press: Buckingham.
27 Sutton, D. (1997) 'Action Learning in search of P', in Mumford, A., (ed.), *Action Learning at Work*, Aldershot: Gower.
28 Harrison, R., Miller, S. and Gibson, A. (1993) 'Doctors in management', *Executive Development*, **6**(2 & 3).
29 Prideaux, G. (1994) 'Action research, organisation change and management development', *Australian Health Review*, **13**(1).
30 Noel, J. L. and Charan, R. (1988) 'Leadership and development at GEs Crotonville', *Human Resource Management*, **27**(4).
31 Froiland, P. (1994) 'Action Learning: taming problems in real time', *Training* (USA), January.
32 Mumford, A. (1996) 'Effective learners in Action Learning sets', *Employee Counselling Today*, **8**(6).
33 Coates, J. (1989) 'How people learn on management courses', *Industrial and Commercial Training*, **21**(2).

34 Marsick, V., Cederholm, L., Turner, E. and Pearson, T. (1992) 'Action Reflection Learning', *Training and Development* (USA), August.

35 Prideaux, G. (1997) 'Making Action Learning more effective', in Mumford, A. (ed.) *Action Learning at Work*, Aldershot: Gower.

36 Argyris, C. (1992) 'Education for leading – learning', *Organizational Dynamics*, **21**(3), Winter.

37 Lee, M. (1995) 'Working with choice in Central Europe', *Management Learning*, **26**(2).

38 Lewis, A. (1994) 'Action Learning in Prudential Assurance', *Management Bibliographies & Reviews*, **20**(6/7).

39 Bunning, C. (1997) 'Turning experiences into learning', in A. Mumford (ed.), *Action Learning at Work*, Aldershot: Gower.

40 Reid, M. (1997) 'Action Learning: a set within a set', in Mumford, A., (ed.) *Action Learning at Work*, Aldershot: Gower.

41 McAdam J. (1995) 'Joint action learning: a collective collaborative paradigm for the management of change in unionised organisations', *Journal of Managerial Psychology*, **10**(6).

42 Meehan, M. and Jarvis, J. (1996) 'A Refreshing Angle on Staff Education', *People Management*, 11th July.

43 Froiland, P. (1994) 'Action Learning: taming problems in real time', *Training* (USA), January.

44 Casey, D., and Pearce, D. (1977) *More Than Management Development*, Aldershot: Gower.

45 Caiae, B. (1997) 'Learning in style', in Mumford, A. (ed.) *Action Learning at Work*, Aldershot: Gower.

46 Mercer, J. R. (1990) 'Action Learning: a student's perspective', *Industrial and Commercial Training*, **22**(1).

47 Mead, M. (1997) 'From colleagues in crisis to the synergy of the set', in Mumford, A. (ed.) *Action Learning at Work*, Aldershot: Gower.

48 Oliver, C., Pass, S., Taylor, J., and Taylor, P. (1997) 'Who cross fertilizes most on MBA programmes', in Mumford, A. (ed.) *Action Learning at Work*, Aldershot: Gower.

49 Mumford, A. (1997) 'Managers developing others through Action Learning', in Mumford, A. (ed.) *Action Learning at Work*, Aldershot: Gower.

50 Gore, L., Toledano, K., and Wills, G. (1997) 'Leading courageous managers on', in Mumford, A. (ed.) *Action Learning at Work*, Aldershot: Gower.

51 Reeves, T. (1997) 'Rogue learning on the company reservation', in Mumford, A. (ed.) *Action Learning at Work*, Aldershot: Gower.

52 Bennett, R. (1997) 'Effective Set Advising in Action Learning', in Mumford, A. (ed.) *Action Learning at Work*, Aldershot: Gower.

53 Kozubska, J. (1989) 'Role of the Set Adviser', *Action Learning Resource*, Bradford: MCB University Press.

54 Donaghue, C. (1992) 'Towards a model set effectiveness', *Journal of European Industrial Training*, **16**(1).

55 Thorpe, R. (1990) 'Alternative theory of management education', *Journal of European Industrial Training*, **14**(2).

56 McLaughlin, H. and Thorpe, R. (1993) 'Action Learning: a paradigm in emergence', *British Journal of Management*, **4**(1).

57 Willmott, H. (1994) 'Management education: provocations to a debate', *Management Learning*, **25**(1).

58 Gregory, M. (1994) 'Accrediting work based learning: Action Learning – a model for empowerment' *Journal of Management Development*, Vol. 13, No. 4.

59 Mumford, A. (ed.) (1997), *Action Learning at Work*, Aldershot: Gower.

60 Reid, M. (1997) 'The IMC Experience' in Mumford, A. (ed.), *Action Learning at Work*, Aldershot: Gower.

61 Gosling, J. and Ashton, D. (1994) 'Academic learning and academic qualifications', *Management Learning*, **25**(2).

62 Raelin, J. (1994) 'Whither management development', *Management Learning*, **25**(2).

63 National Staff Development Committee (Australia) (1995) *Action Learning in Vocational Education and Training*, 4 volumes.

64 Peattie, K. (1996) 'Action Learning in action: the teaching company scheme', *Management Learning*, **27**(1).

65 Kable, J. (1989) 'Management development through Action Learning', *Journal of Management Development*, **8**(2).

66 Dixon, N. (1994) *The Organizational Learning Cycle*, London: McGraw Hill.

67 Watkins, K. and Marsick, V. (1993) *Sculpting the Learning Organization*, San Francisco: Jossey-Bass.

68 Mumford, A. (1995) *Learning at the Top*, London: McGraw Hill.

69 Zuber-Skerritt, O. (1995) 'Developing a learning organization through management education by Action Learning', *The Learning Organization*, **2**(2).

70 Braddick, W. (1990) 'Learning together: practical lessons in partnership in management development', *Journal of Management Development*, **9**(4).

71 Cederholm, L. (1993) 'Personal development', *Action Learning News*, May.

72 Vince, R. and Martin, L. (1993) 'Inside Action Learning: an exploration of the psychology and politics of the Action Learning model', *Management Education and Development*, **24**(3).

73 Noel, J. L. and Charan, R. (1988) 'Leadership and development at GEs Crotonville', *Human Resource Management*, **27**(4).

74 Noel, J. and Charan, R. (1992) 'GE brings global thinking to light', *Training and Development* (USA), July.

75 Downham, T. A., Nowell, J. and Prendegast, A. E. (1992) 'Executive development', *Human Resource Management*, **31**(1 and 2).

76 Lawrie, J. (1984) 'Take action to change performance', *Personnel Journal*, January.

77 Adams, D., and Dixon, N. M. (1991) 'Action Learning at Digital Equipment', in Pedler, M. (ed.), *Action Learning in Practice*, 2nd edn, Aldershot: Gower.

78 Prideaux, G. and Ford, J. E. (1988) 'Management development: competences, contracts, teams', *Journal of Management Development*, **7**(1).

79 Prideaux, G., and Ford, J. E. (1988) 'Work-based learning', *Journal of Management Development*, **7**(3).

80 Enderby, J. E. and Phelan, D. R. (1994) 'Action Learning as the foundation for cultural change', *The Quality Magazine*, February.

81 Boisot, M. (1987) 'Chinese boxes and learning cubes: Action Learning in a cross-cultural context', *Journal of Management Development*, **6**(2).

82 Boisot, M. (1986) 'Action Learning with Chinese characteristics: China – EEC Management Programme', *Management Education and Development*, **17**(2).

83 Pun, A. (1990) 'Action Learning for trainers' development', *Journal of European Industrial Training*, **14**(9).

84 Jones, M. L. (1990) 'Action Learning as a new idea', *Journal of Management Development*, **9**(5).

85 Marsick, V. (1990) 'Experience-based learning: executive learning outside the classroom', *Journal of Management Development*, **9**(4).

86 Rohlin, L. (1996) 'What do we mean by Action Reflection Learning?' MIL Dalby Sweden.

87 Valpolla, A. (1989) 'Management training at Wartsila', *Executive Development*, **2**(1).

88 Mumford, A. (1997) *Management development – how to select the right method*, Self-published, Maidenhead: Honey.

89 Zuber-Skerritt, O. (1993) *Professional Development in Higher Education: A Theoretical Framework for Action Research*, London: Kogan Page.

90 Prideaux, G. (1990) 'Action research, organisation change and management development', *Australian Health Review*, **13**(1).

91 Dixon, N. (1990) 'Action science and learning new skills', *Industrial and Commercial Training*, **22**(4).

92 Codori, C. (1989) 'Three experiences with Action Learning: audit training meets the real world', *Managerial Auditing Journal*, **4**(3).

93 Wieland, G. (1981) *Improving Health Care Management*, Health Administration Press.
94 Wills, G., and Oliver, C. (1997) 'Measuring the ROI from Management Action Learning', in Mumford, A. (ed.) *Action Learning at Work*, Aldershot: Gower.
95 Howell, F. (1997) 'Action Learning and Action Research', in Mumford, A. (ed.) *Action Learning at Work*, Aldershot: Gower.
96 Lamond, D. A. (1995) 'Using consulting projects', *Journal of Management Education*, **18**(8).

Appendix 3 Sources of Further Information

Two principal sources of further information and advice are:

IFAL – THE INTERNATIONAL FOUNDATION FOR ACTION LEARNING

IFAL is a registered educational charity which includes a network of practitioners, in the UK and worldwide. It also maintains a newsletter, a bibliography, a library, provides various advice services and runs workshops in its mission of disseminating Action Learning. IFAL branches are also to be found in the USA and Canada.

Contact:

Krystyna Weinstein
46 Carlton Rd
LONDON SW14 7RJ
UK

Tel & Fax: 0181–878 7358

THE REVANS CENTRE FOR ACTION LEARNING AND RESEARCH

The Revans Centre is in the Department of Continuing Education at Salford University, Salford, UK. Like IFAL it is in touch with large numbers of people interested in Action Learning and also enrols people on post-graduate Diplomas,

Masters' degrees and PhDs by Action Learning. Its archives include all Revans' papers – published and unpublished.

Contact:

Dr David Botham
Director, The Revans Centre for Action Learning and Research
Department of Continuing Education
Salford University
Salford M5 4WT
UK

Tel: 0161–745 5718
Fax: 0181–745 5999

Index

Action Learning at Work

Edited by Alan Mumford

The Action Learning approach to management development, based on the pioneering work of Reg Revans, is well known among human resource specialists. In this book Professor Mumford, himself a leading exponent of Action Learning, has brought together more than 34 articles and papers on the subject from a variety of sources. They reflect the experience not only of those responsible for AL programmes but also of learners and client organizations. A wide range of issues is addressed, from underlying philosophy to evaluation, from the learning process itself to ways of integrating the 'P' and the 'Q' of Revans' famous equation.

All the material in this absorbing collection derives from the work of International Management Centres, a business school dedicated to the Action Learning approach. The result is a treasure trove of insights and practical guidance for anyone involved in, or contemplating, an AL programme – and indeed for anyone concerned with improving managerial performance.

Gower

Developing Managers Through Project-Based Learning

Bryan Smith and Bob Dodds

Every educator knows that the most effective way to learn is by 'doing' – and nowhere is that truth more clearly seen than in management development. This wide-ranging book explains what is involved in planning and running project-based management development programmes and demonstrates the benefits for both the individuals and the organizations concerned.

Drawing on the unrivalled experience of PA-Sundridge Park Management Centre in this field, the authors:

• show how to set up the necessary frameworks
• describe programmes for different levels of management, including 'top teams'
• examine the role of the sponsor
• point out the potential pitfalls and indicate how to avoid them
• look at the influence of national culture.

With summaries and checklists, and case studies focusing on ICI, Allied Domecq, Volvo, Gestetner, Lloyds Bank Insurance Services, The Inland Revenue, London Underground and others, the emphasis throughout is very much on the practical.

For anyone concerned with improving managerial performance, this is a book that will repay careful study.

Gower

Developing Your Business Through Investors in People

Second Edition

Norrie Gilliland

- What does Investors in People involve and how would it benefit my organization?
- How can I make sure that our training and development activities will help achieve our business objectives?
- How can I encourage employees to 'take ownership'?
- How do I prepare for IIP assessment?

These questions and many others are addressed in this revised edition of Norrie Gilliland's highly acclaimed book. Drawing on experience acquired working on Investors in People with more than 50 organizations, the author describes the business benefits of developing employees through systematic communication, involvement and training.

He examines the IIP national standard in detail and suggests numerous ways of meeting it, showing how to align training and development with business objectives, how to assess individual development needs and what should be the role of managers in the process. For this new edition the text has been enlarged and improved to reflect the revisions to the national standard introduced in 1997.

For managers in every kind of business, for HRD specialists and for consultants, Norrie Gilliland's book will continue to be the best available source of reference and guidance in its field.

Gower

The Excellent Trainer

Putting NLP to Work

Di Kamp

Most trainers are familiar with the principles of Neuro-Linguistic Programming. What Di Kamp does in this book is to show how NLP techniques can be directly applied to the business of training.

Kamp looks first at the fast-changing organizational world in which trainers now operate, then at the role of the trainer and the skills and qualities required. She goes on to deal with the actual training process and provides systematic guidance on using NLP in preparation, delivery and follow-up. Finally she explores the need for continuous improvement, offering not only ideas and explanation but also instruments and activities designed to enhance both personal and professional development.

If you are involved in training, you'll find this book a powerful tool both for developing yourself and for enriching the learning opportunities you create for others.

Gower

Facilitating Change

Ready-to-Use Training Materials for the Manager

Barry Fletcher

This is a manual designed to help managers to help their staff, using a range of techniques borrowed from the training professional's armoury, with full explanation of how any manager can use them in a team development context. Introductory chapters describe the principles and methods involved in developing people to cope confidently with change. There are questionnaires and suggestions for diagnosing learning needs and recognizing learning opportunities.

At the heart of the manual is a collection of thirtyfive learning activities. Each is self-contained but can be combined with others within the collection to form a more extensive programme of development. All activities start with a brief description and a note of potential benefits, guidance over who it is suitable for and the time and resources required. This is followed by a step-by-step guide to running the activity. Ready-to-copy masters are supplied for any material to be used by participants. The activities are indexed by subject to make it easy for managers to identify the most appropriate for their own needs.

For any manager who'd like to unlock the full potential of his or her team, *Facilitating Change* provides an excellent starting point.

Gower

Gower Handbook of Management Skills

Third Edition

Edited by Dorothy M Stewart

'This is the book I wish I'd had in my desk drawer when I was first a manager. When you need the information, you'll find a chapter to help: no fancy models or useless theories. This is a practical book for real managers, aimed at helping you manage more effectively in the real world of business today. You'll find enough background information, but no overwhelming detail. This is material you can trust. It is tried and tested.'

So writes Dorothy Stewart, describing in the preface the unifying theme behind the new edition of this bestselling *Handbook*. This puts at your disposal the expertise of 25 specialists, each a recognized authority in their particular field. Together, this adds up to an impressive 'one stop library' for the manager determined to make a mark.

Chapters are organised within three parts: Managing Yourself, Managing Other People, and Managing Business. Part I deals with personal skills and includes chapters on self-development and information technology. Part II covers people skills such as listening, influencing and communication. Part III looks at finance, project management, decision-making, negotiating and creativity. A total of 12 chapters are completely new, and the rest have been rigorously updated to fully reflect the rapidly changing world in which we work.

Each chapter focuses on detailed practical guidance, and ends with a checklist of key points and suggestions for further reading.

Gower

The Management Skills Book

Conor Hannaway and Gabriel Hunt

From managing employee performance to chairing meetings, and from interviewing staff to making retirement presentations, the list of skills demanded of today's manager seems endless. How can you be effective in all these areas?

If you are a practising manager, this book is for you. It is designed to answer your need for support in your day-to-day work.

Over 100 brief guides cover essential management skills. Each guide gives you all you need to know without cumbersome technical details. Look up the subject you need, and apply the ideas immediately.

The Management Skills Book was written with today's busy managers in mind. It is an ideal introduction for new managers, and a great reminder of the essentials for the more experienced.

Gower

New Leadership for Women and Men

Building an Inclusive Organization

Michael Simmons

What are the key attributes of successful leaders in today's organization? The answer to this question is of course hotly debated. But Michael Simmons' ground-breaking book is the first to place the development of a new leadership for women and men at the heart of the argument. In particular, it is the first to focus on the benefits of helping leaders to overcome the negative effects of gender conditioning on the quality of their leadership.

The author proposes that leaders must transform their organizations by learning how to manage a turbulent environment, increase productivity and quality, and build an 'inclusive organization'. Achieving these aims requires that *everyone* is involved in planning the future direction of the enterprise and contributes to its continual improvement. But gender conditioning leads many managers to put up barriers to the full involvement of all their people. Transformation means reaching beyond equality to an organization where boundaries and limitations are not placed upon anyone. It needs a new kind of leadership capable of harnessing the intelligence, creativity and initiative of people at all levels, especially those who have traditionally been excluded.

This timely book provides much more than a searching analysis of women and men's leadership. Using real-life examples and case studies, it sets out strategies, programmes and techniques for improving organizational performance, and describes in detail the type of training needed. In short, it is a book designed to inspire not just thought but action.

Gower

Participative Training Skills

John Rodwell

It is generally accepted that, for developing skills, participative methods are the best. Here at last is a practical guide to maximizing their effectiveness.

Drawing on his extensive experience as a trainer, John Rodwell explores the whole range of participative activities from the trainer's point of view. The first part of his book looks at the principles and the 'core skills' involved. It shows how trainee participation corresponds to the processes of adult learning and goes on to describe each specific skill, including the relevant psychological models. The second part devotes a chapter to each method, explaining:

• what it is
• why and when it is used
• how to apply the core skills in relation to the method
• how to deal with potential problems.

A 'skills checklist' summarizes the guidelines presented in the chapter. The book ends with a comprehensive matrix showing which method is most suitable for meeting which objectives.

For anyone concerned with skill development *Participative Training Skills* represents an invaluable handbook.

Gower

A Real-Life Guide to Organizational Change

George Blair and Sandy Meadows

'Management ideas may change with fashion, but the underlying concepts do not lose their validity. We offer you prepared food for thought for your organizational microwave, rather than exotic dishes that are very difficult to copy.'

George Blair and Sandy Meadows - themselves battle-hardened veterans of the change process - take a refreshingly different approach to most of the new books, videos, seminars and gurus emerging to tell managers how to cope with change. They encourage the reader to start from the reality of his or her own organization and have the courage to design the programme that will work in real life.

Drawing both on proven systems and their own extensive experience, they chart the way forward from strategy to implementation. With the aid of checklists, illustrations and case studies, they show how to diagnose existing problems, how to construct the appropriate plans and how to deal with the politics. They examine the various options, including empowerment, TQM and re-engineering, set out the criteria for selecting the best mix for your own circumstances and then explain the techniques involved in implementation. Unlike many other books on change, they pay due attention to the need for a reward strategy to support the aims of the change programme.

This accessible and often humorous book is firmly grounded in reality, and will be a welcome relief for managers trying to assimilate accepted 'best practice' in change management into their real working lives.

Gower

Requisite Organization

A Total System for Effective Managerial Organization and Managerial Leadership for the 21st Century

Second Edition

Elliott Jaques

Based on Elliott Jaques' latest research, this is a thorough revision of a book that has established itself as a classic in its field.

Jaques has written a practical high-level, how-to book, that applies to all kinds of working organizations – industrial, commercial, service and public. He sets out a totally new way of doing business. Step by step, he builds up the concepts, and then introduces the working procedures to enable CEOs and senior executives, managers, and HR specialists, to develop *requisite organization* for themselves – in other words, organization which enhances creativity, productive effectiveness, human satisfaction and excellent morale.

Requisite Organization challenges all of our current methods and assumptions in the field of organization, leadership and management, and presents a unified total management system built upon a rigorous theoretical base, Stratified Systems Theory.

Any enterprise can gain a competitive edge in the short-term by introducing new products and services. In the long-term, however, an adaptive and successful enterprise calls for soundly structured organization with effective staffing and managerial leadership at every level – a *requisite* organization.

Gower

The Techniques of Training

Third Edition

Leslie Rae

In this third edition of the standard work the author reviews the main methods currently used in training and development. He describes each one briefly, sets out its advantages and drawbacks and shows - with examples and case studies - where and how to deploy it to best effect.

The text has been thoroughly revised to reflect recent developments, including Training and Development NVQs and the changing role of the practitioner. There are new chapters on preparing training events and using training aids. The result is a book that will be of immense practical value to anyone concerned with developing people.

Gower